❧ EROTIC EXCHANGES

EROTIC EXCHANGES

THE WORLD OF ELITE PROSTITUTION IN EIGHTEENTH-CENTURY PARIS

NINA KUSHNER

CORNELL UNIVERSITY PRESS
Ithaca and London

First published 2013 by Cornell University Press

Printed in the United States of America

Library of Congress Cataloging-in-Publication Data

Kushner, Nina, author.
    Erotic exchanges : the world of elite prostitution in
eighteenth-century Paris / Nina Kushner.
        pages cm
    Includes bibliographical references and index.
    ISBN 978-0-8014-5156-0 (cloth : alk. paper)
1. Prostitution—France—Paris—History—18th
century.   I. Title.

    HQ196.P3K87 2013
    306.740944'361—dc23
                                        2013027623

Cornell University Press strives to use environmentally
responsible suppliers and materials to the fullest extent
possible in the publishing of its books. Such materials
include vegetable-based, low-VOC inks and acid-free
papers that are recycled, totally chlorine-free, or partly
composed of nonwood fibers. For further information,
visit our website at www.cornellpress.cornell.edu.

Cloth printing   10 9 8 7 6 5 4 3 2 1

For Joon

✒ CONTENTS

❧ ACKNOWLEDGMENTS

It is with great pleasure that I thank the many people who helped me to write this book, which I began so many years ago. I have had the privilege of being trained as an historian by many inspiring and devoted scholars including Peggy Darrow, Simon Schama, Eugene Rice, Tip Ragan, Deborah Valenze, Martha Howell, and Isser Wolloch. In France, the librarians at the Bibliothèque de l'Arsenal, the Bibliothèque Nationale, the Archives de la Préfecture de la Police de Paris, and the Archives Nationales were helpful and creative in identifying and locating relevant materials. My navigation of the archives and my time in Paris were made immeasurably more pleasant thanks to Ann Morrissey, Jennifer Popiel, Jeff Horn, Paul Cheney, Charles Walton, and Brian Sandberg.

I remain overwhelmed by the generosity of a number of my senior colleagues who read full drafts of this book at various stages and offered substantial comments for its betterment, including Lenny Berlanstein, Katie Crawford, Lisa Jane Graham, Dena Goodman, Daryl Hafter, and the anonymous reader for Cornell University Press. Lisa and Dena in particular helped me to sharpen chapters, correct problems, ask better questions, and develop frameworks in which to answer them. I cannot thank them enough. I also owe a special thanks to Daryl Hafter, who, as we worked together on another project, continued to encourage me to finish this one.

My copresenters, collaborators, friends, and mentors from the Society for French Historical Studies and the Western Society for French History provided wonderful and generative feedback on all the many portions of this book presented at our annual meetings. Clare Crowston's comments on a number of papers pulled the central questions into focus. Clare Crowston and Kathleen Wellman shared their manuscripts with me, and Meghan Roberts shared her dissertation. Kate Norberg and Jeffrey Merrick availed me of their expert knowledge of the police archives. I also thank Christine Adams, Susan Ashley, Rafe Blaufarb, Mita Choudury, Lauren Clay, Julie Hardwick, Nancy Locklin, Rene Marion, Sarah Maza, Jacob Melish, Joelle Neulander, Michelle Rhoades, Charlie Steen, and especially Eliza

Ferguson and Jen Popiel, who graciously and without fail took the time on so many occasions to help me think through ideas. Chapter 3 is all the better for having been subject to the close reading and tough questioning of the graduate students and faculty at the Department of History's colloquium at the University of New Mexico.

At different stages, I received research help and editing assistance from Christine Crabb, Angie Woodmansee, and Steve K.F. Heise. Clyde Marlo Plumauzille jumped in for some last-minute translation help. At Cornell University Press, John Ackerman expertly guided the book through the review process.

I am extremely fortunate to work at Clark University. The university granted me a pretenure sabbatical that launched the writing of this book. The Higgins School for the Humanities awarded me several grants so that I could return to Paris to complete my research. The history department also provided considerable financial support, including awarding me the Hillery Summer Research Fellowship. Holly Howes at Goddard Library managed to find every text I asked for through interlibrary loan and never once gave me the stink eye for my horridly late returns. Drew McCoy and Amy Richter, as department chairs, helped me to create space in a busy academic schedule in which to write. Doug Little, though an American historian, regularly reminded me of Voltaire's dictum that the perfect is the enemy of the good. Janette Greenwood showed me that it is possible to write, teach, and be a mother. Our administrative assistant, Diane Fenner, lightened the load in every possible way. My colleagues Taner Akcam, Norman Apter, Debórah Dwork, Thomas Kuehne, Wim Klooster, Olga Litvak, Ousmane Power-Greene, Paul Ropp, Michael Butler, Paul Posner, Patty Ewick, Debbie Merrill, Shelley Tenenbaum, Ora Skeleky, and Parminder Bachu made writing this book and working at Clark so much more pleasurable. I would especially like to thank Meredith Neuman, Betsy Huang, and Beth Gale for their steady friendship and Beth, in particular, for her help with translations.

To my parents, Linda and Harold Kushner, I owe a great deal, not the least of which was the inspiration to be an historian and the support to pursue this goal professionally. And then there was the babysitting. While I was off reading and writing about prostitutes, they occupied my children with more age-appropriate endeavors, no doubt encouraging them to find their own dreams. My sister, Diana Kushner, always believed this project would be worth the time put into it, and hence helped to make it so.

I had two children while writing this book, Leah and Miles. I thank them for the many long hours and days they let their mother spend at work, and for the joy they provided at those days' end. "The book" became part of their own familial landscape. As a women's and gender scholar, I appreciate the value of children seeing mothers invest in their own careers. Being a working mother also gave me perspective on the kinds of questions that inform my scholarship. But now it is time to spend those extra hours helping my children write their own stories.

Neither the kids nor I would have done so well without the steadfast help of my husband, Joon Bai, who, in his quiet and loving way, created an environment in which this work could be done. It is quite something to share a life with such a person. I am lucky beyond measure. It is to Joon that this book is dedicated.

❧ EROTIC EXCHANGES

Introduction

In February 1762, Paris police inspector Louis Marais returned to the dossier of Demoiselle Varenne after a six-year hiatus. Varenne had been a popular subject with Marais's predecessor, Inspector Jean-Baptiste Meusnier, who in his capacity as head of the Département des femmes galantes, wrote more than twenty reports on the *dame entretenue* (kept woman) in the space of four years.[1] Between the inspectors' dry coverage of the various details of Varenne's work life and their sarcastic rendering of her character, a story emerges from their reports, one of misfortune and desperation, hard work and manipulation, love and, above all, individual agency.

According to her police dossier, Varenne was from Angers, the daughter of a surgeon. By age sixteen, for reasons not made clear in her file, she was a prostitute in the high-end Parisian brothel of Madam Carlier. She did not stay there for long. After a month, Varenne left the brothel as the mistress of an army lieutenant, who paid for her to be treated for venereal disease and then established her in a *chambre garnie* (a furnished rented room). She soon traded the officer for another patron, the son of a *trésorier general*, who, in turn, was quickly replaced by the son of an army lieutenant general. Within a year, Varenne had acquired her own furnishings, a mark of success as well as a source of security in the demimonde. Four years later, at the age of twenty-one, she was the head of a household. It was a small one, just

Varenne and her sister, Demoiselle La Monthe. They lived in a five-room apartment in the Marais district, for which Varenne paid 650 *livres* a year. The two moved a number of times as Varenne's fortune's dictated. Her sister worked as her maid.

Finally, in 1762 at age twenty-six and following a decade of mistress work, Varenne was ready to marry. Her fiancé was not one of the many men who had maintained her. In fact, marriages between patrons and mistresses were extremely rare in the demimonde. Rather, Varenne planned to wed her long-time *greluchon* (boyfriend), a musketeer captain named Montière, the sexual partner to whom she had "sworn eternal love" while the paid mistress of other men. The two intended to elope that May, when Varenne's patron, the marquis de Seignelay (Louis-Jean Baptiste Antoine Colbert, b. 1731), had to report to his regiment. Seignelay was a colonel in the French Army, fighting the Seven Years' War. Varenne's plans were the subject of Inspector Marais's report and, apparently, his disgust.

Seignelay "loved and adored" Varenne, claimed Marais, and had generously maintained her for four years. Relationships of such long duration were uncommon in the demimonde and usually signified a strong attachment on the part of the patron. Nevertheless, the inspector continued, the colonel would soon be "punished by the iniquity" his mistress was planning. Marais referred not just to Varenne's elopement but to her effort to procure a large sum of money in its advance. She had "squeezed" six thousand livres from both her patron and Montière, funds she intended to convert into *rente viagère* (life-time annuities). But before Varenne could get the sum to the notary, her sister absconded with it. Why commit such a crime? According to Marais, La Monthe feared being let go and forced to find work elsewhere following her sister's wedding. Marais concludes: "It would be good for Monsieur de Montière, who is a noble, a cavalry captain, and a Chevalier de Saint-Louis, with an honest fortune, if this loss prevents him from committing such a stupid act that will completely dishonor him. It is true that La Varenne is still attractive, that she has between 12,000 and 15,000 [livres] in *rente*, and considerable personal goods, but these sorts of marriages never work for an honest man."[2]

Did the marriage ever take place? There is no record to suggest that it did. But if it had, it would have represented an extraordinary leap in the social circumstances of a woman of modest social origins who had spent her adulthood as an elite prostitute. The very possibility raises a number of questions: How did a woman like Varenne, who began her working life in a brothel serving whoever walked through the door, accrue wealth, become an independent head of household (in an era in which this was rare for women) and attract a prospective spouse whose status was considerably higher than that of her father, who as a surgeon enjoyed the standing of an artisan and hence was socially inferior to an army officer?

Working as a professional mistress afforded a degree of agency and a potential for financial success unusual for women from such humble backgrounds. The most successful among them became heads of households and enjoyed financial and sexual freedoms uncommon to all but aristocratic women. Some, like Varenne, did quite well. Many, however, never enjoyed her level of fortune. And all were subject to the vicissitudes, violence, and social degradation of their trade. But the structures and social processes that enabled Varenne's rise are the same that shaped the lives of the one thousand or so other kept women working in Paris in the middle of the eighteenth century. It is their story, and its historical significance, that are the subjects of this book.

➥ *Dames Entretenues* and the Demimonde

In the mid-eighteenth century, the *dames entretenues*, or kept women of Paris, famous for their glamour and beauty, were the most highly sought-after mistresses in Europe. Frequently called *femmes galantes*, they earned their living by engaging in long-term sexual and often companionate relationships with men from the financial, political, and social elites, known as *le monde* (high society).[3] In exchange, they were "kept," given material and financial recompense sufficient, at least in theory, to support a household. In principle, these liaisons were exclusive. In practice, they were not. Most dames entretenues at least occasionally took on other kinds of elite sex work—such as *passades* (one-night stands)—with the same clientele in order to earn extra money or make contacts, even while they were being maintained. Nevertheless, a dame entretenue generally limited herself to only a few sexual partners at a time. In other words, her body was not "common to all," which was the definition of a *fille du monde*, or a prostitute. What distinguished a dame entretenue from other elite prostitutes (and from any other type of mistress) were three factors: the nature of her clientele, the constructs that governed her work relationships, and last, her professional status.[4]

A central argument of this book is that being "kept" in the eighteenth century was a profession. Some dames entretenues were theater performers and a few worked in fashion, but with these two exceptions kept women had no other careers. They did not drift into and out of prostitution, as did most streetwalkers, who worked other sorts of jobs, usually in the garment trades, and who tended to engage in prostitution only when they could not earn enough through licit means.[5] Those kept women who did not have patrons (*entreteneurs*) were usually in the process of trying to find them. And, while some became emotionally attached to their patrons, most dames entretenues, like Varenne, carefully nurtured private sexual and intimate lives that they supported financially through their work.

Part of this argument is that both mistresses and their patrons were participating in a sexual subculture—the demimonde—whose practices, customs, and institutions were well defined.[6] In using the word *demimonde*, I am referring to a sexual market in which certain services were sold, as well as the customs and institutions that shaped the market's operation and the community of individuals who participated in it. That community was made up of dames entretenues and other elite prostitutes, their clients and patrons, the madams who facilitated many of their transactions, and the police. Contemporaries often referred to the affairs between elite men and their mistresses—whether professional or social peers—as *galanterie*. Dames entretenues were also called femmes galantes.[7] Answering the question of why Varenne succeeded, and indeed telling the story of kept women more generally, requires situating them in the world that enabled such success and that, at the same time, circumscribed it so profoundly. Reconstructing the demimonde is the fundamental project of this book.

Integral to the process is locating the demimonde on a figurative map of eighteenth-century French society and culture. The demimonde was often depicted as a universe apart, a shadow society of illicit sexuality on the outskirts of le monde. It did have its own institutions, rituals, customs, and jargon, but in some important ways the culture and practices of the demimonde were not particularly exceptional. For example, the business conventions governing patron-mistress relations (which were legal) and the sales of virgins (which were not) were no different from those of any licit small-business deal. The authority of parents, even while they were trying to do something criminal or, indeed, appalling in contemporary thinking—such as selling their children into prostitution—was thought to be as intact in these matters as in any other. The sexual practices and sexual morality of the demimonde are primarily what made it distinct, but even in these areas it was not isolated. While demimonde sexual practices embodied the libertine ethos of pleasure, they were flexible enough, ironically, to be a site in which the elite could experience the emerging family ideal of domesticity.

The demimonde also closely overlapped with several other communities, specifically the world of the theater and that of the royal court.[8] About a fifth of the kept women under police surveillance at midcentury worked in the theater. Most were in the Opéra or its school, as dancers or singers. A few were in other companies, namely the Comédie-Italienne and the Opéra-Comique. Still fewer were in the Comédie-Française. A handful of kept women worked in the low-end boulevard theaters or were members of traveling troupes. Some bounced around, from company to company, trying to work their way up to the Opéra, which for dames entretenues was the pinnacle of success.

Not all theater women were dames entretenues, at least according to the police intelligence. However, police inspectors and the public assumed prostitution until they could prove otherwise. There was good reason to do so. Being on the stage greatly increased what I am calling "sexual capital," the desirability of a mistress and hence the prices she could command for her services. Theater women tended to dominate the top ranks of the dames entretenues in terms of earnings and status. Consequently, getting on stage was a goal of many kept women. But, while being in a theater company differentiated the experiences of actresses, dancers, and singers involved in elite prostitution from those of other women, it did not do so greatly. Theater and nontheater kept women shared the same patrons, and their transactional relationships were structured in the same way. Moreover, the demands of mistress work had women leaving the theater as well as entering it. For theater dames entretenues, the two careers informed each other.

Those dames entretenues who have been subjects of scholarship tend to be theater women, often members of the hyperelite class of mistresses who were paid astronomical sums, and given hôtels and fancy carriages. Focusing on this subgroup of women highlights the power and status of those at the very top of the profession, and ultimately demands some consideration of the question of how some of the greatest self-made women of the era were those who sold sex openly.[9] Considering them exclusively, however, distorts our sense of the degree of agency experienced by most kept women. It also obfuscates the larger structures that made their success, however great, possible. Part of the effort to trace the relationship of the demimonde to the theater involves identifying these structures, and thus looking at dames entretenues—wealthy and poor, on the stage and off of it—as a group.

The relationship of the demimonde to the royal court, in contrast to that of the theater, revolved not around mistresses but their patrons. Many held royal offices or were, like the maréchal de Saxe, important military leaders. The financiers who in the Old Regime often held various lucrative positions of fermiers généraux, or tax collectors, paid for Louis's wars and building projects; they were no strangers to mistress keeping. The fermier général was immortalized as the archetype patron in one of the earliest novels on the subject, Abbé Prévost's *Manon Lescaut*.[10] Princes of blood and other high-ranking aristocrats, including the dukes of Conti, Clermont, Montmorency, Orléans, and Richelieu, were fixtures in the demimonde. It is tempting to think that being at the *parc des cerfs*—where Louis XV met women for short sexual encounters—or becoming a royal mistress was to reach the apogee of the demimonde. It was, but only for a couple of women, namely Louise O'Murphy and Jeanne Bécu who later became Louis's *maîtresse-en-titre* (official mistress), Madame du Barry. Most royal mistresses and even short-term sexual partners did not come from the demimonde. In general, court galanterie and the demimonde were more like parallel sexual economies that overlapped only occasionally. Extramarital affairs at the court were usually between social equals and were often linked to jockeying for position and advantage.[11] In contrast, dames entretenues had no political or social power. While they could, as commodities, enhance (or diminish) the social status of their patrons, they were not participants in these larger political machinations. It is more accurate to argue that dames entretenues were a part of elite culture more broadly. The one thousand or so women who constituted the demimonde consorted with thousands of elite men in Paris. Additionally, mistress keeping supported a sex-gender system embraced by a significant portion of the Parisian elite. It served both to celebrate and define elite male virility while at the same time alleviating marriage from the burden of being the locus of intimacy or even sexuality beyond the needs of reproduction.

✎ Modes of Prostitution and Their Study

The dame entretenue as a kind of prostitute is historically specific. However, mistress keeping is certainly nothing new. Broadly defined as a long-term, remunerated extramarital affair for the purpose of sex and companionship (not reproduction) in which there is little or no possibility of marriage, mistress keeping has been a hallmark of elite male wealth, status, and power in many societies over time. As concubinage, these relationships have often been formalized in law and custom, endowing some concubines with rights while stripping them from others, making their concubinage involuntary.[12] Judicial records, canon law, songs and folk tales, and memoirs provide rich evidence of a continuum of such extramarital relationships in medieval and early modern France, from that of the bourgeois who kept a textile worker to that of his wife, who herself was the mistress of a wealthier man.[13] This practice was particularly in evidence among the elite, especially kings. The eighteenth century was no different. Louis-Sébastien Mercier, that great chronicler of Parisian life, listed no fewer than five types of concubinage in his *Tableau de Paris*, ranging from that of the *grisette* who was looking for a man to sponsor her days off of work to the wife whose added income improved the living standards of the house.[14]

Elite prostitution also has a long history. Defined as expensive transactional sex between elite men and women of lower social origins who appropriated elements of elite presentation in their dress, speech, and decorum, it is often tied to courtesans, who emerged first in ancient Greece and Rome and later in Renaissance Italy. Dames entretenues were called "courtisanes" by the police and other writers. Some contemporaries used the term to refer to a better sort of prostitute, one who earned more money and conducted herself "more decently."[15] Other writers, such as Jean le Rond d'Alembert, who wrote on the topic for the *Encyclopédie*, asserted a difference between Paris's "courtisanes" and the famed women of ancient history. He called a *courtisane* "a woman who gives herself entirely to public debauchery, especially when she practices this shameful occupation with a sort of charm and decency," but noted her lack of artistic and intellectual accomplishment compared with that of her ancient forebears.[16] Courtesans in sixteenth-century Italian city-states, the sites of the first postclassical Western courtesan culture, also embraced strong identities as artists and musicians. As with their Greek sisters, they were trained to provide pleasure, not just sexually, but with educated conversation, music, and dance.[17] The Renaissance courtesans also downplayed and in many cases hid their prostitution, emphasizing instead their own refinement and virtue. There were a few important courtesans, like Ninon de Lenclos, in seventeenth-century France, but there was no established, widespread courtesan culture. Kept women of eighteenth-century Paris, who obtained all (or almost all) of their income through direct prostitution, did little to create an ambiguous status for themselves. Their linkage to the arts was also different. Many dames entretenues were in the theater, many more were not, and very few of the women in either group had sufficient education to converse about literature or philosophy with those of their patrons who might have wished it. Elevated conversation now fell to another cohort, the *salonnières* who ran Enlightenment salons and who rigorously preserved their sexual reputations.[18]

The figure of dame entretenue emerges out of these long histories of mistress keeping and elite prostitution. Her appearance is a function a particular set of sexual relations that develops in this period. What was new about the dame entretenue was that she was a professional mistress who sold sexual services in a highly structured marketplace, one that regularized almost all aspects of elite transactional sex, especially its remuneration. This market probably developed at the end of the seventeenth century and found its full flowering in the middle of eighteenth, spurred by the move of the elite to Paris and by the commercial revolution. It was also a product of a particular "libertine" moment of sexual permissiveness that began with the Regency and continued until the Revolution, in which a significant section of the Parisian elite tolerated premarital sex for males, and adultery for men and some women.

Largely because of the richness of the sources, the history of prostitution in France has been studied primarily from the viewpoint of regulation.[19] This literature is concerned with the relationship of the prostitute to the state or visions of the state and, in some cases, to other authoritative discourses. The regulationist approach—while providing a nuanced understanding of the relationship between sex and gender, and the power and interests of the state—obscures the structure of the trade and the diversity of its various subcultures. In that it defines prostitutes as "object[s] of bureaucratic practice," this approach isolates them from the various communities of which they are a part and buries their voices.[20] Consequently, we know much more about the policing of prostitutes than the kinds of lives that they led.

One study that attempts to reconstruct the world of prostitution is Erica-Marie Benabou's *La Prostitution et la police des moeurs au XVIIIe siècle*. It is impossible to work on the topic of prostitution in the eighteenth century without being heavily indebted to Benabou's impressively researched and important work, in which she explores the working conditions of prostitutes among other topics. Her work is ultimately regulationist, however, because she understands prostitution as a function of regulation. She collapses all prostitution, whether street walking or being kept, into a single activity (sex for money) connected as objects of policing.[21] In doing so, the considerable differences between prostitution subcultures, and even between policing practices, are erased. In contrast, my starting point is the contention that the demimonde was a discrete sexual and social subculture and that its policing had very little to do with the policing of other forms of prostitution. From this perspective, the demimonde starts to look very different. This does not mean, however, that its regulation can be ignored. The police as individuals and as a regulatory body played an important role in the operation of Paris's elite sexual market. My interest is rather in understanding how they contributed to its construction.

↩ Prostitutes and Agency: Women, Work, and the Family Economy

Leaving regulation for a moment, and looking instead at prostitutes within the context of their lives as mothers, daughters, wives, neighbors, and consumers brings them back into the history of women. It highlights the ways in which prostitution was shaped by culture and economics. It also recasts prostitution from a crime or moral problem to a form of work. Thinking of prostitution as work is a newer paradigm in prostitution studies.[22] It is informed, at least in part, by the ongoing debates between sex workers and some feminists over the question of voluntary prostitution: whether it is possible for women to decide to be prostitutes and hence to deliberately engage in prostitution as a form of work, or whether all prostitution is coerced and exploitative.[23] By eighteenth-century standards, elite prostitution did not qualify as work. However, in addition to considering galanterie a vice and a social problem, a wide range of contemporary sources constructed it as sexual *labor*, which the dame entretenue owned and could sell.

What these sources also make clear is that being kept *functioned* as work in the lives of elite prostitutes. Most of these women were professional mistresses only in the years between the onset of adolescence and the age of marriage, during which time many women worked away from home to earn dowries. And, like many other forms of female labor in eighteenth-century France, elite sex work was often part of the family economy. The idea of the family economy, which long dominated women's social history, supposes that women's work was dictated not by the desire for self-fulfillment but by the needs of the family as part of its strategy for survival; a woman's work was tangential, changing and usually subordinated to that of her husband.[24] As we shall see, prostitution was often part of a family strategy, and looking at it from this angle is a useful antidote to the isolation imposed by regulationist arguments. However, not all dames entretenues worked as part of or in service to a family unit. Many kept women disassociated themselves from their parents and spouses and managed, as single women, to become financially independent heads of household. Their success challenges the family-economy paradigm that understands women's labor only within the family. It also challenges the narrative based on the family-economy model, which posits a contraction of opportunity for women in the eighteenth century.[25]

Discussions of women and work usually lead to a historical search for women's agency.[26] The problem of identifying agency in prostitutes is especially difficult, yet the question of how women could control their own lives, work, and sexuality is an important one in this study. Kept women were unusual figures for the period, falling outside of the concatenation of corporations that defined and controlled French people in this era. As single women, many came to be free from the control of the family and the household. As sexual entities, they were generally independent of husbands, brothels, and other institutions that regulated female sexuality at the time. The most elite were celebrities. But they were nevertheless prostitutes—selling sex and maybe even love for a sum—and as such were subject to profound social and legal disabilities.

Moreover, as kept women, they were subject to the rules and pressures of that world. Therefore, while many dames entretenues were able to earn enough money to support themselves, they also were caught up in the demimonde economy of conspicuous consumption, which was necessary to attract new and better patrons. They aped the behavior of aristocrats with material displays of wealth constructed on platforms of debt. And while most were able to avoid incarceration by their families, these women were still at the mercy of their patrons. In sum, choices of kept women were as informed and circumscribed by patterns, expectations, and need as were the choices of their peers who had never left the path to marriage. This study tries to understand how a particular group of women navigated and manipulated the constraints to which they were subject. In doing so, it makes those constraints visible and shows how the operations of gender *and* sexual status were forms of power in the eighteenth century. In this era, the constraints faced by all women were significant. Dames entretenues were subject to more disabilities than most; however, what is important is not their extent, but their difference.

☙ Sources and Method

The main sources for this study are the some seventy-five hundred folio pages of dossiers and other documents generated by a Paris police unit that followed dames entretenues about the city and reported what they did from 1747 through 1771.[27] Inspector Jean–Baptiste Meusnier, who ran the unit from 1747 until 1757, had 550 dames entretenues under surveillance. His successor, Louis Marais, included many hundreds more. The unit produced dossiers on kept women until 1761, at which point the organization, although not the quantity, of the reporting changed. Each dossier consisted of reports from the inspector in charge, *bulletins* (reports) from spies, and occasionally letters from those under observation or other interested parties.

From 1761, instead of adding to the dossiers, the Département began to produce lengthy weekly reports of recent events in the demimonde. Departmental files also contain two boxes of letters and reports from elite madams to various police personnel.

These sources were read against a wide variety of writings that featured dames entretenues, including other judicial documents, novels, satire, *nouvelles à la main* (gossip or news sheets), the writings of commentators, and memoirs. Several voices ring through these documents. The loudest is that of dramatist and journalist Louis-Sébastien Mercier. Mercier was perhaps eighteenth-century Paris's greatest ethnographer. Son of an artisan, he was a strident social critic, deeply antagonistic to the habits of Paris's elite, whose habits of conspicuous consumption he saw as vanity and castigated as examples of the dangers of luxury. Mercier had a particular venom for pretension and so thought very poorly of all prostitutes, except those who stood in rags on street corners, pretending nothing. In contrast, Giacamo Casanova, Alexandre comte de Tilly, and Jean-François Marmontel, each of whom wrote a memoir recounting his experiences in the demimonde, were far less critical of dames entretenues. Casanova and Tilly, both nobles, were sex adventurers, constructing themselves as libertines whose dual purpose in life was seduction and personal advancement. Both had a great deal to say about the women they encountered and the conditions under which they encountered them. While their writings are illuminating of the demimonde, they tended to treat femmes galantes as individuals rather than types, criticizing the system of sexual relations from which they took so much joy rather than the individuals participating in it. Marmontel, a philosophe, was likewise nonjudgmental but also less wry than Casanova and Tilly, and at the same time regretful. As a playwright, he was deeply involved in the world of actresses and their patrons. He was a patron, and his friends were both patrons and mistresses. He reported on the interactions of men and women in the demimonde matter of factly. But as the memoir was framed as a life lesson for his children, Marmontel positioned the "adventures" of his youth as such.[28]

We might consider together the last of these voices, those of Edmond Jean François Barbier and the editors of the *Mémoires secrets*. All of them attempted to record "the news." Barbier was a lawyer and an observer, not a patron, as far as we know. He was focused mainly on legal, diplomatic, and military events but occasionally mentioned a case or an incident that was the subject of popular interest, including some that involved dames entretenues. Barbier was not an overt moralist, or at least his writings about elite prostitution tended to be more muted, focusing less on the scandalous aspects and more on human interest. In contrast, the *Mémoires secrets*, at least with respect to the demimonde, was the eighteenth-century equivalent of a gossip magazine. Its compilers were deeply interested in the lives of elite mistresses and their patrons, partly as a reflection of their orientation as editors of a periodical that covered literature and theater. But their depictions of the lives of kept women were not the same as their coverage of plays. The *Mémoires secrets* recorded "anecdotes galantes," prurient tidbits that mocked the men and women they discussed as a means to entertain the reader and distance themselves from the behavior they described.[29]

Collectively, the nature of the evidence best lends itself to the use of case studies. It is highly qualitative data, inscribing events, identities, and the components of exchange into extended narratives. Occasionally, where enough of a sample could be gleaned from the dossiers, I present statistics based on a representative 265 dossiers. For the most part, however, the sample sizes are too small to be meaningful. Furthermore, there is an unidentifiable skew in the archive. The documents that constituted much of the secret police's output were stored in the *Salle des Archives* (archive room) of the Bastille. Located just to the left of the fortress entrance, the archive room was an easy and early target of the mob that famously ransacked the citadel in July 1789. Efforts were made to reconstitute the archive, but it is clear that there were significant losses.[30]

The broad contours of the demimonde—its central institutions and practices—are discernible across a number of diverse sources. We know about the relationships of kept women with their *greluchons* (boyfriends), for example, from memoirs, fiction, satire, and nouvelles à la main. Police sources, however, are necessary to shade in and detail the picture. Doing so presents the methodological challenge of finding a way to mine regulationist output to explore something other than regulation. This is not a new challenge. Historians of early modern Europe have been using these kinds of records to explore the experiences of the subjects of policing and to recreate their social, mental, and cultural worlds for almost forty years. Emmanuel Le Roy Ladurie and Carlo Ginzburg used Inquisition records to tell us as much about the communities and mentalities of peasants as about the Inquisition.[31] Robert Darnton has used the secret files of the Parisian police to write extensively about the world of letters and to reconstruct communication networks. Arlette Farge and Lisa Jane Graham used similar files to study subversive speech. From their works we learn as much about attitudes toward the king and the nature of popular opinion in the eighteenth century as we do about its policing.[32] In my particular study, the question is how can these sources be read for clues to the experiences of mistresses?

To begin with, the dossiers were not limited to the words of the police. They included letters from mistresses and their patrons, usually asking for help. The police also recorded their utterances. We cannot assume the police were quoting accurately. These sources are suspect, if for no other reason than because they were part of the construction of a larger police narrative about the demimonde. The inspectors understood the events they were following as stories or, rather, as a set of stories. Determining how the police produced the dossiers and their narratives makes it possible to isolate police concerns. Reading these documents against similar files generated by other police departments, on the one hand, and against nonjudicial sources, on the other, highlights police constructions of kept women and their meanings. How and why these reports were put together is the subject of chapter 1.

The aim, however, is not to write a history of discourses about mistresses but instead a sociocultural history that reconstructs the demimonde. Reading the dossiers in various discursive contexts, then, is also a means of decoding their narratives so as to render them into other forms of evidence. The narrative structure of the text is also a form of evidence. Oddities in the text—"loopholes," "omissions," and "exaggerations," in the words of Natalie Zemon Davis, who, along with Carlo Ginzburg, pioneered this method—shed light not only on the attitudes and background of the author but on those of his subjects as well.[33] These approaches, however, take us only so far in trying to investigate the structures of the demimonde. Understanding what kept women did and why requires a sort of thick contextualization, a laying out of the mental, social, and economic world of these women so as to understand their possibilities for thought, action, and meaning. The life histories of these women in turn establish a strategic position through which to reexamine values and habits of eighteenth-century life.[34]

ᴥ CHAPTER 1

The Police and the Demimonde

On Thursday, March 20, 1755, Paris police inspector Jean-Baptiste Meusnier sat down to write a *bulletin* (report) at his hotel on the rue des Canettes, in the faubourg St. Germain. The subject was Demoiselle St. Hylaire, a twenty-year-old woman who was a singer in the Opéra and was working as a dame entretenue. She had been under surveillance for four years.

Meusnier wrote:

> The constant attention of Monsieur Moreau, Officer of the Guard, towards Demoiselle Hugault—he eats and sleeps at her place, refusing to leave—has made it impossible for Monsieur Amelot de Chaillou to continue his relationship with the girl.[1] Amelot has since left her and returned, with a renewed devotion, to his former mistress, Demoiselle St. Hylaire. She lives on rue de Bourbon in the quarter Villeneuve. However, he only comes [to visit her] in the evenings. It was reported that he had supper there yesterday. He arrived at 8:00 and [then] sent his carriage and servants away.
>
> I am assured that Demoiselle St. Hylaire has a new patron, whose name we have not yet been able to ascertain. That will be a task for next week.[2]

The third week in March 1755 was a fairly average one for the inspector. He wrote a report almost every day, each one on a different dame entre-tenue. In his reports, the inspector recorded in exacting detail the emotional and material exchanges that constituted the professional lives of his subjects: Demoiselle Hugault's infidelity supposedly drove her patron back to his former mistress Demoiselle St. Hylaire, to whom he was especially attentive. St. Hylaire, in the meantime, was being maintained by someone else. Demoiselle Maupin, another subject of that week, was fired by her patron, the prince de Nassau-Sarbruck, yet she continued to quarrel with him over a four to five hundred livre bill for a gold-laced dress and a feathered hat, which she had ordered and was expecting to be delivered shortly.[3]

Each report was placed in a thickening dossier, which was filed by subject name in an expanding archive Meusnier kept at his hotel on the rue des Canettes. St. Hylaire, Hugault, and Maupin were just 3 of the more than 150 women Meusnier had followed in 1755, and among the some 550 he observed in his ten-year career with a police unit, the Département des femmes galantes, whose purview was the demimonde. Meusnier was followed in 1757 by his assistant, Inspector Louis Marais, who kept track of an equal number of women, at least until 1761. In that year, he dismantled the dossier system, submitting instead long, detailed weekly reports titled *Notes sur différentes dames entretenues* (Notes on Different Kept Women). These *Notes* reflected a considerable broadening of surveillance, increasing the total number of people under observation.

By 1764, Marais combined these *Notes* with submissions of *Anecdotes Galantes*, reporting the extramarital affairs of men and women in elite society, le monde, as well as those in the demimonde. The reporting stopped, for the most part, in 1771, although there were a few scattered bulletins until 1777. Together, the inspectors reported on the doings of at least one thousand women and an equal number of men in the course of a quarter century. These men included princes of blood, peers of the realm, robe nobles, and financiers, a veritable "who's who" of le monde. Given the ransacking during the Revolution of the archive in which these documents were kept, the total number of individuals under surveillance might have been far more numerous.[4]

Understanding how and why the demimonde was policed is intrinsic to understanding how it operated. This is the case, first, because police operations had a hand in shaping the demimonde. Second, we owe our knowledge of many of the details of daily life in the demimonde to police efforts to record them. The reports are not, by any means, the only source of information on this world of elite prostitution. Police attention to kept women echoed a popular interest much akin to our own obsession with Hollywood gossip. What the most famous femmes galantes did made news. Their affairs, infidelities, sexual proclivities, earnings, and scandalous behaviors were mentioned in private correspondence and recorded by memoirists, chroniclers, and journalists. Nouvelles à la main (handwritten news sheets), including the famous *Mémoires secrets*, reported many *anecdotes galantes*. The habits of kept women and their patrons were frequently mocked by satirists and were also the subject of an entire genre of libertine literature, as well as of more serious works of fiction. Artists like Fragonard depicted galante scenes on canvas. Moralists and police theorists addressed the risks mistress keeping posed to patrimony and society. Madams under police protection submitted regular reports. Notaries recorded the marriage contracts of kept women and the *rente* (annuities) gifted to them by patrons. Kept women and their patrons also spoke for themselves: they wrote letters to the inspectors, and when they understood themselves to be the victims of theft, violence, or fraud, they filed complaints with police commissioners. Collectively, this rich body of evidence paints a clear picture of the grand contours of the demimonde. It is to inspectors Meusnier and Marais, however, that we owe much of our detailed knowledge of this world.

What was the relationship of the police to the demimonde? Why were they interested in kept women and their patrons? What form did their policing take? And what did it mean for those under their watch? These reports were produced as part of an effort by the police and the monarchy, for different reasons, to learn what was happening in Paris, to render the capital visible. Hence the bulletin on Demoiselle St. Hylaire was in many respects not unlike hundreds of others being written by agents in other departments at the very same time. It would be a mistake, however, to assume that the bulletin on St. Hylaire was just like those being produced elsewhere, or to think that it was simply a reflection of larger institutional trends. Report writing had yet to become so bureaucratized as to eliminate the voice of the author.[5] Inspector Meusnier's personality, his worldview, and his social and political relationships informed his construction of the dossier system and its daily workings as much as any long-term evolution in policing. Making sense of these documents, then, necessitates moving beyond understanding why the Département was founded to examining how it operated, both within and against the interests of the police and the monarchy.

The evolution of the modern police force has long been associated with repression.[6] In establishing government over a community that previously had no official oversight, the inspectors expanded the power of the police, the state, and themselves. In creating the dossier system, they "made visible"

to the state the private lives of a good portion of Paris's male elite and so-
lidified the identities of specific women as elite prostitutes. Yet it is difficult
to apply the repression argument—at least in its most aggressive incarnation—
to the activities of the Département. In practice, the police mediated between
the demimonde and Paris's more respectable communities. In doing so they
set the boundaries of permissible behavior, yet these limitations were few. The
inspectors rarely tried to repress behaviors deemed repugnant to outsiders.
More than anything, in fact, the police helped to enforce the demimonde's
own rules. Meusnier and Marais acted as de facto magistrates, commissioners
of the demimonde. As such, they reified the demimonde's institutions and
practices. This benefited many kept women, because the clarity of the rules
and customs made it easier for them to build careers.

✎ The Parisian Police at Midcentury: Why Kept Women?

The Département des femmes galantes was one of many that Nicolas René
Berryer (lieutenant general, 1747–57) and one of his successors, Antoine de
Sartine (1759–74), established at midcentury as part of a general reorganization of the institutions that policed the capital. By 1760, twenty-five of these
departments existed.[7] Six of them handled the city's livestock and food markets, while another six policed groups of people thought to be particularly
threatening or innately subversive. These included charlatans, confidence
men, usurers and pawnbrokers, foreigners, and foreign and French Protestants. There were three departments overseeing the prisons and their oc-
cupants and one that functioned as a military police. Parisian social life was
the focus of at least three departments. A very large one watched over the
theaters. Another policed gambling, and a third, clubs and circles.[8] Sexual
activity was the concern of two, one for the demimonde and another for
public sodomy.[9] A single department monitored and policed the book trade,
and another, which by century's end was the largest, investigated crimes.[10]
Finally, late in the century, the police established a department that functioned
as a wetnurse registry, helping to match newborns to nursing women.

Departmental missions, however, do not represent the full range of police
activity, nor did they absorb all of its personnel. The lieutenant general had
twenty different kinds of officials under his authority and numerous other
categories of employees, ranging from the *Garde* that patrolled the streets
to the men who cleaned them.[11] Among the most important "police" officers
at midcentury were the commissioners and the inspectors. About a third

of the commissioners were assigned to specific departments, but the main duties of these men lay elsewhere. Officially titled *commissiares-enquêteurs-examinateurs*, the commissioners functioned, and had since the fourteenth century, as minimagistrates in each of the city's quarters. Trained in law, by midcentury they numbered forty-eight and were stationed two or three per quarter, where their docket combined judicial, administrative, and to a lesser degree, investigative functions.[12] It was to the local commissioner that anyone with a grievance went first, often for adjudication, and if the magistrate was unable to resolve the conflict, he would initiate the necessary legal proceedings to take it to court. Often posted in the same quarter for decades, many commissioners were well known and trusted by the communities they served.[13]

Inspectors, as the investigatory arm of the police, had an entirely different mission from that of the commissioners.[14] Like Meusnier, most were assigned to different departments where they fulfilled various information-gathering needs in the policing of particular beats. In addition, each had regular obligations in the quarters in which they were stationed, notably open surveillance (for example, checking to make sure the wares sold by dealers in secondhand goods had not been stolen). Inspectors were also tasked with specific investigations, for instance, ascertaining the facts behind a request for a *lettre de cachet* (royal order for incarceration).[15] To gather information, the inspectors relied heavily on networks of informants cultivated over a long tenure in the quarter. The public called all informants *mouches* or *mouchards*, although the police established a hierarchy among them.[16] Mouche networks could be quite extensive. One historian of the police identified fifty-two different informants working "for the police" or "for an inspector" in the notes of Commissioner Chénon.[17] Traditionally recruited from the lowest levels of society, mouches increasingly came from every social echelon as the century progressed, a fact not lost on contemporary observers, who believed mouches to be absolutely everywhere, listening and reporting. Denis Diderot, for example, claimed in his *Mémoire* on policing for Catherine II that "our entire lives and all our habits are reported to the police . . . they know our every action and opinion."[18] While this was hardly the case generally, men like Diderot were under police surveillance.

This brief survey should make clear that the duties of the police in the early modern period extended beyond fighting crime. In the eighteenth century, "la police" referred not to a group of people but to a series of actions, all that was necessary for the good regulation of a city.[19] By the Revolution, the Paris police regulated the city's markets; ensured the honesty of its merchants; lit, cleaned, and made safe the city's streets; fought its fires; regulated its prisons; solved its crimes; kept its wayward elements in order; enlightened its public; and made sure its foundlings were nursed. The police were supposed to maintain some sort of moral order by containing prostitution, preventing Parisians from spending themselves into ruin in the city's many illegal gambling dens, and supporting families in their efforts to discipline unruly members. The lieutenant general was the man responsible for making sure the city was provisioned with all that it needed, even in times of dearth.

When inadequate distribution of flour resulted in riots, criminal gangs controlled certain quarters of the city, and pedestrians were regularly injured fatally by speeding carriages or falling masonry, why did the police devote any resources whatsoever, not to mention an entire administrative unit, to the demimonde? Clearly the demimonde mattered to the police. Our question is why.

Disappointingly, the archives have failed to cough up a definitive answer, and none of the more logical explanations stand up to the evidence.[20] It is unlikely that the dossiers were used for judicial purposes, for example, as *galanterie* was not illegal. Prostitution was. But while officials liked to disparage dames entretenues by calling them prostitutes, they did not treat them as such. Patron blackmail, another possibility, would have been hard to execute, as each dossier was filed under the name of the kept woman and not that of her patron(s). Without a cross-index (if it existed, it has been lost), the only means by which an inspector could retrieve information on a particular man would have been to rely on his own memory. After 1761, when the dossier system dissolved, retrieving information on any one person—man or woman— would have been even more difficult. Moreover, the blackmail hypothesis assumes patrons wanted their affairs hidden. Some did. For many others, however, mistress keeping was a display of status and hence required publicity. Robert Muchembled suggests that the archive was used by Meusnier, Marais, and a cabal of police officials to extort money from kept women and their patrons. While this was certainly possible, it would not explain why the Département was set up. Moreover, the only proof Muchembled offers is either circumstantial—the wealth Meusnier had accrued by the time of his death (which Muchembled claims he faked)—or fantastic, namely some comments from one of the many antipolice "exposés" written at the end of the century, which Muchembled attributes to (the legally dead) Meusnier.[21]

One theory is that the police may have watched kept women so that they could arrest the depletion of those family fortunes made vulnerable by infatuated sons. In his treatise *La police de Paris en 1770*, the police commissioner Jean-Baptiste-Charles Le Maire argued that femmes galantes were dangerous by definition because they supported themselves though bankrupting men. The commissioner instructed police to take action whenever a man "recovered his senses," realized that he had been duped, and sought the "intervention of the magistrate." This magistrate, then, was to stop the woman and punish her, all the more severely if she had taken advantage of the man's naïveté.[22] If this was the intent of the Département, it was never executed. Meusnier and Marais, who ended their assignments decades before Le Maire put pen to paper, anticipated only bits of the commissioner's prescription. They did keep track of their subjects' expenditures and were well aware of who was bankrupting whom. Yet they intervened barely a handful of times, and only when they were asked to do so. Without such a directive, they did nothing, even when they knew a father was desperately trying to stop his son from spending the family's last livre on a prostitute. Moreover, Le Maire's anxiety was misplaced; very few elite prostitutes bankrupted their patrons.

A final theory is that the reports were meant for Louis XV and his mistress, the marquise de Pompadour, Berryer's protector, in order to enliven the reputedly jaded, enervated royal sex life. The belief that the police provided demimondaine gossip to entertain the king dates back to the reign of Louis XIV. Paul Cottin, who edited and published Lieutenant General d'Argenson's letters to Pontchartrain, suggests that the minister was collecting various bits of information—such as updates on the lives of the madams Villefranche and de la Motte, two well-known femmes galantes—for the Sun King's amusement, a practice generally associated with Louis XV and not his great-grandfather.[23] Robert Darnton argued that decades later the comte de Maurepas, a minister who dominated Louis XV's cabinet for decades, held on to power in part because he entertained the king with just such prurient gossip, which he got from weekly secret reports provided by the lieutenant general.[24] After the formation of the Département des femmes galantes, some contemporaries believed that its output—in some cases the madams' reports and, in others, lists or *Anecdotes Galantes*—was for royal consumption. According to literary scholar Pamela Cheek, the rumor gained speed and weight in the first three years of the Revolution, repeated and enhanced by writers like Louis Pierre Manuel and the marquis de Sade, as evidence of the despotism of the Old Regime.[25] The rumor made its way uncritically into nineteenth-century scholarship.[26] Yet even now, scholars who read these reports are taken with their literary quality, their narrative tension, and their biting wit, all of which suggest that they were meant to be read and enjoyed.

If the lieutenants general had been providing *Anecdotes Galantes* for the king's pleasure since the seventeenth century, it is possible that Maurepas had Berryer establish the Département in order to increase his access to this information (and enhance his value to Louis). But the main sources of evidence against this hypothesis are the reports themselves. They contained so many third-party references to the king, and related so many incidents at which he was present, that it is unlikely these documents were intended as a royal read. When an audience is identified in the reports, it is always "le magistrat," meaning the lieutenant general of police. Marais, for instance, wrote to his superior, "I will not discuss the arrangements M. Bertin, *trésorier des parties casuelles*, has made with Demoiselle Arnould of the Opera, because I am assured that *le magistrat* is at least as well informed about them as I am. It is only that I wanted it to be known that I was aware of it."[27]

If anything was destined for the *petit lever*, it was probably the *Anecdotes Galantes*, which were a few pages in length and put together only occasionally—hardly an efficient use of a sophisticated surveillance campaign that required significant police resources. And, while the reports could be entertaining, they were not always so. They contained monotonous descriptions of objects, long back histories on kept women and detailed genealogies of patrons. They were formulaic, and that formula bled through the narratives and the witty turns of phrase that characterized Meusnier's writing. Their purpose was to identify the participants and the exact nature of their exchange in a systematic way. The police wanted to know the same facts about every person under surveillance. Moreover, entertaining police storytelling was not, in and of itself, proof of a royal audience. Around the same time, from 1748 to 1753, Inspector Joseph d'Hemery, charged with the book trade, compiled five hundred dossiers on Paris's writers. His files contain the same odd mixture of data and narrative, merging bureaucratic form and personal voice, as did Meusnier's. Robert Darnton, an authority on the files, speculates that d'Hémery compiled them for himself as a reference base.[28] A run through other police writing yields yet more evidence of this same meld of self-conscious, gratuitous storytelling with police formulae.[29]

The king may have been reading summaries of the reports. The police may have used them to coerce individuals. Berryer may have even intended the squad to aid wealthy, naïve young men in retaining their patrimonies. But rather than being compiled for use as court documents, for blackmail, or to keep track of the most predatory of mistresses, this dossier system, I would argue, was an end in itself. When Berryer began his reorganization of the police in 1747, his protectors and superiors desperately wanted to know what was happening, and what was being said, in the capital. Surveillance and report writing had become standard operating procedure in a great many departments, including those concerned with writers, speech, foreigners, Jews, Protestants, clubs and circles, sodomites, charlatans, magicians, and gamblers. The police gathered information on kept women because they wanted to know what these women and their patrons were doing in the same way they wanted to know what was happening in many other communities and corporations around Paris, especially those that concerned important or dangerous people, or that were behind closed doors. Mistresses mattered because, far from being marginal, the dalliance of a few of the noble elite, these women played an important role in elite culture. Meusnier's and Marais's reports, when combined with those of the madams, reveal several thousand men buying sex, in one form or other, in the demimonde. Their clients included the top echelons of the noble, financial, and judicial worlds, men who individually and collectively exercised a great deal of power. Following mistresses certainly would have been a way to keep an eye on many of the nation's most powerful men at a time when the center of elite society had shifted from under the watchful eye of the king at Versailles to seemingly distant and disordered Paris. It was also a way to keep track of a market through which flowed significant wealth, some of which belonged to principal families.

Why this mattered becomes clear when we step back, for a moment, from the specific problem of "why dames entretenues?" and instead consider several trends in the larger history of the police of Paris. The first concerns the ongoing pressure by the monarchy for the police to function as a royal intelligence agency, a pressure that intensified in the 1740s, right as Berryer initiated his reorganization. The second trend highlights the increasing importance of information gathering, especially covert information gathering, to the police themselves as they worked to establish a "well-governed" city.

✧ The Police of Paris and the Monarchy

Until 1667, the power to police the capital was spread among several dozen competing institutions. From the 1630s, the most powerful among them attempted to work together through a committee called the Assemblée de Police under the gavel of the first president of the Parlement de Paris. This coordination, however, was insufficient to keep order in the city, at least to the satisfaction of Louis XIV, who in October 1666 cast an eye toward Paris and decided to clean up his capital. An advisory group under the guidance of Jean-Baptiste Colbert—Louis XIV's controller-general, naval secretary, and the chief architect of the monarchical state—concluded that the fragmentation of police authority, and the jealousy and competition among cadres, rendered many of Paris's basic safety and sanitation problems unsolvable. Police authority would have to be unified before sufficient progress could be made. Louis established a single office in charge of police, the *lieutenant général de police de la ville, prévôté et vicomté de Paris*, in March 1667. The lieutenant general was an officer of the court of the Châtelet, eventually its chief officer. As such, he was technically subordinate to the higher court of the Parlement, but this relationship existed more in principle than in practice.[30] Louis was able to use the position of the lieutenant general to undermine Parlement, wresting from it much of the control the court had exercised over the city.

To Colbert, the Parlement had also been a competitor in the bid for control of information. This was significant because, as Jacob Soll argues, Colbert linked governance to state control of information, which he worked tirelessly to effect. As part of that effort, Colbert reestablished the Intendancy in 1653. Intendants were royal agents sent to the provinces to shore up the king's authority by enforcing his will. For Colbert, these men were also "bureaucratic informers" and a "corps of information collectors and informants" whom the minister trained in the art of report writing.[31] Colbert consequently understood the position of the lieutenant general not just as a magistrate and administrator, but also as a chief information officer. He auditioned his prospect for the first holder of the office, Gabriel Nicolas de La Reynie, by having him write several reports.[32] The lieutenant general was the intendant of Paris in all but name.[33]

De La Reynie did fulfill the mission, but not always to Colbert's satisfaction. The two corresponded daily on questions of the management of Paris, in particular on censorship and political issues.[34] Colbert's letters to the first lieutenant general were replete with demands for more information on this or that occurrence in the city. Marc-René Voyer d'Argenson, the second lieutenant general (1697–1718), was more accommodating. Independent of his weekly visits to Versailles and the numerous reports he wrote on specific issues, he sent regular bulletins to Colbert's successor, Louis Phélypeaux, comte de Pontchartrain. These were résumés of the information given to him by various agents and officers. They contained the news of Paris, covering a wide range of topics. Pontchartrain, however, was not satisfied. He regularly marked these reports with questions, requesting more material and seeking specific details.[35] Royal demand for information was not limited to those particular ministers like Colbert or Pontchartrain, who either functioned as de facto prime ministers or whose portfolio included the capital city, but extended to all six members of the Royal Council. It was to the minister of war, for example, that the police chief relayed data on recruiting and reports of the behavior of soldiers in Paris.[36]

The ability of the police to produce intelligence, both regularly and on demand, evolved slowly, dependent as it was on a number of factors that together marked the maturation of the institution of the police. This included the integration of existing police cadres under the command of the lieutenant general and the expansion of police competence and jurisdiction. Unification of existing police cadres, however, proved difficult. Those with long histories and deeply rooted institutional cultures actively resisted any degradation of their power and autonomy. It was only after 1750 that contemporaries came to call the men under the lieutenant general's authority "the police."[37] Establishing new police "beats" and enlarging police presence in older ones was also a gradual process in part because of ongoing jurisdictional tussles. The lieutenant general struggled with other urban authorities over the policing of certain domains of activity or areas of the city until the Revolution.[38] And some spheres of activity, like the demimonde, did not become targets of sustained police attention until later. Developing an intelligence system required (and clearly drove) institutional growth and an expansion of bureaucratic competence.

Royal demand for intelligence increased dramatically in the late 1740s. The last few years of the decade were tumultuous both in Paris and Versailles, and it is not surprising that the police reorganization began in this period.[39] The peace of Aix-la-Chapelle, signed in October 1748, which brought the War of Austrian Succession to a close, was deeply unpopular. In May 1749, Louis XV further riled the public with a new tax, the *vingtième*, which replaced the *dixième*, a war tax he had promised to abolish. To make the tax legal, it had to be registered by Parlement, which refused, forcing Louis to perform a *lit de justice*, a legal ritual that compelled Parlement to do the royal bidding but that also smacked of despotism. Added to this was a religious crisis over Jansenism, a form of Christianity that appealed to Paris's robe nobles and professional classes but had been rejected by both pope and crown. In 1749, the archbishop of Paris ordered that last rites be denied to anyone who had not formally rejected Jansenism, resulting in a number of "martyrs" dying without final absolution. Their funerals, attended by thousands, were street protests.[40]

In this tense atmosphere, a poem that attacked the king elicited a massive police manhunt across the capital to find the culprits. The so-called "Affair of the Fourteen" resulted in multiple arrests, adding libelers to prison cells with those imprisoned for speaking out against the Peace, *Unigenitus*—a 1713 papal bull denouncing Jansenism—or the monarchy in general. Robert Darnton, who chronicled the hunt, argues that the arrests did not go unnoticed by the public. The mood was so bad that Parisians jeered the king's cortege as he made his way into the city for the official celebrations of the Peace.[41] In studying the Bastille records for these years, Darnton notes that the police were recording a "welling up of discontent" in 1749.[42] Seeking to quiet discontent and find and arrest those who were speaking out against the king were all compelling reasons for the police to increase their penetration of the city. A more efficient structure would enable more comprehensive policing and information gathering.

A ministerial shake-up at Versailles put further pressure on the police to know what was happening in the city. Jean-Frédéric Phélypeaux, comte de Maurepas, who had been a minister for over three decades, and who simultaneously held the ministries of the navy and the king's household (and hence responsibility for Paris), was ousted in April 1749. The comte had written and distributed a poem mocking the king's official mistress (maîtresse-en-titre), the marquise de Pompadour, his political and personal enemy. Maurepas, like many other courtiers and observers, was alarmed at the political influence the marquise wielded.[43] She had the power to award offices and pensions, had a hand in determining policy, and spent a great deal of money in remodeling various chateaus and mounting theater projects. She had promoted Berryer's candidacy for lieutenant general and, two years later, participated both in Maurepas's fall and the choice of his successor as minister of Paris, Marc-Pierre de Voyer de Paulmy, comte d'Argenson. After 1749, those policing Paris were in her debt.[44] Maurepas's poem, one of many he wrote or sponsored, was part of a wave of anti-Pompadour writings called the *Poissonades*, a play on the marquise's name, Jeanne-Antoinette Poisson, "poisson" being the French word for fish. The marquise was publicly reviled. By 1749, however, the *Poissonades* expanded their vitriol to include the king as well, a development that deeply upset him. According to the marquis d'Argenson (brother of the minister), the king and his mistress very much wanted to know what was being said about them in Paris and relied on both the minister of Paris and Berryer for this information.[45] In December 1749, the marquis d'Argenson recorded in his diary, "My brother . . . is killing himself in the attempt to spy on Paris, which matters enormously to the king. . . . It is a matter of knowing everything people say, everything they do."[46] Between coping with the widespread unrest in the city, the effort to put a halt to the *Poissonades*, and the king's desire to know everything that was happening in Paris, there was every reason for the police to increase its activity in the capital. It was in this context that Berryer, Pompadour's protégé, began to reorganize the police, a reorganization that resulted in the formation of the Département des femmes galantes.

☙ Surveillance and the Policing of Paris

Beyond meeting royal demands for information, the lieutenants general had their own intelligence needs. Information gathered both openly and, increasingly, without the public's knowledge became central to police efforts to order and administer the city. Successive lieutenants general—some more than others—consciously and purposefully developed their intelligence capacities and incorporated them into larger strategies of control over the course of the first half of the eighteenth century. Doing so required innovation, specifically the invention of covert surveillance as a deliberate policing technique. Open surveillance (checking weights and measures at markets, for example) had long been the responsibility of those authorities with powers of police. And the early modern era was certainly not without its spies. But the systematic, secret acquisition of information about the population was new.

It was also not very popular and took a while to establish as a legitimate quotidian police action. This is mainly because covert surveillance emerged together with a regularized and strategic use of clandestine extrajudicial arrest warrants (lettres de cachet) as a means to keep order. The men who spied and those who executed secret warrants tended to be one and the same. As these personnel were directly answerable to the lieutenant general rather than to their own corporations, covert policing came to be a reflection of the power of the police chief as he tried to consolidate his control and coordinate policing. Older policing cadres, led by the Parlement of Paris, pushed back against these developments. One historian of the period, Paolo Piasenza, interprets the conflict as a battle between two policing styles: an older, open, collaborative style represented by the seventeenth-century Assemblée, which had insisted on the transparency of their proceedings and had taken care to inform the city's population of their decisions, versus a new, closed, and more paternalistic style represented by the lieutenant general. Resistance to this new style necessitated a second innovation on the part of the lieutenants general, the establishment of a permanent corps of men who specialized in secret policing. This took four decades to effect, mainly because of the interference of Parlement, which managed to either disband or disempower various cadres established by the police chiefs for this purpose.[47] Eventually, deployment of the new techniques would fall largely to inspectors as part of their wider specialization in investigation.

Despite the ongoing difficulties in establishing a secret police corps, the lieutenants general progressively relied on covert surveillance and policing to control the city. For example, beginning in 1724, police informers produced the infamous *gazetins*, in which they recorded gossip and utterances overheard in cafés, at the barriers to the city, and elsewhere. In studying these reports, Arlette Farge argues that the "systematic reporting of opinions expressed among the common people was not a mere amusement: it was one of the grounding activities of a police system which was obsessed with the detail of what was said and articulated, and required to report the essence of it to the highest authorities of state."[48]

By the 1730s, surveillance and report writing had become part of a police intelligence system, at least with respect to the policing of sodomy. A group of subinspectors under the charge of an inspector named Simonnet systematically coerced men arrested for homosexual solicitation to work for them. These men, usually good looking and young, and now bearing the dubious title of mouche, were forced to return to their cruising grounds. There the mouche allowed himself to be approached by another man interested in sex, and rather than bring this erstwhile partner to some dark corner or tavern, as was customary, the mouche took his catch to Inspector Simonnet, who waited nearby in his carriage. All three returned to the Châtelet. The mouche filed his report while Simonnet interrogated the arrestee, producing another report. A close reading of these documents shows a shift in focus over the years, from a concern with the sin of the individual to the breaking apart of sodomitical networks.[49] In other words, the information gathered was being turned into intelligence: it was collected, analyzed, and used to make new decisions.

When in May 1740 Louis XV suppressed and reestablished the office of inspector, both increasing the price and the qualifications necessary for the position, he put this investigatory arm of the police, and hence covert surveillance and report writing, on firm institutional ground. With the establishment of the departments, covert surveillance became essential to the policing of many "beats." Of the twenty-five departments, at least fifteen engaged in domestic spying.

The development of a surveillance system, however, was not just a question of putting agents in the field. Police historian Vincent Milliot identifies in the 1740s what he refers to as to the "System Berryer," a standardization of the kinds of writing through which police recorded and organized their observations. These "written instruments," which included *registres, journals* (diaries) and bulletins, allowed the police to accomplish their job of control and surveillance.[50] The police's capacity to process burgeoning piles of reports also developed. Founded in 1716, the lieutenant general's paperwork clearing house, called the Secretariat, expanded from eight clerks under Lieutenant General René Hérault (1725–1740) to twenty-seven under Sartine (1759–1774). In the late 1750s, Sartine reorganized the Secretariat, dividing it into six physically separate, independent, and specialized *bureaux*.

How should we interpret the development of surveillance systems, especially in light of the policing of dames entretenues? Historians of the police have argued that at midcentury the lieutenants general desired omniscience and that their surveillance apparatus was deployed particularly toward rendering transparent the lives of those of the lower social orders, for whom hiding anything was an indication of wrongdoing. The police were particularly interested in those individuals who were outside the control of social hierarchies.[51] There were projects from the 1720s to register (*enregistrer*) such individuals with the police, thereby incorporating them, in a sense.[52] Vincent Milliot argues: "If registering them is a way to assign them a place in the social hierarchy, it is also a question of making them visible within the urban space, assigning them a determined and recognized location."[53] Foucault theorized this exact development. He understood police surveillance, the capacity to make everything visible, as elemental to enabling police power to "bear over everything" and to extend the disciplinary apparatus beyond traditionally enclosed spaces like the school, army, or workshop. He argued that this "unceasing observation had to be accumulated in a series of reports and registers," which in themselves represented a new form of writing, "a permanent account of an individual's behavior."[54]

Writing against the "black legend" of the 1770s and the Revolutionary period that depicted police surveillance as a form of despotism, Milliot argues that surveillance practice was understood by those who engaged in it as a form of prophylaxis. Information gave the police a chance to exert pressure or negotiate with troublemakers in order to avoid scandal. The police, he argues, preferred to prevent rather than to punish.[55] In both these contexts, those of identification and of prevention, the founding of a department dedicated to the surveillance of dames entretenues, then, becomes intelligible. Dames entretenues had no natural place in the corporate structure of French society through which the state asserted its authority. Few were married. Those living with families often dominated them, as heads of household. They were not bound by the workshop, nor the brothel. They were free to leave their patrons and often did. In short, they had no "natural" oversight. And, as we shall see in the coming chapters, they exercised a degree of sexual choice unknown to all but elite women, who were bound by family and marriage. By definition the behavior of dames entretenues was scandalous, though acceptable as long as it fell within certain parameters. Enforcing those parameters required an awareness of their behavior. The surveillance of dames entretenues was in keeping with police goals at midcentury. Beginning with the first lieutenant general, de La Reynie, the police had an ear to the boudoir door, occasionally reporting on the activities of kept women. In fact, such information was requested by various ministers.[56] In 1747, the police pushed the door open, putting the demimonde—like other communities—under systematic observation, submitting a group outside of the social hierarchy to surveillance and using information to prevent scandal, when necessary.

✎ Surveillance and the Département des Femmes Galantes

The Département des femmes galantes was one of several whose operations were based largely on covert surveillance and report writing. Its "beat" was the demimonde, the world of elite prostitution. Departmental officers and agents spied and compiled reports on kept women and actresses who were *entretenue*, their patrons and boyfriends, the city's elite madams and their brothels, the *petites maisons* or trysting houses that ringed the city, *petits soupers* or libertine supper parties, and for a short while, libertine priests, although surveillance of this last group was part of a separate operation that had little to do with the demimonde.[57]

The edges of the Département as an administrative unit were not particularly clean. Individual inspectors and subinspectors adjunct to the Département regularly spied on other groups, such as foreigners.[58] More important, there was some engagement by key departmental personnel with the policing of nonelite prostitution. Inspector Marais was a common presence at the mass monthly police court hearings in which streetwalkers, prostitutes working at low-end brothels, and other "debauched" women were tried. Berryer occasionally charged Inspector Meusnier to investigate particular men and women connected to the bottom of the sex trade. That many of these individuals lived outside of Meusnier's quarter and hence did not naturally fall under his jurisdiction suggests the inspector was considered an expert on the subject, a contention supported by his replies to the police chief, which reveal a deep knowledge of prostitution at every level. But while Meusnier and Marais, and some of their colleagues, engaged in the policing of lower-level prostitution, none of these efforts were systematic. Court and prison records attribute the arrest and initial judicial processing of nonelite prostitutes to officers across Paris, indicating that it was carried out within the quarters rather than through the Département des femmes galantes or any other department. Later in the century, at least according to Lenoir, different departments policed street and elite prostitution.[59]

Tasked with policing the demimonde, the Département allocated much of its resources to growing and operating its surveillance system, which was built by one man, Inspector Jean-Baptiste Meusnier.[60] With the probable exception of the intelligence operation of the Département de sûreté (criminal investigation), that constructed by Meusnier was among the most sophisticated of its day. Meusnier may very well have been chosen for the job in part for his writing ability as well as for what seemed to be his "trustworthiness" as an underling. Meusnier first appears on the French bureaucratic map in 1734 as low-level employee—possibly a clerk—connected to the *ferme*, the institution responsible for collecting taxes in pre-Revolutionary France. Six years later, at the age of twenty-six, he joined the police, though in what capacity is unclear, and soon put his *ferme* connections to work, writing reports on various Parisian fermiers généraux (tax collectors). Similar in style and format to those he would later pen on the femmes galantes, these reports were witty, engaging, and above all ironic. Though they did provide basic information on the fermiers généraux and their families, they were so well written that they stood on their own as entertaining character sketches. These reports became public, and by the time they were published as part of Moufle d'Angerville's *La Vie privée de Louis XV* in 1781, they had been so frequently (and inaccurately) recopied that their provenance was all but forgotten.[61]

By 1747, Meusnier had begun to work with the newly organized Département des femmes galantes, though he did not purchase the office of inspector until two years later, in 1749. By at least 1751, he was living on rue des Canettes—not so far from the Comédie-Française—and had charge of the Luxembourg quarter. Berryer appears to have trusted Meusnier and assigned him several missions to gather information explicitly on behalf of the police chief's own patron, the marquise de Pompadour. Meusnier's loyalty, however, did not stop him from spying on his boss, keeping track in his private journals of Berryer's sexual affairs.[62] The dossier system started up, meekly at first, in 1748. In that year, at least seventeen kept women were of interest to the police. Meusnier submitted reports on ten of them. The following year, the inspector opened another forty-six dossiers. Eventually, Meusnier had dossiers on 550 women. Reports from the madams begin in 1749. As part of the Département's efforts to keep track of kept women, they had many petites maisons under surveillance.[63] These were small but well-provisioned country houses in the villages (not yet faubourgs) of Passy, Clichy, Chaillot, La Petite Pologne, and the Barrière Blanche, just beyond the city's boundaries. They were popular as secondary (and in some instances primary) residences for wealthy Parisians, many of whom had nothing to do with the demimonde.

Who were Meusnier's subjects? For the police, there were two administrative subject categories: women in the theater and nontheater femmes galantes. Of the 550 remaining dossiers compiled by Meusnier, 115, or 20.9 percent, are on theater women, and more than two-thirds of these on women of the Opéra.[64] Meusnier did not routinely follow the actresses of the Comédie-Française. Most theater women under surveillance were members of the Royal Academy of Music (the Opéra and its school), while the rest were performers with the Opéra-Comique or Comédie-Italienne. These latter two companies merged in 1762. Meusnier investigated almost every woman who trod on the stages of these three companies, but he did so with differing degrees of attention. Those who were big stars of the demimonde, with the best-paying patrons, were the subject of regular, sometimes monthly, reports. Those who never became entretenue slid off of his radar quickly, oftentimes without having become a dossier subject. For example, Meusnier limited his comments on Demoiselle Rolle, a dancer in the Opéra ballet, to his annual summary, in which he listed the name, age, address, position, and *amant* (patron) of every woman in the troupe. For Rolle, he wrote, nastily, "has no one. She is ugly."[65]

It was widely understood that any woman in the Opéra, and to a lesser degree the other theater companies, was a dame entretenue, or at least wanted to be. Most contemporaries assumed that performers took on patrons because they needed the money and because, in the very act of being on the stage, they were already at some level prostituting themselves. A principal singer or dancer was paid only one thousand to three thousand livres a year. A member of the chorus or corps de ballet earned a pittance, from one hundred to eight hundred livres, while those in "supernumerary positions" were not paid.[66] Women in the Opéra earned considerably less than their counterparts in the Comédie-Française, for example, and certainly not enough to support themselves in the manner in which they were expected to live.[67] These salaries were so low that Giacomo Casanova, who had quite a bit to say on the matter, thought that "a girl who is there [in the

Opéra] must, by her position, renounce what the lower classes call 'virtue,' for if one of them tried to live virtuously she would die of starvation."[68] Actresses in the Comédie-Française were in a different position. As recent scholarship attests, they not only earned more, they sometimes enjoyed creative control. Some, like Demoiselle Brillant (née Marie La maignon), did lead sexual lives that conformed to those structures which governed patron-mistress relationships. Other actresses, who had lovers and patrons, did not fit the kept-woman model.[69]

If the women of the stage constituted one category for Meusnier and later Marais, "everyone else" constituted the other. The latter comprised all the women whose dossiers were labeled dame entretenue, or *fille* or *femme galante*. The first category was discrete. Either a woman was a member of a company or she was not. The second category was broader. It included women from diverse backgrounds who engaged in a variety of transactional sexual relationships, experiencing different levels of financial success as prostitutes. Some did not easily fit the profile of a dame entretenue, and their dossiers were closed almost as soon as they were opened. Emerging through these records, however, is an ideal type. These women formed a group on the basis of four factors: their clients, prices, professional status, and nature of their liaisons. The clientele were members of le monde from whom high sums could be commanded. While some of these women did drift into marriage, they tended not to drift into and out of prostitution, as did most streetwalkers.[70] They were dependent almost entirely on their patrons for their livelihoods; they were professionals. The liaisons formed between these women and their clients often lasted for some time. They could be companionate, and even if not, there was the expectation that they might be. In theory, these liaisons were exclusive.

Following the surveillance practices Meusnier used with theater women, the inspector also prepared annual rolls of filles entretenues. When a particular woman on the list had no current patron, Meusnier simply noted, as he did with Demoiselle Rolle, "she has no one." The identification as a kept woman remained as such even if she was, at the moment, without a patron. Membership in a theater company separated the two groups; in all other ways, however, they were integrated. Singers, actresses, and dancers often had the same patrons as nontheater kept women. They attended the same parties, shared apartments, and were friends.

After 1757, Meusnier's adjunct, Louis Marais, took over management of the Département des femmes galantes. Marais had neither the skill nor the insight of Meusnier. He painted his subjects in broad, often crude, strokes, especially when compared to the subtle portraits composed by his predecessor. He followed Meusnier's routines for the first year or so, but by 1759 Marais gradually began to shift the focus of police surveillance, writing his lengthiest reports on women at the edges of the demimonde, those whose earnings, on average, would scarcely have made them competitive with Meusnier's subjects. As for the latter, they were still observed. In fact, Marais widened surveillance of theater women as well as of the highest paid non-theater dames entretenues.

In writing their reports, the inspectors had two major areas of interest: the identities of their subjects and the terms of exchange, or who was maintaining whom and of what did that maintenance consist. Identity depended first on a name, and this was not always so easily acquired. Sometimes regular investigative means failed, especially when a couple took pains to hide their affair by meeting out of town or by wearing disguises. Such was the case with the dancer Catherine Ponchon. Meusnier wrote, "The mystery and circumspection with which Demoiselle Ponchon has conducted her amorous intrigues . . . has thrown in error for quite some time [the identity] of her principal patron."[71] It was only after Meusnier had the dancer followed for over a week that he learned her patron was the chevalier de Mocenigo, ambassador from Venice.

A name, however, was not an identity. The inspectors construed identity differently for patrons than for their mistresses. For patrons, establishing identity required locating them in a nexus of family and corporate relationships. The inspectors ascertained a patron's office and rank, his geographical origin, his financial and marital status, his past affairs, and most important, the station and business of his family. Only then might an inspector remark on the patron's habits or lifestyle, noting that he was *libertine* or a *mauvais sujet* (trouble maker or scoundrel).[72]

Mistresses were identified by a different set of criteria. While the police were still interested in basic background details such as age, geographical origin, and parental occupation, they constructed mistresses as single entities, each the function of a particular history that propelled her into a highly specific set of social relationships. That particular history, a teleological narrative, explained how the woman in question left her family and became a dame entretenue, listing all the men with whom she was known to have had sexual relations—marital or transactional—along the way. The inspectors understood entry into the demimonde as a process. A girl first had to leave her home (usually the parental domicile but sometimes a marital one). Then she had to become a kept woman. What drove her through these stages, as they saw it, was either some wretched misfortune or a weak character.[73]

A second investigative axis was the terms of exchange, structured around the *contrat* (contract), the oral agreement between patron and mistress that delineated her remuneration. These were not legally binding. The inspectors went to great lengths to find the terms of the contract and, in addition, to record what was exchanged extracontractually, namely gifts. Meusnier detailed these items, describing them vividly down to the number of *aunes* of silk in a summer dress, and he always estimated their value. The inspectors also tracked emotional exchange, or at least its impact on material recompense. Both Meusnier and Marais spoke of love in only the most cynical of terms. They saw it as a lever to the contract. They used the intensity of a patron's romantic sentiments as a gauge to determine whether a dame entretenue would secure a contract, fix a damaged one, or "draw" (*tirer*) additional riches from her patron. If he is impassioned enough, they imply, she will get her way.

Running through these reports was a stable construction of the femme galante. Although he endowed them with real and varied personalities, Meusnier, the writer, mocked his subjects. He seemed to think that many of the women in his jurisdiction were mercenary and inexhaustibly materialistic, and that, to some degree, they enjoyed the physical demands of their profession. In his mind, they were professionals and as such knew how to manipulate their clients' emotions to maximum advantage. Speaking of the relationship of Demoiselle Magdelain to her boyfriend, for example, he wrote that the woman charged her lover as if he were a patron because "she did nothing for the glory of it."[74] Meusnier did leave room for a few who were, by his reckoning, "sweet" or "innocent" (and the many who were "stupid"). And he clearly felt sorry for the girls whose poverty forced them into prostitution, regardless of the prices they were commanding. However, he had no romantic illusions, of the kind that Alexandre Dumas would generate a century later, about the business that he was policing.[75]

To gather information on kept women, the inspectors relied on their employees, and their mouches, the most important of whom were the madams who ran the city's elite brothels. The madam-inspector relationship was the foundation of police efforts in the demimonde, and like so much else in that world, it was based both on an exchange and on the fiction of power. In theory, the police tolerated the elite brothels in return for information on their pensioners—women who lived and worked in the brothels—and clients, as well as on other players in the demimonde. Madams, for their part, took pains not to provoke the police into shutting them down. They were good neighbors. They ran quiet establishments, calling the Guard when necessary to remove gangs of drunken soldiers and other rowdies from their doorsteps. However, in practice, these establishments' powerful clientele, which included princes of blood, would have made closing them all but impossible.

The madams themselves responded to the inspectors in different ways. Some were wary. Madam d'Osment, a personal informant of the lieutenant general, was still afraid of Meusnier. When a client once skipped out without paying, she resorted to ambushing him on the street rather than approaching him at work for fear that Meusnier would be called.[76] Madam Hecquet, on the other hand, was insouciant. When Meusnier once demanded she come to his hotel, she replied that she was busy, having promised to take her "petite famille" ("little family," by which she meant her pensioners) on a picnic.[77] Regardless of particular attitudes, all the madams fulfilled their obligations. D'Osment provided the lieutenant general with information on a bimonthly schedule. Several madams were assigned specific inspectors—perhaps because many of these women were barely literate—to produce a steady stream of reports for Meusnier's files. At least seven of the madams also produced regular brothel reports, writing down who came to their establishments, what they did, and how much they paid, and recording any other seemingly important information.[78] Remaining documents suggest that several other madams provided the police with these brothel journals, but that they have since been lost.[79]

Collectively the madams created something akin to an intelligence grid that underpinned much of the inspectors' activity. It established categories—of buyers and sellers, libertines and troublemakers, women who were up-and-coming and those who were about to end their careers—into which the inspectors added the fruits of their investigations. The intelligence supplied by the madams served as the basis for the dossier system. Any girl coming out of a brothel would have had her history investigated by her prospective employer during the initial hiring process. D'Osment wrote, "I have taken back Marie-Françoise Moisson, *fille*, as a pensioner," and then proceeded to relate Moisson's sexual history.[80] Such interrogations may have been mandated. Brothels were not supposed to accept virgins, although, of course, they did, and with regularity. Nor were they to take women from respectable families. The madams were so well situated in the demimonde that their investigative reach extended beyond those who were or had once been in their custody. They were able to unearth the backgrounds of girls who had never been in the brothel system.[81]

Madams and police spies were the foundation of an intelligence system to which many other agents contributed. Meusnier and Marais sought information directly from those who served the dames entretenues. Servants were especially important in this regard and were the most likely source of information on the internal dynamics of patron-mistress relationships. The inspectors also queried furniture makers, jewelers, and other artisans who produced the luxury goods that were aggressively acquired by kept women (through the auspices of their patrons). The police talked to neighbors and friends and sometimes to the kept women themselves, as well as to their patrons. They talked to their subjects' masters, parents, and commanding officers.

The inspectors did not take this information at face value. They marked up incoming reports, correcting some facts and demanding verification of others. Meusnier made notes in his own journal regarding what information he was lacking and which source he planned to ask.[82] The final product often deviated from the original source. For example, in June 1751 Berryer sent Inspector Meusnier a note requesting more information on a particular man, named Destourneau, whom police informants had heard criticizing the government's handling of the War of Austrian Succession. Such an investigation would have been part of Meusnier's regular duties as an inspector, and he assigned the case to Jean-Charles Pean de La Jannière, *exempt de robe courte*, one of the officers he used frequently in his surveillance of kept women.[83] Seventeen days after receiving Berryer's order, Meusnier submitted to his superior his own report and that of La Jannière, having corrected the latter.[84]

The processes of information verification did not stop once the report was written. Both Meusnier and Marais wrote drafts and edited them heavily, adding and altering information as it became available. Final reports corrected mistakes of earlier ones, sometimes written years before. That inspectors worked hard to get at what they thought was the truth is perhaps best evidenced by their regular use of the phrases such as "on dit" ("they say" or "it is said") and "on comte" (it was reported), parenthetical markers that separated gossip or rumor from what was verifiable. For example, in speaking of Demoiselle Le Clair, a dancer with the Comédie-Italienne, Inspector Marais wrote, "It is said that presently she is very well *nippée* [provided for in clothing and furniture]."[85] In the report that opened this chapter, for example, Meusnier carefully separated the facts from pieces of information from which he thought he should distance himself. "It is assured," he wrote, "that Demoiselle St. Hylaire has a new patron, whose name we have not yet been able to ascertain. That will be a task for next week."[86]

Given their processes, the inspectors' standards of proof were probably better than those of most police departments and certainly superior to those of any other serious news-gathering entities of the day. But, ultimately, the final reports were only as good as their redactors. What information the inspectors sought, as well as how they wove their "facts" into a narrative, were informed by the reports' intended purpose and readership. Once finished, the reports went to the Secretariat and then on to the lieutenant general. Sometimes Chaban, the bureau's chief clerk, wrote notes in the margins or indexed the names of all those mentioned in the report. The lieutenant general intermittently appended notes of his own, often requesting that his clerk ask the inspectors for more information. Occasionally, he would order the staff to investigate a woman who was not in the dossier system. Nevertheless, the movement of information was overwhelmingly from the bottom to the top. Whatever role the lieutenants general initially had in shaping the Département and its mission, their role in its operation was reactive.

What we have, then, is a fairly significant police operation that was designed to produce documents specifically for police consumption as part of a larger mission of policing the demimonde. Understanding that mission requires untangling what was happening on the ground level, determining the extradiscursive relationships of the police and the policed.

☛ Beyond Report Writing: Police Actions in the Demimonde

While surveillance no doubt took up a good portion of their time, the inspectors' reports and ancillary documentation reveal a larger mission of the Département des femmes galantes. Its officers functioned both as de facto regulators and as commissioners. The line between these two roles is often difficult to draw, especially since the inspectors generally respected the customs of the demimonde and allowed business to transact without much police interference. As regulators, the only rules that they imposed and regularly enforced concerned the operation of elite brothels. These establishments had to be orderly. They had to submit reports, and they could not accept certain classes of girls and women as sex workers: the very young and those from middling and upper-class families.

There was a double and mutually reinforcing logic at work in these rules. Commentators, judicial officers, and even "public opinion" as recorded by diarists considered pedophilia, as well as the prostitution of girls from "good" families, to be morally repugnant. Such acts violated fundamental notions of family and honor and constituted a line the crossing of which was unacceptable. The Parlement of Paris prosecuted cases of pandering in both instances. Some police officials, such as Lenoir, argued that the protection of the honor of such girls was a purpose of the *police des moeurs*.[87]

But more broadly, the policing of sexuality at midcentury and, in particular, the actions of the inspectors were about preventing scandal. The scandal inherent in selling sex bothered some moralists and religious thinkers, though its permanence and necessity seemed to be accepted by most. For urban authorities, street prostitution was problematic largely because it was on the street, in public, attracting attention and upsetting neighbors and passersby. For the state, the problem took on a slightly different hue. Many of the late-seventeenth-century laws that criminalized prostitution and established punishment regimes juridically lumped sex workers together with other *gens sans aveu* (vagabonds, people without jobs); prostitutes posed a problem because they were outside the network of corporations that extended hierarchical social control over the population. Being on the street only highlighted their threat to order.[88] Collectively, the Paris police directed their energies toward arresting those prostitutes and madams whose activities drew attention, showing little concern for those who did not. Orderly brothels, those which kept the noise down and prevented the congregation of soldiers and other rowdies, were less likely to scandalize neighbors and the quarter.

With respect to the demimonde, however, the scandal argument has to be tempered. This is largely because, above and beyond unruly prostitution and pimping, many of those scandalous behaviors one would expect the inspectors to halt, if not prevent, were never cause for arrest, nor even warning.[89] Meusnier and Marais did not stop madams from selling virgins (as long as the girl was at least twelve, it seems), nor did they keep elite prostitutes from spreading venereal disease. They stood by as dames entretenues committed fraud, using pregnancies, for example, to game funds from numerous men, each of whom had been led to believe he was the father. Meusnier allowed a sex worker to remain in a brothel as he noticed that her father was searching for her.[90] Both inspectors tracked the efforts of parents to stop the financial hemorrhage occasioned by a son's reckless spending on his mistress, yet did nothing. In cases that involved families, the inspectors did not get involved unless specifically asked to do so.

The case of Catherine Mahüe, known professionally as Virginie, is a good example of the inspectors' policing policies. Once a dame entretenue, Virginie's fortunes had faded, and she eventually ended up a low-end prostitute working from a *chambre garnie* (rented, furnished room). Each day she sent her maid down to the street to trawl for clients. After a few months, when Virginie again found a patron who could maintain her, she secretly sold her furniture on the eve of its repossession. All the while, she had been causing scandals in various taverns and dives. Meusnier wrote that Virginie's "dominant passion" is to go to different disreputable places in Paris and "cause a ruckus." Streetwalking (even by proxy) and selling goods belonging to another (theft) were criminal offenses warranting arrest. Furthermore, women who spent time in "disreputable places" and repeatedly made public scenes were often caught in night raids by the Guard or arrested via lettre de cachet at the request of their families or neighbors. In short, Meusnier had the right to apprehend Virginie for any number of reasons in the year she was under surveillance. However, it was not until she dressed as a man that he arrested her, and he did so immediately.[91] Transvestism was a crime that the police took seriously. Cross-dressing prostitutes were sent to the Hôpital.

It was not that the inspectors were unaware of these events as they transpired; they were, and they took notes. But instead of acting to suppress those illicit sexual activities that defined the demimonde, Meusnier and Marais regulated them. Sometimes ex officio, sometimes on the request of a particular party, they managed instances in which kept women or their patrons deviated from demimonde custom or when their behavior caused problems in the wider community. This sort of regulation, which kept the demimonde running smoothly, was an alternative to repression in preventing scandal, or at least containing it. For example, in determining where brothels could be located, Meusnier anticipated and sometimes dealt with the reactions of neighbors. In running interference between kept women and those who opposed their presence in certain quarters, they diffused tensions. In this, they acted like commissioners.

Complicating their role, the inspectors did not always share the same definition of scandal as did complainants who sought their adjudication, nor did they necessarily rule in the favor of the members of the dominant community. For example, the curé of St. Benoit wrote to Meusnier demanding that the Italian, Angélique Lambertini, an actress in the Comédie-Italienne and a friend of Casanova, be forced from his parish. Knowing the curé's intentions, Lambertini went to see the inspector on two different occasions and, having found him out of his office each time, wrote him a letter defending herself. She claimed that she was not living scandalously in that she was maintained by a single person. Meusnier allowed her to stay; her address in the police files remained the same.[92] What are we to make of this decision? The inspectors functioned as magistrates or commissioners of the demimonde. In doing so, and in ruling on behalf of kept women, they moved beyond tolerating galanterie to making a tacit claim for its acceptability. Mistress keeping and elite prostitution were not so scandalous, after all, as long as elite prostitutes and dames entretenues operated within boundaries, which police presence and activities helped to make clear thereby assuring the wider public. This stance served to benefit kept women both practically— Lambertini did not have to move—and more generally, by validating their profession. The reports reflected a similar positioning. The inspectors, in their obsessive reporting on contracts, conceptualized the demimonde on its own terms.

The inspectors did not handle all disputes involving kept women. Those that had the appearance of legal squabbles, specifically those that concerned the delivery of services or payment for those services, tended to be handled by actual commissioners. But in his role as faux-commissioner, Meusnier was the officer to whom kept women went when they needed help. When Suzanne Elizabeth LeGrand, known professionally as Beaumont, wanted to return to Paris after having absconded earlier with a thousand écus (three thousand livres) of other peoples' money in order to marry a man Meusnier described as a good looking mauvais sujet, she wrote to the inspector. She hoped, in the inspector's words, that he would protect her "from the bad mood of her creditors and from the wrath of the police" who would arrest her for theft should she enter the capital.[93] She was trying to annul her marriage, she claimed, maintaining that the man her "big heart" and "credulity" led her to believe would give her a "happy ending" was nothing but cruel and abusive. She wrote to the inspector, "I pour out my heart to you as a man in whom I know there are feelings of honor and goodness." She also offered something in exchange for his smoothing the path of her return. "I wait for the great service I ask of you" and "I will do anything to please you."[94] Such statements of devotion were almost formulaic in letters asking for help, though LeGrand's language may have been deliberately ambiguous. Meusnier did not help her, at least for a while. After reading her dossier, he was convinced that she was trying to separate from her husband so that she could come back to Paris to take "advantage of its resources," meaning moneyed men and opportunity. He wrote, "The letter attached . . . proves that she has not repented."[95] When Meusnier received LeGrand's first letter, he had recognized her handwriting. This is not surprising. He corresponded regularly with quite a number of women.

While the cumulative effect of the inspectors' surveillance and intervention may have been beneficial to many kept women, there was a darker side to their engagement in the demimonde. LeGrand was not reaching when she seemingly offered her sexual services to Meusnier. The role of confidant and helper did not stop the inspector from taking advantage of the sexual opportunities available to a man holding his office. He was a cus-

tomer at the brothels he was supposed to police. This was expected. Madam
d'Osment actually held up Meusnier's conduct during his visits as exemplary in comparison to that of his successor.[96] But, while frequenting a
brothel was not particularly scandalous, some of his other actions were.
Madam Montbrun, while following standard procedure and informing the
police of an impending sale of a virgin, appears to have offered the girl to
the inspector. After explaining how the girl, Demoiselle Perrin, was brought
to her, she wrote, "There you go. You now know everything and you can take
a keen interest in it if you think it is appropriate." Apparently, the inspector
did. A note later appended to the bottom of the file read by Marais stated,
"For a louis, Meusnier fucked the niece of La Perrin." Perhaps Meusnier
anticipated his involvement with the girl and was either conflicted or simply
wanted to cover himself in case his decision became known to his superiors
or the public. A week prior to Montbrun's offer, and for the first and only
time in thousands of pages of writing, Meusnier morally condemned the
actions of his subjects, in this case the aunt who sold her niece, the child he
would later buy.[97]

Engaging the services offered in the demimonde did not make Meusnier
particularly corrupt. What it did do was indelibly blur the line between the
police and the policed. In buying the virginity of Demoiselle Perrin, Meusnier assumed the role of client or patron. Like any other client, Meusnier
paid, though in this particular case the currency was as much the promise of
protection as it was cash. Yet this did not separate the inspector so greatly
from other patrons who complemented their material offerings with other
intangibles like status, protection, or security. Moreover, Meusnier learned
about the sale in the way any other client would have, through the broker,
Madam Montbrun. LeGrand's offer of sexual services in exchange for police protection more firmly entrenches Meusnier in the role of patron. Its
acceptance would have been almost banal in this period in which the exchange of sex for other services was commonplace. But when the client is
the inspector in charge of policing the greatest and most formal assemblage
of such exchanges, it takes on an added importance.

Meusnier's relationship with his wife further obscured the line between
the police and policed. His wife, Geneviève Longagne, was the illegitimate
child of a speculator who had amassed and then lost millions under John
Law, the Scottish financier who had tried and failed to establish a French
national bank in the 1720s, bankrupting many in the process. Longagne
began to have affairs soon after she married Meusnier. As an aggrieved husband, the inspector had his wife repeatedly incarcerated via lettre de cachet
for libertinage. She was only released from her final imprisonment after his

death, when she appealed directly to Lieutenant General Sartine. As a police inspector, Meusnier actually started a dossier on his own wife, observing her actions with the same level of objectivity as with those of his other subjects. All that distinguished this particular file from any other is a small note added by a clerk in the upper right hand corner: "femme de Meusnier."[98] In one way, the matter seems quite simple: Meusnier used all of the resources at hand to control his wife. In doing so, however, he collapsed any walls separating his official and personal lives.

Meusnier's tenure as the Département chief ended with his death. According to Inspector Marais, his predecessor was murdered in March 1757 by Monsieur Herment, a prisoner he had been escorting to the Chateau d'If. Herment had been under surveillance since 1751, as had his mistress, Catherine Winter.[99] Nineteenth-century historian and archivist Paul d'Estrée contested this account, claiming that a few years later Meusnier was spotted alive and well and living in Hamburg, where he was duly employed as a recruiter for Catherine II.[100] Whatever happened, police investigation into the murder was minimal.

Inspector Marais stands in stark contrast to his predecessor. So much of what Meusnier did depended on his own immersion in the mores of the demimonde. He respected the contracts and corporations that constituted both the demimonde and those Parisian societies beyond it. Much of his job, aside from the surveillance, was to make sure those customs were followed. Marais performed this job, but in an entirely different spirit. The inspector continued to mediate between the world kept women were in and that from which they came, but there is little documentary evidence to suggest that he helped any in need. It seems that most of his extrasurveillance energies were engaged in building up his own power base and taking advantage of the fruits it had to offer.

For example, Marais rarely paid for the sexual services he engaged when he went to the brothels. This so outraged Madam d'Osment that she complained to Lieutenant General Sartine. As Marais was in the habit of making these forays in the company of his clerk, a good-looking man, d'Osment wrote, "It seems they think that the position of one and the beauty of the other enable them to dispense with the necessity of paying." Nor did Marais stay for a meal with the madam and her pensioners as was the custom. D'Osment found this insulting and argued that Marais had become the inspector "only to enrich himself and to pay less for girls." She was particularly horrified by his abandonment of the pretense of wearing a disguise when passing an afternoon with her pensioners.[101] It was not the inspector's corruption that upset her. Rather, it was his disdain for the conventions of

corruption, his arrogance, and his assumption of power that led him to reject the very social niceties that would affirm his part in the community.

Marais's disregard of the conventions of the demimonde changed his relationship to the world he was policing. In not paying for services, he ceased
to be a client in the way his predecessor had been. This new attitude was
shared by those under his protection. When Anne Bonard, known professionally as Mon Royal, was denounced as a prostitute, she seemed drunk
before Commissioner Sirebeau and announced that she no longer feared
punishment for her actions, for "she had as a friend and protector Sir Marais,
inspector of the police, with whom she had sexual relations." She was so
involved with him, she claimed that "she called him by no other name than
Papa" and "she came in the mornings to find him in his bed."[102]

Disdain for convention, however, was not the totality of Marais's transformation of the office of inspector of the Département des femmes galantes. Marais actually offered his policing services to various wealthy and
important patrons. In so doing, he moved from objectively observing and
recording events to intervening in them. For example, he had his mouche
watch the house of Louise Régis (Demoiselle Raye), a dancer in the Opéra,
in order to aid her patron, the marquis de Romey, in ascertaining whether
or not she was cheating on him. (She was, and he fired her.)[103] In another
example, the duc de Fronsac asked the inspector to use his encyclopedic and
up-to-date knowledge of the demimonde to help him determine who had
given him venereal disease.[104] Marais, it seems, liked the company of powerful men. Lieutenant General Sartine, writing a report on his inspectors to
Lenoir, the man who was to succeed him, said that Marais was a good officer
but that he was too interested in attending parties thrown by the comte du
Barry and other "seigneurs," to which he was often invited.[105]

It is possible to see Meusnier and Marais as examples of old and new
policing. Meusnier enforced the rules of a world from which he could not
separate himself. Marais effected that separation mainly through a new corruption. Yet their personal differences cannot efface a fundamental similarity. Both inspectors spent the majority of their time engaged in surveillance
of kept women.

In practice, policing shaped the demimonde in a number of ways, each of
which will be explored in detail in following chapters. Taken as a whole,
the Département's actions served both to authorize and legitimize elite transactional sex and, indeed, even facilitate it. The inspectors' policy of toleration enabled madams to grow substantial businesses. In intervening in
conflicts between dames entretenues with those inside and outside the

demimonde, the inspectors tacitly recognized being kept as a *métier*, as a way of life that differentiated these women from others. Recognition and labeling by the police were not necessarily beneficial, as we saw in the case of women who were assimilated to street prostitutes and incarcerated in the Hôpital. However, police action with respect to the demimonde accorded the community a certain legitimacy. Police surveillance and the information dialectic with the madams that it embodied set the boundaries of the demimonde, both in terms of personnel—the buyers and sellers of elite sex— and in terms of acceptable practices. Policing formalized the demimonde as a community with which others engaged. In observing the terms of and sometimes helping to adjudicate the oral contracts that governed patron-mistress relations, the inspectors clarified and fixed the means by which kept women could accrue sexual capital and advance their careers as elite prostitutes. They contributed to the standardization of mistress keeping and its professionalization. In doing so, they fostered the formation of a work identity and an agency—however limited—for kept women.

The police presence was not all helpful, of course. As in the case of Suzanne Elizabeth LeGrand, the inspectors did not always rule in favor of kept women. They extorted sexual services and possibly money. Nor should we overstate the benefits their policing effected. They did not and, indeed, could not keep mistresses safe from the exploitation and violent behavior of their patrons, boyfriends, and families, nor from the dangers of pregnancy and venereal disease. They had no interest in helping these women find other lines of work, and the ways in which their policing professionalized galanterie may have militated against this. They did not seem to have any positive power over the trajectory of careers; they could not make women more desirable. They allowed and sometimes oversaw the prostitution of preadolescent girls. But in a world in which the alternative for many of these women— from virgins to established femmes galantes—would have been street prostitution with all its attendant dangers, policing of the demimonde advantaged mistresses more than harmed them.

Effect, however, is different from intent. While it is unlikely that the Département was established or saw its mission as that of "helping" elite prostitutes, it is equally clear that it was not intended to repress elite transactional sex. As such, the actions of the Département conform to theorizations of surveillance. De Tocqueville associated surveillance with increasing efficiency of the state.[106] Writing two centuries later, Foucault articulated the emergence of a disciplinary society in which even those outside traditional disciplined spaces, such as the workshop, came to be objects of a disciplinary apparatus.[107] For both the monarchy and the police, the goals of rendering

the capital visible and of supporting corporations and families, those fundamental constructs of social control, were intertwined. Individuals outside
these structures, the gens sans aveu, whose actions by definition were not
visible to the state, had to be "incorporated" in some way. So whether we
choose to see the demimonde as a de facto corporation or as its antithesis, a
chaotic body of women without natural oversight, the inspectors' job was a
familiar one. They were to make sure that the demimonde followed its own
rules, for by doing so it would remain controlled. At the same time, the
inspectors opened up that world by reporting what was happening behind
the metaphorical doors of the demimonde. Both these processes made the
inspectors at once a part of the world they were policing and mediators
between it and other corporations and communities.

From this perspective, their regime was not particularly repressive, at least
in context. Yet it was this sort of surveillance, and its companion practice,
covert arrest, that constituted the basis of the "black legend," a depiction of
the police, beginning in the 1770s and gaining momentum during the Revolution, as despotic, arbitrary, and abusing their power.[108] Modern scholarship on this period has revisited the relationship between the police and the
policed, emphasizing their mutual interdependence and even the ways in
which the policed manipulated new institutions for their own purposes.[109]
Police personnel later in the century, including the lieutenants general,
absorbed certain Enlightenment ideas and came to understand their missions, at least in part, as making men better and improving their lives.[110] But
it is important to remember that however we judge the work of several inspectors and several dozen mouches—whether as being repressive or helpful—
their impact was inconsequential compared to what happened to these
women in the hands of others. Both the police and the policed were part of
a larger system of values and morals in which women who lost their sexual
honor were marginalized and consequently suffered enormous social disabilities and financial penalties. In other words, the most severe policing had
been effected long before Meusnier and Marais entered the scene. It is to
that policing that we now turn.

✒ Chapter 2

Leaving Home

In 1744, when she was fourteen years old, Anne Michelet traveled to Paris from the village of Nesle-en-Brie to find work.[1] If she walked, the journey might have taken her a week. If she went by *poste*, perhaps she could have covered the seventy-five miles within several days, depending on the roads. In other ways, the journey was even farther. Anne left the small town where she had grown up. She left her father, the local school teacher, with whom she lived alone; her mother had died some years before. She left her friends, her family, and the way of life of the Picard village to live in France's biggest city, an entirely different world. At more than one-half million people, the very size of the capital, its density, its pace of life, and its culture would prove challenging, if not shocking, for Anne and the tens of thousands of others who immigrated to the capital each year.[2]

Thanks to an aunt, Anne found work as a servant (*servante*) with a hat-maker, for whom she might have provided industrial labor as a *coupeuse, arracheuse,* or *repasseuse* responsible for removing fur from pelts after they had been soaked in a mercury solution.[3] These were arduous tasks and, with the risk of heavy-metal poisoning, dangerous ones. Alternatively, Anne's responsibilities might have been entirely domestic, relieving the master's wife of the most grueling work of cleaning, lighting fires, fetching water, doing laundry, and running errands. The French term *servante* comprehended both domestic labor and industrial work; the two were not clearly distinguished.[4]

Whatever her duties, Anne performed them for only three years before finding a new position, and then another. Finally she left service altogether to share a *chambre garnie* (furnished room) with a friend with whom she worked "en linge," that is, in linen production or maintenance, most probably sewing linen products such as tablecloths, napkins, and undergarments.

Up to this point, there is nothing striking about Anne's journey. Girls from her background, those who had to earn their own dowries, left home between the ages of twelve and fourteen to find work. Nor was changing jobs any sort of red flag; it was common among those engaged in such low-skill work. For Anne Michelet, success at this point would not have been measured by employment stability but rather by maintaining her sexual honor and saving enough money for a dowry. If Anne had stayed steadily employed, and had been lucky, she might have put aside one hundred livres for a dowry by the time she reached the age of marriage, twenty-five or twenty-six.[5] Anne, however, was not successful, at least not in these terms. She never finished the cycle of working and saving that was supposed to lead to marriage. Midway through, at around age nineteen, she made a decision that opened the way to a different future. As a result, twelve years after leaving home, rather than having become the wife of a tradesman—a usual match for women in domestic service—Anne was a professional dame entretenue, a kept woman maintained by a Flemish marquis at the price of five hundred livres a month. What happened? How did this daughter of a Picard schoolteacher become a well-established and well-paid femme galante?

Anne's turn toward prostitution, we see in retrospect, began with an irregular relationship, when she left her chambre garnie to live with Vielbans, a twenty-six-year-old soldier in the Black Musketeers.[6] The couple shared an apartment together for two years in the neighborhood of Saint Antoine—a part of Paris populated largely by working people—where they passed for man and wife. The line between canonical wedlock and socially sanctioned cohabitation was blurred in some plebian districts of Paris, where "free unions" were common and could be recognized by friends, family, and *le quartier* as marriage.[7] In this milieu, even after Anne had a child, she would not have been socially disqualified from marrying.

But this changed in the summer of 1752, when Vielbans abandoned Anne, leaving Paris to visit his family. Anne turned to prostitution to support herself, first working in brothels and then streetwalking in men's clothing (including a sword and wig), for which she was arrested and incarcerated for eight months. We are given no explanation for what seems like such a dramatic shift in behavior. Why prostitution rather than domestic service? And how did Anne even find the elite brothels? Anne may have been recruited, but Vielbans is also an obvious link. Musketeers were notorious personae in the demimonde, filling the ranks of petty patrons or serving as gigolos (greluchons) to the mistresses of other, wealthier men. Anne's association with Vielbans could easily have exposed her to Paris's elite sexual underworld.

Exposure, however, did not equal approval. When Vielbans returned to Paris and learned of Anne's conduct in his absence, he decided he no longer wanted to support her and instead became one of her customers, paying Anne for *passades* (one-night stands).[8] If Anne's experiences in the brothel, on the street, and in prison had changed her personally, they also did so in other respects, fundamentally shifting her status in a way that being a girlfriend-mistaken-for-a-wife could not. Culturally, socially, and judicially, Anne was now a different creature from the *servante* working for her dowry.

Vielbans, however, was not Anne's only client. She also saw Pierre Henri de Tourmont, *président de la cour des aides* (president of the coinage court), who took her on as his mistress.[9] For Anne this relationship was extremely profitable. While Tourmont was not known to be rich, his support allowed Anne to acquire some of the clothing and jewelry that were the unofficial uniform of kept women. Perhaps more important, keeping Tourmont's company—he was rarely without a mistress—publicly marked Anne as a dame entretenue and gave her access to other candidates for patronage. Tourmont was followed (not directly) by the prince de Rohan-Cabot, who kept Anne for a year, paying her six hundred livres a month and giving her six thousand livres in furniture.[10]

How and why did Anne Michelet become a dame entretenue? The inspectors structured their own investigations into this very question by looking at "what went wrong" on the path to marriage. They envisioned loss of sexual honor as stepping off of that path. They imagined its natural outcome, prostitution, as a discrete, instant, and permanent transformation, one which prevented a woman from ever marrying. What drove a girl to such extremes was either her love of pleasure and luxury, or a pitiful desperation. Yet the details of the inspectors' very own reports belie such simplification. Anne's entry into the demimonde was clearly gradual, a slow shift from one life course to another. It was the result of a number of decisions, each made within the context of the institutions, social practices, and cultural expectations that were supposed to turn daughters of the modest poor into brides. The questions of how and why Anne Michelet became an elite prostitute are consequently embedded in the larger narrative of her own subjectivity. How did Anne imagine her future when she left for Paris and then, later, at each juncture where she made a choice that pushed her further from the course laid out to marriage? Studying the constructs that shaped female adolescence, we can hope to stitch together how Anne might have seen her options and to understand the mental horizons that informed her navigation of them.

To understand the course taken by Anne and other women we must examine contemporary imaginings of the "marriage plot" and its opposite, "harlot's progress." Like the inspectors, we will look at "what went wrong" on the path to marriage, in trying to chart Anne's mental world. But we will also use Anne's story to interrogate this very framework and to challenge the assumptions on which it rests. Anne's story and those of women like her complicate and in some instances subvert the conventions of normative heterosexuality at midcentury. They show that marriage was not always the most immediate goal; it competed with a desire for love, money, security, adventure, or simply the need to survive to the next day. The stories of these women reveal that a great deal of living occurred between the careful (and chaste) cycle of working and saving that was to lead to marriage and its putative antithesis, streetwalking.

☙ Profiling Dames Entretenues

Marriage was the ultimate goal of most women in eighteenth-century France.[11] The pressure to marry came from every level. In religious, political, and contemporary social theory, women were meant for marriage and the male oversight and government it provided them. It was considered the natural order of things, divined by God, urged and supported by the state. Economically, being in a long-term stable relationship was often the only way in which women were able to survive. Many enterprises required the labor of both partners. Those industries in which single women could find employment rarely paid a living wage.[12] And while some female artisans, like successful mistress seamstresses, were able to support themselves alone, such independence was unusual among never-married working women.[13] Socially, marriage established husband and wife as adults and granted them the rights of full community members. Through marriage, women attained social respectability and their own households. Remaining single often meant a life of poverty, low social status, and dependence on relatives.

In principle, marriage had two prerequisites: sexual honor and a dowry. Although women were able to marry without either, this was rarely their intent from the outset.[14] Sexual honor was a form of reputation, specifically the perception that a woman was following the rules of sexual decorum for her social community. Girls from peasant, laboring, and artisanal

backgrounds—backgrounds typical for families that produced kept women—
were not forbidden from premarital sexual intercourse, as long as the couple
eventually married. However, sexual decorum comprehended a great deal
more than sexual activity. Clothing, speech, and carriage were all indicators
of sexual probity. A woman who frequented *mauvais lieux* (disreputable
places) or had rendezvous with different men incurred a poor sexual reputation, regardless of what she actually did with her body. A girl or a woman
with a good sexual reputation was thought to make a good, faithful wife,
one who would not cuckold her husband, impugning his honor and creating the possibility of a false heir. So important was reputation that women
went to court to defend themselves against insults to their sexual honor.[15]
They did this in part because legal and religious thinking conceptualized
sexual honor as being binary: a woman had honor or she did not. This was
especially the case for unmarried girls. A girl's bad reputation, for example,
could contribute to the legal nullification of certain charges of rape.[16] In
theory, any girl who lost her virginity without marriage was barred from
respectable society, making it difficult for her to marry anyone but her se-
ducer or even find employment, for which good morals were often a quali-
fication. However, this was not always the case in practice.

As for a dowry, the second standard requirement for marriage, expectations varied greatly. For girls from modest families, dowries usually consisted
of a lump sum of cash and some objects necessary for setting up a household: linens, possibly a bed.[17] Ideally, the dowry, combined with the groom's
portion, would set the new couple on a sound financial base, enabling them
to support themselves so that they would not tax their families and extended
communities.[18] In many instances, a skill set could substitute for a portion
of the dowry. Undowered and unskilled women did marry in eighteenth-
century France, but they often married men who were similarly without
resources. Sometimes this was possible because the couple lived in an area of
plentiful wage work through which they could support themselves.[19] Rarely,
couples entirely ignored the heavy weight of social tradition in addition to
their own economic interests and married without any clear financial strategy for survival. Nevertheless, while not every marriage was contracted with
a dowry, a dowry always was seen as desirable.

Exactly how a girl safeguarded her sexual reputation while accruing a
dowry was determined by socio-professional background. The police reports
provide the only systematic survey of social data on kept women. In a sample
of 265 dossiers, police recorded parental occupation in 110. Of these, about a
third of the fathers were artisans, ranging from glaziers to dyers to belt makers. They included butchers, carpenters, glass makers, and masons, among

other professions. One was a tunnel digger. Five happened to be wigmakers. These families came mainly from Paris and France's other big cities.

After artisans, servants of varying ranks made up the second largest group of fathers, almost 20 percent of the sample.[20] Three were doormen. Another three were or had been gamekeepers. Many were valets, some serving high-ranking aristocrats. The father of Marie-Antoinette Moreau had been a manservant to the duc d'Orléans, while his wife had been the duchess's maid.[21] Like Mère Moreau, some of the wives were servants. Several were washerwomen or, like Anne Michelet, worked "en linge." A few had small businesses. With the exception of the gamekeepers, these were largely Parisian families. Eighteen fathers (about 15 percent of recorded cases) were merchants or otherwise involved in commerce. These families originated outside of Paris. They ranged from a Lyonnais silk merchant to several small-time to-bacco retailers. For the most part, police records do not identify the size of their enterprises and hence the social background of the families running them. The few wives in this group who were professionally identified were in business with their husbands. The last large group of fathers (10 percent of the sample) was that of theater performers, actors, singers, dancers, and musicians. Most were or had been married to theater women, and almost all had immigrated to Paris from cities in the provinces or from abroad. These were theater families. Sons and daughters followed their parents onto the stage.[22]

Only a handful of fathers were described by police as nobles or officeholders, and each of these cases was atypical. Demoiselle Minot, for example, was reported to be the illegitimate daughter of a *conseiller de Parlement* and supposedly grew up unaware of her father's identity. She had not been raised as a daughter of a robe noble. In fact, her father only revealed his relationship out of desperation, to stop an affair between Minot and his son, her half-brother.[23] At the other end of the social spectrum, very few kept women claimed or were reported to be from families that made up the rootless and criminal elements of urban society, the *gens sans aveu* (people without positions), beggars, vagabonds, pick-pockets, and street prostitutes who were rounded up in the *Grand Renfermement*. If we include in this category those without stable employment, such as day laborers and water carriers, this finding is striking. This group, constituting between 33 and 50 percent of any urban population, was significantly underrepresented among the natal families of kept women.[24]

In fact, if we consider paternal occupation as an indicator of status, most kept women were not from the very bottom of the pile, the "people" or "populace," as one might expect. Rather, like Anne Michelet, they came from families that hovered between the middle and lower end of contemporary social hierarchies, with the exception of theater performers.[25] Perceptions of performers were complex and changing but any ranking of occupations in the mid-eighteenth century would have been certain to classify them toward the bottom. Although they were celebrities, actors carried the shame inherent in their profession. The Gallican church considered actors to be outside of the Christian community.[26]

The lower-status families, those with servant or theater fathers, tended to be, in modern parlance, the most functional among those that produced kept women. Few of them seemed to have been terribly poor. Perhaps this was because most of the parents' marriages still were intact at the moment their daughters entered adolescence. The families had the income and labor of both partners. In fact, many of them were wealthy enough to apprentice their daughters in trades. Marie Jeanne Treppier, daughter of servants, was apprenticed to a Parisian dressmaker.[27] Meusnier claimed that the family Moreau were financially comfortable and that through the mother's connections they were able to set up their daughter in a lace-making apprenticeship.[28]

In contrast, the merchant families, though of higher social standing, were quite poor and in great disarray. Most had businesses that either were failing or disordered. Adding to family financial pressures, many of the merchant fathers simply were absent, either dead or having abandoned their wives and children. Marguerite Madeylaine Jacob's father, a silk merchant, declared false bankruptcy and disappeared. Her mother turned to elite prostitution, according to Meusnier, to support the family.[29] Authorities incarcerated a *marchand mercier* (haberdasher), leaving behind five children. His wife dead, four sons were sent to the colonies, and the only daughter, the future dame entretenue Montigny, was farmed out to a relative.[30] Demoiselle Roux's father, once "dans le commerce" (in business), was dead, as was the father of the sisters Crousol. Upon his death, Père Crousol had left twelve hundred livres in rente to his two sons and nothing for his daughters, whom the mother eventually brokered into patron-mistress relationships at the suggestion of her neighbor, an infamous Parisian procuress.[31] It was usually fathers who broke homes in eighteenth-century France. A father's disappearance from an economic unit that required the work of both spouses could tip, or in some cases catapult, the family into poverty.[32]

The police recorded social data on families—occupation, geographic origin, age of parents, and number of siblings, for example—as well as more descriptive items such as the family's financial status, whether the parents were separated, and the relations between parents and children, as part of their effort to understand the making of kept women. This information formed part of a "backstory" found in most dossiers, usually contained in the third or fourth report, its delay perhaps a function of the time it took to undertake such an investigation in a preindustrial society. Several pages in length, the backstory recounted the events by which a woman ended up in the demimonde and can be understood as part of the larger effort by the police to "identify" the king's subjects. For workers and those of lower social milieu, that effort consisted of the process of "enregistrement"—bureaucratic inscription in a register or in identity papers.[33] When it came to sex, however, the police added a layer. In addition to labeling women as "dames entretenues" or men as "pedarastes," they required what can be thought of as a "narrative of descent," the story of how the person in question became sexually deviant. This approach shaped the questioning of men entrapped by the police for the solicitation of sodomy. Their confessions suggest they were asked when and how they first engaged in same-sex sex and then to recount all subsequent homosexual acts in order, their chronologies serving as explanations for how they came to be soliciting on the quays or in the Tuileries.[34] In some respects, police sensibilities can be likened to the practice of confession. For inspectors Meusnier and Marais, the narrative answered the question of how a girl became a prostitute rather than a bride or a nun. They wanted to know specifically what happened such that their subject abandoned her respectable life to lead the paradigmatically disreputable one, prostitution. In reading these records, literary scholar Pamela Cheek argues, "Understood as an unambiguous indicator of identity, the scene of a woman's earliest sexual activity was the moment at which she became recordable."[35]

The principle event the backstory is meant to explain is the girl's initial prostitution, however it occurred. How she came to be a high-class prostitute was the subject of the rest of the dossier. Although they investigated thousands of cases, each with its own particular nuances, the inspectors managed to inscribe the events and what they perceived as their causes into four different narratives. In the first, the "leaving home" narrative, a girl departs from home at the onset of puberty, her honor intact, with the intention of finding honest work. Then, through a series of events, she becomes a kept woman instead. In the second, the "lost honor" narrative, a girl runs away from home with a man, either a boyfriend or a patron, with whom she was sexually involved. Then, she ends up a dame entretenue. Third was the "pleasure seeking" narrative, in which girls left home with the specific intent of becoming kept women. The fourth and final narrative collapsed the three stages, as parents sold or pushed their children into elite prostitution. This will be the subject of the next chapter.

In the act of structuring their backstory narratives around "what went wrong," the inspectors reinforced the notion that sexual honor was binary. They constructed the loss of sexual honor as an inevitable prelude to prostitution. They imagined prostitution—defined as streetwalking, working in a brothel, or offering the sexual services of a dame entretenue—as a state inherently opposed to that of respectability. Engaging in prostitution defined the moment that a girl fully lost the life she could have had. Yet despite its Procrustean tendencies and aggressive reductionism, the inspectors' narrative typology has considerable explanatory power. For those women who, like Anne Michelet, were neither married nor sold into prostitution, it was in the period between leaving home and settling as an adult that they were most vulnerable. If we reject the inspectors' moral grammar, and look at their first three narratives entirely as social histories, slightly different patterns emerge. Collectively, these revised narratives highlight the conditions that led to prostitution. In the first, renamed the "no connections" narrative, girls from outside Paris came to the capital hoping to find work but become prostitutes instead. In the second narrative, "from work to prostitution," girls and women working in Paris, some of whom were migrants and others native to the capital, left their jobs or were fired and became prostitutes. In the last narrative, "professional enhancement," girls who were already elite prostitutes came to Paris to advance their careers. It is to these three narratives that we now turn.

✦ No Connections

In the first narrative, girls and women came to Paris to find work. They did so to acquire money for dowries. Girls who came from families with scanty resources and no trade in which to train their daughters were sent off to earn for themselves. Like Anne Michelet, these girls left home between the ages of twelve and fourteen.[36] Many set off for regional industrial centers like Lyon, Bayeux, or Millau, where they could find work in the silk, lace, and glove-making industries, respectively.[37] Others went to the nearest town in which the demand for servants outpaced local supply. Domestic service employed more women than any other sector in eighteenth-century France. In towns north of the Loire, female servants constituted up to 13 to 15 percent of the population.[38] Service, as we explored in the case of Anne Michelet, meant any number of things. Even the poorest family with some discretionary income hired a female servant to be, in the words of Olwen Hufton, "a resident drudge."[39] In larger households with numerous servants, the goal was to obtain a position as high in the hierarchy as possible, a feat never accomplished by girls who became dames entretenues. Those kept women who, like Anne, began their work lives as servants were employed in small or modest households, passing their days in hard and low-status labor.

The hope of those who left home was to find work nearby. Most girls ventured no more than thirty miles.[40] But, whether traveling near or far, work seekers, especially female ones, tended to journey within well-established circuits, fixed over decades, that tied a particular community to another of greater employment opportunity; all over France, the work cycle determined migratory patterns.[41] In our sample of the girls who became kept women, about half of those whose origins are known were born or raised in Paris. In most respects, the geographic origins of the rest of the sample conform roughly to the general patterns of immigration to Paris outlined by Daniel Roche. Roche found that two-thirds of all immigrants to the capital were born and raised north of the Loire.[42] As Daniel Roche made clear, though it might have taken them some time, perhaps punctuated by stops in other urban centers, men and, to a lesser degree, women seeking work in an urban area in the north of the country often came to the capital. This was especially true of unskilled and low-skilled laborers. Roche also found that the sizes of Parisian immigrant communities from other parts of France and abroad were inversely proportionate to the distances between their homes and the capital.[43]

Girls from outside Paris who became kept women, especially those who were unskilled, hailed predominantly from provinces north of the Loire. The rest came from cities outside this zone, mostly Lyon and Marseilles, their numbers likewise being in inverse proportion to their hometown's distance to the capital. A small percentage came from foreign cities, especially Florence, Venice, and Brussels. The geographic distribution of kept women's origins, however, defies general trends in two ways. First, these women traveled farther than most. Both Roche and Cissie Fairchilds have shown that female migrants to Paris generally came from the surrounding countryside, while men traveled from farther afield. Secondly, the sample has an unusually urban character. In a period when 85 percent of France's population was rural, how is it that almost 80 percent of kept women came from urban areas?[44] It is possible that either the police or their informants were rounding off geographically, using the nearest large city to identify someone who came from a nearby village. This is unlikely, however, as the distribution of paternal occupations suggests urban origins for most of these women. But whether from the country or some provincial city, it was how they got to Paris that introduces us to the problem.

It was as part of this epic nationwide movement of girls away from their homes and villages in search of work that many who became the subject of police dossiers as dames entretenues first encountered difficulty. The inspectors, alongside moralists, novelists, judges, and girls themselves as they testified in paternity suits, rightly target the journey from home to work as a moment of extreme vulnerability. For many, the trouble began when they arrived in Paris alone, with little or no money and no connections to which to turn. Finding employment depended on knowing someone in the capital— a friend, relative, or countryman—who either knew of a job or would help to find one and who in the meantime could provide food, shelter, and protection. The danger of fleeing to Paris without a support network, either at home or in the capital, was a common theme in the police reports. For example, Inspector Marais wrote sympathetically that Julie Brebant, the fourteen-year-old daughter of a wigmaker, left her rural community in Champagne to find work as a servant in Paris. But "having not a single acquaintance, she soon fell in with bad sorts who led her to libertinage."[45]

Problems began the moment a girl passed the city's barriers, where she would have been identified as a migrant from the provinces by those lying in wait to take advantage of unwary and inexperienced newcomers.[46] And these women were inexperienced. Their average age on arrival was sixteen. From the police reports, it appears few of them stopped along their journey to work, a process Daniel Roche argues allowed immigrants to acquire the skills and acculturation necessary to survive and prosper in the capital. He found that 25 percent of servants in Paris had arrived in the city after the age of thirty.[47] Traveling from the barrier to a particular neighborhood offered immigrants even less chance of blending in; in the nosy quarter in which everyone knew each other's business, strangers stood out.[48] For women like Anne, it was not just a question of needing to find employment and protection from the capital's more aggressive elements, but also of learning the ways of the city.

Anne had help. Her move to Paris was facilitated by her aunt. But not every immigrant girl or young woman searching for work possessed such a vital connection. They ended up alone in Paris for any number of reasons. Often a girl arrived in Paris without an address because she left home before one could be arranged. Inspector Meusnier reported that Geneviève Châtelain, for example, escaped a deteriorating domestic situation. Her father's remarriage created tensions in the household, and the girl, aged fifteen, fled to Paris to make it on her own.[49] However, many of those running away did so less to escape domestic strife than to avoid punishment for disobedience or promiscuous sexual behavior. Edmée Liotard was one such case. Inspector Meusnier reported that Liotard was sexually active, wild even, as she had had sex with the domestics of the prince de Clermont and had attended parties of a disreputable neighbor. He claimed her father had tried regularly to "remind her of her duty," in Meusnier's words, by beating her and locking her up with only bread to eat.[50] Finally, Meusnier added, Père Liotard remarried, thinking a stepmother might help him with his problem daughter, at which point the latter fled.

Some girls fled with men. According to Marais, Julie Morel ended up in Paris alone because she had run away from home with her boyfriend. She had fallen in love with the coachman of her father's *seigneur* and accompanied him to the capital.[51] Marie-Louise Prévost also followed a coachman, though more, it seems, to get away from home and a new stepfather than from love. "The poor treatment she received from her stepfather saddened her," wrote Inspector Marais, who was following the case, "and made her vulnerable to the sweet nothings of Cadet la Violette, a coachman of the duc de Villeroy." They absconded to Versailles.[52]

How did Julie Morel and Marie-Louise Prévost imagine their flights? Did they think they would marry these lovers, or through their connections find respectable work? The nature of courtship in this period was processual. Its various elements—courting, betrothal, publication of the banns, church ceremony, and sexual intercourse—did not always take place in that order. Between 10 and 20 percent of brides were pregnant on their wedding day in the second half of the eighteenth century.[53] Penetrative sex was often considered as a promise of marriage. Evidence of this comes from testimony by women, pregnant and abandoned, before the Paris police commissioners. In submitting petitions, these women hoped to obtain compensatory payment or child support from the father, and to reestablish their own honor. They did this by trying to show that the pregnancy was a part of a courting process they had been certain was leading to marriage. The father's testimony supported the mother's assumptions, but not by agreeing that there had been a promise of marriage. Instead, the father's testimony positioned his partner as unmarriageable, if only because she had had sex with him. Were she libertine or a prostitute, sexual intercourse carried no promissory burden.[54]

What casts any doubt on expectations of marriage for Julie Morel and Marie-Louise Prévost was not that they engaged in premarital sex, but that they ran away from home to do so. Any marriage contracted under these circumstances, regardless of the age of the woman, was illegal, a form of *rapt*, and was a capital offense for the groom.[55] While the Catholic Church recognized clandestine marriages—marriages contracted without the permission of parents or guardians—the state did not. From 1556, it imposed on those wishing to marry a series of requirements specifically intended to prevent such unions.[56] By the eighteenth century these included multiple proofs of permission and publication of the banns three consecutive Sundays prior to the ceremony. It is likely that in Marie-Louise's case, running away seemed like the only option. She might have hoped Violette would help care for her. But he did not. He deflowered her, gave her an *écu* (six livres), and then sent her packing. Since Marie-Louise felt she could not return home to Saint-Germain-en-Laye, he put her on the road to Paris.

It is possible, even in the face of flight and the crime that it constituted, that Marie-Louise hoped to marry Violette. His social background would have made him an appropriate candidate for marriage. But any such desire could never have been realized when a girl fled with a man of much higher rank. In her study of *procès de gravidation* in Languedoc, the legal process by which a pregnant woman (or her family) tried to compel her lover to marriage, Nicole Castan found that a difference in rank between man and woman, especially when accompanied by a gross difference in fortune, was sufficient grounds for a judge to drop the case. In such instances, there could be no promise of marriage. Defendants argued that since the union could have no legal future, the woman was by definition a libertine. When the defendant did not make this claim, the judge did.[57] In eighteenth-century society, with all the meanings and significance attached to marriage, high-status men did not marry poor, low-status women. The state had an interest in preventing such unions and discouraged them in the Ordinance of 1639.

Moreover, the behavior of these seducers belied any intent to marry. For example, Radine de Chennevière, a cavalry captain, abducted Demoiselle Monginet from her home in Normandy, brought her to Paris and set her up as his mistress in the Hôtel des Trois-Milords on the rue Traversière.[58] In another example, a foreign noble took sixteen-year-old Demoiselle Prioré from her home in Brittany. Inspector Meusnier reported that the abductor had wanted to marry the girl but for the objections of his family, and so instead he maintained her. She had a child. Eventually he brought to her to Paris and abandoned her, at which point she found another patron.[59] Prioré and Monginet were treated as mistresses.

Were Prioré and Monginet coerced or willing accomplices? It did not matter to the police who assigned fleeing girls varying degrees of culpability. Julie Morel was in love and ran away of her own volition, having "followed" (*suivi*) her boyfriend. Demoiselle Monginet was "taken away" (*enlevée*) from a respectable home. The police did not judge more harshly those who followed boyfriends. Morel, who was a willing participant in her own downfall, was painted the victim just as much as was Monginet. Within a few months of arrival in Paris, both girls had been abandoned by the men who had brought them there, according to Inspector Marais. He reported that Morel, "overwhelmed by poverty," decided to find a madam who could help her attend some parties (for which she would be paid).[60] Monginet faced "the most hideous poverty" and allowed herself to be recruited and introduced to Monsieur le Caze, *directeur général des Grands Gabelles* (general director of the salt tax collection). He maintained her for a while.[61]

The inspectors' sympathy stemmed from an awareness of the dangers facing young women in this period. Meusnier and Marais pitied not just the obvious, pathetic victims, those who were sold by their parents or kidnapped by some passing acquaintance. They also evinced compassion for the simple and incredulous under their watch, girls who ran off with men thinking it would end in marriage. They tended to highlight the gullibility of these women by describing their putative boyfriends as adventurers, scoundrels, and mauvais sujets. The inspectors were unusual in thinking that some kept women were victims, forced into prostitution as the only way to support themselves. Most novelists and commentators reserved the apology of poverty for prostitutes who remained in poverty. For example, Louis-Sébastien Mercier argued that *filles publiques* were the "unfortunate victims of indigence or parental abandonment."[62] Dames entretenues, despite often being victims of the same forces of immiseration, were, like the fictional Manon Lescaut, Mademoiselle Brion, and other prostitute protagonists of libertine literature, thought to be driven only by a love of pleasure and luxury.[63]

Despite such a framing, the inspectors instead saw these women as completely unprepared to survive on their own in Paris, having neither the knowledge nor the social connections to find work. The inspectors were right. Not only were these women without support systems in Paris, which were critical to survival, but most had none at home to which they could apply for help or even return. Even though some runaways did go home in times of need, using neighbors as intermediaries to broker a rapprochement, this was not an option for the women in this study.[64] They had families that were broken by death, contentious remarriage, poverty, and violence. A woman in this group was twice as likely as any other kept woman to have lost her mother by the time she entered the workforce. Those with families intact feared returning home would mean punishment and incarceration.

✒ From Work to Prostitution

Turning to the second police narrative that explained how women became dames entretenues, we see that not every femme galante entered prostitution as a result of having arrived in Paris unprepared. Some, like Anne Michelet, managed to find work. Others, about half the kept women for whom the police recorded geographic origin, were born in the capital and hence did not face the hazardous transition of their immigrating sisters. Parisian girls had a fundamentally different experience of adolescence. Some, especially daughters of artisans, lived and worked at home until marriage. Others lived at home and worked elsewhere. A family with a little bit of money, like that of Marie-Antoinette Moreau, might try to apprentice their daughter in a craft. Girls raised in Paris notoriously avoided service, looking instead to work in textile and clothing production.[65] But whether urban girls lived at home or with their employers, they still could go home on occasion. Many continued to work in the same job or industry after marriage. With adolescence spent in the capital, these girls had multiple networks on which to rely for help: friends, neighbors, relatives, and work associates. They were living and working in their own culture and were less likely to suffer the isolation and loneliness of immigrants. For these individuals, the shift away from preparation for marriage and into prostitution had little to do with the preparations themselves and the social and cultural dislocation they often engendered. What unites this group together with women who, like Anne Michelet, came from the provinces and successfully found work in the capital, were struggles with employment and the problems posed by illicit sexual relationships.

Employment, as we have seen, was precarious and, at times, entirely wanting. Girls once employed, but no longer, turned to prostitution simply because they were poor and opportunity presented itself. Marie Viot, for example, was an orphan. The police reported that her father had been a master shoemaker and her mother a washerwoman, but both died, impoverished and in state institutions, her father at Bicêtre and her mother at the Hôtel Dieu.[66] Such deaths suggest that the Viots were not just poor (and her father possibly a criminal) but among the group who were in "a state of absolute poverty," described by Olwen Hufton as being with "no food or adequate clothing or proper shelter, that one had parted with the few battered cooking-pots and blankets which often constitute the main assets of a working-class family."[67] With so few assets, one wonders what they could have done for their daughter, what connections they might have had who still would have been willing to help them. According to the police, Marie decided to prostitute herself to earn money for food, and first became the mistress of a clerk.

Yet even with a steady position, working women in Paris remained vulnerable to seduction, abandonment, and rape by their peers and superiors. There were a great many opportunities for meeting men in the big city. Urban living conditions, which closely quartered multiple families in cramped apartment buildings, facilitated these encounters. A woman who rented a room, like Anne Michelet, met men on the stairs, the landing, and the foyer as she came and went each day. The occurrence was so common it was immortalized in prostitute fiction. It was just such a meeting that launched the Parisian career of the "La Belle Allemande," the protagonist of an eponymous novel. Arriving in Paris, where she and her mother shared a chambre garnie, she was noticed by the man next door, who eventually sent an intermediary to broker a patron-mistress relationship.[68] Working women had greater freedom of movement than did their social superiors. Daily errands and rounds about the quarter brought them into contact with men of all classes. Thérèse Levasseur met Rousseau, her lifetime partner, when he was staying at a hotel in which she was a washerwoman. However, this contact was not always friendly. David Garrioch argues that among working men a sort of sexual predator mentality predominated. And while families relied on neighbors and relatives to look out for their daughters and employees, the demands of work or the pursuit of entertainment might lead a girl beyond the gaze of her direct community.[69] Illicit sexual relationships, whether voluntary or coerced, proved a common thread linking working women in Paris to prostitution.

Servants were particularly susceptible to seduction and assault by both social equals and superiors. Arlette Farge found that of one hundred petitions submitted by abandoned pregnant women, more than half were from servants, most from the bottom of the servant hierarchy, "kitchen girls, shop hands or chambermaids at best."[70] Male servants used enormous pressure, and sometimes violence and other means of coercion, to compel female servants to have sex.[71] For servants who became kept women, however, the problematic sexual engagement was not usually with a social equal. Differences in fortune and social status, and the prospect of unemployment, all exacerbated by dangers posed by proximity, increased the potential for coercion in affairs between masters and employees.[72] Seduction of a servant by a master was illegal, but in most cases—at least in medium-sized cities across France—masters were able to fire their pregnant servants with a promise to pay for the maintenance of the child. If she took her master to court, a pregnant servant was likely to receive fifty livres or less.[73]

The employment problems that pregnancy presented for a servant were often insurmountable, leaving many with little recourse but prostitution.[74] Depending on the year, a servant leaving a position had to obtain a certificate from her former master or risk imprisonment. Even with a certificate, she was legally obligated to find work within a certain period of time or leave the city. Yet everyone in the quarter would have known her situation. Neighbors took an intense interest in what was going on in their streets, their buildings, and their neighborhoods. They listened at (thin) walls, watched out windows, and kept track of comings and goings. Any change in routine was observed, analyzed, and discussed.[75] Pregnant or thought to be sexually promiscuous, a girl would not be able to find another position. Moreover, her reputation—"le bruit public" (rumor)—in the quarter actually served as a form of legal proof of prostitution.[76] If she had contacts in another quarter, she could move and be virtually anonymous, working until her pregnancy became obvious. But without any such contacts, a move to a new quarter would make her a migrant, and leave her isolated and without prospects.

In trying to understand how girls became kept women, the police inspectors simply positioned sex with a master as the moment a servant was socially ruined. Demoiselle Deperville, for example, came to Paris to be a domestic and worked in the house of a surgeon. "He took her virginity," Inspector Meusnier simply reported. And then she became a prostitute.[77] We do not know how or why. Because it became a legal matter, however, Meusnier provides more detail in the case of Rosalie Blondet (*dite* Rougi), who was impregnated by her master, the newly married comte de St. Felix. Following his tendency to dichotomize sexual guilt, the inspector depicted Demoiselle Blondet as a seductress who easily manipulated the young master of the house by virtue of her "pretty figure" and her "experience"—she already had a child "by some other intrigue," though one wonders if it was indeed illicit. Had such a history been known, it seems unlikely she would have been hired by a noble family in Languedoc.

According to Meusnier, the comtesse de St. Felix fell ill shortly after her wedding, and Blondet, a *femme de chambre* (maid), "knew how to profit from this situation to insinuate herself into [the comte's] heart."[78] The relationship was short lived. Blondet became pregnant and was dismissed by the marquis de St. Felix, the comte's father. Blondet went home and gave birth to a boy. Due to an unrelated legal matter, St. Felix eventually went with his father to Paris, where he later met up with Blondet, whom he kept secretly as his mistress. Meusnier writes that she "recaptured the young man in her net" and cost him fifteen thousand livres over three months. To break up the affair, the marquis had Blondet arrested. Blondet's own father, a game warden, then came to Paris to file a complaint with the police against the comte for seducing his daughter and against the marquis for firing her.[79] Claiming his daughter had always been virtuous, he demanded damages.

Was Père Blondet right in praising the virtue of his daughter, or was he just trying to turn a bad situation to his financial advantage? Meusnier's repeated insistence that Blondet was the sexual aggressor inverts traditional hierarchies in a noble household, giving a lowly maid power over an aristo-

crat, power that she supposedly exercised cleverly and persistently even as
the venue for their relationship moved from the south of France to Paris.
Moreover, we have the problem of how Blondet, a servant from Languedoc,
found St. Felix in Paris. There is no evidence that Blondet had ever visited
the city before. Their meeting could hardly have been accidental. Did he
send for her? Did she come because this affair was her best option? Studies of
affairs between masters and servants both support and challenge Meusnier's
interpretation. Arlette Farge found cases of individual women deciding to
have sex with an employer because "of the rather subtle but dependent
relationship the woman had with him on account of the domestic service
she provided."[80] But rape and coercion, a rewriting of Meusnier's tale, also
are well represented in judicial records. Whatever the case, what is clear is
that Meusnier understood that seduction paired with pregnancy and dis-
missal resulted in Blondet's entry into the demimonde.

Most kept women who began their work lives as servants found their way
into prostitution less dramatically, through a series of smaller events, following
a trajectory similar to that of Anne Michelet. Like Anne, Marie Marguerite
de Villers was reported to have left her job, in this case as a servant in a *gar-
gottier* (cheap inn), with a chevalier who been a guest there. According to
Meusnier, the man had "neither manners nor position" and so "follow[ed]
the vicissitudes of fortune . . . and liv[ed] off of intrigues and swindling."[81]
When this relationship soured, de Villers became the mistress of another
chevalier in the same regiment.

What were de Villers and her chevalier to each other? She may have
been his mistress, supported in exchange for sex and company. Or perhaps
their relationship was closer to that of Anne Michelet and Vielbans. Irregular
relationships played a role in the shift from work to prostitution. We might
define an irregular relationship as a long-term, stable, sexually and emotionally intimate union in which the female partner was either economically
self-sufficient or was dependent on her lover. These relationships were neither
marital nor explicitly commercial, although the boundaries between transactional and nontransactional sex can be extremely difficult to draw. While
they have not been the subject of sustained scholarly interest, we know
from studies of *déclarations de grossesse* (the forms single women had to fill
out declaring their pregnancy), for example, that irregular relationships
occurred with great frequency and sometimes lasted for many years, occasionally with a promise of marriage, but more frequently without.[82] Requests
for lettres de cachet—the legal instrument by which a concerned party could
have a person incarcerated—from aggrieved husbands and wives reveal spouses
having lived with other partners, for decades. Irregular relationships occurred

all along the female life cycle. They preceded marriage with the same man, or with a different one.[83] As we saw in the case of Anne and Vielbans, they could also function as a marriage.

A good example of an irregular relationship is that between Thérèse Levasseur and Jean-Jacques Rousseau.[84] Thérèse had a great deal in common with many kept women. Like a number of those whose stories we examine in this chapter, Thérèse met her lover through her work. In the spring of 1745, she was employed as a washerwoman at the Hôtel Saint-Quentin, where Rousseau took some of his meals. She caught his attention. Like many kept women, Thérèse was poorly educated—she was barely literate—and her family was experiencing hard times. Her father had lost his work as a coiner in the mint in Orléans, and her mother's business had failed. Thérèse lived with her parents and siblings, contributing toward their upkeep with her meager earnings. Like many kept women, she had had sex out of wedlock, and she was famously so embarrassed by this that she initially resisted Rousseau's advances. After moving in with Thérèse, Rousseau would, with enduring loud complaint, support the family Levasseur for the rest of his life, much the way patrons supported their mistresses' families, although both Thérèse and her mother worked for Rousseau in various capacities, labor Rousseau would have hired others to do.

Thérèse's relationship with Rousseau has been hard for scholars to figure out, perhaps because Rousseau himself provides conflicting accounts of his affections for Thérèse. Thérèse worked for Rousseau as a servant, and she shared his bed, but had she married someone of her own social station, the duties of servant and wife would have also overlapped. One even might argue that Thérèse and Rousseau were from the same social background, the difference being that his sex and his brilliance allowed him to advance. Thérèse stood by Rousseau as he had affairs with at least one other woman. They married after twenty-five years together, but Thérèse's relationship did not lead her into prostitution. Two factors distinguish Thérèse from Anne Michelet. First, Thérèse's family was present and not only encouraged her illicit attachment, they were dependent on it, suggesting that had the relationship failed, Thérèse would still have been welcome at home. Second, the relationship did not fail. Dominique Godineau points out that irregular relationships rarely benefited women.[85] However, in the case of both Anne and Thérèse, one has to question this conclusion; the alternative to being without such financial and social support was often worse. The problem for Anne was not that she was in such a relationship. It was that the relationship ended.

Servants were not the only girls and young women susceptible to illicit sexual affairs and irregular relationships. Those working in textiles or the needle trades—most from Paris—also came to prostitution through illicit sexual affairs. The connection between prostitution and the garment trades is illustrated by Erica-Marie Benabou's survey of women sent to the prison of Saint-Martin for prostitution or debauchery in the years 1765, 1766, and 1770. She found that 97.9 percent of the 2,069 women arrested declared an occupation. A little more than half of them claimed to be textile workers or involved in the making and decorating of clothing. The largest number of these were, like Anne Michelet, linen workers. Another large group were fashion workers.[86] After textile workers came washerwomen and then servants. It is possible that so many prostitutes claimed past training or work in the clothing trades because it was such a substantial employer of women. Clare Crowston estimates that, in the first half of the century, between 7,500 and 8,500 Parisian women worked as or for seamstresses. Many more worked in other branches of the garment trade, for linen drapers, tailors, or fashion merchants.[87]

With girls in the textile industry, the initial relationship could be between equals, or as in the case of Henriette Lécuyer, with a man of higher social status. According to Inspector Marais, Lécuyer came from a poor family, though not one that was demonstrably destitute. At age fifteen, she quit both her home and her job with a seamstress to live with an "old" tobacco merchant named Gautier. It is possible she saw this relationship as something long term, that the move-in established a free union, which, in some cases, did lead to marriage.[88] The difference in social standing was not so significant. But their ages weigh heavily against such a conclusion, as does the fact that Lécuyer relied entirely on Gautier for support. Urban plebeian wives, some of whom did marry young, but rarely this young, continued to work after marriage.[89] According to the police, Lécuyer paid his mistress so poorly that she sought out Brissault, a tailor and, with his wife, an elite pimp, to find additional sex work. Meusnier claimed that Gautier did not go back to sewing because she was lazy and preferred prostitution.[90] The topos of the indolent, vice-loving prostitute often obfuscated the realities of unemployment and the presence of semipermanent irregular relationships. It is likely that the police misrepresented the situation, that Lécuyer did not leave her job but was fired or laid off and could find no other. Like many other girls, when she found the situation with her lover unsatisfactory, she might have feared returning home and thus have been pushed into prostitution.

For girls in the textile industry, however, it was not only relationships of inequality that drove them to prostitution. As with servants, relationships with their peers had similar consequences, and for the same reasons: seduction and abandonment. Marie-Barbe-Sophie Faillon was a lace-making apprentice living in Paris. In September 1759, after having sex with a journeyman printer "whom she liked a lot," she fled, anticipating that the anger of her aunt and mistress would result in her being incarcerated.[91] It is possible that Faillon and her printer were courting, and that sexual intercourse in this instance was understood, at least by Faillon, as a promise of marriage. Women apprenticed in the clothing trades did marry craftsmen.[92] Moreover, the ways in which sex imbedded itself in plebeian courtship blurred the line between girlfriend and mistress. Faillon was recruited into an elite brothel.

Demoiselle Blanchard was in many ways like Marie Faillon. She had an affair with a journeyman wigmaker.[93] Because Blanchard could one day have married her boyfriend, it is tempting to think that the two were courting, and that perhaps, under the hope or promise of marriage, Blanchard had slept with her wigmaker only to be abandoned. If this did happen, it is not revealed in the historical record. But what this and several other cases have in common, and hence what suggests itself as at least one derailing factor, was proximity to men and women who were active participants in the demi-monde. Blanchard's lover convinced her to quit her job at a *marchande de modes* (fashion merchant) and take another as a femme de chambre in the home of Demoiselle Minot, a dame entretenue.

Why Blanchard turned to galanterie is not clear. Her entry was likely facilitated by her contact with the demimonde through Minot. It is possible that Blanchard might have found her employer's lifestyle attractive. A series of wealthy patrons had left Minot occupying two floors of a house whose furniture she owned. At the time Blanchard came to work for her, the ex-dancer was being maintained by Monsieur Duvaucel, *grand maître des eaux et forêts du département de Paris*, who had given her fifteen thousand livres worth of silver, linens, and jewels and was trying to find her a house.[94] Or perhaps it was just a function of exposure. It seems likely that Blanchard met another dancer, Jean-Denis Duprès, through Minot. Blanchard moved in with Duprès, who had her enrolled in the Opéra ballet school. Her matriculation marked her as a kept woman, one of significant sexual capital, which she used to procure sex work that supplemented the couple's income, but not for long. Blanchard soon found a better patron, a German baron.[95]

It is ironic that Blanchard's shift into elite prostitution came after she left the marchande de modes, since girls and young women working in these establishments, commonly called *grisettes*, regularly were pulled into the demi-monde. The marchande de modes was a fashion purveyor, the female owner of a boutique that embellished women's clothing. While some marchandes de modes functioned as general clothing contractors, responsible for having dresses made and decorated, most just enhanced the garments brought to them. Without such embellishment, dresses were unfinished. When fashions changed, dresses were sent back to the marchandes de modes for updating. In doing so, in picking the right trim or ribbon, adding touches here and there, marchandes de modes were stylists in the modern sense as well as makers of fashion.[96] They also sold various finished goods, such as hats, shawls, and headpieces, which could complete an outfit.

Clothing and fashion were extremely important to dames entretenues. Successful kept women not only followed the latest fashion trends, but they also set them. Perhaps this is why some kept women became marchandes de modes on retirement from prostitution. The connections between the two worlds were many. Dresses and dress accessories were common gifts from patron to mistress, and these were acquired from the marchandes de modes. Patrons sometimes brought in their own clothing for finishing. Hence, they were frequent visitors to the boutiques, where they interacted with the girls who waited on them and saw the others who were sewing at the counter.

But a prospective patron did not have to cross the threshold of a shop to see the women working inside. These shops were fronted by big glass windows in which the marchande showcased her fashions. "Sitting at the counter in a line, you see them through the windows," wrote Mercier of the grisettes; "they arrange the pompoms, trinkets, and decorations that fashion creates and varies. You eye them freely, and they meet your eye." The window situated the grisettes as consumables, just like the fashions that stood in the foreground. Mercier, seeing "the young faces next to the ugly ones," imagined the grisettes as a harem. "The pretty ones would be the sultan's favorites and the others would be their guardians."[97] The objectification of grisettes did not go unnoticed by contemporaries. Jennifer Jones argues that libertine writers were "aware of the potential for seduction when hundreds of young women fell daily under the gaze of customers and passersby in the boutiques of Paris."[98] But to contemporaries, the grisettes were not just objects of sexual interest. Mercier claimed that they enjoyed and cultivated the attention, fantasizing about passersby, and that they were active agents in creating sex lives for themselves, looking to be maintained "for very little and without scandal."[99] But while Mercier celebrated the "independent spirit" of the grisette, he also condemned her, claiming that what drove her to prostitution was not only boredom, but also—along the lines of the old luxury critique—a taste for libertinism and a desire for more clothing and accessories.[100]

These shops were not only found in bustling commercial districts; many were also concentrated in the demimonde epicenter of the rue Saint Honoré and the galleries of the Palais Royal.[101] The Opéra, a central institution in the demimonde, was housed in the Palais Royal, and the rue Saint-Honoré was a popular address for mistresses. Perhaps this was to keep them within walking distance. The rue Saint-Honoré was also the city's financial district. Colin Jones reports that, in 1789, nine-tenths of the capital's financier/tax collectors, the fermiers généraux, lived there or in the neighboring faubourg Saint-Honoré.[102] And if a prospective patron was not in the neighborhood, he might have encountered grisettes at his home; marchandes de modes and *revendeuses à la toilette* sold accessories door to door in some of the wealthier neighborhoods.[103]

Several kept women began their work lives as grisettes. Jeanne Béroud (*dite* Fouassier) worked first for a seamstress and then at a marchande de modes, where, according to Inspector Marais, "she behaved very well for two years." However, she eventually became the mistress of the vicomte de Sabran, who often came to her store.[104] The most famous grisette of all was the most successful kept woman of the eighteenth century: Jeanne Bécu, Madame du Barry, maîtresse-en-titre to Louis XV.

Unlike those who fled to Paris and ended up in prostitution as a result of having no connections in the city, the police portrayed women who left work to be kept as willing adventurers, understanding their decisions as deliberate and informed. There were of course a few instances in which they attributed the move to gullibility. Marie Jeanne Treppier, seduced and abandoned twice, was made out to be a dupe. While working in a dress shop, a neighbor promised her "more butter than bread" if she dined alone with him that evening. Once he slept with her, he alerted her father so that the girl would be forced to go home and he would not have to keep her as his mistress. Her father then apprenticed her to Madam Epinay, a hairdresser. Madam Epinay, however, did not teach the girl her trade. Instead, she convinced Marie that her previous "misfortune" made her forever ineligible for marriage and then sold her to a lawyer in the Paris Parlement.[105]

The central issues underlying all these cases do not concern character, nor whether the girl was stupid or wishing for an adventure, despite the irresistible pull of these explanations to the police. Their reports instead highlight the volatility of semipermanent relationships and the instability of employment, the dangers of which are highlighted by the counterpoint offered in the story of Thérèse Levasseur. Textile manufacture and clothing production, the two industries that hired the most women, were subject to sudden contractions. That more than half the women incarcerated in St. Martins for prostitution claimed they worked in these trades is telling. Poverty drove many women into prostitution, but not always permanently. For some it was a way to supplement what income they had, or to compensate for what wages they did not.[106] Some events, such as incarceration in the Hôpital, could, as in the case with Anne, push a woman into professional prostitution by irreparably damaging her reputation so that it was impossible to acquire work, were she even to have the contacts necessary to find a position. Lastly, we should consider that some women may have thought being entretenue, with the food, housing, and clothes it could provide, was an attractive option, not over the unremitting and crushing poverty of street walking, but over a life that was several steps above, in a chambre garnie sewing pieces of linen.

In contrast to those girls who came to Paris looking to work for a dowry, there was a small group of women who migrated to the capital specifically because of the opportunities in the demimonde. Many of them had been dames entretenues somewhere else.

❧ Paris: Center of the World

Successful provincial kept women often migrated to Paris. Many of these women were actresses, singers, and dancers from great provincial cities like Rouen and Marseilles. They might have come by way of a patron whose business or social interests had drawn him to the capital. Paris was by far the largest city in France. Its population exceeded 600,000 people in the last quarter of the eighteenth century. Lyon, the next largest city, which was expanding at the same rate as the capital, weighed in at a mere 140,000 inhabitants. The great provincial seats were certainly centers of local power in their own right—judicial, political, and in some cases economic—but none could compete with Paris, even in these spheres. Paris was the nation's cultural and social center as well. It supported the most prestigious salons, the royal theater, and opera companies as well as royal academies. It was the locus of luxury production. Aristocrats forced by Louis XIV into the social labyrinth of Versailles followed the Regent's move to Paris. While court life was still the avenue to advancement under Louis XV, Paris remained the center of elite sociability. The best sort of patron would probably move back and, in this context, might try to relocate his provincial mistress. Demoiselle Roux, for example, a dancer in the Lyon Opéra, was brought to Paris by her patron-to-be, Lord Hyde, an English nobleman.

When Roux's mother did not approve of the match, the girl tricked her by arguing that the move was for the advancement of her dancing career. In Paris, she argued, "her talents would shine" as opposed to being "buried in a provincial town," as she referred to Lyon.[107] Only after they arrived in the capital did Mère Roux realize she had been manipulated. Yet the efficacy of Demoiselle Roux's argument is suggestive. For performers, success on the

Parisian stage was the furthest they could take their careers. Such was also the case with nontheater demimondaines. Paris was the center of the demimonde not just of France but of Western Europe. It was there that women could find the highest-ranking and best-paying patrons and live the most luxuriant lifestyles.

Often, the two aspirations—stage and demimonde—were inseparable. For example, Demoiselle Alart, a young Marseillaise who moved to Lyon and danced in the theater there, eventually found herself maintained by Sir Lamarche, Roux's former patron. Lamarche, a wealthy manufacturer, had reportedly been extravagant in his expenditures on Roux. He supported Alart for fifteen months. They had one child. Nevertheless, soon after Alart was made principal dancer in the Comédie, she wanted to go to Paris to try her fortunes there. "Although Sir Lamarche left his mistress desiring nothing," wrote Meusnier, "and although she has the title and salary of principal dancer in the troupe of Demoiselle Destouches, she could not resist the desire to go and try her luck in Paris."[108] Only in Paris could members of a variety of professions reach the top of those fields.

We now have a sense of Anne's options: when Anne went to a brothel after Vielbans left her, it is possible that it was a choice, that this was the work she wished to do over any other kind available to someone of her background. But, just as likely, she was unable to find a new position in service or en linge. She had a child to support and no partner. Perhaps as a result of her relationship with Vielbans, Anne already thought of herself as a prostitute, making her transition back to respectable work more difficult. That relationship was the stepping stone into the world of elite prostitution and mistresshood, in which it took connections both to succeed and to withdraw to anywhere other than the street.

What happened to Anne? The last we hear of her is in 1756. Anne was twenty-seven and nearing the age of retirement for most dames entretenues. Her daughter was six, and they lived together. Inspector Meusnier, with a typical epistolary smirk, claims that Anne Michelet liked to play the wit, and that everyone pretended she was. However she comported herself, she was finding work. She was being maintained by Monsieur Peillot de la Garde, *auditeur des comtes.* And she had a *greluchon* (boyfriend), the marquis de Custine, a *maréchal de camp*, who, according to the police, was in love with her.[109]

What Anne's story makes clear is that, contrary to depictions of kept women in literature and their construction by moralists, dames entretenues were made and not born. They were the functions of the failure of the very institutions that were meant to shepherd girls to a life of married respectability. Prostitution manifests the weaknesses of those institutions in part because they were inflexible; they were unable to absorb the shocks and quakes that were family troubles, unemployment, failed courting, sexual predation, and possibly, hopes for a different life. What they were meant to protect, sexual honor, was instead exploited, showing that the most valuable possession of these girls was their sexuality. The weakness of these institutions was exacerbated by the limited employment opportunities for a single woman with no real skill and equally by the dominance of employment networks. This raises a critical question. In studying the difficulty of dowry accumulation, Olwen Hufton argued that while there is no way "of calculating how many succeeded and who failed" in putting together a dowry, "there is enough to indicate that the odds of success were low."[110] So what happened to the rest of these women? Did they simply go home? Did they marry without dowries, enter irregular relationships, or become prostitutes?

Prostitution, then, was on a spectrum of failure for these institutions. Yet Anne's story is evidence that the lines between the economy of sexual honor and that of sexual capital were not hard and fast. For a long while, Anne— like many other girls in the police files—existed in a liminal relationship state, one in which transactional sex, free union, and courting were indistinguishable. Her incarceration in the Hôpital, the event that pushed her firmly into the world of prostitution, would mark her forever, making it difficult if not impossible to go back. Nor were the boundaries between the worlds of low-level and elite prostitution firmly drawn. For a while, when Anne frequented elite brothels, she straddled the two worlds; not until she became Tourmont's mistress had she definitively become a dame entretenue.

Anne's story also evinces a degree of agency, a series of choices made from among a string of not very attractive alternatives that led her ultimately to galanterie. But not everyone's journey into the demimonde was a process. As we shall see in the next chapter, some girls made the transition in a single, violent leap.

✐ CHAPTER 3

Being Sold into the Demimonde

One June evening in 1753, Inspector Meusnier was urgently called to the house of a woman named Fleurance, a madam, to settle a dispute that fell within his unique purview. Fleurance was sheltering twenty-one-year-old Louise de la Tour (née Devaux), who had run away from her patron, Captain Dargent, Fleurance's neighbor. From this hideout, Louise had complained of the abusive behavior of both Dargent and her own father. Exactly what Louise hoped to accomplish is not clear. That she ran away to a brothel, however, suggests a certain level of desperation. Madams were often the only resources available to runaway kept women. They could offer protection from patrons. They also were willing to provide the financial help or matchmaking services a kept woman might need to get back on her feet. None of this, however, appeared to matter to Dargent. Upon discovering his mistress's whereabouts, the captain immediately, and angrily, went to retrieve her. He was accompanied by friends and, more important, by Louise's father. In addition, he brought with him the note that Père Devaux had given him the month before. It read: "I consent of my own free and pure will to leave my daughter Louise Devaux with the Sir with whom she lives at present. If she leaves him or if she enters any convent she wishes, this will be done by her will alone, and will be done without any hindrance. Written in Paris. Signed Devaux. Father of Louise

Devaux."[1] It was this note, Louise claimed, that was the source of the problem. She accused Dargent of interpreting it as a legitimate transfer of paternal authority. With it, he was claiming "an unlimited power over her."

When Dargent arrived at the home of Madam Fleurance, he was wild. He "threatened to kill everyone and break everything if Demoiselle Devaux was not turned over to her father" and if her father did not then "honor his word" and give the girl to him.[2] It was in the middle of this scene that Inspector Meusnier finally arrived. He ruled that Louise, who was just twenty-one and still a minor, would go with her father. (The age of majority was twenty-five.) Père Devaux then compelled Louise to go with Dargent. Meusnier made a copy of the document for his files and then left. Meusnier subsequently reported that Dargent, Louise, and her father had all reconciled later that same night. Dargent agreed to move Louise to an apartment and pay her 36 livres a month. Madam Fleurance was reimbursed the 120 livres Louise owed her. Louise gave her father 12 livres. Meusnier concluded: "At present it remains to be seen on this last subject if the deposit is worth more to the father than the fight; he ceased his interference in return for the twelve livres his daughter gave him."[3]

This incident was not the first time Père Devaux had prostituted Louise, if we are to believe Meusnier. Six years earlier, Devaux had lost his position as a *valet de chambre* (manservant) and found himself "out on the street without any resources but the face and youth of his daughter."[4] He sold the girl, who was fifteen at the time. The buyer was a commercial ship captain named Millon, who paid in a lump sum of cash. How Devaux knew Millon is not clear. Nor do the police give details of the transaction. But we do know that Devaux spent his money quickly, and then wanted more. Reneging on his "traité verbale" (verbal agreement) with Millon, he demanded cash or the return of his daughter. Millon refused to release Louise. Louise, for her part, was reluctant to go. Upset, Devaux threatened to have the girl incarcerated in the Hôpital, presumably for debauchery. "Alarmed by these threats," Millon hid Louise (in a brothel) and began his negotiations anew with her father. They quickly agreed that Devaux would be provided with a weekly allowance in return for giving his written consent to Millon to keep Louise.[5]

This case raises the question: Who had authority over the sexual body of Louise de la Tour? Did Père Devaux legally have the right to transfer authority over Louise to another, even for such illicit purposes as those intended by Captain Dargent? In other words, could parents sell their children into prostitution in eighteenth-century France? Since the answer is no, why did all the parties in this story act as though it was "yes"? Why did they take such pains to make the transfer of authority "valid"? And, why did Inspector Meusnier force Louise back to her father when he knew the latter would prostitute her against her will?

Understanding how Louise ended up at Madam Fleurance's that night and what happened there requires telling a bigger story, that of the elite sexual market in girls. As this case shows, not every girl or woman entering the demimonde did so on her own and only as a last resort. Many, like Louise, were pushed. Sold to individual men or to brothels, or forced to become mistresses, procured daughters made up about a fourth of those who ended up as subjects of the inspectors' files, although many never became successful dames entretenues. We will sketch the contours of this market, looking at the mechanisms by which girls were bought and sold, the attendant price structures and networks of buyers, and what in fact being "sold" meant.

The case of Louise de la Tour makes clear that understanding the market necessitates putting it into the context of both the family and policing in the Old Regime. It was parents, usually mothers, who sold these girls. For these families, the prospect of prostitution functioned as a part of the family strategy for survival—the plan for making ends meet while seeing that each child was provided for. More than any other factor, assumptions about family authority shaped the market in its legal and most human aspects. Additionally, it was against their families that procured daughters struggled for independence. But policing also played a significant role. Faced with terrible parents, the inspectors did nothing to stop these sales except under very specific conditions. Nor was their prime motivation the enforcement of parental authority as much as it was to avoid scandal and to keep the demimonde running smoothly. Yet through their actions, the police reinforced the idea that parental authority was operative in the demimonde.

✒ Pimping Parents: The Family Strategy of Prostitution

Père Devaux could count himself a member of a very special group of parents, those who sold their daughters into prostitution. Familial prostitution of daughters generally followed three patterns, each of which involved increasing effort and investment. Some parents directly prostituted their children themselves. Others relied on professional brokers, and a third group pushed its daughters into the demimonde by forcing them to join the Opéra.

We tend to know the least about this first group, as the initial act of prostitution occurred elsewhere, beyond the media grid of the demimonde. When a madam brokered the sale, she was supposed to report it to the police. However, private transactions, those exclusively between parents and a buyer, came to the attention of the police much later, and then only when the girl in question had become a dame entretenue or was arrested as a street prostitute. The inspectors recorded such beginnings as part of the back history they tried to compile on every dame entretenue. The number of girls who were sold into prostitution and ended up in the lower ranks of the profession, or met some other fate, better or worse, we cannot know. The cases that comprise the inspectors' historical record, therefore, represent the success stories of a sort.[6]

Collectively, families who sold their daughters without professional help were not distinguishable from the sample of 265 dossiers taken from the police files. Like most families that produced kept women, half were single-parent families. Paternal occupations were similarly distributed. And, like so many other families, they were poor.

With this first group, the selling of a daughter was usually less a question of a carefully developed strategy to combat poverty than desperation coupled with ready opportunity. This was the case, at least initially, with Père Devaux. After losing his job and supposedly exhausting all other resources, he sold his daughter to Millon. Whether he approached the captain or was approached by him is unclear; however, as with most cases of this sort, Devaux appears to have invested little time and energy in the initial transaction. In many instances, parents simply gave in to the wishes of a man who was pursuing their daughter. When Dame Noël was widowed and found herself sinking into poverty, she forced her daughter, according to Inspector Marais, "to surrender to the demands" of Monsieur Rondé, *garde des diamants de la Couronne* (Guard of the Crown Diamonds) who was "deeply in love" with the girl.[7] All but a few Parisian neighborhoods in this period were socially integrated, not just by street but also by dwelling, with the better-off occupying the ground floors and the poorer living in the upper ones.[8] Classes mingled at popular entertainment venues such as taverns. Police and judicial records show men meeting their future mistresses, women who had not yet engaged in any (steady) form of prostitution, walking in the street and in parks, in their own buildings, and most famously, in dress shops.

Parental objectives in such sales varied. Some wanted a quick livre and others a steady income. In the case of Devaux, one goal shifted into the next. After the initial sale to Millon, Devaux, wanting more money, must have realized Louise's earning potential. His realization fit general patterns of familial pimping. In almost every case, parents who sold their children or forced them into some form of sexual servitude did not do so to get rid of them (simultaneously increasing family income and alleviating the family of the burden of the child's maintenance). Proffered girls almost always remained a part of the family, at least, for a while. Many lived at home. Others had regular contact until they broke away from their parents. In one of two backstories for Marie Emilie Duneboc de Carville, for example, Inspector Meusnier claimed that she ran away from home in Normandy at around the age of fourteen to escape both her father, who was prostituting her, and the household poverty that her prostitution was supposed to alleviate.[9] She later became a dancer in the Opéra corps de ballet, putting herself legally out of reach of her family.[10]

Not every case of direct parental prostitution was an impulsive response to opportunity. Mère Dumont, a marchande de modes, was reported to have brought her daughter from Soissons to Paris for the purpose of prostituting her, presumably to better-paying men than could be found at home. She was successful. According to police files, the fantastically wealthy fermier général Grimod de la Reynière paid fifty louis (twelve hundred livres) for her virginity (which had already been sold to another) and then maintained her for two years at quite a high rate.[11]

But Dumont's case was unusual. Those for whom prostituting a child was premeditated, as opposed to part of an "economy of makeshifts," generally used brokers, specifically the madams of Paris's most expensive brothels.[12] Collectively, families who used brokers stood apart from the other pimping parents in that they were almost all families headed by single mothers, the fathers dead or missing.[13] The procuresses they retained were able to secure buyers from a very specific and well-known clientele among the upper echelons of Paris's financial, judicial, and social elites. For example, in the spring of 1758, according to police records, Dame Boujard presented her virgin, thirteen-year-old daughter Marie to Madam Varenne, a procuress and owner of an elite brothel in Paris. She wanted the madam to find someone who would pay for the right to take the girl's virginity and then hopefully keep her as his mistress. Madam Varenne, an experienced broker in the virgin market, accepted the charge. She moved Marie into her brothel for safekeeping (and possibly to prevent her mother from employing a competing madam) and then "mounted a campaign to find someone who would suit the three of them," mother, daughter, and pimp.[14] If the mother approved the match, the pimp would earn a commission. The daughter had no say whatsoever.

Inspector Meusnier, who reported the case, followed it with little sympathy and great prurience. Madam Varenne, he wrote, first presented the "victim that should be sacrificed" to the marquis de Bandol (Francois–Auguste–Hilaire de Boyer), whom she knew to be "an avid lover of virgins." Bandol negotiated a price of four louis (ninety-six livres) for which he was to have sex with the girl, with the vague promise of some future maintenance. Neither deal was honored. Apparently, it was not just Marie's youth and body that attracted him; it was also the specific experience of having sex with a virgin. The marquis was sadistic.[15] In the words of the police, "but not encountering the resistance he had anticipated, especially since he himself was of an enormous nature, or so said the dozens and dozens of girls through whose hands his 'nature' had passed, he became furious at La Varenne and rather than granting her proof of his generosity, he threw twelve livres on the floor, and left cursing at her and swearing to add no more in the future, no matter what she said."[16]

The police do not report Marie's reaction. Madam Varenne, however, was concerned for her reputation as a virgin broker or perhaps for her ability to sell Marie, either being evidence of the importance of these sales to her business. Marie's subsequent visit to a surgeon revealed something about her sexual physiology that disqualified her from this market; most probably she was not a virgin.[17] Dame Boujard gave her permission in writing for Madam Varenne to keep the girl as a brothel worker. Marie's name was changed to Belleville.

While Dame Boujard left all the arrangements up to Madam Varenne, other pimping parents took more active roles in negotiations. Over the course of two weeks, Dame Perrin employed two madams and conducted interviews with three prospective buyers in trying to sell the virginity of her niece, with whose education she had been entrusted by her brother, the girl's father. She was supposed to find the girl some "honest occupation." Ultimately, Dame Perrin sold the girl's virginity twice through Madam Montbrun. The second time was to an Italian marquis who paid an incredible 30 louis (720 livres) to have sex with the girl.[18] While 30 louis was an unusually high price for sex with a virgin, madams generally were successful at negotiating significant sums, at least compared to what kept women earned on average. That they could do so more than once was good for business. Selling a maidenhood repeatedly was a common practice. It was a theme in literature. Pidansat de Mairobert, in his satirical description of Madam Gourdan's famous brothel, claimed the procuress had a specific room dedicated to making girls virgins once again.[19]

The few prices recorded for virgin sales range from cash payments of 240 to 720 livres, sometimes accompanied by dresses or jewels, whose prices are impossible to determine from the police reports. Other payments were in kind and included objects such as clothing, gold watches, or help with daily expenses. When a virgin girl was brokered into a patron-mistress relationship, as were the sisters Crousol, for example, the price paid for the maidenhood was not always distinguishable from the gift that often accompanied the beginning of a relationship. Both girls received a *pot-de-vin* (a "pot of wine" meaning, in this case, a signing bonus) of 600 livres of cash, as well as furniture and dresses, which could have been worth several thousand livres.[20]

Madams could negotiate these prices in part because they had access to a cohort of men willing and able to pay them. This access was not surprising. Madams were the very centers of those social networks that constituted the demimonde in mid-eighteenth-century Paris. Their establishments served not just as sexual emporia, but, perhaps more important, as the demimonde's core of sociability, where wealthy men threw parties or simply had an after-theater meal (supper) with one another and a few select female guests. Madams were also particularly motivated. The higher the price, the greater the reputation of the broker. Rumor of a high price also contributed to a kept woman's sexual capital—her value as a sexual commodity and hence the prices she could command for her services. Most girls sold in this manner never became kept women. However, the practice was mythologized in backstories so that the most successful kept women were attributed legendary debuts into the demimonde. Demoiselle Alart, a dancer in the Comédie-Française, for example, was reputedly sold at the age of fourteen for fifty louis (twelve hundred livres).[21] The inspectors reported these highest prices only as rumors.

Of course, like Dame Boujard, many a mother was less interested in such a one-time deal than in having a procuress make her daughter a rich man's mistress. This was the strategy of Mère Godeau. She quit her job as a femme de chambre with the intention of living off of the talents of her fifteen-year-old daughter, who recently had debuted as a dancer in the Opéra-Comique. However, when no patron immediately presented himself and Dame Godeau found herself in financial need, she turned to Madam Varenne for help. Varenne arranged a match for the daughter with the marquis de Chailleux, a Dragoon officer, who promised to pay 12 livres a month.[22] Varenne concluded a more lucrative match for the daughters of the Widow Crousol, who had four children and only 1,200 livres in *rente* (annuities). The powerful aristocrat, military leader, and well-known libertine, comte de la Tour d'Auvergne (prince de Turenne) gave the older daughter an impressive initial gift of 25 louis (600 livres), as well as furniture, clothing and jewels, which was a lot for Crousol but little in terms of what Turenne usually paid his mistresses. A year later, Monsieur Sibire paid Varenne 12 louis (288 livres) for the younger sister, whom he maintained at 130 livres a month.[23] One hundred and thirty livres was high for such a match. Usually, unknown girls brokered by madams ended up with patrons who would maintain them at much lower rates, between 12 and 50 livres a month. Men willing to pay more than 150 livres a month generally sought higher-profile mistresses, women already established in the demimonde. The comte de Coubert, for example, paid his mistress, the dancer Deschamps, 1,000 livres a month.[24] Deschamps's pension eclipses Crousol's; nevertheless, the younger Crousol alone managed to double her family's income.

For Dame Godeau, the trip to Madam Varenne's establishment probably involved walking no more than a few blocks. The psychological journey may have been even shorter, at least for the mother, who, as a former maid to various women of the theater, had lived for years on the edge of the demimonde. For Dame Crousol, it was a similarly simple journey. Varenne was Crousol's neighbor. The procuress initiated and executed the deal. Crousol's entire participation consisted of approving, though, possibly, this may have cost her something. For most parents, however, this route toward financial betterment demanded an investment of time, energy, and often money: expenditure of family resources for a trip to Paris if the family did not live there, familiarizing oneself with the demimonde, the review and then negotiation of possible offers. This work and financial cost was less than would have been required had they tried to place a daughter in an apprenticeship or set aside a portion of their wealth for her marriage. It required more, however, than using connections to find the girl a job and expecting that she support herself thereafter, which, as we have seen, often was the case with girls from poor families. Then there was the emotional investment. This was not, it would seem, distress at pushing a daughter into prostitution. Not one police report shows a pimping parent evincing even a single moment's regret (though, of course, this may have been a choice in reporting). While the reports do occasionally try to separate "bad" greedy parents from the terribly desperate ones, the inspectors' profiling stops there. Whatever concern these families had for their daughters' honor or for their own failures as parents in light of the increasing importance placed on children in this era, their desire for money was greater. Rather, it was a question, as in the case of Dame Godeau, of the hope that prostituting the child would save the parents from work or, more seriously, end the family's financial woes. As for the daughters, the records are mostly silent, with the single exception of Demoiselle Perrin. After she had sex with Monsieur Darnet, the first to whom her virginity had been sold, she was "allowed to eat and she cried for her brother who lived in Paris."[25]

As a family strategy, however, use of a madam to prostitute a child did not involve the type of advance planning required in the third pattern of prostitution, that in which parents prostituted their daughters and soon thereafter (or sometimes concurrently) enrolled them in the Opéra. Families who engaged in this sort of prostitution also stood apart from the sample at large, being more likely to contain two parents and, not surprisingly, being wealthier. That wealth, however modest, was necessary because this strategy involved considerable financial investment: music or voice lessons, a move of the entire family to Paris, the steady cultivation of acquaintances and the manipulation of the social networks through which the girl would obtain a place in the Opéra school. It required early and careful allocation of family resources.

That the Opéra, the Opéra-Comique, and to a lesser degree, the *comédies* were vehicles to success in the demimonde was a well-known fact. In his memoires, the Italian adventurer Giacomo Casanova mentions seeing girls of thirteen and fourteen who thought nothing of being pregnant at rehearsal at the Opéra school, accompanied by their mothers.[26] When the Opéra singer Marie-Antoinette Petite was fired for having been caught having sex with the marquis de Bonnac in her *loge*, she supposedly hired Abbé de LaMare, librettist of *Zaïde: Reine de Grenade*, to pen a public defense. Though clearly a satire and doubtfully authorized by Petite, the apology is telling nonetheless as it claims that Petite joined the Opéra "only with the goal of imitating her colleagues and achieving happiness like them through the route of pleasure." When she got her place in the choir, the author continued, Petite assumed her fortune was made.[27] In his satire of the demimonde, Turmeau de la Morandière called the opera school, which took four times more students than there were positions in the company, "the harem of the nation, the bazaar where *les Grands* of the Empire buy their slaves."[28]

Dame Godeau is a good example of an Opéra mother. She quit her job only when she saw that her daughter was sufficiently talented in dance to become a professional and hence earn a living for them, both as a dancer and as a dame entretenue. The Raye (née Régis) family is another example. In his backstory on Louise Régis (known professionally as Demoiselle Raye, *l'aînée*), Meusnier reported that the family had been living in Paris, in horrible poverty, "waiting for the oldest daughter to master dance which they endeavored to have her learn so that they could live comfortably." When, at the age of fourteen, Demoiselle Raye successfully debuted as a dancer in the Comédie-Italienne, wrote Meusnier, she also "took particular care, in accordance with her mother's lessons, to accept the tributes of all those the rich leches who approached her, getting out of them whatever she did not have." Her earnings as a kept woman enabled the family to move to a very nice, well-furnished apartment.[29] However, Raye had trouble professionally and personally, as her multiple lawsuits attest.[30] She bounced from company to company, was embroiled in a bitter marriage and separation with Antoine-Bonaventure Pitro, a principal dancer of the Opéra, and apparently spent enormous sums of money on gifts for boyfriends and greluchons. She died in 1768, at the age of thirty-one.

Meusnier penned a Raye family saga. Anticipating for a quite a while the "profligacy of her eldest daughter," he wrote, "[Madam Raye] did not neglect in these times of plenty to have her youngest also trained in dance." Shortly after the younger Raye, then thirteen, enrolled in the Opéra school, her mother, who wanted to "reestablish the financial footing of the household as it slipped from view so quickly you could see it [disappearing]" began working to find someone to take her virgin daughter as his mistress. Madam Raye visited several elite madams and even did some legwork herself, spending time at the apartments of various Opéra performers. Eventually, she landed for her daughter Monsieur de Courchamp, *conseiller de Parlement*. He paid twenty-five louis (six hundred livres) a month maintenance and gave the girl a new wardrobe both as a pot-de-vin and as compensation for taking her virginity. He also gave her some furniture. It was a very lucrative match. According to Inspector Marais, Madam Raye insisted on keeping her younger daughter at home, regarding her as the "last resource of her fortune" and not trusting that Monsieur de Courchamp could prevent the girl from engaging in the kind of behavior that would destroy the relationship.[31]

So did this family strategy of pushing daughters into the demimonde work? Were these families supported by their daughters' earnings? Whatever happened to Dames Crousol and Perrin, the mother and aunt who used brokers? Unfortunately, we do not know. The police do not tell us. The police opened dossiers on brokered girls, but few of these dossiers contained any additional entries. Since the inspectors tended to report whenever a subject under surveillance made some news (a new patron, problems in a relationship, a breakup), lack of further reporting suggests that these girls never fully established themselves as kept women.

What about the *mères de l'Opéra*? Did Dame Raye achieve her goal of being supported by her daughter's wealthy lovers? Unfortunately, in her case and so many others, we also do not know. While the police continued to report on both daughters, they stopped reporting on their mother. This very lack of information is itself important evidence. If a girl was having (or trying to have) sexual relations with men of the right caliber for which she was being paid at a certain rate, parental involvement was, all by itself, news. Take, for example, Demoiselle Dascher. Demoiselle Dascher entered the demimonde with the help of Brissault, one of Paris's few male procurers. Her career got off to a promising start. For a fee, Brissault had arranged a number of passades with the comte de Jumilhac de Cubjac, governor of the Bastille from 1761 to 1776, and other high-profile noblemen who frequented elite brothels. One of these men, the marquis de Voyer, son of the secretary of war and governor of the Château de Vincennes, eventually took her as his mistress. The girl soon found herself on her own again, however, and shortly thereafter Brissault began to pressure her to repay him the money she owed. Dame Dascher, desperate to find her daughter a new patron, sought out Jumilhac, and, in the words of Inspector Marais, offered the girl to him. Marais thought the interchange sufficiently important to be the subject of an entire report.[32] When parents disappeared from the police reports, it probably signified the cessation of their active involvement in the demimonde.

If we assume that the lack of information about parents in the reports meant that the parents had disengaged from managing their daughters' lives, then we can make some observations about the success of pimping as a family strategy. First, the strategy did work. As in the case of the sisters Crousol, pandered girls became primary breadwinners for their families. Monsieur Sibire, the notary who took the younger daughter as his mistress, paid for her by supporting the Crousol household (which included her mother).[33] Second, while this strategy did work, and many patrons dramatically improved family fortunes, they rarely did so for long. On average, parents who prostituted their children disappeared from the historical record after a year. In about half of the cases, as with the family Crousol, this is because the dossier was closed. What became of the Crousol sisters we do not know. As they appear in no records concerning the demimonde, it is unlikely that they had very successful careers as elite prostitutes. In the remaining cases, the police continued to report on each subject, saying nothing more of her parents.

☙ Patterns of Authority in the Demimonde

How can we explain these patterns? Why did this strategy work at all, if only for a year? It is an especially pressing question when we consider that pimping, even of one's own children, was illegal. In their respective commentaries on the law of the Old Regime, Joseph-Nicolas Guyot and Daniel Jousse include pimping by parents among the most serious forms of the crime of procurement (*macquerellage*), one deserving capital punishment.[34] Both this criminalization and the practice of pimping daughters that occurred in spite of it have to be understood within the larger context of the increasing power and authority of parents in this period and the state's enforcement of it.

Fathers had always held enormous power in Western societies. This power was both highlighted and augmented amid the intense civil strife of the sixteenth century as patriarchalism was used to support and justify monarchical power in France. In his *Traité de la République* (1576), Jean Bodin argued that the monarch's political authority over his subjects was the same as that of a father over his family. Royal and paternal power legitimized each other; the family served as the first school of absolutism. A series of royal edicts beginning in 1556 and ending in 1639 with a statement by Louis XIII, which paraphrased Bodin, enhanced parental power, specifically in the realm of spousal choice.[35] In the decades that followed, *parlementaires* and other judicial officers began to enforce these laws through the courts, translating parental authority (the right to do something) into parental power (the ability to do something). Sarah Hanley attributes the enhancing of parental control through these laws to a "family-state compact" between the families of the *noblesse de robe* and the monarchy. The monarchy needed these families to staff the bureaucracy with which it was centralizing institutions and bringing them under royal control. These families in turn needed full control over the marriages of their children in order to build the alliance and patronage networks through which they advanced themselves. They used their positions as judicial officers to effect a revolution in paternal authority and power up until the early eighteenth century.[36]

By the eighteenth century, fathers had formidable legal rights over their children.[37] They could not kill their offspring, nor sell them into slavery, but they did have control over every other facet of their children's lives. In Paris, parents retained control over a child as long as he was an *enfant de famille*, meaning until the child married, reached the age of majority (twenty-five), joined a religious order, or went through a specific judicial process separating him from his parents. In all other cases, the father controlled the property of an enfant de famille, as well as any income that property gener-ated, with the exception of wages.[38] Children did not possess legal person-alities and thus were not able to make legal contracts, borrow, lend, or testify in court. Nor did they have the right to choose their marriage part-ners without parental consent, even after reaching the age of majority.

Yet, in the face of the state's efforts to support parental and especially paternal power, that very power was coming under attack from various and unrelated quarters. Catholic moralists across Europe articulated greater responsibilities for parents. Beyond providing a religious and moral educa-tion, parents now had the duty to establish their children in a profession.[39] Philosophes also attacked the idea of a patriarchal absolutist father. They did so in conjunction with their attacks on monarchical power. As the family model had been used to legitimate and consolidate monarchical power, so it now was being used to undermine it.[40] Linked to this shift was a growing interest, especially after the publication of Rousseau's *Émile* (1762), in children and children's education. The cumulative result of all these movements—the emergence of children's literature, larger attacks on the family model from a political standpoint, and protests by Catholic moralists against forcing children to marry—was a growing individualiza-tion of the child.

Historians of the family point to the call for expanded and more in-volved parenting as evidence that the family had fundamentally changed, or modernized, over the course of the early modern period. Though the tim-ing and exact character of this change are still widely debated, the general argument is that by the late sixteenth or early seventeenth century the nu-clear family had individuated itself against the household and larger kin networks to become the center of family life, responsible for raising offspring and for mutual support and protection.[41] At the same time, the nature of the relationships within the family became more emotionally intense as conjugal and familial affection replaced husbandly and paternal authority.[42] The shift seems to have accelerated in the middle of the eighteenth century, when the nuclear family made increasing demands for privacy, hence isolat-ing and privileging itself further. This was reflected, for example, in interior architecture, which began to include corridors in order to isolate rooms and allow for more privacy.[43]

The scholarship on this subject has primarily concerned middling and elite families. How far down the social ladder did this "modernization" extend? Was the power granted by the state also attenuated by the expecta-tion of affection and mutual respect among artisan and working families? We know the least about working or artisan families, backgrounds from which kept women tended to originate. Arlette Farge, in studying attitudes of poor people towards their children, argues that there was a tension between families' "hope for life" and a "contraction of their hope," due to the perils of life in the capital.[44] The former resulted in attentive caretaking and the latter in neglect. In her study of parental reaction to the abduction of children by the police in 1750, she found that while some parents ran after their children, doing whatever was necessary to liberate them, others did nothing.[45] Suffice it to say that there were many working and artisanal families in Paris in which parents deeply loved their children and did their best for them. Whether these sentiments tempered the authoritarian potential is unclear.

The original question is even more curious. If pimping was illegal and use of force, legal or not, was increasingly frowned on, why did these families consider prostitution as part of a family strategy, and why did the strategy work, if only for a year? It worked for two reasons. First, the state did not frown on use of authority by parents; rather, they encouraged it. Second, although pimping was illegal, the police of Paris acted as though it was not.

While the church and Enlightenment thinkers increasingly criticized authoritarian parenting, the police of Paris were its foot soldiers. They helped parents control children through the use of the lettre de cachet, a legal instrument by which people of all social ilk sought to incarcerate relatives whose behavior threatened to bring dishonor or some other disaster down upon the family.[46] Officially, a lettre de cachet was a direct order of the king used to effect a wide variety of actions, from dictating forms of ceremony to compelling an assembly to register an edict. Beginning with Louis XIV, however, they were most frequently issued to incarcerate individuals. The monarch used lettres to silence and punish political opponents, mainly writers. This practice became a regular policing tool in Paris after the late 1740s.[47] The police employed lettres de cachet in *affaires de police*, to preserve *le bon ordre*, prevent riot, or hush up scandal. For example, police inspectors used them to lock up prostitutes caught in night raids immediately rather than wait for them to be tried and convicted in the Friday morning police court. These royal orders also authorized inspectors Meusnier's and Marais's harassment and arrest of libertine priests.

Starting from the 1720s, a family wishing to have one of its own incarcerated had to apply for the privilege in writing to the king (often through the lieutenant general of police) with the submission of a *placet*, a particular form of request. That such an application was necessary cannot be overemphasized. Unless the problem at hand was of sufficient magnitude that it caused scandal in the district, the police would involve themselves in family affairs only if they were specifically asked to do so. (And, more than likely, if the problem did spill out of the house and into the street, it was probably the complaint of some other party—the local priest or an aggrieved neighbor—that brought the police to the scene.) Parents who applied for orders of incarceration did not receive them automatically. Their requests were investigated and had to meet certain criteria. Nevertheless, sales of children were occurring in a climate in which parents also had the power to have their own locked up. Because the orders were extrajudicial, a function of the king's will (or whim), it was possible to have someone arrested clandestinely and imprisoned indefinitely without any publicity.

Operation of parental authority in practice concerned protecting family honor and financial assets. Arlette Farge and Michel Foucault looked at ninety-three placets resulting in lettres de cachet to incarcerate a family member in the year 1758. Most described a pattern of dissolute behavior as opposed to a single instance of it. They were concerned with a general *dérangement* (disorder) of the child. Incarcerating him or her was intended not as a punishment but as a way to prevent his behavior from ruining his family. If, however, the child used his time under lock and key to reflect and change his ways, his reform was generally lauded and often resulted in the call for a second lettre de cachet, this time for his release. A series of recognized traits constituted such *mauvaise conduite* (bad behavior). For boys, these included violence, especially in the home; regular or prolonged absences; theft; and drunkenness. For girls, mauvaise conduite usually had a sexual connotation. Sometimes it was a question of protracted absences, or a fondness for spending the entire night out. It was assumed that such a daughter was spending her nights in a mauvais lieu, such as a tavern. Absences from the home were especially problematic if the woman in question had children. Even *concubinage* (a man and woman living together without being married) had to be qualified before it was seen as a problem. It was not so much the cohabitation itself that upset parents as much as some of the events that accompanied it. Perhaps the man was married, or maybe the couple produced children out of wedlock.

The registers that listed individuals incarcerated via lettre de cachet (though not necessarily at the insistence of a relative) confirm that the police generally arrested women who had displayed mauvaise conduite.[48] For the year 1756, for example, seventy-four women were arrested for sex-related crimes. Under the heading *sujet de leur détention* (reason for detention), the term *macquerelle* (procuress) appears thirty-three times, *prostituée* (prostitute) fifteen, *libertine* (libertine) thirty-nine, *mauvais commerce* (transactional sex or disreputable trade) one, *vivre* or *livré en debauche* (to be or cause someone else to be debauched) eight, and *cause du scandale* (causing a scandal) fifteen. Three women were accused of debauching others, two of drunkenness, and six of theft. Of the seventy-four, four had sold their furniture, which was seen as a mark of general disorder endangering the family's economic welfare. Three had threatened their families, and two had dressed as men. In all, these 74 women were accused of 142 different types of improper behavior. Marguerite Langlois, for example, was said to be a "prostitute, pregnant, passing her days with libertines, and mistreating her mother."[49] Catherine l'Equiller (Femme Chaveau) was accused of being a "libertine who left her husband several times and turned toward prostitution."[50]

In the eyes of the family, the evil of mauvaise conduite was compounded by the physical proximity of the subject to her family's dwelling. The closer a wayward child lived to home, the greater the chances the neighborhood would associate her with her family.[51] There develops a circularity. Aside from the obvious nature of problems such as theft, child neglect, and violence, the behavior of children, especially female children, was problematic because it was thought to be so by the community in which the family lived. Reputation was made by the neighborhood. It was to avoid public awareness of a child's misbehavior—in other words, scandal—that the family sought the lettre de cachet in the first place. When supporting parents' efforts to incarcerate a child, the state simultaneously supported, if not reinforced, certain community moral standards. Consequently, the age of the child was not an issue. Of the ninety-three lettres studied by Farge and Foucault, 30 percent concern children over the age of majority. (Six were over the age of thirty-one!) The history of the most famous subject of the lettre de cachet, the marquis de Sade, shows that an individual was legally vulnerable to his parents (or in this case his strong-willed mother-in-law) at any age.[52]

The placets transcribed by Farge and Foucault show that state and family interests intersected in controlling children (and spouses) whose behavior threatened to destroy the family. In doing so, the state set the limits on what sorts of behavior it would tolerate from children. However, it did not set any such limitations on parents, as such. If parents had no objection to their children's wild though not illegal behavior—and that behavior was not the subject of a neighbor's or employer's placet—the state would take no action. An extension of this formula was that, short of killing a child, parents could treat their progeny as they chose without the expectation of state interference. This was not entirely true, but buyers and sellers of girls seemed to think that it was. They believed that police support would extend even to those parents forcing their daughters into prostitution, a belief fostered by the very actions of the police themselves. The police did not always support parents nor did they always turn a blind eye, but the perception that they did shaped pimping as a family strategy.

That perception was likely based on the fact that the main policing bodies in mid-eighteenth-century Paris, those men under the lieutenant general of police and the city's Parlement, did not generally prosecute parents from lowly social origins who sold their children on their own or through certain madams. The police were aware of many of these cases as they unfolded. Let us turn back to the case of Perrin. As we have seen, this forty-two-year-old woman engaged a series of procuresses to find a buyer for her fifteen-year-old niece, whom she passed off as her daughter. On November 23, 1752, Inspector Meusnier recounted a set of negotiations in which he participated, pretending to be the agent of a Polish noble, a possible buyer. Over the course of the week, Meusnier continued to track the negotiations.[53] Later, he described the incident in which the girl was violated.[54]

Meusnier did not stop the sale, nor did he prosecute Dame Perrin. His lack of judicial intervention, however, did not signify a disengagement from the virgin market. On the contrary, the inspector oversaw it. In the case of Perrin, he even worked undercover. The inspector's reports evince his careful attention to these sales. Reports from madams indicate a well developed, albeit corrupt, oversight system. For example, in November 1755, Madam Lafosse wrote to Meusnier to report the details of a virgin sale in progress, involving herself, Madam Gautier, and a man named Dumetz.[55] Lafosse gave the inspector the dates and places where meetings were to take place and made clear that she did not want the girl in her brothel, "fearing scandal." In her phonetic French and rough hand, Lafosse both sought permission to proceed and, like Montbrun, who brokered the sale of Perrin, offered the girl to the inspector. "I am sure that Gautier will be as happy to leave her [the girl] in your hands as those of M. Dumetz."[56] Meusnier, as we saw in chapter 1, had had sex with Demoiselle Perrin. Whether Lafosse was suggesting the inspector save the girl or contribute toward her prostitution was unclear.

Meusnier's tolerance of virgin sales, however, was not a specific endorsement of the practice. Rather, it was an extension of the general police habit of ignoring all but the most scandalous and public of sexual activities. This would appear to be incongruous as virgin sales were scandalous by any measure, that is, until we consider two other principles that informed police practice: the Département's obeisance to social hierarchy and the instrumentalization of toleration.

The inspectors' reactions to parents were framed by a larger pattern of supporting social hierarchy, the authority of parents over children and that of elites over nonelites. The inspectors tended to allow parents to do as they wished with the sexual bodies of their female children but in some instances, they wanted to be sure of parental consent. For example, if a parent was prostituting a child, as was the case with Marie Boujard, the parent's permission had to be assured and continuing. This could be problematic. Madam Lafosse, for example, took Anne Bourlans at the request of her father. They agreed that Lafosse would keep the girl and clothe her, and that in exchange she would "please those who came to see her." Yet Père Bourlans—like Père Devaux—returned, threatening to put the girl in the Hôpital should she not provide him with more money. Lafosse protected herself by reporting their exchange to Meusnier. She claimed that she threatened to evict Anne should her father continue his harassment, after which Père Bourlans supposedly declared himself "ravi" (delighted) with their current arrangement.[57]

When parents were not present, however, their actual consent rarely seemed to matter. In other words, consistent with police practice regarding the lettres de cachet, when parents did not press the issue, neither did the police. But they were sensitive to it. In these cases, instead of seeking parental permission, the madams were obliged to explain its absence. They produced for their police handlers long teleological histories—backstories—on each of their pensioners, explaining why it was acceptable by community standards for the girl in question to be a prostitute. The answers were standard. Either the girl was sexually experienced and hence had lost her sexual honor, or she simply had no other option. The historian Erica-Marie Benabou argued that madams were banned from taking inexperienced girls and that this was to avoid parental complaints, which were "a major concern for the administration."[58] The need to prove a girl was experienced or, I would add, desperate and unattached, is a logical explanation for all the paperwork required of madams. But Benabou's argument should be qualified. The police sought to avoid the kinds of complaints that could result in scandal. Parents who did not live in Paris mattered little.

If police were willing to support the authority of "bad" parents as they sold children into prostitution, why did not they equally support that of the "good" ones who were trying to retrieve daughters from brothels or patron-mistress relationships? The number of instances in which a parent tried to stop his or her child's prostitution were few. What evidence there is suggests that when the inspectors failed to support these parents it was for one of two reasons. The first was that the parent had not asked for the inspectors' assistance. As with the lettres de cachet, the Département would not interfere in the life of a kept woman or brothel pensioner who was playing by the demimonde rules, unless they were specifically asked to do so. Even if, through their own investigations, the inspectors came to be aware that a parent was searching for a child, they would take no action ex officio.

The police also failed to support "good" parents when the parents' interest in their daughter clashed with that of a social superior. This was the second reason. When Demoiselle Roux ran away to the home of Lord Hyde, who was assisted in this plot by the duc de Richelieu, one of the most powerful aristocrats in France, Meusnier noted in his report both the girl's where-abouts as well as her mother's frantic search for her, a search in which Mère Roux had tried to involve the authorities.[59] In another example, Inspector Marais did not intervene when he knew Julie Morel's father was searching for her. A peasant farmer, Père Morel had asked his seigneur, with whose coachman Julie had absconded only later to be abandoned, to find the girl in Paris. He did, at the elite brothel of Madam Hecquet, where, according to Marais, he was taken with the girl, "amused himself with her" and "became her protector" as she continued to work at various brothels, all the while tell-ing the father he had failed in his task.[60] It is likely that Marais had little con-cern for the complaints of a peasant farmer in Normandy over the desires of a nobleman in Paris.

A final consideration in understanding why the police allowed parents to sell their children lies in the very functionality of the policy of toleration. Meusnier and other inspectors stood by and allowed Perrin and Boujard to sell their girls. However, these same inspectors arrested parents when they worked with madams not affiliated with the police. Limiting toleration to certain madams could have corralled the virgin market so that it came under official observation. Whatever violation and assault these girls experienced was far less important to the police than their own ability to track such events and render them "visible."

All these explanations serve to show why the police did not interfere in virgin sales and how their actions helped to foster the impression that these sales were licit. But the police did endorse the elite sex market, or at least validate it, in another sense. Police magistrates helped to regulate it, at least passively, as commerce. For example, the parents of Marie-Catherine Reg-gièri, called Colombe, sold her to an Irish aristocrat, Lord Massareen, for 10 louis (240 livres). The fifteen-year-old girl then left her paternal home to live with her patron, to whom she bore a baby and for whom she seemed to have genuine affection. When her parents demanded more money, Mas-sareen and Colombe resisted. The conflict, like thousands of others over small business matters, ended up before Leger, a local police commissioner. Leger listened to the testimony of both sides, drew up a *procès verbal* (the deposition necessary to begin legal proceedings), and declared for the girl and her patron. That was the end of it.[61]

Perhaps it was police practices that encouraged elite buyers and sellers of girls to assume that parental authority operated in the demimonde exactly as it did in the world of licit sexual relations. Returning to the case with which we opened this chapter, when Père Devaux threatened to incarcerate his daughter should her patron not provide more money, Millon (the captain to whom he had sold his daughter) took the threat seriously. Could Devaux actually have incarcerated for debauchery the very daughter he himself debauched? Millon seemed to think so. The captain retrieved his mistress, whom he had hidden in a brothel, only after he had negotiated a new deal with her father. As we have seen, this deal included the father's written permission for Millon to live with his daughter.[62] In another example, Dame Boujard gave her permission in writing to Varenne when she left her daughter to work in the latter's brothel.[63] Even such a rich and powerful patron as the English aristocrat and Jacobite politician Lord Hyde sought written permission to live with his teenage mistress from the girl's mother, with whom he was battling for control of the girl.[64]

Would Devaux have in fact been able to have his daughter incarcerated? Probably not. The police investigation would have revealed the facts. But it was the assumption behind the threat that is important. Devaux, Hyde, and Varenne—individuals from very different backgrounds—all seemed to think, or at least worry, that the law was "on the side" of the parents. The perception that the law operated in the demimonde in a sort of regulatory capacity was further supported by participants' adherence to legal forms in the making of these deals. In other words, transactions—which in this case were the buying and selling of girls—conformed to contemporary legal structures for other business deals.

✎ Unkept Daughters

Let us return to our second question posed at the beginning of this chapter: Given the extent of parental investment in the project, why did it usually fail after one year? In some cases, it failed because the girl being prostituted never became a dame entretenue. Being sold as a virgin, even into a patron-mistress relationship, did not make a prostituted girl a kept woman. What did was the ability to translate that initiation into a series of high-paying sexual relationships governed by a verbal contract with men from the social, financial, political, and judicial elites. That so many newly sold girls disappeared from the record so quickly emphasizes how difficult it was to become a professional mistress, despite the best efforts of parents and brokers. But with regard to those who "made it," there are several explanations as to why parents did not long reap the benefits of their labors. Some parents may have died. It is possible that others did continue to profit but had relaxed into more passive roles uninteresting to the police. Lastly, some daughters managed to forcibly eject their parents from their lives.

There is a good likelihood that parents who disappeared from the record did so because they were either sick or dead. Daniel Roche and Annik Pardailhé-Galabrun both used notarial documents to determine that the average life span of a Parisian was from forty to fifty years. Paris, with its crowded, poorly ventilated housing, its polluted water systems, its open sewers, and its dangerous streets was a perilous place. The late age of marriage combined with the fact that girls were prostituted, on average, at age fourteen meant that most parents were, at the very youngest, in their early forties by the time they sold their daughters. If a child was late in the birth order, her parents would have been even older.[65]

A second possibility is that many of these parents, specifically mothers, may have stopped actively managing their daughters once the latter were established. As we can see not only from the police reports, but also from complaints kept women made to the commissioners, a good many dames entretenues lived with their mothers or other close relatives, sometimes on and off, for years. These relatives often functioned as support staff, cooking, cleaning, managing the household and taking care of children. In return, they received shelter and food. Almost all of these mothers were single, either abandoned or, more often, widowed. One thinks again of Thérèse Levasseur living with her mother and her lover, Rousseau, who paid their bills and employed them as domestics.

Part of the arrangement might involve support but separate living quarters. A patron might set up his mistress in an apartment and not wish to spend time in the company of her mother. Such appeared to be the case with Demoiselle Amédée, a dancer in the Opéra. By the summer of 1749, she was twenty-two and had been working in the demimonde for eight years. She lived with her mother, who did her cooking and managed her expenses.[66] At this time, Inspector Meusnier thought that Amédée was meeting her patron, the duc d'Olonne, three to four times a week in a house he rented on the outskirts of Paris. Amédée left Paris for a brief spell to live with Olonne on his lands in Normandy. When she returned to the capital, she moved from her old apartment to a new one, where Olonne came to sleep several times a week. At least this is what Meusnier suspected. With the move, Amédée's mother—one of the few "support mothers" who was not single—returned to live with her own husband on the rue Princesse in the faubourg St. Germain. They were poor. Amédée "sent what little help she could."[67]

These relationships of mothers living with daughters and daughters comfortably supporting indigent parents bring to light another set of family dynamics in the demimonde, one that contrasts sharply with the brutal sale of teenagers by their parents. Without denying the importance of the child's contribution to the family income, we see examples in which parents provided support and comfort to their daughters. This was especially the case among theater families, families in which one or both parents, and often several siblings, were theater performers. For many of these children, becoming a performer was no different than it was for millions of others who went into the family trade or business. That many children from these families became exceptional artists, principal singers and dancers, suggests an authentic interest in the arts. That many made their debut in the demimonde more or less concurrently was hardly shocking either to family members or to the police, given the importance of these affairs to the family's survival. Prostitution, as it was part of the culture of the theater, was normalized in many of these families.

Parents and children in theater families demonstrated enduring, tight emotional bonds. Theater families moved about to accommodate their children's careers. This in itself was not unusual. Many a nontheater family worked to put an attractive, talented daughter on the stage, moving from town to town, following the best opportunities. But these families usually fell apart soon after the daughter debuted. With theater families, however, daughters (and sons) often remained loyal, living with their parents and siblings for years after debuting, and supporting them long after that. Rosalie Astraudi, star of the Comédie-Italienne, for example, held a nine-year lease and paid the rent on the house on the rue Grande-Truanderie in which she lived with her siblings and parents, former theater people themselves. Comte d'Egmont, Astraudi's patron, paid many of the household's bills.[68]

A third reason why many parents disappeared from the record after about a year is that their daughters made them leave. There are numerous cases in which kept women tried to free themselves of pimping parents. Some were able to gain this freedom through the assistance of their patrons. As we have seen, patrons clearly believed in parental authority, so much so that they often used their primary lever, economic pressure, to co-opt it. By definition, these men were significantly wealthier than the families who produced kept women. Sometimes a patron simply bought off a parent. Other times it was more complicated. Take, for example, Demoiselle Roux. Until she ran off with Lord Hyde, her mother managed her career for her. Hyde first tried to buy off the mother, offering her a carriage and twelve hundred livres of *rente* (an annuity) if she would return to her native province and renounce all rights to her daughter in writing. The mother refused. Hyde then tried to have her incarcerated via a lettre de cachet on a bogus charge, but Meusnier saw though it. Finally, Hyde made it impossible for her to earn a living, forcing her to leave town.

Other girls may have used the Opéra as means to escape their parents' power. Membership automatically conferred the protection of the king. Hence, a girl inscribed on its rolls could not be incarcerated by her family, or by anyone else for that matter. Scores of girls, dishonored or even pregnant, fled to Paris to join the Opéra specifically for that purpose. Marie-Louise Guénon de La Chanterie used this right when she went to Commissioner Louis Cadot to file a complaint against her parents, who, she asserted, had been harassing her for money for three years. Their most recent behavior, she claimed, had made her so upset that it "prevented her from doing her duty at the academy." Because she was a minor—La Chanterie was only twenty—her parents had a right to her earnings. But as a member of the academy, she had royal protection. Cadot investigated and, when neighbors confirmed her story, spoke to her father and got him to back down.[69] However, unlike La Chanterie, those put on the stage by their mothers rarely took advantage of the legal protection it offered them to free themselves of meddlesome parents, perhaps because the residue of parental authority was too strong and they were too young.

For others, becoming a kept woman might have been part of a larger process of maturation. The world of licit sexual relations was based on an economy of sexual honor. Women derived power and status through marriage. The demimonde, on the other hand, was predicated on an economy of sexual desirability. The greater a girl's sexual desirability, or sexual capital, the more likely she would attract wealthy patrons, obtain a position in the Opéra and, finally, make her parents money. Girls with the greatest capital rapidly moved their families from the ranks of the working (or often nonworking) poor to a more comfortable life. Crousol, who was put into a far from brilliant match, lifted her family out of poverty. Sometimes the girl herself was rapidly catapulted into luxurious surroundings, attended to, at least for a while, by a powerful aristocrat. Being the family breadwinner or being ultimately responsible for the profound changes in her own life could not but give the girl an awareness of the power of her own sexual capital, and this may have helped, in the right circumstances, to shatter parental authority.

Unfortunately, Louise de la Tour did not find herself in those circumstances. So how do we explain the events of that June evening in 1753, when Louise de la Tour fled her home for the brothel of Madam Fleurance? Both Père Devaux and Captain Dargent believed that Devaux's written note constituted a licit transfer of authority. The captain paid Devaux for that authority. As the inspector's later report clarifies, Père Devaux was not trying to rid himself of Louise. What he wanted was a regular stipend from her. The inspector returned Louise to her father knowing full well what would happen next—that he would give her to Dargent—because what might happen next was not his concern. Meusnier was not interested in Louise's wishes as she contested this transfer of authority, nor in preventing her "corruption." He was enforcing paternal will.

When he turned Louise back to her father, Meusnier proved deaf to older discourses that stipulated the duties of parents and to the new, louder ones that encouraged mothers and fathers to nurture and respect their children. In supporting parental will over all other considerations, the inspectors made no claim about the kind of parents his subjects ought to be. As such, they clashed with their own superiors. In investigating and executing lettres de cachet, the lieutenant general revealed a stable vision of the family, one in which parental authority would be supported only if the child were risking the family's honor or its financial footing. The irony is that Meusnier and Marais, as inspectors, investigated these very same cases and drew conclusions about their merits based on the state's criteria. But when wearing their Département hats, they were more concerned about hierarchy. When drawn into family issues, they supported the social hierarchy, ignoring a parent's wish when it conflicted with that of an elite. In only one way did the Département's approach to families and that embodied in the execution of lettres de cachet overlap. Both protected the family's viability as an economic unit.

It would be a mistake, however, to argue that the Département was part of the larger state effort to ensure the power of parents over their children. The inspectors engaged only when asked to do so. In almost all other instances, they stood on the sidelines and took notes. The inspectors' larger purpose with respect to families was to contain sales of children to the demimonde where they could be watched, their actions inscribed in bulletins, journals, and registers. The cumulative effect of this approach contributed to the perception that structures of parental authority and power, which were embedded in the legal and customal fabric of the world of licit sexual relations, remained intact and operative in the demimonde. This perception was the armature of the elite market in girls, shaping it, forming it and enabling it.

So we are left with one question. Why did Louise run to Madam Fleurance? It is to this question and the ways in which elite prostitution was connected to female networks that we will turn in the next chapter.

► CHAPTER 4

Madams and Their Networks

Let us return to the case of Marie Boujard. In the fall of 1758, Mère Boujard had engaged Madam Varenne to find a buyer for her thirteen-year-old daughter's virginity. After failing to please the marquis de Bandol, who thought the girl was not a virgin, Marie was examined by a doctor and found to have some genital anatomical problem that made her unfit to be brokered into a patron-mistress relationship. Her mother left her in the brothel under "pecuniary conditions." The exact meaning of this is unclear. Perhaps Marie was to earn back the money spent on the doctor. Alternatively, if Marie had claimed to be a virgin when she was not, she might have been forced to earn money to compensate Varenne for the damage to her relationship with her client. Or Marie could have been simply earning money for her mother.

Known as Belleville, Marie Boujard spent more than six months living as a pensioner in the brothel, required to have sex with whomever asked for her.[1] She also was sent on outcalls, specifically to *petits soupers*, the small supper parties that were a core of sociability in the demimonde. Like most other brothel prostitutes, Marie eventually contracted venereal disease, probably syphilis. Unlike most, she was not fired immediately when customers began to complain about her sores. Madam Varenne must have thought Marie an important asset to her business. She arranged to have the girl treated twice, subjecting her to the painful, debilitating, and expensive mercury cure, the cost of which was added to Marie's debt. Though she must have been exhausted and emaciated, and possibly disfigured from her two treatments, two weeks after returning to work Marie attended a petit souper at which she met the marquis de Persenat.[2] Persenat "found her to his liking" and decided to take her as his mistress. Marie Boujard was fifteen years old.

To do so, Persenat had to negotiate Marie's release from Varenne. He paid Boujard's now staggering debt of twenty-five louis (six hundred livres) and promised to pay Varenne an additional twenty-five louis for the girl herself. Persenat offered Marie a contract of three hundred livres a month, in addition to presents, which she accepted. But there was still the problem of her mother. At fifteen, Marie was a minor, and would be so for the next ten years, the usual span of a demimonde career. Persenat, however, wanted nothing to do with Mère Boujard. Rather than return his mistress to her mother's custody, or find an apartment for the two of them, as was often the custom, he relocated Marie to his own home. Several months later, when Persenat left Paris to report for military duty (it was the Seven Years' War), he moved Marie to an Ursuline convent at Saint-Denis to wait for his return.

With Persenat out of town, and Mère Boujard out of the way, Madam Varenne began making secret visits to the convent. Perhaps Marie was lonely. Perhaps Madam Varenne visited of her own volition. Whatever the case, the bond with her former madam overpowered that with her patron, and Marie decided to return with Varenne to work at the brothel, though she never actually succeeded in doing so. She was stopped by a coordinated effort of the marquis (from afar) and her mother, who boarded her elsewhere. It seems that Marie did not want Persenat. Or maybe she believed he no longer wanted her. The text is not clear as to why, but the couple broke up shortly after Persenat returned to the capital in September 1760. Inspector Marais reported that the marquis gave Marie some money and "granted her the freedom to be her own mistress."[3] Marie rented a chambre garnie above the brothel of Madam Eudes and, like many other women, worked as an independent contractor, using the city's elite madams as agents to find sex work. We know that she was still working in some capacity for Varenne because it was at her old brothel that Marie met Monsieur Desjeans and became a mistress once again. He gave her 12 louis (288 livres) a month, enough for Marie to move to an apartment and hire a single servant.

More than any other factor—more than poverty, desire, or random chance—what shaped Marie Boujard's life as an elite prostitute and a femme galante was a person, Madam Varenne. In this way, Marie's story was not unusual. As we saw in the preceding chapter, not every woman who entered the demimonde did so via the brothel. But few dames entretenues fully escaped the influence of these powerful older women. Some kept women used madams as brokers, to procure patrons or, when times were mean, to find part-time work. Those femmes galantes who worked as free agents, finding entreteneurs and customers entirely on their own, were sometimes approached by madams acting as brokers for prospective patrons. Hence, even when they wanted to manage their own affairs, dames entretenues could be brought into the orbit of the madams. Madams were the hubs of overlapping networks of buyers and sellers of elite sexuality.

Relationships between madams and prostitutes were complicated and at times contradictory. Madam Varenne sold Marie, then hired her when she seemed unsellable, then sold her again, possibly lured her back to work, then worked as her agent. Each of these transactions prostituted Marie in a different way, according Marie varying degrees of agency. What did Madam Varenne want with Marie, and equally important, what did Marie want from Varenne? In the effort to understand how kept women negotiated the demimonde, we must begin with a study of the madams, lay out the networks and relationships they fashioned, and explore how these both aided and hindered the careers of dames entretenues.

Madams played an important role in helping the demimonde cohere as a subculture. Their commercial dealings, in large part because they transpired on such a wide scale, worked to standardize both the kinds of services that were available and the means by which these services were acquired. In cultivating a workforce, and in bringing together networks of buyers and sellers of elite sex, madams literally held the demimonde together. However, they were only able to do so because of police forbearance. In their dealings with the madams, the police continued to act like magistrates, enforcing a set of shadow rules that, though common practice in the demimonde, were in complete violation of royal law and local ordinances.[4] They managed the madams, usually arresting those who violated the rules, especially when the transgression came to public light. Ironically, that toleration fostered some of the most successful businesswomen in the city and the very rare domination of an entire (and extremely lucrative) business sector by them. Unlike that of many other businesswomen, however, the madams' success was contingent neither on the rights of a family member nor on the exploitation of some loophole in the legal code. They were successful in their own right in an informal, criminal economy that was shaped both by an open market and by more traditional forms of economic organization. The relationship of Varenne to Marie, of madam to sex worker, was determined by the needs of these businesses.

◆ The Madams and Police Toleration

Paris's elite madams were few in number, perhaps twenty or so women (and two men). What we know about them comes largely through the reports they submitted to the police, sometimes to inspectors Meusnier or Marais, sometimes to another inspector or the lieutenant general himself.[5] Beyond the twenty protected madams for whom we have evidence, there were a number of others who appear occasionally in police reports and whose relationships to the police were unclear. What collectively distinguished the privileged madams from other pimps and procurers was with whom they did business. From the weekly journals many submitted to the police, we know that nobles, officeholders, financiers, and military officers represented a good share of their customers, men who patronized the brothels. Madam Dufresne identified more than half of the men who visited her brothel in the summer months of 1753 as nobles or military officers (56.8 percent). Another third were officeholders or financiers (29.5 percent). She counted among her customers quite a number of high ranking courtiers and military officers, including an army brigadier.[6] Nobles and military officers similarly constituted about half (51 percent) of Madam d'Osment's customers in the last quarter of 1750.[7]

However, these establishments did not provide services only to the elite. Brothels were locales of mixed sociability, though all the customers were wealthy enough to afford the services they purchased. Casanova, who spent the winter of 1750 in the capital, noted that Madam Justine Paris "welcomed all who came to visit her." But, he added, "she was some distance from [the city of] Paris, hence she was certain that those who came to her establishment were people of means, for it was too far to go on foot."[8] Men of both elite and middling backgrounds visited the brothels. In the case of valets and masters, sometimes they did so together. In July and August of 1752, nobles and military officers constituted only 16.7 percent of the men who visited Madam Montbrun's brothel. Another 16.7 percent were officeholders, while 15 percent were identified as students or sons of professionals.[9] In those two months she had five clerks, four professionals (notaries and engineers), and two unemployed men come through her doors. And, while the président de Tourmont—Anne Michelet's first patron—visited Madam Babet's brothel, as did several marquis and military officers, most of her customers were not men of particularly high social status. They were members of various military cadres including the musketeers, the gendarmes, and the Swiss Guard. The presence of a clerk, however, did not obfuscate that of a marquis. These were the brothels to which the elite went for sex and entertainment. And, while customers may have come from varying social backgrounds, the madams' clients—those who used the services madams offered beyond the brothel—did not. Madam Baudouin, for example, counted the marquis de Paulmy d'Argenson as a client, and Montbrun catered to the duc d'Orléans. Clients were nobles, officeholders, officers, wealthy merchants, and financiers.

Because of their unique position in elite culture and the importance of their customers and clientele, these madams and their businesses were tolerated by the police. They were given the privilege to operate, and although this was not a formal, legal privilege, it still had to be paid for: in this case, with information.[10] The madams provided the police with considerable intelligence. At least a few submitted monthly spreadsheets detailing brothel operations and written reports on their other business dealings.[11] Some were assigned particular inspectors with whom to work, presumably because these madams were barely literate. The reports of Madam Baudouin were edited or transcribed by Inspector Durocher, for example. Madams investigated the women who were in their employ as well as men and women who were not, some of whose lives touched the demimonde only peripherally. Madams also gathered information on and from their customers and clients. When Inspector Marais wanted to know whether the duc d'Orléans was going to recognize his mistress's child (the paternity of the child was in doubt), he turned to Madam Brissault. Madam Brissault and her husband, a tailor, ran one of the most fashionable brothels in the capital. Madam Brissault had a close relationship with the marquis de Vierville, who seemed to know what was going on.[12] Marais reported to his superiors, "I charged the wife of this tailor to get the marquis to gossip since he trusts her and to pull from him all the details that she could about this event." A week later, Marais reported back that Madam Brissault had learned nothing. When the subject was broached, Vierville had responded that he did not want to talk about the duke's mistress (Demoiselle Marquise) as "this creature" was "a devil" and the duke "a frenzied person."[13]

But the madams were not merely passive purveyors of information. As operatives in an intelligence system, they exercised a great deal of influence, even though Meusnier and Marais, assisted by several other inspectors, checked their information. Lies could be uncovered. Detecting the careful selection of information meant to bias the police would necessarily prove more difficult. Moreover, regardless of what they said about people, the madams were powerful because they decided, in part, which people about whom something needed to be said. They identified subjects for surveillance, determining if they were participants in the demimonde. They also manipulated their positions as information brokers both to secure and, when possible, to advance their own standings. For example, they reported madams who were not privileged, edging out competition. They also informed on each other. Madam Lafosse wrote Meusnier that she had been asked by Madam Gautier to help negotiate a virgin sale and to keep news of it from the inspector.[14] Hiding such transactions from the inspectors was against the rules.

Of equal importance, madams used information to strengthen ties with some police agents while discrediting those they considered threatening. By informing Meusnier of Gautier's actions, Madam Lafosse engaged in an open betrayal of her natural ally to their mutual adversary. Doing so was an obsequious display of loyalty to the inspector, the kind that could enhance her usefulness and serve as the basis of a bond with Meusnier. Madam d'Osment, once left alone in the office of Inspector Dumont, took the opportunity to read his mail and report its contents to Lieutenant General Berryer, to whom she regularly reported. Her letters to the lieutenant general contain frequent inquiries into his health, solicitations for advice and, once, an apology for having been drunk.[15] Madam d'Osment wrote scathing reports to the lieutenant general regarding the behavior of Inspector Marais: He had sex with pensioners, did not pay, did not bother to disguise himself, and was only after women and money. In her reports, d'Osment depicts herself as honorable, or at least constant, in the face of Marais's corruption and incivility. At their first meeting, Marais swore repeatedly and was very rude, but was shocked, she claimed, that his rudeness did not discomfit her.[16] As she defined their characters, she also put their relationship into context. Marais, she wrote, "hated her" because "he did not find [her] as tractable as he imagined [she] would be" in his campaign to arrest libertine clerics. It was easy then to claim that Marais was filling his reports on her with "lies and calumnies" including the accusation that she had brought a girl, dressed as a boy, to a monastery, which was a forbidden practice.[17]

All businesswomen in the Old Regime had to deal with peers and with those who had power over them, such as the police, guild, or royal officials, and usually husbands. In the Comédie-Française, for example, actresses owed their positions not just to talent, but to the ability to secure parts and privileges through negotiation with colleagues, spouses, authors, patrons, and overlords.[18] Madams had an especially tricky line to walk. They were tolerated, but they had no proprietary right to their businesses. At the end of the day, they were criminals. The police stymied competition by limiting their total number, but these women still had to contend with each other in an effort to capture a market share. One weapon at their disposal was informa-

tion. (The other was sex.) With information, they created certain relationships within the demimonde, making themselves valuable on the one hand
and undermining threats on the other. Ironically, police demand for information may very well have strengthened the position of these women as
much as toleration did. It would have forced them to extend their reach into
the demimonde and to cultivate new contacts among prostitutes, customers, and clients as well as among the servants and neighbors of their quarry.
Because these women were charged with supplying information and often
tasked with specific fact-finding missions, they would have come to know a
great deal about quite a number of people, beyond what they would have
gathered in their day-to-day operations. Succeeding in this game, manipulating the police policy of toleration to their advantage, took a particular
kind of intelligence.[19] One could only imagine that it was also empowering.

But we should not forget that there were profound limits to the madams'
power. Pimping, procuring, and running a brothel were illegal activities.
They were outlawed specifically in the Edict of Orléans (1560). This law
was reconfirmed in later royal declarations, and in municipal and police
ordinances.[20] While the application of these laws was usually limited to unauthorized madams who disturbed the peace, it bears repeating that they
were still enforced. Madam Lacroix, for example, was arrested and sent to
the prison of Saint-Martin after neighbors complained and the police veri-
fied that she was causing a "great scandal."[21] To deal with unauthorized and
noisy brothels, the police staged *visites de nuits*, the infamous night raids.[22]
Madams caught in these operations who were guilty of nothing more than
simple pandering ended up with their employees in police court along with
numerous other women similarly (and vaguely) accused of prostitution, libertinism, or debauchery. Customers other than clerics and priests were let
go. Once a month the lieutenant general held a mass hearing in which dozens
of women were condemned and then taken, heads shaved, to the prison of
La Salpêtrière or forced to leave Paris.[23]

Toleration, however, did not mean that madams could run their establishments any way they wished. Inspectors had a say concerning both where
brothels were located and the terms under which they operated. Madam
Lafosse reported that her colleague Dupont had agreed to set up her brothel
under Meusnier's protection in a particular house on rue Pont-aux-Choux,
but that the terms of their agreement did not suit her.[24] When, following
the 1750 riots, Madam Paris moved her establishment out of the city, it was
Meusnier who decided which madam would take over the space Paris had
occupied for twenty years on the rue de Bagneux, faubourg Saint-Germain.
He offered it first to Lafosse, the madam with whom he had the closest

relationship. She declined, claiming the rent was too high. Meusnier eventually allowed Madam Carlier to take over the premises, even though Madam d'Osment had been campaigning Berryer for it.[25]

The inspectors also expected the madams to follow certain rules, all of which were designed to prevent scandal and to organize the elite sex market so that certain practices occurred only where the police could keep track of them. Aside from a prohibition against allowing the businesses to be seen or heard from the street, there was a set of rules that addressed who could come into the brothel, as a customer or worker. Madams were not supposed to receive monks or abbés and, if they did, were to inform the police at once. Particularly important, madams could not take on girls from middling or upper-class families. Madams could broker virgin sales, but as we saw in chapter 3, they had to inform the police while doing so, allowing the authorities a chance to stop the deal should they see fit.[26] The police shut down nonprivileged madams engaging in virgin sales, even when the young women had the written permission of their parents.[27] Virgins were not supposed to be too young. Judicial officials occasionally prosecuted madams who pandered girls ages thirteen and younger. However, under the inspectors' watch, age twelve was to be the bottom of the range. A virgin had to arrive at the brothel through no ploy of its madam; such solicitations were forbidden. Judicial officials did prosecute madams who kidnapped girls. The most famous midcentury case was that of Jeanne Moyon, a madam not among those tolerated by the police. The case was discussed by diarist Edmond Barbier and cited by the legal scholar Daniel Jousse, among others.[28] Moyon was convicted of kidnapping an eleven-year-old girl from her catechism lesson on behalf of a wealthy client who then raped the child. The madam was sentenced to be whipped, branded, and banished. Moyon's crime was considered particularly egregious because of the extenuating circumstances: the age of the child, the status of her family, and the fact that she was kidnapped. Madams accused of crimes like these, those with aggravating circumstances, found themselves not in police court but before the Chambre Criminelle du Châtelet. Their sentences were automatically appealed to the Parlement of Paris, which usually confirmed them. The total number of these cases, however, was few.[29] This suggests a number of possibilities. The crimes may not have been reported, or the police may have ignored reports coming in. Alternatively, at least among the demimonde madams, the policy of toleration may have worked to encourage these women to comply with the rules.

If the first set of rules was not to disturb the peace and the second set involved who could enter a brothel, a third set concerned under what conditions girls and women were allowed to work there. As we saw in the preceding chapter, madams needed the permission of parents who were in their daughters' lives. The rules that prohibited employment of certain classes of women and girls, and those that governed how madams acquired their workers collectively, although probably not deliberately, prohibited cases of pimping under "aggravated circumstances," in the words of legal theorist Daniel Jousse.[30] Formally, "aggravated pimping" was not a class of crime, but such pimping was considered to be more heinous and scandalous, and was consequently more likely to be prosecuted and severely punished.

When tolerated madams broke these rules, when they allowed their establishments to be noisy, or when they engaged in aggravated pimping, what did the police do? Noisy madams were given a warning. Aggravated pimping was an entirely different matter. It did not appear to be prosecuted in every instance but it certainly was when the crime became public knowledge. The sensationalized case of Dame d'Oppy is emblematic. In 1775 Madam Gourdan (Marguerite Stock) was tried and convicted alongside two other privileged madams, Montigny and Eudes (above whose brothel Marie Boujard had rented a room), for prostituting Dame d'Oppy, wife of the *grand bailli d'épée de Douai*. Madam Gourdan had procured d'Oppy on behalf of a chevalier who wanted to have an affair with her. The two met at Gourdan's brothel. D'Oppy was discovered by her brother-in-law and incarcerated via lettre de cachet, beginning years of legal battles between her and her husband. The affair and Gourdan's role in it not only became public, it was a huge scandal, widely discussed and reported. The trial records reveal that Inspector Marais had ordered Gourdan to receive d'Oppy so that the latter could be arrested in the act. But the madam's exposure in procuring a married woman of rank implicated her in such a public violation of the tacit rules by which tolerated brothels were allowed to operate that she and the madams who had testified against d'Oppy (and therefore knew of the affair) were prosecuted.[31] In another case, Madam Paris was arrested and incarcerated in February of 1752 for "having seduced a young person, age twelve, from a good family," in the words of the diarist René-Louis comte d'Argenson. D'Argenson, former minister of foreign affairs, recorded the news of the court and capital.[32] The crime and arrest of Madam Paris were common news.

Contemporaries were aware of police toleration of the elite brothels, though the value of that toleration was a subject of debate. Mercier wrote of a "tacit regulation" by which madams were allowed to take only girls who had already been sexually active and by which they were required to report to the police any newcomers who were not. In this, he claimed:

They tried to establish a kind of order right in the midst of disorder, to pare down the worst abuses, to protect innocence and weakness, and to prevent a brazen licentiousness that destroys civil bonds and the very heart of families. Thus fathers have no complaints to make, as the misconduct of their daughters never begins in such disreputable places. It is an important point and every observer who thinks about it should praise the police for it.[33]

Clearly, the case of Marie Boujard belies Mercier's optimistic representation. But the impression of the brothel as a place for ruined women persisted. In part, this impression was supported by the backstories in which prostitutes stepped over the brothel threshold only when they had nowhere else to go. Most were reported by the police to be sexually wayward by the time they came to the madam's door, hungry, wearing rags, and clearly needing help. Yet the similarity of their stories, many of which were based on intelligence provided by the madams themselves, suggests that the madams may have colluded with the police in the creation of something of a salvation narrative. Certainly, the madams had an interest in portraying themselves as saviors of desperate, deflowered girls. Aside from removing the need for parental consent, it was a fiction in which they were social benefactors and one which, as a staple of contemporary discourse on prostitution, helped to ensure continued tolerance of their establishments. On the one hand, they saved individual girls who might otherwise have died on the streets. On the other, they supported society at large by preventing these girls from plying their trade wantonly, scandalously, and without oversight on the city's thoroughfares. The salvation narrative also positioned the brothel as an institution of recontainment, a place where girls and women loosened from the path to marriage, and hence sexually independent, came back under supervision.[34]

The police were similarly invested in the narrative. It gave them an excuse to tolerate the disreputable institutions that were the chief suppliers of intelligence on the city's demimonde. It made them seem, in the words of Mercier, to "establish a kind of order right in the midst of disorder." As we can tell from the story of Marie Boujard, perceptions of the nature of tolerance were both completely on and off the mark. While publicly barred from selling virgins, elite brothels did so frequently and with police knowledge. Contrary to Mercier's claim that fathers need not worry about losing their daughters to brothels, police records make clear that elite brothels were in many instances allowed to keep pensioners being sought by their parents. But in another sense, police actions did "order right in the midst of disorder."

☙ A Community of Madams

The elite madams formed a professional community within the demi-monde. It was informal, nothing like a guild, for example, but rather was built upon mutual recognition and shared practices. Their community predated organized police engagement with them. Many of the madams under police protection, like Justine Paris, had operated brothels for years before the dossier system they supported came into being. However, police toleration encouraged further cohesion among these women as copractitioners of the same occupation. Working together to acquire information or colluding to get around police rules strengthened their ties. Alternatively, working against each other to gain advantage stressed those bonds. Both sets of actions forced the madams to identify each other as allies or as competition. It required that they recognize themselves as a group with shared interests, if they had not done so already. At the very least, toleration reified identity. Successful elite madams gained protection in the first place because they were successful elite madams. Granting these women informal official status only confirmed their position and contrasted them, as a group, to all other madams. One could also argue that toleration encouraged community by helping to standardize the types of services madams offered; police expectations set outer limits on what was acceptable and pushed madams to monitor each other's adherence to those limits.

Community, however, was not only a function of toleration and shared clientele. The elite madams also hired the same women. Many brothel workers bounced from house to house, often changing their names each time, sometimes cycling back to their establishment of origin. For example, Marie-Barbe-Sophie Faillon began her career as a prostitute in the brothel of Madam Vaudry. After several months she contracted a venereal disease and was let go. She applied to the house of Madam Villette, who kept her for a few nights and then "ceded" her to Madam Montigny, who thought the girl had sufficient earning potential to merit lending her the money for medical care.[35]

Madams also helped each other with staffing problems, lending each other workers when needed. Madam d'Osment reported that she had to borrow a "girl" from Madam Montigny to send to a party at the hotel of Monsieur de La Poupelinière. Madam Lafosse sent for Sayre, a pensioner at Madam Dupont's, in order to provide her best client with another prostitute.[36] Madams also attended each other's parties. When Montbrun threw a ball, six other madams attended, each bringing along one or two pensioners to staff the party and advertise their own brothels. Montigny, for example, brought two prostitutes: a woman called La Petite La Tour, who regularly attended brothel parties, and a second girl who was fourteen or fifteen years old.[37]

But while the madams formed a professional community, they had very little in common with each other personally. If their ability to write is any indication, they came from vastly different social backgrounds. Some had no education whatsoever. Others, like Lafosse, had learned the rudiments of writing; she wrote French phonetically, in a big messy script. D'Osment, on the contrary, claimed she was the daughter of a schoolteacher. She had good French and a fairly neat hand. The police records reveal little biographical data on most of the madams, aside from tidbits here and there. Inspector Meusnier suspected Madam Montbrun of being a lesbian. He wrote, "They say La Montbrun is a tribade," "tribade" being a term for women who preferred women as sexual partners.[38] About Madams Baudouin and d'Osment, we know much more. The former was engaged in a lawsuit against her husband, and the latter included an autobiography among her official reports.

Both women had been elite prostitutes in their youth, and both had retired and then married. Madeleine Baudouin married late, at age thirty, to a widowed *limonadier*, putting most of her savings, some two hundred louis, into the marital fund. Her marriage fell apart quickly. According to Inspector Durocher, who submitted a report on the madam, Baudouin soon realized her husband was heavily indebted and "a drunk libertine." She legally separated from him and moved into a convent, where she lived off of her savings until she ran out of money in 1747. It was at this point, the report claimed, that she became a procurer.[39] Similar to the stories she would tell about her pensioners, it was only after her other options ran out that she turned to the sex trade. While we have little information on Baudouin's youth, d'Osment, in her own telling, began to earn money from attending parties after her father died, leaving the family with few financial resources.[40] In her autobiography, d'Osment asserted both humble and prestigious origins. Her father was a schoolteacher who eventually bought the office of *huissier*, but her parents had many noble friends and patrons. It is unclear if d'Osment was claiming a sexually active youth or if she was merely frequenting an aristocratic libertine crowd, but the fact that she was earning livres and spoke about her own "galanterie" suggests the former. Whatever the case, d'Osment claimed that her foray into the demimonde was cut short by her mother, and although she claimed a fundamental aversion to wedlock, she did finally marry. Like Baudouin, d'Osment eventually left her husband and sometime later became a madam.[41]

For d'Osment, Baudouin, and the rest of the elite madams, running a brothel was only one component of a larger business. Madam Varenne brokered virgin sales and patron-mistress relationships, staffed parties with sex workers and found passades for women who were free agents. In trying to understand what Marie Boujard and Varenne wanted from each other and how their work and personal lives intersected, we must regard their relationship within the context of Varenne's business. We know how toleration created a space in which madams could operate as businesswomen and how it facilitated community. Now we must understand how Varenne's various commercial dealings were related to each other and how each fostered relationships of dependence with sex workers. In turn, this will help us to understand how madams standardized what they sold, how they were able to build such successful businesses, and how these businesses served as central institutions in the demimonde.

✎ Paris's Elite Brothels

In his entry on "madams," Louis-Sébastien Mercier included women engaged in a range of activities, from those who acted as companions to dames entretenues to those who worked the sidewalk recruiting customers for a single prostitute in a chambre garnie.[42] Madams are most frequently identified with owning and managing brothels. Most elite brothels for which records remain were small establishments. Babet and Montbrun each had only two pensioners and several women on call, prostitutes who lived outside the brothel and were summoned when the madam needed more sex workers. According to the spreadsheets the madams submitted to the police, it was rare for more than three prostitutes to be working in one of the brothels at any one time unless there was some sort of event. There were some exceptions. Casanova reported seeing fourteen prostitutes during his visit to the Hôtel de Roule, the brothel of Madam Paris. Barbier asserted that twelve girls worked there and noted that the support staff was also fairly sizeable. He wrote that Madam Paris employed a cook, a porter, four maids, and masters of writing, dance, and music to educate the girls, as well as a doctor to visit them every two days.[43] Pidansat de Mairobert claimed Madam Gourdan had twelve women working for her. Madams Paris and Gourdan also rented larger houses for their brothels than did most madams. The Hôtel de Roule had a drawing room, in which the pensioners underwent review by customers, as well as a garden, a dining room and individual bedrooms on the ground floor.[44] According to the postdeath inventory of her property, Madam

Gourdan's establishment was also sizeable, a four-story house with many richly furnished bedrooms. The commissioner who drew up the report, however, left out many of the details, opting not to describe items he thought scandalous.[45] Mairobert's largely satirical description of Madam Gourdan's brothel also depicted a large establishment, with several rooms in which prostitutes were washed, made up and dressed, and various rooms in which they fulfilled customer fantasies. Mairobert was concerned mainly with the mechanisms of dissimilitude by which prostitutes fooled customers and by which customers disguised themselves. His writing on this topic was both criticism and a form of pornography.[46]

The nine brothels whose operating records survive had relatively few customers each day. In the early winter of 1754, Madam Babet's brothel averaged three to four customers on days she did business. She was either closed or without customers several days a week. Madam Montbrun's operation was similarly small. In the first ten days of January of 1754, she had an average of two to three customers a day.[47] These businesses shrank even further when officers were called back to their regiments, as happened with the marquis de Persenat, or when the royal court was at Fontainebleau. At least one madam, Payen, packed up her operation and went with the court. Madam Carlier took five or six women and followed the army of the maréchal de Saxe to Flanders during the War of Austrian Succession. Saxe was a noted libertine and often had several mistresses at once.[48] It was, nevertheless, not a successful venture; Saxe forced the madam to leave.

Men usually went to the brothel alone, or in small groups of two to three. Most stayed for an hour and had sex with one or sometimes two of the pensioners, interactions that Madam Montbrun called "parties," anticipating current terminology.[49] Customer visits started in the late afternoon and ended around midnight. Many brothels were in the center of town, on the rue St. Honoré or nearby, making them convenient for men leaving the Opéra. Customers had the option of spending the night. Those who did usually left at around eight or nine in the morning. Depending on when they arrived and how long they stayed, customers sometimes supped or had other meals in the brothel with the prostitutes. Dinner (*dîner*) was the meal served in the afternoon, between 1:00 and 3:00. Supper (*souper*) was a late evening meal, often following the Opéra.

The madams, especially Lafosse, were not shy about describing what customers paid prostitutes to do. Anne Bourlans, like many other prostitutes, became a specialist in flagellation, and among her customers was the philosophe Claude-Adrien Helvétius, who was a devotee of the practice. Several of Anne's other customers sodomized her, which was also a common sex act in brothels.[50] Customers engaged in vaginal intercourse with prostitutes, but quite a few paid to be masturbated as well. Oral sex was so rare that when it did occur, informants, even one as jaded as Lafosse, expressed surprise. In describing how a pensioner named July fellated Monsieur de Boullongne (*controleur général des finances*), Lafosse commented that "I am no longer astonished he sees her so often as few girls would have complied."[51] A few customers preferred women of color. Lafosse complained that "the taste of the century has entirely changed" in that none of her clients wanted European women anymore. One of her customers, the marquis d'Asfeldt, a *maréchal de camp*, wanted what she described as someone from the "coasts of Brazil," and she had to look all over Paris for a "negresse."[52]

Many of the men visiting the brothels were regular customers. Over the course of a month, the marquis de Langaret twice went to Madam Babet's, while Monsieur Dalainville and Président St. Lupin went to Chez Montbrun together twice in one week. Regular customers often had close or at least congenial relations with the madam. In August 1753, Madam Baudouin reported that Monsieur Foquet, *secretaire du roi*, visited her. He "complained of his chest and did not at all want any girls," instead telling Baudouin about his "adventure" with a kept woman named Beauvoisin.[53] Some repeat customers were in the process of attaching to a particular pensioner whom they would later take on as a mistress, as the marquis de Persenat did with Marie Boujard. But while madams worked hard to place pensioners as mistresses, they often had little patience for customers who monopolized their workers without such intentions. For Babet, Monsieur Montigny proved to be just such a problem. In December 1754, he came to the brothel to visit a prostitute named Celie almost every other day, four to five times a day. He usually spent the night. Babet warned Montigny of the "indecency of his behavior," but in vain. When Montigny tried to prevent a group of men from having sex with Celie, Babet had him forcibly ejected from the brothel. He returned and was thrown out again.[54]

Montigny, at least, was paying his bills. The madams complained bitterly in their reports of cheating customers. Montbrun was particularly upset with Monsieur Vauberg, lieutenant general of the police of Orléans, who frequently visited her brothel with friends and left without paying.[55] Perhaps unaware of the protected nature of these businesses, men like Vauberg who were with other policing bodies often offered the exchange of protection for sex. Brothel fees could add up. Most customers paid a louis (twenty-four livres) per session.[56] Casanova claimed that Madam Paris charged by the hour. "One paid six livres to breakfast with a girl, twelve livres to dine there, and a louis to sup and spend the night." He paid when he arrived in the morning. At midday he was asked to pay again, and again in the evening if he wished to stay the night.[57] Barbier reported the same prices, adding that for thirty-six livres there were carriages-for-hire to take customers back to Paris from the Hôtel de Roule.[58]

In addition to paying, the second requirement of brothel customers was that they conduct themselves "decently," which was defined largely in the negative. Decent customers did not cause a ruckus nor make noise in the street. Brissault banned five marquis who frequented his brothel together because they were "too rowdy in their pleasures."[59] Decent customers, moreover, were not abusive to the madam. Abuse of prostitutes was another matter. There is almost no discussion of violence toward sex workers in these records. It is unclear if this was because it never happened or because the madams and police did not care if it did. Montbrun certainly cared, however, about Vauberg's treatment of her. In June 1752, she reported that the lieutenant general had come to her brothel with four other men and

> he spouted nonsense and made the most brutal threats, saying that he would burn down my house if I did not let him do everything he wanted. He pushed his insolence so far that those of his companions, who were very calm, told him in front of me that if he continued to insult me, they would throw him down the stairs.[60]

In September, when Montbrun finally refused Vauberg's business, he threatened to send for the Guard and have the madam arrested and taken to the Hôpital. Since her brothel remained open the rest of the month, it appears that Vauberg did not carry out his threat.

The primary function of brothels was as sexual emporia, but madams did use them to provide other services. Specifically, they sold privacy, or at least its illusion, as the madams reported these goings-on to the police. They allowed their brothels to be used as occasional *maisons de rendez vous* for couples wishing to keep their affairs secret. Demoiselle Parmentier, the mistress of the marquis de Paolucci, had passades at Chez Brissault.[61] Demoiselle la Tournelle, who was maintained by the marquis d'Orville, had a passade with the Baron Boëhme at Chez Montbrun, where he was a regular customer.[62] Customers also used brothels to house women whose positions in the demi-monde were transitional or in question. As we saw in chapter 2, Captain Millon hid his mistress, Louise de la Tour, in a brothel to keep her from being incarcerated by her father. Monsieur de Nancy, an officer in the Musketeers, had Manon Maison return to the brothel of Madam d'Osment—she had just left to live with someone else—for a few days until he was able to get a room for her.[63]

↝ Outcall Services

In addition to operating brothels, Paris's elite madams ran what in modern terminology are "outcall" services. These were businesses in which madams sent sex workers on request to a party, or out for a passade in which they spent a few hours or an entire night with a client. In some instances, clients asked for a specific prostitute. In others, they asked only for a prostitute. For example, Lafosse reported that the fermier général Monsieur Le Normant d'Étiolles, husband of the marquise de Pompadour, told her one Tuesday that he would like a girl sent to him the following Monday.[64] The practice was immortalized in Théveneau de Morande's satire *Le Porte-feuille de Madame Gourdan* (*The Correspondence of Madame Gourdan*), which comprised a series of letters supposedly received by Madam Gourdan. In one, a fictitious marquis wrote to complain that the prostitutes Gourdan had sent were neither pretty nor accommodating of the marquis's fantasies, and that he requested better-looking and more libertine women be sent to him the following Thursday for a party he was having with several other nobles.[65]

In a sense, separating the brothel and call aspects of a madam's business is something of an artificial division. As the case of Marie Boujard shows, pensioners went on outcalls. Some went to have sex with men at their homes or other locales. Most, like Marie, were sent to staff supper parties—petits soupers—where they would have sex and a late-night meal with guests. The madam's participation in facilitating these parties gets lumped into her call service. But what makes the category of the call service analytically useful is not just that it highlights that pensioners worked for madams outside of the brothel. It also captures the sort of work Varenne and Eudes arranged for Marie Boujard and women like her, who were neither mistresses nor pensioners.

Women who took outcalls fell into a number of categories. Some were established kept women with patrons who simply wanted to earn extra money. Usually these women avoided the exposure risked by party work, taking only those passades that could be carried out in secret. Others, like Marie Boujard, were between patrons and engaged in whatever part-time work they could find. Some women specialized in petits soupers and balls. Montbrun was the agent for a woman named Regnault, who had been married for several years and made her living attending parties and balls.[66] Some women looking for part-time work sought help from those madams with whom they had the closest relationships. Éléonore Boismilion was one of the few who relied on a single madam, a limitation she literally could afford. Having recently returned to Paris from America, she was rumored to have one thousand louis (twenty-four hundred livres), but she also had considerable expenses. She was spending a great deal on furniture and jewelry, and taking music lessons in an effort to get a place in the Opéra chorus. Meusnier claimed Boismilion sought out the madam, because she had lost all her connections, was no longer "known" in the demimonde and wanted Lafosse "to find her appointments while waiting for a happier outcome."[67]

Prostitutes often looked for work from a number of different madams. Demoiselle Marquis was typical in her efforts. After having been dismissed from the ballet corps at the Comédie-Française, she could not find a patron. She procured work from madams Montbrun, Hecquet and Brezay, who arranged for her to have passades and attend parties in the "Bois de Bolougne and other similar places," wrote Inspector Meusnier. Demoiselle Marquis also did in-calls for Madam Baudouin, who sent for her when an extra prostitute was required in the brothel. She did just this one afternoon in September 1753, when her customer, the writer and diplomat Augustin-Louis Marquis Ximènes, having had sex with a pensioner, requested another. Baudouin reported that Ximènes was so pleased with Marquis that "he took her in his carriage to dine with him at his house in the country. They did not return until 1:00 p.m. the following afternoon, when they slept together again." For this work, Ximènes paid Marquis 8 louis (192 livres). Soon thereafter she found herself a patron and stopped taking outcalls.[68]

A large portion of the madams' call business consisted of staffing petits soupers. These were small gatherings consisting of two to four male guests and an equal or fewer number of women. In contrast, the supper parties thrown by the duc d'Orléans in the early 1750s, to which he invited eighteen men and women, were known as "grands soupers."[69] Sex was strongly associated with these events. Reports by the police and madams depict women dining in various states of undress, sometimes completely naked, with sex taking place before, after and sometimes during meal.[70] While staffing petits soupers was important to the madams' businesses, the importance of the madams to the production of these events across the demimonde is hard to gauge. In the early 1760s, Inspector Marais began the practice of recording in his *Anecdotes Galantes* guest lists of petits soupers that featured kept women, women of the theater, prostitutes and the men who associated with them. It is unlikely that he listed every party. Given the gossipy nature of the *Anecdotes Galantes*, however, it is likely that he listed all those that made for juicy news, those which involved male or female demimondaine celebrities. Of the sixty-four women who attended fifty-three events between January 1761 and February 1762, thirteen were brothel pensioners.[71] A handful of others had been sent by the madams as free agents; Baudouin sent demoiselles Beauvoisin and

Marquis, both professional kept women, to the petit souper of Monsieur Ignard so that he could choose between them.[72]

More than a third of these women attended parties in venues provided by the madams. Madams held these parties at their brothels. For example, the princes of Nassau, who were brothers, arranged to have a petit souper at the brothel of Montbrun in January of 1754 for four men. Montbrun was asked to provide four women. The madam also catered the party and supplied the lighting, among other amenities.[73] In addition to their brothels, madams also made available their *petites maisons*, houses in the villages that surrounded Paris, especially in Chaillot, La Petite Pologne, Passy, Montmartre, and around the Barrière Blanche. The connection between the petites maisons and the petits soupers was so strong that in a 1754 report listing the lessees of these houses a police inspector made notes about the supper parties held in several of the locations.[74] At least half of the petits soupers noted by Marais took place in petites maisons (though only a quarter of these were let by madams).[75] Madams were not the only ones to rent these houses. They were popular as secondary (and in some instances primary) residences for wealthy Parisians who had nothing to do with the demimonde.[76] As they afforded privacy or, when necessary, secrecy, they also were popular as trysting houses with dames entretenues and men who kept mistresses.[77] Madams let theirs out to couples for this purpose. Brissault even let himself be used as a front to rent a petite maison in La Petite Pologne for the marquis de Duras.[78] Men and women associated with the demimonde tended to rent the same properties. There is no evidence that this was a result of police influence but it is in keeping with their practice of trying to direct certain forms of transactional sex to locales under surveillance. For example, number 8 rue St. Lazare near the Barrière Blanche, was rented in succession to the dames entretenues Dame de la Ferté, Demoiselle Coupée, and Demoiselle Devaux, the last two of whom were dancers in the Opéra.[79]

Petits soupers were instrumental to the madams' business. In staffing and arranging petits soupers, madams had the chance to increase their clientele by exposing male guests to services on offer. In a social universe in which an elite madam's standing was determined largely by reputation, and this by word of mouth, these parties were important advertising. Male guests were made aware of the venues a madam had at her disposal and were introduced to at least some of the sex workers whom she employed or for whom she served as an agent. Prospective clients could also get a sense of the discretion and competence of various madams. But for madams, petits soupers were not just an opportunity to attract male clients. They were also an occasion to recruit female ones, those women hired or invited to the party by its male host. The parties assisted madams in making connections with elite prostitutes and femmes galantes, women who might need a madam at some later point.

For the pensioners, call girls and kept women attending petits soupers conferred benefits beyond money. The base pay for a supper party was one louis. This would have been a significant sum for someone like Marie Boujard, though little to the woman she replaced as the marquis de Persenat's mistress, Marie Dascher. But perhaps more important, petits soupers introduced women into demimondaine circles. As was the case with Marie Boujard, these parties provided pensioners and other sex workers whose circulation was limited—either because they lived in a brothel or because they had just started out—a chance to meet future clients and patrons. Women new to the demimonde could not gain entrance to these events, in part because no one knew who they were. Madams provided these women access to the networks of sex buyers they needed to make a "career" of galanterie. This idea was even represented in fiction. In the novel *Histoire de Mademoiselle Brion*, the prostitute protagonist, a brothel pensioner, was sent to a petit souper "not as the prettiest, but as the least well known" and there managed to make the connections that would allow her to be maintained.[80]

As we have seen, there were other ways to break into these networks. Women who had recently debuted in the Opéra or were mistresses of the right kind of patron were able to do so without the aid of madams. But even for these women, connections were established and nurtured at supper parties. Petits soupers, then, were means of accelerating the process by which a prostitute built sexual capital or, in the case of established dames entretenues, increased that capital. Inspector Meusnier reported that, as a result of having supper with the duc d'Orléans, Demoiselle Deschamps, one of the most famous kept women of the day, was able to partially restore her reputation after a slow period.[81] Lastly, the instrumentality of the petit souper was not just in the visibility it provided. For women new to the demimonde, petits soupers offered an opportunity to meet career kept women. They provided a means of acculturation.

Despite their importance, there is little evidence that madams organized their own petits soupers to drum up clients. However, they did arrange balls for just this purpose. Balls were meant to be income-generating events. Entrance required a ticket. Madam Betrand, who threw two balls a week, charged six livres.[82] Some madams complemented the food and wine with gambling or lotteries in order to increase their earnings. Most of these affairs were too big to be held in brothels. Madam Beaumont threw a ball with eighty men in attendance. Baudouin gave a ball in which fifty men paid the entrance fee. Like most others, it began in the late evening, at eleven, and ended at six in the morning.[83] Like Betrand, Montbrun threw several smaller balls on a regular basis, at least during the winters of the 1750s, for between twenty and thirty people at a time. The men in attendance came from the middle to upper end of her clientele. Auguste-Louis Bertin de Blagny, who was *trésorier des parties casuelles*, a German baron, several musketeers and army officers, and the Spanish ambassador were among her guests at a ball in February 1757.[84] Blagny at this time was the patron of the Opéra star Demoiselle Hus, their affair immortalized in Diderot's *Neveau de Rameau*. Most women who attended balls were elite prostitutes but not professional mistresses. Montbrun had her pensioners, as well as other madams and their pensioners, at her events. Those dames entretenues who attended were searching for patrons or passades. For madams, pensioners, and professional mistresses, balls, like the petits soupers, functioned as important networking events.

The outcall service gave women who were starting out in the demimonde an agent to find them work. It helped those dames entretenues who needed more work. And it provided clients with sex workers. It explains why Varenne would want to keep in touch with Marie Boujard, who had proven herself a desirable call girl, even if the latter did not want to go back to the brothel. The outcall service also highlights the complexity of the madams' businesses and the ways in which these businesses were similar to and different from work done by other women. Between the brothel and the petites maisons, madams had to rent and manage multiple properties in different parts of Paris or, given the locations of some of the petites maisons, in different municipalities. Each of these properties had a domestic staff that had to be hired, managed, and paid. Madams had to find and retain competent servants who were not averse to the scandalous nature of their work environment yet who would keep quiet about what they saw. The outcall service also made madams event planners. They provided meals, people to serve them, and light and heat by which to eat them, all in a well-furnished, well-maintained space. Doing this at a profit demanded some command of math and budgeting.

In many of these aspects, the work of madams was not unlike that of other women. Leasing and managing property was necessary for many *marchandes publiques*. Wives of craftsmen and small-time merchants traditionally managed their husbands' businesses and accounts. Widows of craftsmen and some single women ran their own businesses. Property management and party planning were among the duties of elite women.[85] Madams brought these components together. But madams were operating tolerated, not legal, businesses, and this complicated things. For example, for those madams who were married, leasing property legally required a husband's permission or, alternatively, claiming the status of *marchande publique*, which endowed married women in commerce with legal personalities for the purpose of running their businesses.[86] Since most madams were estranged from their husbands, and because it was illegal to rent property to anyone running a brothel, tolerated madams did so only with the help of the police, who had a say in where they set up shop. But what most differentiated an elite madam from any other businesswoman was not the compromises she had to make because of the criminal nature of her enterprise. It was the enterprise itself and its particular demands. Madams sold sexual services. To do so, they needed a steady stream of young women whom they could compel to engage in activities that were illegal, socially stigmatized, physically dangerous, and personally disgusting to many of them. Madams also needed access to elite men. The outcall service helped to build both worker and client networks. These networks were the basis of the last piece of the madam's business, matchmaking, and it is to this that we now turn.

✒ Matchmaking

Separating the madams' matchmaking from their outcall services imposes clearly bounded categories of commercial sex on a situation in which these activities overlapped a great deal. By "matchmaking," I am referring to three sets of practices distinguished by madams' efforts to connect specific buyers and sellers of sex. These include efforts to broker women into patron–mistress relationships, efforts to procure certain prostitutes for men who wanted them for passades or as mistresses, and last, virgin sales, examined in the preceding chapter.

Madams worked to place both their pensioners and call girls into patron–mistress relationships. Practically, the shift from pensioner to kept woman was not a complicated one. All a pensioner had to do was find a man willing to maintain her, and she met many candidates every day. It would seem, then, that all advantage lay with the pensioner. She had exposure, "face time," with potential patrons. Since a patron often shared dinner or supper with the woman he had selected, she had numerous opportunities to get to know dozens of men, and to present herself as charming and later as sexually skillful. Yet the process of becoming a pensioner handicapped many of these girls in their efforts to become kept women. On moving into a brothel, they quickly were bound to the madam through a system of debt that prevented them from leaving to seek their fortunes elsewhere.[87] In this way, madams were able to tie workers to themselves in what was essentially an open market system. Prostitutes could choose which madams for whom they wished to work, although as we will see, those choices were often informed by a number of factors. Prostitutes were not servants who needed papers to leave their positions or risk arrest. They could come and go as they pleased, though, of course, if they worked the streets or became vagrants they could be arrested. However, because of debt, despite whatever exposure a girl may have had to patrons, her future lay entirely in the hands of her madam.

The primary disadvantage pensioners faced in trying to become kept women stemmed from the conditions that brought them to the brothels in the first place, desperation and poverty. We already have explored the ways in which these histories were overplotted, neatly matching a salvation narrative. But the existence of a salvation narrative should not hide the fact that the brothel did provide refuge for those in need. It offered its boarders food, clothing, comradeship of other women, a place to sleep, and freedom from the worst violence of the trade at a moment when these protections were wanting. It may even have offered a (corrupted) form of maternal strength and affection. Social relations inside the brothel replicated that of a family. New pensioners, like Marie Boujard, usually were in their early teens and were orphans or runaways, or had been abandoned. They traditionally called the madam of the house "maman" (mama). Madam Hecquet, in turn, called her pensioners "my little family."[88] Madams looked after their employees, probably motivated more by good business sense than by any maternal feelings. This security, in the face of few independent resources, left pensioners dependent on the madams.

Even if a pensioner had some relatives to whom she could turn, or some livres stashed somewhere, these hardly could have helped her out of the debt she would accumulate as a pensioner. Some girls, most in fact, arrived indebted. For example, when d'Osment accepted Françoise Gilette as a pensioner in her brothel, the madam had to pay the seventy-five livres the girl owed to her creditors.[89] In this way, madams, like other businesspeople, acted as moneylenders and creditors, except that madams used debt as a means to secure a workforce over whom their only other form of control was emotional. Gilette was then expected to work off the sum. The custom of debt assumption was so well established that girls occasionally abused it in order to relieve immediate financial pressure. In a letter to the lieutenant general, d'Osment expressed concern that Gilette might be using her in this manner, but she decided not to worry about it.[90]

What debt pensioners brought with them, however, was often minor in comparison to the costs they accrued as brothel workers. Women staying in brothels had to pay for their rooms, board, and specialized clothing such as negligees, as well as makeup, which madams provided to increase the sexual capital of their workers as well as to bind them to the brothel. Casanova reported that the prostitutes at the Hôtel de Roule wore matching white muslin dresses.[91] These costs could be considerable. Occasionally, madams made special and costly investments in their pensioners that the latter would be expected to repay. Madam Montigny, for instance, fitted Geneviève-Agnès Deschaux with a denture made of three teeth.[92] The problem of debt among pensioners was so widespread that it penetrated literary culture. Rétif de la Bretonne satirized the problem when he depicted his fictional prostitute Eglantine spending 59 livres more per day on clothing and food than she earned.[93] Yet the most significant cost for pensioners did not even make it onto Eglantine's list; this was medical treatment, specifically for syphilis.

Venereal disease was endemic in the brothels. Once a worker showed symptoms, she could be dismissed outright. Madam Lafosse fired Catherine Mahüe when customers began to complain about her ulcers. Mahüe was forced to rent a room and seek medical help on her own.[94] Those without resources were left with no choice but to go to the prison La Salpêtrière, where they might wait up to a year for an appointment to get treated. If a madam wanted a girl cured without paying for it, she could use her privileged relationship with the police to have a sick pensioner put at the head of the queue and be treated immediately.[95] If a girl was a good earner, however, she usually was spared the trauma of the Hôpital system and instead was sent to a private surgeon under contract.

The treatment, wherever it was received, was brutal. One round of the *grands remèdes* took six weeks, and a full cure often required several rounds. The patient was first bled, purged, and bathed. Then, for four weeks, she had regular applications of a mercury-based ointment rubbed into her skin. This was followed by a two-week recovery period during which her food was severely restricted.[96] Patients emerged from this course emaciated, often sick and disfigured from mercury poisoning, but better. Mercury is an effective bactericide. Erica-Marie Benabou found that 56 percent of the women leaving La Salpêtrière in the second half of 1765 were declared cured.[97] Whether they actually were cured, however, is open to debate. Regardless of treatment, syphilis has its own life course, and the symptoms of initial infection disappear after a few weeks even without medical intervention. Girls sent to surgeons were responsible for the costs, and these were significant. Marie Boujard entered the brothel of Varenne most probably without debt. She left six months later owing six hundred livres, mainly on account of her two treatments. Illness trapped women in the brothels. Once sick, they had to stay and work off the debt. In the process they were often reinfected and required additional treatment, which only further indebted them.

In being indebted, pensioners were just like most other people in eighteenth-century France, of every social level. The role of credit was particularly essential to the survival of the working poor, who obtained a variety of types of loans and often proffered credit themselves. Julie Harwick argues that "the management of complex and fragile networks of debt and credit was a crucial element in early modern households." Legal action for debt was common, as was the sight of creditors seizing items.[98] According to the police reports, demimonde custom was that any pensioner indebted to her madam could only quit the brothel with her permission. What separates prostitutes from many other debtors, then, is that their bodies, rather than their possessions, were a form of collateral.

A very few, like Françoise Gilette, worked off their debts and left to try business on their own. Many pensioners were simply expelled from the brothel due to illness or age. Ironically, any girl thought to have become too libertine also was let go, as were those who had been at the brothel for too long. Benabou, in her study of brothel rosters, found that madams generally liked to have new pensioners every six months or so, although there is also plenty of evidence of particular individuals remaining at certain houses for more than one year.[99] Mercier claimed that madams "keep women for all tastes under their own roofs" and this was Casanova's observation of the prostitutes of Madam Paris. He wrote that the women "were all about the same age, and all pretty—some tall, others of middle height, others short, some were brunettes, some blondes, some auburn hair."[100]

Despite the need to obtain permission to leave, some girls simply ran away. On January 1, 1762, Inspector Marais reported that Brissault was devastated. His best earner, Demoiselle Dangeville, who later became a successful dame entretenue, had fled, owing five hundred livres. To add insult to injury, she sent some men the following day to retrieve her possessions, which Brissault normally would have held as collateral for her debt.[101] Dangeville may have fled because, at least according to Marais, Brissault wanted her as a mistress, set her up in an apartment and had sex with her twice. He reported that Dangeville had come to him "in tears, asking for advice." She found her former pimp both "ugly" and "disgusting."[102]

Like those who were expelled or left on their own, those women pulled out of the brothel by a single client to be set up as a mistress similarly could not leave without the permission of the madam. The marquis de Persenat had to negotiate with Varenne to take Marie Boujard as his mistress. He eventually agreed to pay Boujard's debt and to give the madam another twenty-five louis in the form of two *lettres de change*.[103] The Dutch business-man who took Marie Lelache out of Madam Préville's brothel agreed to pay the madam the ten louis (240 livres) Lelache owed her. He then set the girl up in a chambre garnie, engaged several domestics for her service, and paid her a stipend of two hundred livres a month.[104]

It is interesting to speculate why patrons bothered getting permission. These were powerful, wealthy men dealing with women who were crimi-nals and were socially abhorred. In the case of a runaway pensioner, the only legal recourse a madam might have would be to seek repayment of the girl's debt, although this did not always work out. Madam Préval went to the home of a former pensioner to retrieve clothing she had provided. When she found that most of the clothing had been sold, she called the local commis-sioner, who arrested Préval rather than her ex-employee.[105] The madam's business was not protected in the way other sexual commerce was. Madams feared seeking official help even when they clearly were wronged. Pension-ers and prospective patrons did not ask permission and go through elaborate negotiations out of fear of legal retribution. Most probably, it was custom and the prospect of social retaliation that concerned them. Neither patron nor pensioner wanted to damage his/her relationship with the madam. Why this was so important we shall see shortly.

That permission had to be sought, debts paid, and fees negotiated and tendered would seem a hindrance in attracting prospective patrons. But these hassles were more than balanced by the marketing efforts of madams to place their pensioners. For example, through the winter months of 1753–54, Madam Baudouin launched an impressive campaign to do just that for her pensioner "La Petite Monçan." She publicized the girl's availability by taking her to the Opéra ball. She wrote letters to various men who she thought might be interested. If they replied, she sent Monçan to visit them for a day or a night. She asked men who came and slept with the girl at the brothel if they knew anyone who would want her as a mistress. By the time Monçan was spirited away (or stolen, in Baudouin's telling) by a Swiss Guard three months later, the madam had found four prospective patrons, including a man she referred to as the "duc de Paulmy" who probably was the marquis de Paulmy (Antoine-René de Voyer de Paulmy d'Argenson, 1722–87), son of the former foreign secretary.[106]

At first glance, the outplacing of pensioners would seem a poor business strategy for the madams, especially when evaluated in monetary terms.

They did make quick, tidy sums from these sales, often eight or nine louis a head. Varenne's fee for brokering Marie Boujard, twenty-five louis, was unusually high. But even the most conservative estimate of pensioner earnings suggests that these women accrued more profit for their employers by working for them than by leaving. Monçan was earning from twelve to as much as forty-eight livres per service she rendered in the brothel. Why, then, did Baudouin make such an effort? The successful placing of a woman like Monçan with a socially prestigious and wealthy client such as the marquis de Paulmy was what sustained a good portion of Baudouin's business. It was how she built networks of buyers and sellers of sex, and it was these networks that were at the center of her business.

Commanding these networks enabled madams, as businesswomen, to dominate the market of providing sexual services to men of the elite. It also helped the demimonde cohere as a community. In constructing these networks, madams did not just identify buyers and sellers of sex, they labeled people as participants in this highly specific subculture. Moreover, in brokering exchanges and having both parties adhere to certain formats—such as paying debts and a fee to take a pensioner as a mistress—they reinforced the standards by which these exchanges were tendered.

❧ Buyers and Sellers

Let us look first at buyers: if Baudouin were indeed able to find a mistress who very much pleased the marquis, he would (and did) use her services again, trusting she knew his preferences. Théveneau de Morande satirized this relationship in his *Le Porte-Feuille de Madam Gourdan.*[107] Once hooked, patrons showed remarkable loyalty to their brokers, even when common sense would have them seeking another. For example, the marquis de Montmorin, governor of Fontainebleau, had a long business relationship with Baudouin. In the fall of 1750, five days after dismissing the last mistress she had placed with him (whom he kept for four months), the marquis ordered the madam to find him a new one and deliver her to his house in Paris on the tenth of the month, the day he expected to be back in the capital. Baudouin brought him Demoiselle Rozières. The marquis liked her, but she had syphilis. Two weeks later, having grown impatient with her rate of cure, he demanded that the madam find him someone else. The next candidate (whom the marquis chose, Baudouin merely arranged the meeting) got drunk at the end of their first supper together and told the marquis that he disgusted her. To smooth relations with her longtime client, Baudouin offered the marquis the virginity of a girl named Dassigny, who was not a virgin. In fact, she was five months pregnant and had just been released from the Hôpital. Moreover, she had the reputation of "lying like a lackey." The marquis, nevertheless, was charmed. Apparently a poor judge of character, he thought the girl sweet. He was touched by her story and set her up with clothes, furniture, and an apartment. Within two weeks, however, he sent his son to Madam Baudouin, complaining that Dassigny was too libertine. The madam was directed again to find him a new mistress. Eventually, she made a successful match.[108] Baudouin either did not know Montmorin's taste in mistresses, or she did not care. But the kind of service she provided required a level of intimacy between an elite man and a nonelite female merchant that was unusual and that was important to the madams' success.

In part it was this intimacy that kept clients loyal, turning repeatedly to the same madams to arrange passades and petits soupers. Of the forty-four hosts of petits soupers recorded by Inspector Marais in 1762, each used the same madam for every event he wanted organized in all but two instances. For every passade arranged or party organized, the madam received a substantial sum. Of course, there were circumstances in which a client might engage a different madam from his usual one. This was often the case when a man wanted a liaison with a particular dame entretenue. He might hire the madam he thought had the best relationship with her. The duc de Grammont, for example, often used the services of Brissault. When he wanted a liaison with Demoiselle Beauvoisin, however, he hired Madam Surville to make the necessary arrangements. Surville was not entirely successful, and Grammont was forced to settle for a passade rather than something more substantial.[109] Marquis Ximènes asked Baudouin to find Demoiselle Grenier and ask her to come to his place the following day between one and two in the afternoon "for urgent business." In this case, Baudouin, annoyed that Ximènes had not paid the four louis he had promised her prostitute (paying two instead), simply sent the marquis Grenier's address with a note that he had lackeys to execute his orders.[110] Brissault, generally, was known to have the best connections with women of the theater. Madam Gourdan, claimed Pidansat de Mairobert, was most expert at acquiring anyone, even women who were not normally associated with the demimonde, like Dame d'Oppy.

The example of Grammont and Surville illustrates the importance to madams of developing a wide network of sex sellers. As a madam was able to place more women, she would attract more buyers, impressed with her connections. In turn, having a large number of buyers coming to her looking for mistresses, passades, and partygoers would attract even more sex sellers, hopeful that this particular madam, with her huge network, would be able to find them work. It was not, however, just a question of numbers.

The importance of satisfying such a high-profile client as the duc de Grammont lay as much in the status it bestowed on the madam as it did in the
return business of a single loyal customer. The sexual capital of prostitutes
and dames entretenues was based on a number of factors, including maintenance history. In other words, the higher the status of her past patrons and
the higher the salaries she had received, the more a dame entretenue could
command from her future maintainers. The importance of maintenance
history shows the degree to which status in the demimonde reaffirmed itself. In part, it was the fact that these women were desired that made them
desirable. Madams profited from and indeed manipulated this male culture
of narcissistic self-definition and affirmation. Therefore, placing an unknown
or a debutant like Monçan with a man like the marquis de Paulmy accomplished much for Baudouin. It defined Monçan's sexual capital as being very
high and thus Baudouin as a madam who trafficked in women of this status,
cementing the latter's reputation and hence her business.

Let us now turn to the sellers: sellers' networks seemed at once tighter
and more fluid than those of buyers. Women who emerged from the brothels
often maintained close relationships with their former madams. Many seemed
to turn to their ex-madam as a first resource, whatever the problem. According to Inspector Meusnier, Geneviève-Agnès Deschaux, for example, asked
Madam Montigny to visit her in her new apartment where she talked with
her former madam about her relationship with her patron.[111] Sometimes
these relationships were almost maternal, fostered perhaps by the forced intimacy and family structure of brothel life. For example, Demoiselle Agathe,
later known as Marbourg, looked to Madam Paris as something of a mother,
or at least a wealthy aunt endowed with good sense. Agathe left the brothel
of Paris as the mistress of Monsieur Klinglin, premier président au Conseil
souverain d'Alsace, who had set her up lavishly, hired her singing and dancing
masters, and then seven months later, abruptly quit her, claiming financial
hardship. (He later resumed their relationship.) Agathe was devastated and
disoriented. Even worse, she owed over one hundred écus (three hundred
livres) to various local merchants. She turned at once to Madam Paris, who
not only "reassured her of her future," but offered her shelter from creditors
and finally advanced her the cash to pay her debts. Over the next four years,
as Agathe struggled both with her unsteady relationship with Klinglin and
with her debts, Madam Paris was a steady support and source of advice,
helping her plan strategies to recapture her patron and supporting her for
months at a time. In all, Paris lent Agathe more than five thousand livres.[112]

Those who used madams to launch their careers more directly also
remained loyal, at least for a while. As we saw in chapter 2, some of these

girls—like Marie Boujard—came to Paris (or were brought by their mothers) in hopes of finding a patron to maintain them. The mother of Demoiselle Dascher believed that her daughter was fit for the king, so she bought
the thirteen-year-old an expensive gown and paraded her up and down the
halls of Versailles, but to no avail. She never caught the king's eye. When their
funds ran out, they approached Brissault, who thought the girl worthy of some
significant investment. He set her up in a furnished apartment and lent her
cash to buy clothing. He then introduced her to his most elite clientele. By
investing in her, he was building his buyer and seller networks. Brissault was
successful. The comte de Jumilhac de Cubjac, a noted libertine who was
governor of the Bastille and brother-in-law of Bertin de Blagny (also a
noted libertine), had a short affair with the girl. The marquis de Voyer took
her as his mistress, as did Marie Boujard's patron, the marquis de Persenat.[113]
Brissault was not the only broker who invested in new prospects as a way
to build networks. Madam Paris, for her part, loaned twelve hundred livres'
worth of furniture to her former pensioner Judith Leoni, who eventually
became Demoiselle Matini, a dancer in the Opéra-Comique.[114]

Madam Varenne prostituted Marie Boujard in every way possible. She sold
her virginity, kept her as a pensioner, sent her on outcalls, worked for her
as an agent, and brokered her into a patron-mistress relationship. Some of
these actions seem counterintuitive, at least from a profit-minded perspective. Placing Marie as a mistress, for example, deprived Varenne of the income
the girl earned as a pensioner. But each transaction was valuable to Varenne
in a different way. Each helped her to develop and sustain a network of sex
buyers and sex sellers. The three components of Varenne's enterprise—the
brothel, the outcall, and matchmaking services—built on each other by drawing men and women into Varenne's network, encouraging them to use more
of her services. The networks were the core of her business. Since Varenne
worked in an open market in which buyer and seller could use any madam
they wished, or no madam at all, the madams had to find a way to retain
them. Buyer loyalty was assured through satisfaction. This in turn necessitated having sexual services to sell. Seller allegiance was more complicated.
Madams attracted some elite prostitutes, those who were more experienced,
by being good agents and finding them the work they needed. But the madams also fostered bonds of dependence, especially with girls new to the
demimonde. These bonds were predicated on debt and desperation, at least
initially, but could endure through an entire career. Marie clearly had a personal bond with Varenne. She was fourteen or fifteen when she was left in
the brothel. That her mother abandoned her there suggests a brutal home

life. And it was only through Varenne that Marie was able to access elite buyers and ultimately rise within the prostitution hierarchy. In their professional lives, Varenne and Boujard had a symbiotic relationship. Of course, Marie's relationship with Varenne was not symmetrical. It was predicated on exploitation and the worst form of dependence, although probably not forever.

Varenne's impact on Marie's life extended beyond their personal relationship to the ways in which Varenne and her co-madams shaped the demimonde, affecting even those buyers and sellers with whom they had little or no direct interaction. Madams structured their enterprises in similar ways, providing the same sorts of services for around the same prices. In doing so, madams may have simply been reflecting general community practices. Even if this was the case, the volume of their business and the reach of their networks gave them the power to further standardize these practices, not just in terms of the services being sold, but of the very structure of their purchase. Standardization within the market of elite prostitution stabilized it. Buyers and sellers knew what to expect and how to negotiate sales. This helped dames entretenues advance their careers. That the madams were a community brought further stability. In their efforts to make money and satisfy the police, they identified those who were part of the demimonde. In policing each other to adhere to the toleration policy, they agreed what was for sale and what was not.

What was for sale was the sexuality of young women and girls, most of whom, like Marie Boujard, the madams horribly abused. Yet it was this relationship that made madams so successful. I am not referring here to the dependence that turned these girls into sex sellers, but rather the nature of the market in which their sexuality was sold. Madams were impressive businesswomen by eighteenth-century standards. They operated complex commercial enterprises that demanded a range of skills from budgeting to event planning, from controlling young girls to ingratiating themselves with elite men. The conditions under which they operated required another set of skills, including the ability to manipulate all the players—fellow madams, buyers, sellers, parents, the police—in their universe. All of this took formidable emotional intelligence. But what made such success possible was not only the talents of the madams but also the market in which they were practiced. The madams operated in a space defined by the police policy of toleration, which both limited competition and imposed a very light regulation. Within those limits, the madams contended in an open market with what seemed like an unending supply of potential prostitutes and a huge demand for them. It would not be until the end of the eighteenth century that the police and the state began to consider regulating prostitution more formally, thereby curbing potential profits. Until the Revolution, elite madams, with very few restrictions and indeed with police support, could take girls, sell their sexuality, and reap the rewards.

We do not know what sort of contact Marie had with Varenne after Marie became the mistress of Monsieur Desjeans. It is possible that Marie came back to Varenne periodically, for comfort or help, or simply for work. But from this moment, with her mother out of the picture, a second construct began to structure Marie Boujard's engagement in the demimonde. This was the patron-mistress contract, a subject to which we now turn.

☙ CHAPTER 5

Contracts and Elite Prostitution as Work

By the spring of 1754, Monsieur Dumas de Corbeville, *fermier général des postes*, had been supporting his mistress, nineteen-year-old Demoiselle Gautier, for two years.[1] He was, by contemporary standards, an extremely generous patron and spent so much on his mistress that he had to mortgage his carriage and rent a cheaper one to get around Paris. Dumas established Gautier in a Paris apartment leased for six hundred livres a year, which he furnished. She had on the outskirts of town a secondary residence, a petite maison that he rented and also furnished. He paid the wages of her three servants, a cook, a lackey and a femme de chambre. (These households were in addition to Dumas's own, which he shared with his mother.) Over the years Dumas gave Gautier jewelry, silver, linens, and quite a few dresses. Yet, despite the outlay of such significant sums, Gautier left the relationship with surprisingly little. Usually kept women emerged from lengthy relationships with well-paying patrons considerably enriched.

The cause of the breakup was Gautier's infidelity with a man the police identify as chevalier Darques, a former army captain. Oddly, Gautier had been having sex with Darques (and others) for the entire duration of her relationship with Dumas. It was only in February 1754, after two years together, that Dumas either caught on or, equally possible, decided to care. He set a trap to catch his mistress. Telling Gautier that he was going to the country, Dumas said his goodbyes, leaving her in their petite maison, only to secretly double back later that evening. After watching the house all night, Dumas forced his way in to discover Darques hiding in the lackey's bed. Dumas's reaction was to dismantle his relationship with Gautier systematically and quickly. He paid what wages were owed to the servants and summarily fired them. He kicked Gautier out of the house. She was allowed to keep about half of what he had given her, including some dresses, linens, and jewelry. A waiting carriage then took her and her things to her sister's house.

Shortly thereafter, possibly within days, Dumas had a new mistress, fifteen-year-old Demoiselle Raime, a dancer in the Opéra. He installed Raime (and her mother) in Gautier's old apartment.[2] He allowed her to choose which of Gautier's remaining dresses and furniture she wished to keep and engaged a *tapissier* to make what furniture was lacking. (Gautier was later given the unwanted objects.) Wary of Gautier's experience, Raime insisted on having all the furnishings, old and new, put in her name. Police reports imply that Dumas provided Raime with the same maintenance he had given Gautier: an allowance of six hundred livres a month, the wages of her three servants, an apartment, and furniture. When Dumas died a few months later, Raime profited enormously. She was left ten thousand livres of furniture, quite a windfall for a kept woman who had debuted in the demimonde only a few months before.[3]

How do we explain Dumas's actions? Why did he take half of what he had given Gautier over two years and how was he able to do so? If the answer is obvious, that she cheated, we might wonder why she was allowed to keep anything at all. The question is complicated by the fact that mistress infidelity was one of the most common justifications for breakups, yet it rarely resulted in the confiscation of goods. So why did Dumas find it necessary to set a trap when most patrons hardly required such proof for ending a relationship? The interactions of Dumas, Gautier, and Raime raise the question as to what conventions governed patron-mistress breakups and, for that matter, their relationships.

That March night, Dumas acted out a well-rehearsed script. Relationships in the demimonde were highly patterned, and their public performance was ritualized. The discovery of infidelity and the repeated firing of the same unfaithful mistress were such common occurrences as to be literary topoi.[4] Even the ways in which Dumas and Darques related to each other through Gautier followed certain conventions. Numerous factors shaped these conventions, including notions of honor, contemporary gender relations, libertinism, and shifting ideas of marriage. But perhaps it was in the world of work that we find the most significant determinant of how these relationships were organized and lived.

Patron-mistress relationships were governed by what the police called a *contrat* (contract), which, despite the term, was not a proper contract. These were verbal agreements, negotiated and assented to by patron and mistress (or sometimes the mistress's parent), that stipulated remuneration. They were not legally binding, nor did breaking them carry any serious long-term social stigma. Nevertheless, they were customary. These contracts were recognized by the community, the police, and sometimes other judicial officials as valid agreements. Each party expected the other to follow the terms, called *conditions*. In providing both of his mistresses with servants, an apartment, furniture, a monthly wage, and gifts, Dumas was adhering to the stipulations of the individual agreements that he made with each of them. In sleeping with Darques, Gautier failed to live up to her obligations, and this brought into question her ownership of the items that had been her remuneration. Contracts, like madams, organized and stabilized social and sexual relationships across the demimonde.

The impact of the contract on the lives of kept women and their patrons, however, lay beyond its regulatory function. Whatever the private feelings between patron and mistress, these relationships were organized around an exchange, the value of which was partially monetized in a paralegal form. In this way, patron-mistress relationships were similar to marriage. But there were crucial differences. In patron-mistress relationships, the contract, or its absence, actually shaped behavior, influencing how patron and mistress interacted with each other and even how the couple interacted with other sexual partners, like the chevalier Darques. It informed and infused meaning into interpersonal dynamics. But it also worked the other way around. The emotional relationship between patron and mistress could affect the execution of the contract, the flow of money and goods. As an economic instrument, the contract made mistresses into sex workers yet at the very same time confused their status. In this ambiguity lay the potential for profit and the limited exercise of power by women who otherwise would have lived the short and dangerous lives of streetwalkers.

✒ Patron-Mistress Contracts

The agreement that governed patron-mistress relations was called by several different names. *Les arrangements* (arrangements) was often used in satire and prostitute fiction. The police referred to *le contrat* (contract), *la traité* (treaty), *les arrangements*, or even, somewhat crudely, *le bail* (lease), all of which were terms used in contemporary commercial language. "Bail" also appears in street songs about kept women.[5] The borrowing of commercial language in this instance is not surprising. Prostitution itself had long been called *le commerce* or *le mauvais commerce* (illicit commerce or business), derivations of an earlier connotation of the word meaning illicit sexual activity.[6]

The contract was standardized, and its terms, called *conditions*, were never particularly inventive. They simply settled the details of preexisting categories. Future patron and mistress filled in the blanks, the most significant of which was the *honoraires*, a monthly allowance given at the first of each month, usually a month in advance. Use of the word *honoraires* in this circumstance was ironic as it primarily referred to the fees owed an *advocat au conseil du roi* for writing a brief or those collected by a doctor or a member of another "honorable profession."[7] The police were not the only writers with a sense of humor. The term is used similarly in fiction.[8]

In a sample of one hundred of these verbal agreements as reported by the police, the size of honoraires varied from as little as 48 livres a month to as much as 2,400. The median stipend was 600 livres, which was what Dumas paid Raime. The mean was 623 livres. Slightly more than three-quarters of these stipends were between 200 and 800 livres a month, with about a third being between 600 and 800 livres. Another fifth were between 800 and 1,200, and only in a few cases were kept women paid more than 1,200 livres a month.[9]

Evidence of the size of honoraires for the hyperelite mistresses—the dozen or so women at the very top of the profession who were given richly furnished mansions and multiple carriages, and who accrued vast material wealth—comes from the *Mémoires secrets* and other "journals" of the day. With the exception of Demoiselle Deschamps (Marie-Anne Pàges) and Rosalie Astraudi, these women tended to have thin police dossiers or none at all, most likely because their fame made their files particularly attractive for those who raided the archive in 1789. According to the *Mémoires secrets*, the prince de Soubise paid the famous dancer Marie-Madeleine Guimard six thousand livres honoraires.[10]

Comparatively, honoraires were high, especially when measured against what women from such backgrounds could typically earn. Wet nurses were paid 6 livres a month. Clare Crowston found that girls working for mistress seamstresses in skilled and semiskilled positions were paid between 36 and 100 livres a year. The annual salary of a shopgirl (*fille de boutique*) at a *marchande des modes* (fashion merchant) was between 150 and 200 livres. Honoraires were high even in comparison to what men from the same backgrounds earned. Michael Sonenscher estimated that a journeyman in the building trades earned up to 472 livres a year, and at midcentury, a master silk maker might bring in 1800 livres annually. Robert Darnton reported that when Monsieur and Madame Suard earned an income of between 10,000 and 20,000 livres a year, they had reached the pinnacle of the literary world.[11]

Honoraires tended to remain fixed for the duration of a relationship. Kept women did not get raises, a practice that was in keeping with the customs of pay in other industries. According to Michael Sonenscher, journeymen hired at a certain rate, whether into a workshop or for a certain project, were paid at that rate until they left, at which point they might be able to negotiate a different wage with a new employer.[12] In industries based on annual contracts, workers sometimes could negotiate raises during their yearly contract renewal. Lauren Clay found this to be common practice among actors and actresses in the provinces. They were most likely to be successful in these efforts if they were popular or in demand by other theaters.[13] In theory, servants, many of whom were on annual contracts even though they often received their pay only at the end of their service, could negotiate raises. However, in her study of households in Aix, Sarah Maza found that wages of unskilled servants "tended to remain fixed by custom at the same level in any given household over years or even decades."[14] The patron-mistress contract, unlike most others, was of an indefinite duration, giving the mistress little chance to push for a raise, at least in her honoraires. However, the complexity of the pay package afforded numerous opportunities for increasing total remuneration.

While honoraires served as the contract's foundation, patrons contributed to their mistresses' maintenance in other ways. In about a fifth of the cases, new mistresses were given a pot-de-vin (sometimes called an entrèe-de-jeu), a present that marked the beginning of the relationship; it could be considered a "deal sweetener." The pot-de-vin was received in advance of any sexual activity and generally was worth between five and ten times the honoraires. At the bottom end (i.e., in contracts with honoraires of less than 100 livres), patrons frequently offered their mistresses-to-be a dress or two. Women accepting such low stipends were by definition poor, at least according to dame entretenue standards. Many were just starting out and, coming from artisan or working-class families, they necessarily lacked the habiliments of their new trade. Consequently, a pot-de-vin for a recently debuted dame entretenue was sometimes akin to a kept-woman starter set. The comte de la Tour d'Auvergne, for example, promised the fifteen-year-old virgin Demoiselle Crousol some furniture, a dress, some linen, and some jewelry. Her younger sister, consigned to a local notary, was given "all that she needed" in addition to her monthly stipend of 150 livres.[15] For some, the pot-de-vin was a small sum of cash with which to pay the most pressing debts. When the philosophe the duc d'Uzès decided to take as his mistress the fourteen-year-old Geneviève Vallée, a pensioner at the brothel of Madam Baudouin, he gave her twelve louis (288 livres) with which to pay her creditors.[16]

At the higher end (contracts with a minimum of 800 livres in monthly honoraires) the pot-de-vin was almost always a large chunk of cash, occasionally supplemented by an expensive piece of jewelry. Demoiselle Sire, for example, a dancer in the Opéra ballet, was given 10,000 livres and some diamonds (perhaps in the form of a necklace or earrings) as a deal-sweetener by her patron-to-be, a man the police identify as a German, Count Bentheim de Steinfurt.[17] The *Mémoires secrets* reported that in 1768 the comte de Lauraguais gave the German dancer Marie Heinel for a "present de noces" (wedding gift) 30,000 livres in cash, some 20,000 more livres to her brother, "exquisite furnishings" and a carriage. The total value of the pot-de-vin was estimated to be 100,000 livres.[18] Sometimes, as in low-end cases, the cash gift was earmarked for debt payment. No kept woman was free of debt.

There were other additional forms of compensation attached to the contract. In slightly fewer than a quarter of the contracts in this sample, a patron agreed to pay the rent of his mistress's current apartment or to move her to a new one, as Dumas did with Raime and Gautier. In a subset of Marais's reports transcribed and published as the *Journal des inspectors*, Erica-Marie Benabou found fifty-nine instances in which patrons paid rent ranging from one hundred to twenty-four hundred livres a year. (More than half the leases were between four hundred and seven hundred livres, slightly more than a quarter were between eight hundred and thirteen hundred livres, five were between thirteen hundred and twenty-four hundred, and three were more than twenty-four hundred livres.) Thus while Raime's honoraires were about average, she lived in a much more expensive apartment than did most of her peers. But even kept women in lower-end apartments still were housed better than most Parisians. In 1790, more than half of Parisian residences were rented for between forty-two and two hundred livres, only 10 percent were between four hundred and six hundred livres, and 5.6 percent were between six hundred and eight hundred livres, with very few costing more.[19] Some patrons agreed specifically to provision these new domiciles, paying the grocery, butcher, wine and fuel bills, as well as servants' wages.

Rent and bearing household expenses were not the only additional form of compensation. In about a fifth of the cases, the patron bought his mistress new furnishings or promised to do so within one term (four months) of the beginning of the contract. Dumas bought furniture for both Gautier and Raime. When Monsieur Villemure, identified only as a wealthy man from Britanny, wanted to take Demoiselle Leoville from the brothel where she was a pensioner, he agreed to rent and furnish her an apartment and pay her 100 livres honoraires.[20] Count Aprakseim, who the police identify as a Russian admiral, agreed in February 1761 to put Demoiselle Chédeville, a dancer at the Opéra chorus, in an apartment leased for 1,500 livres a year, which he promised to furnish "elegantly" by Easter. He also gave her 36 louis (864 livres) a month.[21]

At the highest levels, accommodations were lavish. In 1753, the duc d'Orléans took over the lease for the building on the rue du Four in which his new mistress, Demoiselle Deschamps, lived. He evicted all the other tenants, and then gutted, remodeled, and furnished the premises. Her next patron, the comte de Coubert, bought her a petite maison in Pantin, for twenty thousand livres.[22] At this level, patrons were often expected to continue financing building and renovation projects begun under other patrons. Such was the case with the various residences of the famous dancer Marie-Madeleine Guimard, first with her house in Pantin paid for by the prince de Soubise, and later with the Hôtel Guimard in the Chaussée d'Antin, designed by Charles-Nicolas Ledoux. The mansion, which was widely discussed in the *Mémoires secrets* and in another news journal, the *Correspondance littéraire*, contained a five-hundred-seat theater, and paintings by the artists Fragonard and Jacques-Louis David. The furnishings cost twenty-seven thousand livres. Historian Kathryn Norberg notes that in comparison, the eighty-five pieces of new furniture ordered by Princess Kinsky in 1777 to furnish her entire house cost only six thousand livres.[23]

Additional compensation could be conditional and on a delayed schedule. Phillippe Barthélemy Lévesque de Gravelles, *grand maitre des eaux et forêts* for Touraine, Anjou, and le Maine, had Demoiselle Gallodier stay under the close watch of a matron. He gave her honoraires but was waiting to see how she behaved before paying off her debts and fulfilling other elements of the contract.[24] In January 1754, Auguste Brissart, the fermier général, who famously would later foot Deschamps's bills, promised to move the dancer Marie Perrette Granier into a new and better-furnished apartment at Easter were she to stop seeing her ex-lover. When Brissart caught him at her place a week later, he canceled the arrangement.[25] In a déclaration de grossesse, the dancer Marie-Adélaïde Le Monnier claimed that a man named Roseville had promised her a number of items were she to continue her "exemplary conduct." When he failed to keep his word, Le Monnier turned to the local commissioner to compel her patron to pay the costs of the birth and support the baby she claimed was his.[26]

Beyond the contract, informal custom dictated still further remuneration. Many patrons gave their mistresses *étrennes*, a traditional New Year's gift. The prince de Soubise gave Marie-Madeleine Guimard a six thousand livres étrennes.[27] The giving of étrennes was a widespread custom in the eighteenth century within the court, among families, and from employers to employees. Journeymen in certain trades expected to collect them from their masters or from their masters' clients.[28]

Complex modes of pay, in which wages were combined with other forms of compensation, were standard in the eighteenth century. Many journeymen received meals and lodging. They could be paid both by piece and by time, and they might receive wages, raw materials, and finished products, or some combination of the three. Servants were paid wages and were given food, lodging, and clothes. Provincial actors and actresses were awarded per diems for extended performance runs in other cities.[29] These forms of remuneration were in addition to the rights and protections conferred on individuals by virtue of belonging to a workshop, household, or company.

From the perspective of work remuneration, however, patron–mistress contracts were comparatively interesting in several ways. The patron–mistress contract was, by definition, of an indefinite length. This was one way in which it stood apart from formal and legally binding work contracts of the period. Another was the ease with which either party could be released from it. Provincial performers often had to pay a fine if they broke their annual contracts. Servants could be dismissed at the master's whim, but if they left on their own could be liable to prosecution and risked losing any accrued wages.[30] Workers in various trades could not simply leave. Depending on when, where, and in what trade, a worker might have to give notice, finish current projects, and then get a certificate (the *congé* and later the *livret*) without which legally he would be considered a vagabond.[31] In his diary, journeyman glazier Jacques–Louis Ménétra recounted his difficulties in leaving employment, including the need to give two weeks' notice and being forced to stay because he could not obtain permission to leave.[32]

Yet another difference was that the contract never stipulated total pay. Rather, it determined base pay. Whether "gifts" were formally included, they certainly were expected, and it was not uncommon for the value of gifts to increase as a relationship intensified. Patrons in love with their mistresses notoriously gave so extravagantly that they ruined themselves financially. Dumas's need to hock his carriage (and his mother's consequent ire) presents only a mildly cautionary tale in light of the scores of stories in which infatuated patrons spent themselves right into prison. A man Meusnier identifies as the nineteen-year-old son of a fermier général named Roussel was forced by his family to leave Paris after his infatuation with Catherine Ponchon, a dancer in the Opéra, led him to buy her a bracelet worth ten thousand livres and a horse and carriage, among many other very expensive gifts.[33]

Many mistresses actively encouraged gift giving, coercing, by whatever means, an entreteneur into providing beyond what he had originally intended or expected to provide. This practice had a name, *tirer* or "drawing," as in withdrawing from a bank. Writing about the separation of Monsieur de St. Jean and his mistress Demoiselle Pelissier, Inspector Meusnier speculated that the loss would be significant for her because "it was rumored that in the course of the six months that they were together, she had the talent to draw more than 8000 livres from him."[34] Drawing seriously concerned contemporary commentators. They envisaged an exaggerated ability of kept women to bankrupt sons of important families, an ability they imagined greatly endangering France.[35] But for the moment, and considering the contracts and not the debate over luxury, gifts were a form of bonus. These bonuses could be considerable.

Gifts (and furnishings) were often the only means through which kept women could accrue wealth over the course of their careers. Dames entretenues rarely budgeted so as to put aside money from their honoraires. Moreover, their remuneration was not designed to help establish and maintain households but was meant to entertain the patron and sometimes his friends. Furniture, even the bed, was often intended for his use rather than that of his mistress or her family. Gifts, on the other hand, were portable wealth. Patrons gave material objects—such as dresses and clothing, linens, jewelry, silver plate, additional furniture, decorative objects—and *rente* (annuities). Gautier's case demonstrates that possession of material gifts could be contested under certain circumstances. Rente, however, was established legally in the name of its beneficiary and, unlike a bowl, could not be retrieved easily. The notarial document in which the duc de Mazarin gifted three thousand livres in *rente viagère* (annual life-time annuities) to Marie Allard, a dancer in the Opéra, declared that they were "for life, pure, simple and irrevocable."[36] Gifts were also an important source of wealth in another way, as capital. The specific items that tended to be proffered as gifts had symbolic meaning in the demimonde and consequently helped to build social status. Possession and public display of diamond earrings, for example, indicated sexual capital and hence enabled the wearer to attract better-paying patrons.

The enormous variety and profit potential in the receipt of gifts stands in sharp contrast to the specificity of payments in kind in other sorts of work contracts. For example, as a result of a dispute in 1786, corporate officials in the Nantes shoemaking guild specified what meals masters had to provide for their journeymen: "an *ordinaire* of two meals a day, with meat on the five *jours gras* and soup on the remaining *jours maigres*." Eventually the masters converted the meals into an extra wage of ten *sous*.[37] Whether the ten sous was a fair price for those meals is not clear, but the effort to monetize the benefit, regardless in whose favor, helped to specify its value. Meals made up a certain defined proportion of the total remuneration of journeyman shoemakers. In the case of patron–mistress contracts, both parties agreed more generally to "gifts" or "furnishings." Social convention made greater specificity unnecessary as patron and mistress seemed to share a general sense of what kinds and quantities of gifts were appropriate. However, gift giving was a source of tremendous tension, in part because it functioned as a form of bonus pay and hence was interpretative. "Lack of generosity" and "failing to live up to promises" were the most common explanations given by dames entretenues for leaving patrons.

The balance of benefits differed depending on the contract. In some cases, honoraires constituted the bulk of remuneration. In other cases, material objects did, especially if the relationship was short lived. Furniture or expensive jewelry given at the start of a relationship made up a greater percentage of the remuneration of a mistress maintained only for a few weeks, over one in a longer-term arrangement. Similarly, food made up a greater proportion of the total pay of women with low honoraires, though wealthier dames entretenues generally kept better tables.

Some of these pay packages were of enormous value. Satirists took ready aim at the most lucrative of them, exaggerating their worth. In his mock petition by femmes galantes to the lieutenant general of police, Turmeau de la Morandière laid out a contract in which, among other expenses, the patron had to pay 40,000 livres worth of his mistress's debts; furnish an apartment "magnificently"; give her 30,000 livres in diamonds and another 30,000 in silver plate; allow her to get twelve new dresses a year, three per season; pay the wages of ten servants; give her still more diamonds on her birthday; and pay her 40 louis (960 livres) in honoraires.[38] But while few contracts represented this kind of wealth, in most instances, the lack of specificity as to the value of furniture and gifts makes the total value of kept-woman pay packages difficult to estimate.

Equally difficult to determine is the total net worth of any kept woman. After-death inventories and reports of robberies give us snapshots of wealth, or portions thereof, for particular women at specific moments in their lives. For example, a few years after bankrupting the Russian prince Belonsiski, Demoiselle Lacour reported a theft of 50,000 livres worth of items, mainly jewelry, including a diamond necklace (15,500 livres) and a pair of earrings (9,600 livres).[39] In another example, the notaries who inventoried Marie-Joseph Laguerre's belongings after her death declared that had 300,000 livres' worth of goods and 30,000 livres in rente.[40] From this sort of evidence, we know that women who secured more lucrative contracts were better able to accrue considerable material wealth. But these women were rarely as rich as these "snapshots" suggest.

The material wealth of kept women necessarily expanded and contracted, sometimes dramatically. Rarely were dames entretenues continuously employed, forcing them to hock items to pay bills. Some were terrible wealth managers or got caught up in the relentless acquisition of luxury items. In fact, one hallmark of the hyperelite was their riches-to-rags tendencies. In 1760, Deschamps held a ten-day auction of her items to pay what the police estimated to be 300,000 livres' worth of debts.[41] Four years later she would die in poverty.[42] In 1768, Guimard had to auction off her house through a sort of lottery, selling 2,500 tickets for 120 livres each.[43]

Further destabilizing their wealth, kept women rarely owned outright items listed in police reports and after-death inventories. Like every other Parisian, dames entretenues lived on credit. The dancer Marie-Louise Denis, for example, was arrested for debt in October in 1768 because she had paid back only forty-two hundred of the eighty-two hundred livres she had borrowed to buy a pair of earrings.[44] Many mistresses owed rent to landlords. Demoiselle Lacour, who had experienced a considerable drop in fortune after the theft, filed multiple complaints against her landlord after he seized some of her things as surety for her rent.[45] Even the famous Sophie Arnould was successfully sued by her landlord for back payment of a year's rent (twenty-four hundred livres).[46]

The value of the contract, however, was not limited to the material wealth it conferred. There is one last component of the exchange between patron and mistress to consider. While it was nowhere in their formal agreement, patrons sometimes provided legal protection and patronage for their mistresses. Both could be of inestimable value. The infamous altercation between Jeanne Vaubertrand and her landlord, Monsieur Roger, a *procureur* at the Châtelet, is illustrative. Vaubertrand responded to Roger's complaints regarding the noise coming from her apartment by throwing a full chamber pot at his door. When his wife complained, Vaubertrand's patron, Monsieur Séguier, *avocat général* of the Châtelet, slapped Dame Roger. The Rogers sought justice from multiple policing cadres, all of which declined to intercede—as did the lieutenant general of police—once they learned Séguier, who as avocat général was a high ranking official at one of the two most powerful courts in the capital, was involved. Barbier reported that across Paris, people thought Vaubertrand should be evicted, while Séguier should make amends to Roger and his wife. Yet nothing happened.[47]

Numerous patrons tried to get their mistresses onto the stage and, once there, continued to intervene to advance their mistresses' careers. The philosophe Jean-François Marmontel reported in his memoirs that his friend Barthélemy-Augustin Blondel de Gagny, *trésorier de la caisse des amortissements*, was "one of the most faithful devotees of the Opera," and "had taken as a mistress an aspirant to this theater, whom he wanted to debut playing the great roles of Lully." Gagny invited Marmontel and some other friends to his home in Garge in order to hear his mistress, Mademoiselle Marie-Madeleine Saint-Hilaire, and "give her lessons."[48] Saint-Hilaire did become an opera singer, and thereafter Meusnier kept a file on her. Not every patron offered such services. Nor did every dame entretenue aspire to a stage career or face legal problems. For those who did, such help was critical. It also put the patron-mistress relationship, at least in this one aspect, squarely into the context of the patron-client relationship, which was a motor of advancement and identity in the Old Regime.

Even in this final aspect, then, the demimonde contract reflected wider practices of worker remuneration. It differed, however, in ways that were important in enabling some dames entretenues to achieve financial success. The contract assured that whatever the personal feelings of patron and mistress, their relationship was fundamentally a financial one. Yet the vagueness of certain parts of the agreement made it a particularly flexible instrument through which a patron could express his feelings, whether good or bad, in material or monetary terms. It was in the promise of gifts and furnishings that lay the greatest potential for wealth, because the value of these items was not specified. In principle, they were pay for a job well done, either in satisfying a patron or in having mastered the ability to "draw" additional support from him. In fact, this is not entirely true. Many a patron embellished his mistresses to enhance his own status or lifestyle. Whatever the case, under the best of circumstances, a mistress could "hit it big," so to speak, through expensive gifts and extras. Of course, unhappy or financially strapped patrons could just as easily leave their mistresses with little more than the base pay stipulated in the contract. But even when things went badly in a particular affair, the fundamental economic basis of these relationships benefited dames entretenues by stabilizing remuneration, at least for a month, which was more security than many female workers enjoyed.

The tension over the value and quality of previously unspecified gifts makes clear that mistresses were not necessarily passive parties in either the negotiation or execution of their agreements. That tension was a function, in part, of the ambiguity of the mistress's status, between lover and employee, wife and whore.

✎ The Mistress's Side of the Contract

To what did a kept woman agree when she accepted a patron's honoraires and extras? The police never enumerated her responsibilities. This may have been a particular quirk of police reporting, but that is doubtful. It would have been uncharacteristic of the inspectors, who otherwise were focused so tightly on the details of the exchange between patron and mistress. Perhaps mistress obligations were not reported because, unlike those of the patron, they were never spelled out. Rather, once a mistress agreed to accept honoraires, she agreed not to a specific subset of dame entretenue services—say to have sex three times a week—but to every service kept women offered. In other words, she agreed to become a mistress. By the time the police began to devote considerable resources to following kept women around town in the 1740s, galanterie was a well-established occupation. The duties of a kept woman were defined and standardized by convention and tradition, and reified in fiction and satire.[49]

First among these was the duty to have sex. But what kind of sex? The inspectors' reports are rather silent on this front. It seems clear that a certain degree of amatory skill was expected. After having slept with Demoiselle Dubois, Monsieur de Rochefort supposedly told Brissault that he did not want the girl as a mistress because "she was not at all pleasing to bed."[50] A mistress also was supposed to have a more developed sexual repertoire than a wife. This was the complaint of the duchesse de Montmorency. After her husband began to maintain Rosalie Astraudi, star of the Comédie-Italienne and former mistress of Le Normant d'Étiolles, the duke apparently demanded that his wife perform the same sorts of sexual acts as his mistress. The duchess was horrified and complained to her father-in-law, the duc de Luxembourg. He was horrified as well, so much so that he threatened to incarcerate the actress were she ever to see his son again.[51]

What exactly did Montmorency ask his wife to do? Well-read Parisians in the mid–eighteenth century were aware certainly of a wide range of sexual behaviors. Manuals of sexual positions had been available since the sixteenth century, with the publication of Aretino's (in)famous *Sonetti lussuriosi* (1524) and Marcantonio Raimondi's *I Modi* (1524).[52] According to Robert Darnton, a modern version of Aretino's work, *L'Arrétin moderne* was among the nation's best sellers in the later part of the eighteenth century along with such salacious, prurient works as *La Putain errante (The Wandering Whore)*, a work sometimes attributed to Aretino, and *Thérèse Philosophe*, which includes vivid depictions of sex acts. In fact, Darnton includes ten pornographic works among the top thirty-five best sellers of the period (though not all these works had clear descriptions of sexual acts).[53] In her work on Renaissance pornography, Bette Talvacchia notes a "literary transvestism" in the *Sonetti*; Aretino gives women authoritative voices that they use to articulate male sexual fantasies. In doing so, they are both subverting sexual order and supporting it by praising male sexual prowess. This textual tension is evident in much eighteenth-century pornography and in many ways parallels power dynamics in the demimonde, in which women were construed as sexual aggressors but in which their very existence is tied to reinforcing "exaltation of male sexual prowess and praise of the phallus."[54]

Familiarity with a panoply of sexual positions, however, does not necessarily mean that patron and mistress were putting them to the test. The police are largely silent on this topic.[55] Contemporary observers are equally unhelpful. Even Casanova and the comte de Tilly, both of whom recounted their "conquests" with gusto in their respective memoirs, rarely related the intimate physical details of these affairs. We can get a sense of the sorts of acts in which people engaged from the *procès verbalux* of libertine priests arrested by the police in various lower-end Parisian brothels, as well as from the reports the madams submitted to the police. The most common sexual practices aside from vaginal intercourse were masturbation and intercrural intercourse. Flagellation, which was a mainstay of pornographic literature, was, as we have seen, also fairly common among customers in eighteenth-century brothels. The madams who discussed their customers' and clients' sexual tastes reported, in addition to vaginal intercourse, sodomy and masturbation. Oral sex, as Lafosse indicated, was uncommon. The police confirm its rarity by saying that prince de Carignano had "unique tastes" since he "demands of the mouth the services most women prefer to render with their hands."[56]

What is more important than what a couple did in bed was that they shared expectations of what should happen there. In the police reports, instances in which a couple broke up because of reported sexual dissatisfaction were few. Half concerned a mistress who was problematically modest, while the other half concerned women who were thought not to be modest enough. In these instances, "libertine" could include any number of characteristics in addition to a desire and willingness to engage in an expanded sexual repertoire. It might refer to a woman who was crude in speech and decorum. She might eat or drink too much or be excessive—spilling over rigid cultural boundaries—in some other manner. According to Inspector Marais, Demoiselle Raye turned down the offers of Baron Warseberg because his sexual proclivities were too libertine (and he was not paying enough), although she accepted him eventually.[57] If reporting is any indication, the majority of couples either had no sexual problems or none that were serious enough to merit separating. This suggests a number of possibilities. Either sexual performance was not very important in patron-mistress relationships, or performance matched expectations. The latter seems more likely. The role of reputation in the demimonde was such that any patron seeking an experienced mistress with particular sexual skills or inclinations easily could identify such a woman.

While we cannot be sure exactly what the patron and mistress did in bed, we do know that they spent time together, usually at her residence. Most men saw their mistresses three times a week, often for a few hours in the evening or midafternoon. The marquis de Voyer visited his mistress, Demoiselle Puvigné, a dancer in the Opéra ballet, three to four times a week. He arrived in the evening but never slept there.[58] Some patrons stuck to schedules or gave advance notice. Others came and went as it suited them. Some couples regularly supped together. The comte de La Marche (Louis François Joseph de Bourbon-Conti), a prince of blood and the son of the prince of Conti, always visited his mistress, Demoiselle Coraline, an actress in the Comédie-Italienne, at night. He would sup there and generally leave between two and three in the morning. Like most patrons, de la Marche rarely slept at his mistress's house.[59] Those patrons who did spend the night were in the minority. Patron and mistress also left the house to attend supper parties and the Opéra, or to walk on the boulevards or in the Palais Royal.

Beyond amatory and companionate services, patrons understood that their honoraires, furniture, gifts, and payment of household expenses also purchased fidelity. Patrons cited infidelity more often than any other grievance when breaking off relations. Expectations of sexual fidelity, however, were complex. Some patrons found being cuckolded humiliating. In his memoires, the comte de Tilly described a friend's reaction to learning that Tilly had slept with his mistress. The man "felt humiliated" and had wanted to fight the young chevalier. Instead the two men got drunk together.[60] Monsieur Dumas, whose story opened this chapter, however, simply told Darques to "get dressed."

Most patrons were infuriated. In his typically understated way, the philosophe Jean-François Marmontel reported in his memoires that his affair with Marie de Verrière cost the aspiring actress her patron, the maréchal de Saxe. When Saxe, who had several other mistresses at the same time, found out about the relationship, he swore to never see his mistress or their child again. This was a promise Marmontel claims the military leader kept, more or less, reuniting with his daughter only after the death of her mother.[61] According to the file Inspector d'Hemery kept on Marmontel, the breakup cost Verrière twelve thousand livres a year, although he said that the couple reconciled.[62] Nevertheless, patron anger could be quite expensive, as Gautier found out when Dumas took half of her things.

Yet with time, many cuckolded patrons reconciled with their mistresses. Some even came to resign themselves to their mistresses' infidelity. For example, Monsieur Courval and Demoiselle Aubin broke up repeatedly, not over her infidelity, supposedly, but over its public nature. At a party marking their reconciliation, Aubin publicly vowed to be more discreet in seeing her greluchon, rather than promise never to see him again. Courval, for his part, vowed to be more generous and less violent.[63] Extrapatron affairs were so common that, while many men were angered by their mistresses' behavior, few were surprised. And while some kept women went to extraordinary lengths to hide their infidelities, others barely could be bothered. Infidelity was more acceptable in some instances than in others.

Of the various factors that shaped expectations of fidelity, the most significant was money. A primary patron, like Dumas, who a spent considerable sum on his mistress (and even sacrificed his financial health for her), expected that she would have sex with no one else, regardless of how often he saw her. In part, he expected fidelity because he gave her enough money to maintain herself in luxury. She had no need to take on additional work. That insufficient honoraires authorized extrapatron sex was demonstrated in the case of the fermier général Laurent-René Ferrand. Ferrand paid his mistress Demoiselle Rossignol fewer than 8 louis (192 livres) a month. Inspector Marais reported that, as a consequence, the tax collector gave his mistress "permission to find a patron who accommodated her better, permission which she used fully in taking all the passades that Brissault could arrange for her."[64]

How little was little enough to validate cheating, however, has to be considered in context of household budgets. The sum of 192 livres may not have been enough for Ferrand's mistress, but such a salary was more than enough for the younger Demoiselle Crousol who, maintained at 130 livres a month, did not seek additional clients, at least according to her dossier.[65] Dumas's expectation of fidelity also was based on convention. Emotional attachment, the subject of the next chapter, also informed patron reactions to infidelity. Besotted patrons often put up with a lot, including being put into secondary positions. But emotional attachment also could work the other way. A very attached patron might be more likely to dismiss a cheating mistress. It was acceptable for a mistress to sleep with other men, as long as she did not love any of them. Any such attachment destroyed the fiction on which the patron-mistress relationship was based.

The extent to which a particular couple circulated in libertine circles also helps explain how they valued fidelity. For some Parisian libertines, no amount of money would (or was necessarily supposed to) secure exclusive access. Perhaps Courval and Aubin were of this ilk. The guest list of their reunion party was a "who's who" roster of the demimonde. Cécile Rotisset de Romainville, an Opéra singer, clearly articulated these sentiments. When her patron, Étienne-Pierre Masson de Maisonrouge, *receveur général des finances* for the *généralitie* of Amiens, bitterly complained of her open infidelity with the comte de Coubert, Romainville reportedly said that "she had never intended by attaching herself to him to be sequestered from the rest of humanity and to live in slavery, and that Monsieur Coubert would come to her place as would many others."[66] Despite his objections to her behavior, Maisonrouge married Romainville two years later, causing an enormous scandal.[67]

Finally, some men may simply have had a higher tolerance for infidelity than did others. The fermier général Thiroux de Montregard paid Demoiselle Astraudi twelve hundred livres honoraires but the police doubted the relationship would last. "Monsieur de Montregard will not hear of any substitute," wrote Meusnier, "and Demoiselle Astraudi is not of the same mind. Nevertheless she promised to comply on this point."[68] The relationship lasted less than two months.

The expectation of fidelity always was in tension with a counterexpectation that kept women regularly would seek out and engage in extrapatron sex, as though they were constitutionally incapable of doing otherwise. The expectation of cheating was so normative that it challenges the use of words like *infidelité* (infidelity). In fiction and contemporary documents, the dame entretenue was constructed as a woman who was eternally unsatisfied. She might have sex with other men for money because whatever she was earning, it was not enough. Or she might have sex for pleasure, because her sexual desires were thought to be considerable. In police writing, it was only the rare mistress who was both modest and remained faithful to her patron. A closer reading, however, reveals a more complicated situation. Kept women cheated for money, for fun, and for love. Many, as we shall see, tried to maintain private intimate lives alongside their professional ones. Others understood that certain forms of cheating helped in establishing their sexual capital. For many, it may indeed have been part of their professional ethic. In the open market that was the demimonde, most kept women, even those who were paid quite well, eventually turned an eye toward the prospect of a better patron—one who paid more, bothered her less, or was, for any number of reasons, found to be more agreeable. Landing a new patron often involved some passades in advance of a contract.

The contract, as an instrument that systemized the material expression of sentiment, carried the potential to greatly enrich some dames entretenues, while providing a certain security of payment for most others. Ironically, what enhanced the potential for a big payoff was the unilateral structure of the contract, in that it specified the patron's obligations while leaving those of the mistress undefined. In doing so, the contract—the very instrument that made the patron-mistress relationship transactional—had the capacity to downplay its own transactional nature. Failing to enumerate a mistress's sexual duties confused her status and made the relationship ambiguous. It separated her from the prostitute, and in some ways made her closer to a wife. Marriage contracts also defined an economic relationship while leaving the parameters of the sexual and intimate one to custom (although marriage contracts detailed the economic contributions of both parties). Differentiating the mistress from the prostitute created space in which to imagine that she was not fully mercenary, laughing at her patron behind his back, but that she might share at least some of the sentiments that inspired him to spend so much. The contract, then, conferred respectability on the mistress, making her a better candidate for emotional and financial investment. But if it was the structure of the contract that allowed mistresses to gain wealth, it was in its execution that they had the potential to exercise power, however limited.

☛ Execution of the Contract

The central assumption to which all parties assented when forming an agreement was that sexual services were to be rendered only in exchange for money or goods and, unlike many other business transactions, they would not be delivered on credit. The first sexual engagement traditionally occurred only after a patron had provided his future mistress with an initial gift or her first honoraires. The two transactions might take place on the same night, or within days of each other. Money, then sex. Moreover, were the patron to stop paying, his mistress would owe him nothing, regardless of what had transpired between them. This was demonstrated clearly in the case of a man Inspector Marais identifies as the Russian prince Belonsiski, who, over the course of a few months, had spent as much as eighty thousand livres on dresses and furnishings for his mistress, Jeanne Tellefert (Demoiselle Lacour), a singer in the Opéra. When he found himself out of both money and credit, Lacour "completely dismissed him." According to Inspector Marais, who had taken a specific interest in the prince, there was little the latter could do about it; Lacour's behavior was "by the rules." Marais paid a visit to the prince and asked him how he found "French manners," to which the prince supposedly replied, "I would be charmed . . . if she were to take another lover. I was not made to be with her forever. I advised him [the new lover] myself in order to ease the way. I see her now only rarely."[69]

The expectation that kept women would only have sex for money also was shown in a battle over some jewelry between the dancer Demoiselle Deschamps and her patron, Denis-Joseph de La Live d'Épinay, husband of the writer and educational theorist Louise d'Épinay, who was Rousseau's protector. According to Inspector Marais, Monsieur d'Épinay had been charged by a relative to buy a particular piece of diamond jewelry worth sixty thousand livres. Deschamps convinced her patron to let her wear it to the Opéra, after which she refused to give it back. D'Épinay thought of having a police commissioner forcibly retrieve it, but the fact that he was sleeping with Deschamps complicated matters, as did d'Épinay's history as a patron. He was a well-known figure in the demimonde, having supported numerous opera singers and dancers at such expense that d'Épinay's father sent him from Paris to stop the financial hemorrhage. D'Épinay had bejeweled his previous mistress, Demoiselle Briseval, yet offered Deschamps nothing. All this constructed the loaned object into a gift, and hence payment for services rendered. D'Épinay eventually negotiated a resolution with Deschamps. The jewelry was to count as her étrennes.[70] Deschamp's nineteenth-century biographer claimed the dancer bragged about her exploit.[71]

The understanding of sex as a commodity was in evidence not only in interactions of dames entretenues and their patrons, it was explicitly theorized in satire. The *Mémoires secrets* published a letter supposedly, though doubtfully, from Marie-Claude Saron in which the Opéra dancer explained why having had sex with a notary should have canceled the debt of eighteen hundred livres she owed him. "Of everything I have, nothing belongs to me more than my favors," argued faux-Saron, "I have the incontestable right to dispose of them freely and by consequence to give them away or sell them." Anyone who saw the notary, she continued, would realize that "nothing could inspire such generosity" in her and that "I sold what I was unwilling to grant for free."[72]

Both parties may have submitted easily to the fundamental principles of the contract as they carefully negotiated its specifics. They did not always agree, however, on whether the contract was being properly executed. Of particular concern was timing of payment. When Alexandre Jean Joseph Le Riche de La Poupelinière proposed maintaining Angelique Coignard, known as Beauchamp, a dance student at the Royal Academy, he promised her an apartment with new furnishings. Poupelinière expected that Beauchamp would begin to have sex with him shortly thereafter, but she chose to wait, she said, until he had fulfilled his promises and the apartment was ready (which would have been some time as the furniture was being built). According to Inspector Meusnier, who was following the negotiations, Poupelinière was quite taken aback and claimed that he was not used to "being refused and that she was the first to doubt his word."[73] Beauchamp and Poupelinière never resolved their differences.

Equally problematic, as we saw with Gautier and Dumas, was the question of the ownership of certain objects. When ownership was openly contested, the argument pulled on both explicit and implicit elements of the contract, because at issue was whether the mistress had earned the item in question. When, in March 1765, the dancer Marie-Catherine Lachau (called Adélaide) accused her patron, the comte de Sarmeny, a retired Spanish colonel, of stealing jewelry from her, the latter defended himself by arguing that Adélaide had not sufficiently pleased him, and hence the items were not really hers. In the context of the demimonde, the case was a serious matter. Adélaide filed a complaint with Police Commissioner Jean-François Hughes in which she stated that Sarmeny had taken a key from her pocket as she slept, emptied out her cabinet and left a note. Adélaide accused Sarmeny of theft and nothing more. She did not mention their relationship. In response, officers of the Châtelet armed with a warrant searched Sarmeny's apartment.

In his inevitable countercomplaint, Sarmeny made his case: he had already spent a great deal on Adélaide, having paid for the renovation and furnishing of her current apartment and much else besides. When the dancer asked for diamonds and other jewelry, the count refused doubting he would receive an adequate "return" from such an investment. He was willing to lend her diamonds and the other valuables in question. However, he would not give her their receipts—and hence full ownership as he construed it—as he had done with the furniture. When she demanded the receipts, he reiterated the point that "he was not suitably satisfied with her to give her these objects." They had supper, slept together, and again fought in the morning, at which point, the count claimed, she was verbally abusive, told him to leave, and gave him back the jewelry. Sarmeny's defense is telling. Despite his vastly superior status to that of his accuser, he did not simply claim that the items were loaned and expect to be taken at his word. Instead, facing conventions in which mistresses were paid in just such objects, he explained *why* they were only loaned. Adélaide did not please him. As she had not adequately fulfilled her sexual and companionate duties, she did not deserve extra pay. Sarmeny further supported his own case by depicting Adélaide as greedy, ungrateful, and rude and in so doing, made the assumption that the authorities would understand that gifts were a form of payment for certain services, services that she had not rendered.[74]

Adélaide was not the only person who sought help from local officials. If a couple could not resolve their dispute (and if, it seems, they were on relatively good terms), they might together go to a local police commissioner, hoping for some sort of adjudication. In many cases, the commissioner recorded his intervention in his logs but would not necessarily draw up a *procès verbal*, the paperwork required to start a legal proceeding. Suzanne Elizabeth LeGrand (Demoiselle Beaumont) and the German baron de Wolfsdorf had such a disagreement. One night after the theater he asked to take her home, presumably to have sex. She assented, and the baron ate and slept at her apartment. A few days later, he gave her a small ring containing three diamonds worth 7 or 8 louis (168–192 livres). When he did not pay her honoraires (at 300 livres) on the first of the month, as they had agreed, she stopped sleeping with him. He then asked for the ring back, and she refused, having, in the meantime, set up a "fixed appointment" every Monday with the duc de Grammont. Wolfsdorf took LeGrand before Commissioner Cadot, who ruled in her favor.[75] Wolfsdorf was a baron, but LeGrand, a part-time actress and dancer and full-time sex worker, got to keep the ring. In making this ruling, Commissioner Cadot affirmed the custom of the contract, even if it was not a legal instrument. In resolving this case between patron and mistress, the commissioner acted as he did in a thousand other disputes between small-business owners and their clients. Cadot acknowledged that in providing sexual services, LeGrand deserved compensation.

In some cases, police agents were asked by patrons to retrieve items at the end of a relationship. A former infantry captain Meusnier identifies as Monsieur Le Bretonnier, involved the police in an effort to recover items he left at the house of his mistress, Agathe Rigotier, known as Zélie. These included three horses and various items of silver. He claimed in a letter to the lieutenant general that he had not given Zélie these things, nor had he ever intended to. He did not, however, contest her continued possession of other gifts valued at more than twenty thousand livres.[76] As the case of Adélaide and Sarmeny reveals, what constituted ownership was not always clear. Sarmeny claimed receipts were required, and similarly, Raime, following Gautier's "humiliation," wanted the new furnishings put "in her name." Yet, the police assumed Adélaide's ownership without the paperwork.

It was standard in eighteenth-century France to take a dispute to an arbitrating body. Most industries had one. In her article on the business of acting, Lauren Clay shows how the Comédie-Française became the arbitrating body in disputes between actors and the directors of provincial companies.[77] In the trades, there were many bodies and institutions that had policing powers. Depending on the nature of the conflict, the first attempt might be to resolve it within the guild itself. Outside authorities who might be called on should internal resolution mechanisms fail included municipal officers or sometimes the lieutenant general of police, and failing this, the courts. Kept women did not form a guild, nor did their work world mirror one. They participated in a sexual open market, meaning that in principle almost any woman could hire herself out as a mistress to any man. The demimonde had no internal mediating authority. The police came to fulfill that role.

Submitting to the police for mediation, however, was voluntary. While the police investigated what they considered to be legitimate accusations of theft, as they did with Adélaide, they would not help a patron sort out a property dispute unless asked to do so. Very few patrons asked. As we saw in the case of Dumas and Gautier, other patrons recovered contested items themselves, although there are few such cases in the police reports. That patrons could recover such items, even items specifically enumerated in the contract, puts their very ownership in doubt. It emphasizes the degree to which the contract was not binding even if most parties respected it as a convention. There were no legal ramifications and almost no social ones for breaking it. Moreover, we should not forget that by definition, Gautier and her colleagues entered into relationships with men who were economically, politically, and socially superior. Dames entretenues were extremely vulnerable. If a patron decided to mistreat his mistress, there was often little she or her family could do.[78]

It is tempting, then, to argue that the convention could break down under the will of a determined and powerful patron but what little evidence there is suggests the opposite. Sarmeny claimed Adélaide did not earn the jewelry. Dumas took back his gifts only after proving to himself and to witnesses his mistress's infidelity. In retrieving or trying to retrieve items, these men did not break the contract; they honored its forms. They claimed that the goods in question had not been earned and in doing so, they revealed an understanding that Adélaide and Gautier owned their own sexual labor. Kept women claimed this ownership through their actions, specifically in cheating on their patrons and, as we shall see, in ranking them.

❧ Contracts and Patron Ranking

Kept women like Gautier, who had more than one entreteneur at a time, ranked them. That ranking determined how a mistress related to each of her patrons and how they related to each other, if only indirectly, through her. In deciding who had what kind of sexual access, and who she might humiliate, Gautier and other successful kept women exercised power.[79]

In the case of Gautier, Dumas was a primary patron. Dumas was a primary patron because he had a contract, the terms of which were sufficient to maintain Gautier at a level she accepted, because he honored those terms and was granted, at least in theory, exclusive sexual access to his mistress. A primary patron always was accommodated. As such, Dumas was entitled to see his mistress when and where he wished and she organized her other affairs to support his belief in her exclusivity. But what of the chevalier Darques, hiding in the bed of a lackey? Although he was rich, there is no indication that Darques paid Gautier, which would make him a greluchon, a "lover of the heart" or boyfriend. In many cases, mistresses had secondary and even tertiary patrons, defined by the fact that they paid less and that they paid less reliably. Such men rarely were beholden to a contract and hence to the payment of honoraires. They often gave cash and gifts on an irregular but necessarily frequent basis.[80]

But even a patron with a contract could be explicitly denied exclusive sexual access if he did not pay enough. A poorly paying primary patron, like Ferrand, usually accepted his mistress taking on additional professional engagements to pay the bills. In theory, she would do so discreetly and without inconveniencing him. Secondary patrons, on the other hand, were discommoded openly, a regular reminder of their inferior status. However, well-paying secondary patrons were rarely cooperative in this regard. Monsieur

Pelletier de la Houssaye, *maître de requêtes*, supported Catherine Ponchon, a dancer in the Opéra, at 720 livres honoraires. He also provided her with a letter of credit with which she purchased more than 3,600 livres of food and wine over the course of several months. Yet Houssaye was only the secondary patron. The primary, the chevalier de Mocenigo, ambassador from Venice, supported the dancer at a cost of 1,200 livres a month. Despite the size of his honoraires, Ponchon would not grant Houssaye "honors of the Louvre" (allowing him to see her publicly). She required that he take various precautions to avoid being seen, the most onerous of which was visiting only after eleven in the morning so as to avoid any possibility of running into the ambassador, who supposedly left at this hour. Already impatient with such restrictions, Houssaye rejected them altogether when he learned that Ponchon had been lying to him. The morning slot was regularly taken by a third man, either another patron or a boyfriend, who simply hid when the ambassador was around. According to the police, Houssaye said "I paid lavishly enough to go to her house with my face uncovered when it pleased me."[81] When sums from a secondary patron were considerable, the pecking order and its associated privileges were not always clear.

While secondary patrons, regardless of what they paid, may have been annoyed by inconvenience or frustrated by working around the primary patron, in one sense they actually held privileged positions over their better-paying brethren. Together with his mistress, the secondary patron engaged in the process of hoodwinking a more powerful man. The dangers and pleasures of this form of alternate adultery were explored widely in contemporary libertine novels.[82] The complicity suggests that the secondary patron had greater emotional access to his mistress, since together they deceived another. Emotional access increased as payments decreased, culminating with the greluchon.

A man wanting to have a relationship with a kept woman negotiated which position he would occupy. Whether he took the position of primary patron depended on a number of factors, the first being whether the job was available. Another consideration was cost. Women long in the business had established costs, determined by the size of the household they had to support, the lifestyle they wished to maintain, and their own status. While women new to the demimonde or those with low sexual capital might accept the best offer, more experienced kept women rarely budged from a certain range of honoraires. Demoiselle Raye, for example, demanded twelve hundred livres a month from at least one prospective patron. Inspector Marais claimed that the cost of her household, which included a mother, grandmother, two sisters, and several servants, repulsed many potential suitors.[83] The idea that kept women had set costs was evidenced by the few examples of copatronage, when two men split the cost of maintaining a dame entretenue. Some patrons allocated a set amount of money to pay for a mistress, regardless of who she was. For these men, mistress keeping was a fixed cost like rent or food.

Men often changed patron positions. When Dumas fired Gautier, Darques was suddenly tasked with her maintenance. In another instance, when Monsieur Pressigny de Torigny, a gendarme officer, started to support Demoiselle Villet, a dancer in the Comédie-Française, at 360 livres a month, he told her that she was at liberty to find a better patron, but with one caveat: were she successful, he wanted to "retain the post of greluchon" at 10 louis (240 livres) a month, just until he had to report for duty.[84]

Mistresses used the contract as a way to rank patrons. In doing so, they regularized infidelity, making tacit a claim of ownership over their sexual bodies and labor. By ranking and cheating, mistresses exercised agency. We should not, however, overstate its degree. Since all but a few mistresses needed patrons to survive, few had the option of leaving prostitution, which was the ultimate display of empowerment. Moreover, as cheating was both expected and usually done privately, without the intention of public notice, it is perhaps best characterized as form of systematic resistance, one enabled by the contract system. The contract then served the interests of kept women in multiple ways. One more we must consider is its role in the development of sexual capital.

❧ Contracts and Sexual Capital

The range in the size of honoraires and the value of gifts raises the question of what determined whether a dame entretenue would be maintained at 130 livres a month like Demoiselle Crousol or 2,400 livres like Demoiselle Deschamps. No doubt experience, patron wealth, and bargaining skill were important. But focusing on the particularities of the negotiation distracts from the bigger question of why some women regularly secured patrons who would pay 2,400 livres while others lived precariously. Mercier was of the opinion that it was completely random, a matter of luck and fads.[85] A larger part was surely savvy and a certain kind of aggressiveness. Some women must have had the knowledge and gumption to create opportunities to meet patrons and the skill to land them. But it was not all luck and operational know-how. The value of the contract both reflected and determined sexual capital. The higher a dame entretenue's sexual capital, the greater the demand for her services and the more she could command for them.

The concept of sexual capital is minimally developed in scholarship. Pierre Bourdieu argued that beauty was a form of cultural capital but was not concerned with sexuality more generally. Working from Bourdieu's arguments about forms of capital, British sociologist Catherine Hakim developed the idea of "erotic capital," which is conceptually akin to my theory of "sexual capital."[86] Like Hakim, I understand sexual capital to be a personal asset, similar to social, economic, or cultural capital. It was extremely important for all women, not just for professional mistresses, because its core component was virginity. When virginity was lost without marriage, a girl moved from an economy of sexual honor to one of sexual capital and the nature of that capital changed.

In the demimonde, the construction of this asset was complicated. Dames entretenues with high sexual capital tended to have certain physical and character attributes valorized by demimondaine society. Or more accurately, they tended to have a high sum total of these qualities, strong areas compensating for weak ones. There were no descriptions of kept women with unattractive faces *and* bodies, or women who were unattractive *and* insipid. But beyond body and personality, sexual desirability hinged on an equally important second layer of social determination, a self-reflective mechanism by which the demimonde established value. The most desirable kept women were desirable in part because high-status men or important institutions like the Opéra identified them as such. As far as the sources permit us to understand it, sexual capital was a multilateral construct in which the body was read as attractive not just because of its innate qualities, but because its owner's success as a mistress rendered it thus. Let us start, then, with the physical qualities.

Ideals of beauty in the mid-eighteenth century come down to us from art and are described at length by contemporaries.[87] However, if there was an aesthetic ideal for dames entretenues, like the high foreheads and blond frizzy hair of sixteenth-century Venetian courtesans, it had little impact on how these women actually looked. The most detailed account of the appearance of these women as a group comes, not surprisingly, from the inspectors, who regularly described their surveillance subjects. In the inspectors' view, what counted as pretty varied greatly. Inspector Meusnier declared that Demoiselle Raime was, at age fourteen, just when Dumas had met her, "fit to be painted" with her blond hair, her small but lively eyes and her delicate features.[88] The inspectors preferred blond hair to black or brown, although Meusnier praised dark eyes, as long as they were not too small. Eyes that were, like Raime's, "vifs" and "spirituelles" were ideal. In his writing, pretty women had good eyebrows, faces that were not too long and pale skin. Snubbed noses were undesirable, as were those that were flat, long or too small (aquiline was okay). Both inspectors preferred "fine" features, considered freckles as disfiguring as smallpox scars, and clearly appreciated a good set of teeth, which were a symbol of youth.

Nevertheless, beauty, at least as Meusnier perceived it, was less significant than one might think. In a small sample of forty descriptions, he labeled only one-third of the women as "pretty enough," "pretty," or "very pretty," while one half were "not pretty" or even "ugly." A greater proportion— about half the sample—had desirable bodies in his opinion. Yet many of the women Meusnier considered unattractive had successful careers. For example, the inspector claimed that Marie-Thérèse Biancolelli, an actress of the Comédie-Italienne, had a "foolish and inane looking face." She was, nevertheless, supported by a series of high-paying patrons, at least one of whom appears to have lost control of himself over her, spending so much that he had to flee Paris and was later locked up by his family, presumably to stop his devouring of the family's patrimony.[89] It may be that Meusnier had a different standard of female beauty than other men, or that his contempt for various kept women biased his assessment. The inspector's disdain, however, was not consistent with his assessments of attractiveness; some women he considered beautiful were also those he most despised.

The inspector did, however, provide an explanation as to why women who ranged, in his opinion, from being physically unremarkable to downright ugly *were* sexually attractive to a host of patrons. In many instances, it was a question of liveliness. For example, Inspector Meusnier described Demoiselle Villers's face as having been so devastated by smallpox that she was heavily scarred. She was "hardly pretty," he wrote somewhat sarcastically, but then added, "what is most pleasing about her is her vivacity."[90] From both police reports and other sources, we get a sense of the highest paid dames entretenues as animated individuals with strong personalities. For the inspectors and indeed other observers, however, liveliness was multivalent. In addition to being a personality trait, it was an aesthetic quality. They used the word *vif* to describe eyes. Deschamps had "les yeux vifs et beaux" (lively, beautiful eyes). "Yeux vifs" referred as much to a quality of mind as to appearance, the eyes being a mirror of the soul. The 1762 dictionary of the *Académie Française* connected the two, stating a person with "les yeux vifs" had eyes that were "brilliant" and the ability to understand things quickly and deeply.[91] "Les yeux vifs" implied a certain intelligence and presence, and these were qualities attributed to most successful kept women.

Liveliness, however, did not refer to sexual performance, about which the inspectors said surprisingly little, providing nothing more than an occasional prurient quip. Inspector Marais, for example, reported that Demoiselle Marie Lelache "passed for being a very good lay."[92] But Marie Lelache's amatory skill yielded no great career. For the short duration that she was under police surveillance, she was never paid more than two hundred livres a month and experienced periods of unemployment during which she had to move into a brothel. At the moment police reporting stopped, she was being supported by an ex-hairdresser. In a counterexample, Inspector Meusnier wrote of the actress Demoiselle Brillant, age twenty-nine, that "formerly she enjoyed the reputation of being good to seduce, but three children and long service has, according to those who would know, quite changed those things."[93] Yet four years later, Brillant—now thirty-three—was being maintained by the marquis d'Hautefort, former French ambassador to the Habsburg court. He paid her one thousand livres a month.[94]

The paradoxical careers of Lelache and Brillant should not imply that sexual skill or compatibility was unimportant. Rather, it suggests that sexual skill was only part of a constellation of factors that made a dame entretenue desirable. This argument is supported by the contract, which was negotiated *before* any sexual activity took place. Of course there were patrons who had sex in passades or at brothels with women they later maintained. But in most instances, a patron would not have had the opportunity to sleep with a prospective mistress before hiring her for a full month. Some of these women had been at work for a while and hence had established reputations. Others did not.

Beyond the physical body, sexual capital was also a function of social presentation, specifically taste. In looking at both the furniture and home decorative objects of a dozen of the hyperelite mistresses, Kathryn Norberg showed how their consumption of fine furniture was highly visible, the focus of much public interest and discussion. These women exercised careful choice, drawing on a range of cultural influences, in working with artisans to execute their desires; part of their public identity was as consumers of these objects.[95] For many kept women, much of what they wore and possessed were gifts the design over which they had limited influence. However, even for the dame entretenue who had little say over her wardrobe and furnishings, social presentation was still a component of sexual capital. This is because *what* she owned—beyond its design—and how much it cost mattered a great deal. Many tried to direct gift giving over the course of one relationship or across many relationships to acquire the kept-woman "panoply," the set of items that publicly marked them as dames entretenues. The panoply included certain kinds of clothing, furniture, jewelry, and decorative objects. The monetary value of the panoply constituted a form of sexual capital.

Of particular importance to kept women were diamonds. In his work of literary criticism, the author Abbé Clément joked that there was a "council" of *filles d'Opéra* (female Opéra performers) that met in the wings of the theater. The singer, Mademoiselle Coupée, was president and joining required the possession of forty thousand francs in diamonds.[96] In another example, Demoiselle Lacour supposedly told the duc de La Vallière that "diamonds were the Cross of Saint-Louis of our profession."[97]

While some patron gifts were enjoyed privately, many, like diamond jewelry, were intended for public display. In this way, patrons decorated their mistresses and displayed them as they might some other luxury possession. In that the Opéra audience clapped and shouted the name of a patron when his bejeweled mistress appeared on stage, the mistress was an expression of the patron's wealth and, in some instances, his taste. The value of a kept woman's panoply, above and beyond its styling, simultaneously enhanced her own sexual capital and that of her patron. In other words, social presentation constituted sexual capital because it represented the value other elite men placed on a particular commodity, in this case, a kept woman.

This was the case for another component of sexual capital, salary history—meaning honoraires—established though the contract. While a dame entretenue could not display her honoraires as she did her diamonds, police reporting signals that the size of these monthly stipends was a subject of demimonde gossip. Some were mentioned in the *Mémoires secrets*. Honoraires, then, established a femme galante within a certain category of value known to others in the demimonde. Some women had unstable earnings, their honoraires varying wildly from patron to patron, but most did not. What evidence we have from the police reports suggests that in the majority of cases, salary remained stable or climbed steadily until reporting stopped. For example, in three years, Demoiselle Raye was paid either 600 or 720 livres by five different patrons.[98] Honoraires were a simple (though inaccurate) means of comparing the value of contracts and hence provided kept women with a way to take advantage of what were perceived as better offers. In leaving one patron for another who offered higher honoraires, kept women increased their own sexual capital. They showed not only that they were worth more but that they would leave when they could to earn more, making them a harder-to-acquire commodity. Although the police reports were secret, their general existence was widely known. One wonders if the attention their inquiries brought to the terms of the contract, specifically the honoraires, helped kept women see them as a way to assess relationships.

In addition to appearance, personality, and salary history, artistic talent and membership in a theatrical company also contributed to sexual capital. That sexual capital accrued from membership in the Opéra was so well known, mothers wishing to establish their teenage daughters as mistresses tried to enter the girls in the Opéra school. The mothers were right. Girls in the ballet school attracted enormous attention from potential patrons, debuted with much higher honoraires than other girls, and tended to have much longer careers in the demimonde. Actually being on stage increased sexual capital so much so that when Deschamps started to have serious financial difficulties, she asked for her old position in the Opéra corps de ballet. Meusnier reported that Deschamps arrived at the Opéra wearing what he estimated to be 100,000 livres in diamonds and bribed Jean-Barthélemy Lany, the old dancing master, with a snuff box worth 1200 livres, all to secure a position that paid 200 livres a year.[99] Why was membership in the Opéra so valuable? Casanova was puzzled by this, noting that even "ugly and untalented" dancers were so popular they could cheat on their patrons. He concluded, "What chiefly makes French noblemen eager to have a girl at the Opéra to their credit is the fact that all the girls there belong to the King as members of his Royal Academy of Music."[100]

Inspector Meusnier also acknowledged the considerable increase in sexual capital inherent in Opéra membership. He reported that Marie Hernie, known as "Marie Trois Tétons" because she supposedly had three breasts, had been residing in the worst parts of town (where she was presumably a low-end prostitute) until she met Claude Javillier, a principal dancer in the Opéra, who trained her and got her onto the stage. Soon after she made her debut, and while still living with Javillier, she came to be supported by the comte d'Estaing, whom she supposedly bankrupted. Meusnier reports that she took 100,000 livres from her next patron.[101] In this narrative, entry into the Opéra lifted Marie from her down-and-out existence into a luxurious one.

The inspector put considerable stock not just in the allure of the stage, but in the power of actual talent. Meusnier had described Marie-Thérèse Biancolelli as unattractive but added, "nevertheless, she had talent."[102] He wrote of the stunning talent of the famous principal dancer Marie-Anne de Cupis de Camargo. This was important, he claimed, as it was only her talent that, in his words, "made more than tolerable, we wouldn't dare to say likeable, a figure as ugly and as without merit as hers."[103] Other sources contest Meusnier's descriptions of these two women, which suggests that he was either wrong in his assessment of their beauty or right in his assessment of the power of their talent.[104] The inspectors were not alone in seeing talent as an aphrodisiac. Jean-François Marmontel admitted that he could not distinguish his love of the actress Mademoiselle Clairon from his love of her talent.[105]

While it is interesting to note what patrons found sexy, more significant to the themes of this chapter is what dames entretenues did with this knowledge. Sexual capital, like other capital, could be increased. In other words, dames entretenues were not passive subjects of their own biology and market forces. They actively invested in themselves. Many tried to join the Opéra. All sought the highest paying patrons they could, regularly leaving relationships to take advantage of better propositions. In tough times, kept women were more inclined to engage in passades to survive than to be hired at considerably lower honoraires, which could damage their salary histories. They worked to acquire panoplies of the best possible quality, displaying them whenever possible to make a public statement of their worth.

Dames entretenues could also develop those components of sexual capital that were body based. Beauty could be enhanced through makeup. Women new to the demimonde might very well have studied their more experienced peers, or even have been tutored by them, in how to dress, hold their bodies, and conduct themselves. Such exchanges might have included discussions of sexual technique. It was an old theme after all, the subject of Aretino's foundational work of modern pornography, a modern version of which was a best seller in the eighteenth century.[106] Those mistresses who came up through the brothels or who worked with madams may have been coached. Body-based attributes were a form of capital that could be increased with investment. Kept women, then, were both consumers of commodities and commodities themselves. To complicate the picture, their consumption was part of their own self-fashioning as commodities, designed in part to increase sexual capital and hence their worth. Both aspects involved active engagement with markets.

Of equal importance was the recursive nature of sexual capital acquisition. Bourdieu posited that his three forms of capital—social, cultural, and economic—were fungible, meaning that social and cultural capital could be turned into economic capital.[107] This was also the case with sexual capital. When kept women exchanged access to their sexuality for money and material gain, they turned sexual capital into economic capital. When they used sexual desirability to gain access to networks of aristocrats and financiers, connections that resulted in numerous benefits, they converted sexual capital into social capital. They were also able to transform sexual capital into cultural capital—*institutionalized* in the sense of membership in the Opéra, or *objectified* in the sense of ownership of decorative objects.[108] What is central to the argument is that these conversions occurred in both directions. Kept women converted economic, social, and cultural capital into sexual capital as well. Owning certain objects, being in the Opéra, and being seen in the company of certain elite men increased one's sexual capital. Bourdieu argued that "economic capital was at the root of all the other types of capital."[109] In the case of kept women, the underpinning construct was sexual capital. This helps to explain how women who started with nothing (who inherited nothing) were able to become members of the hyperelite. They and their less successful sisters did not simply invest in themselves. They leveraged and releveraged—the process was recursive—all the resources available to increase and advance their wealth and status in the demimonde.

So at last we turn back to the story of Dumas, Gautier, and Raime, and their scuffle over sexual access and property. It is possible that Dumas was furious with Gautier, having suddenly learned of her longstanding affair. More likely, he staged the entire scene as a means to retrieve wealth from a mistress of whom he wished to rid himself so that he could maintain someone else. Even beyond the initial ruse, the entire scene required planning: money on hand to pay the servants, a waiting carriage, and an exit plan. That Raime moved in so quickly suggests that Dumas had already negotiated an agreement with her before leaving Gautier. In giving Gautier's apartment and things to the young dancer, Dumas spared himself a great deal of the expense necessary to establish a new mistress at a moment when he was supposedly having financial difficulties. But whether he was animated by anger or calculation (or both) that March night, his behavior was telling. He confiscated items he had given to Gautier only after a very ritualized scene that gave him public justification to do so. In cheating, Gautier had violated a tacit element of the contract. Dumas used her behavior to nullify her ownership of his gifts. The contract was not legally binding, yet Dumas's behavior provides evidence of its strength in governing patron-mistress relations.

The central argument of this chapter is that the contract helped kept women earn money and establish agency because it simultaneously constructed sexual acts as services that could be sold, establishing their public value, and yet left the status of the mistress ambiguous. Officials adjudicating disputes, as well as patrons engaging in them, similarly construed what mistresses did as a form of sellable service. The conceptualization of sex-as-commodity mattered to mistresses. It meant that they had a right to what they were given and what they were promised. Honoraires and gifts were not gifts in the true sense of the word; they were earnings. The idea also established the mistress as the owner of her sexual body. In cheating, for whatever the reason, kept women challenged the notion that ownership could be sold to another, even temporarily. Moreover, it turned the sexual body into capital, which the mistress owned and in which she could invest.

One direct benefit of the way in which the contract constructed sex as work was a certain level of security. As workers, elite prostitutes were extremely vulnerable, not least to competition. They operated in an open market into which new girls entered every day. For most kept women, those who lived from patron to patron, the contract provided the promise of payment, at least for a month, since they were paid a month at a time. As a flexible instrument that materialized the expression of emotion, it enabled some kept women, like Raime, to do quite well quite quickly. Expensive gifts could catapult a novice to the top of her profession, something more difficult in other industries in which women worked.

Because of the contract, the patron-mistress relationship was at once a clearly defined exchange and a very hazy one. It was a commercial construct, but it was based as much on emotional and sexual attachment as it was on predetermined visiting times, a payment package, and a pretense of fidelity. Its structure differentiated the mistress from a prostitute, leaving her somewhere between a worker whose pay had been negotiated and a wife, whose economic relationship to her husband was written into a contract while her personal one was not. It endowed the relationship with a certain level of plasticity, allowing its participants to experience it as something more personal and meaningful than the exchange of a louis for a passade. This ambiguity was central to the success of mistresses. Mistresses tended to accrue the most wealth in long-term relationships, in which the interpersonal relationship mattered a great deal.

This might explain why patrons stuck to the convention of the contract when they did not need to. As we have seen, these agreements were not legally binding nor was there any social retaliation for breaking them. Moreover, they were made with women who had little power to demand such an arrangement. Some, the stars of stage, had cultural stature and leverage, but just as many were living in brothels, serving whoever came through the door. Pensioners were the dregs of Parisian society. The contract system was in place because it benefited patrons. It facilitated the establishment a household in which to enjoy the company and body of a mistress. It was also a way to win the favor of a woman rather than coerce her into a sexual relationship. But the real issue lies elsewhere. The contract did certain cultural work. It made mistresses respectable and more appropriate as intimate partners. It thereby allowed for the possibility that these relationships were not merely mercenary, but meaningful. It is to the experience of these relationships that we now turn.

✒ CHAPTER 6

Male Experiences of Galanterie

On January 16, 1750, Demoiselle Dallière, a dancer in the Opéra ballet, was rumored to be leaving her patron of long-standing, Pierre Henri de Tourmont, président de la cour des aides (president of the coinage court). He had failed to cough up the twelve thousand livres in rente viagère he had promised. This fight was just another episode in the long stormy history of the couple. The man for whom Dallière was leaving Tourmont was Alexandre Jean Joseph Le Riche de La Poupelinière. Poupelinière, an extremely wealthy fermier général, is quite well known for his patronage of the performing arts in the period. In his private theater at his home in Passy, he mounted musical productions with an orchestra directed by Jean-Philippe Rameau drawing major talent from all the Parisian companies. Writers, composers, and performers flocked to his salon, and some even resided in apartments there. Dallière, like so many other performers, had attended parties at Passy, possibly with Tourmont. About Tourmont less is known. He was married and, by the time he became involved with Dallière, had three children. He was from a Parisian robe noble family, his father having held the position of *conseiller* to the Parlement de Paris. He frequented brothels and was rarely without a mistress. Two years later, he would become the patron of Anne Michelet.

It was not long after receiving Poupelinière's first honoraires that Dallière reconnected with Tourmont. Giving her "what he could in order to preserve his former privilege," according to Meusnier, Tourmont easily slid into the position of secondary patron.[1] By August of that year (1750), Demoiselle Dallière added to her regular roster of lovers a third man, a greluchon named Villeclos. Described by the police as a mauvais sujet, Villeclos had the dubious distinction of having been expelled from the army only to support himself through "various schemes on the streets of Paris" and through Dallière, who rented him an apartment.

That Dallière had two paying patrons and one "eating one" (in the words of the police) did not stop her from engaging in passades. One night after the Opéra, the dancer was approached by a German baron, Schmitt, who proposed that they return to her house. They did, only to be interrupted at 2:00 a.m. by Villeclos, who arrived demanding to see his mistress. He screamed from the street and banged on the door "like a deaf person," according to Inspector Meusnier. Although Dallière's maid told him that her mistress was with company, Villeclos insisted on entering anyway, "to ascertain the extent of her mutiny." According to the police, the baron was told that the wild man was Poupelinière's valet come to warn that his master was on his way. The baron quickly dressed and went home. In the words of the police, "Villeclos got into bed and found it already warm."[2]

At some point in that spring, Poupelinière finally became aware of his mistress's infidelity, or perhaps of its extent. One of Dallière's competitors informed the fermier général that his mistress had been sleeping with Tourmont every night and was now pregnant. (She was quite far along. How Poupelinière failed to notice this is puzzling.) Poupelinière's reaction was swift. He cut off his former mistress, and to great effect. By the beginning of April 1751, Dallière was broke and about to give birth. Villeclos, the baby's purported father, had left town. It was Tourmont who helped her, though Dallière abandoned her baby in the *Enfants-Trouvés* (foundling hospital).[3]

Two years later, we learn that Poupelinière had gotten back together with Dallière only to break it off, again on account of her infidelity.[4] The couple eventually came to be on good terms. The rest of Dallière's story, however, really belongs to Tourmont. In his book, *Daughters of Eve*, Lenard Berlanstein describes their affair as alternating periods of domestic harmony with those of turbulence occasioned by Dallière's efforts to increase her income by taking on additional clients.[5] Tourmont was not wealthy enough to support her in the style that she desired. When Dallière became pregnant by another man, Tourmont left, but he eventually returned to support her, emotionally and financially, through her pregnancy. Dallière later became pregnant with his child. At this point, police reporting stops.

How can we understand the experiences of these men: Tourmont, Poupelinière, Villeclos, and even the German baron? What did each expect of his dealings with Demoiselle Dallière? Were they pursuing love, pleasure, companionship, or even status? Was the relationship most meaningful in public or in private? Each of these four relationships with Demoiselle Dallière was unique. Yet, as we explored in chapter 5, each also exemplified an ideal relationship type determined in part by the contract. Poupelinière was the primary patron, Tourmont the secondary, Villeclos the boyfriend, and Schmitt a passade. Interactions between kept women and their clients were structured by well-known conventions. In addition, the public performance of these relationships often was ritualized.

Yet within these fairly heavy strictures played out a sequence of human dramas. We have to wonder if Tourmont did not love Dallière or if Poupelinière's feelings as well as his pride might have been hurt by her behavior. Only two years before, he had been publicly humiliated by his wife's affair with their neighbor, the duc de Richelieu.[6] In this particular case, the feelings of these men are not recoverable. What we can do is try to determine the parameters of their expectations by focusing on the social and cultural meanings of these relationships. We have seen already how the conventions that structured patron–mistress relations contributed to flexibility of experience. Now we will put these relationships into the context of the shifting terrain of elite sexuality to ask why patrons wanted mistresses and what these relationships may have meant to them.

Male experiences of galanterie varied a great deal. To make sense of them and to try to establish parameters of expectation, we will analyze these relationships in two particular contexts. The first considers what happened between patron and mistress without the thought or presence of others. We might awkwardly refer to this as their "private life," embracing the full weight of the concept. The primary component of this private life was emotional attachment. For many patrons, keeping a mistress was about sex and pleasure. It was a normative practice of old aristocratic culture that allowed men (and to a lesser degree women) to seek sexual satisfaction outside the marriage bed.[7] Yet for others, the experience was completely different, infused with an intensity of emotion made popular in midcentury novels. Patrons who fell madly in love with their mistresses showed themselves willing to sacrifice family fortunes and, indeed, safety to be with them. For still others, these were less intense, passionate affairs than deeply important and loving relationships; some patrons found with their mistresses an emotional intimacy they could not create in their marriages. In terms of emotional attachment, then, male experiences of mistress keeping ran along a spectrum. At one end, sex was disassociated from everything but pleasure. At the other, it was part of a larger, meaningful relationship.

Intensity of emotional attachment was not the only element that differentiated male experiences of galanterie. The relationship of patron and mistress to their communities and the media provides a second context in which to consider those experiences. We might call this the couple's "public life," and assess their relationship in terms of its public meaning. For some men, patron-mistress relations seemed to be entirely public constructs, significant only as a mode of sociability and engagement within the demimonde. For many others, publicity not only gave the relationship meaning, it shaped its internal dynamics making mistress keeping as much about status and reputation as about personal pleasure. Yet at the same time, a sizable number of patrons went to great trouble to keep their relationships secret from spouses, family, friends, and the public at large. In the male experience of mistress keeping, emotional attachment and public consideration deeply influenced each other, and both existed along spectrums from open to secret, from detached to attached. Mistress keeping could enhance a patron's status or damage it; as such, it was a function of masculinity.

What follows, then, is an attempt to look at and analyze types of relationships as they fell across both spectrums, keeping in mind that these groupings emphasize dominant patterns but do not encompass the full range of male experience. We will begin with a discussion of the most common social practices of mistress keeping.[8]

✒ Social Practices of Mistress Keeping: An Overview

Broad parameters defined the social practices of mistress keeping. Most patrons visited their mistresses several times a week, though a sizeable minority visited more often, sometimes every day or even several times a day. Relationships in which a patron visited either more than once a day or less than several times a week rarely endured long. Regardless of how often they saw each other, the couple passed most of their time in the mistress's apartment and secondarily, if they could afford it, in a petite maison. In both places, they might entertain guests. Time together in public was spent at the Opéra or at other spectacles where the patron watched his mistress on stage or, if she was not a performer, where they sat together in the audience. Other sites of public sociability included the Palais Royal and the "viewing" boulevards where the couple rode or walked together, as well as assemblies, petits soupers, and balls. In the fall of 1750, a night's entertainment for Demoiselle Amédée and her English patron, Laval, consisted of eating together, attending the Comédie-Italienne, gambling at her house, and then going to the house of a friend.[9] Most men shared meals with their mistresses during their visits, and just as in brothels, eating together was an important prelude to sexual activity. It was far less common for a patron to spend the night, though some certainly did; most patrons slept in their own homes.

Mistresses provided company and sex but not usually other forms of entertainment. They were not courtesans, like *courtigiane honorate* in Renaissance Italy and the *heterai* in ancient Greece, who were hired as much for their musical and conversational abilities as they were for their amatory skills.[10] The image of the French mistress-as-courtesan was popularized in the seventeenth century by Ninon de Lenclos. Like her Renaissance forebears, she integrated sex into a wider language of manners and a series of integrated performances.[11] But Lenclos was exceptional. In the eighteenth century, a very few dames entretenues, namely stars of the Comédie-Française and Comédie-Italienne, were educated and clearly brilliant. Singer and actress Sophie Arnould, interpreter of Gluck, knew Latin and Italian. She was known for her witty conversation—some of her witticisms were later published—and for a while she ran a salon.[12] Marie-Madeleine Guimard also hosted weekly gatherings of artists and intellectuals.

Being an educated conversationalist, however, was neither a requirement nor even an expectation of any kept woman. The duc de Montmorency, for example, maintained for one year a woman who had come directly from the country to Paris seeking work as a maid.[13] It is unlikely they discussed the works of Voltaire and Rousseau. Even Rousseau, as he was writing these very works, shared his bed and sometimes his heart with Thérèse Levasseur, a woman who was barely literate and not, in his estimation, very intelligent. Mercier claimed that it was the unsophisticated (and hence uneducated) girls fresh from the country who made the best mistresses.[14] The education available to most kept women would have made it difficult for them to demonstrate the sort of refinement that made Lenclos famous.[15] At best, those from artisan or working backgrounds could anticipate by age fourteen to have had several years of schooling, in which they may have learned the rudiments of reading, writing, and counting.[16] Their letters to the inspectors reveal minimal literacy.[17]

Whatever a patron expected of time spent with his mistress, there were three general patterns in the frequency of mistress keeping. Patrons following the first pattern rarely kept mistresses. For some in this category, mistress keeping was a deliberate (and single) act that served as a rite of passage prior to marriage. For others, it was the attachment to the individual, and not the larger culturally defined practice of mistress keeping, that held meaning. A much larger group of men were engaged in patron-mistress relationships episodically—the second pattern. For some in this second group, frequency was dictated by fortune; when an individual had the resources, he spent his money on mistresses, passades, gambling, and other expensive pleasures. For others in this group, the rhythm of mistress keeping was shaped by lifecycle. A mistress often was the purview of the bachelor, and perhaps of the widower. Career demands were also determinative. Army officers or officials reporting to posts outside of Paris sometimes dismissed their mistresses when they left town, probably to save money, often with the hope of reestablishing relations on return.

Serial mistress keeping characterized the last pattern. Like Tourmont, men in this last group were rarely without a mistress, spending very little time "single" between relationships. They budgeted for their relationships in the same way they budgeted for their other regular expenses making mistress keeping as much a part of their daily experience as having an apartment or hotel in Paris.

In sum, mistress keeping fit into the elite male lifecycle at every point, with affairs lasting from days to years. Hence, whatever the meaning of the experience, mistress keeping functioned more generally as part of a marriage system. It was defined by the very fact that it was not marriage. Without an officially sanctioned form of heterosexuality, unsanctioned forms, like concubinage and mistress keeping, could not exist. In theory, a man engaged in different activities with his mistress than he did with his wife. In practice this was not necessarily the case, depending on the man, the marriage, and the mistress. Again, the case of Rousseau and Thérèse Levasseur is brought to mind.

In the demimonde, mistress keeping could serve as a substitute to marriage for single men. It was also its complement, the secondary relationship to which various components of marriage could be outsourced. These included recreational sex, companionship, and for some, emotional intimacy: components that were considered the domain of marriage but were not yet part of its general practice. A mistress with high sexual capital could—under the right circumstances—enhance her patron's prestige. This was a very different prospect, of course, from the way in which a bride of high social rank benefited her husband's standing. But the prospect is telling. In the mid-eighteenth century, if sex and intimacy on the one hand, and the enhancement of male status on the other, were the commission of the wife, they were also the claim of the mistress. It is the balance that we will explore below.

⚓ Between Patron and Mistress: The Private Experience of Mistress Keeping

Outlining the social practices of mistress keeping reveals little about the qualitative experience of it for men. How did they feel about their mistresses? Many clearly felt sexual desire, if nothing else. In a letter to Demoiselle Gautier, one suitor copied the style of contemporary pornographic literature as he wrote of his "violent desires when deprived of seeing her." He reported a "burning fire" that "ran through his veins" and "devoured him." Not surprisingly, the suitor was writing to get an appointment.[18] Lust, then, is in evidence, but what of love?

The contours of emotional engagement in these relationships were broad. Some men declared that they had no feelings for their mistresses. Others seemed to care deeply. The marquis de Persenat, the patron of Marie Boujard, was reported to have had a "close connection" to another of his mistresses, Demoiselle Lacroix. He made her quit her position as a dancer in the Opéra several months into her pregnancy. He had her retire to his petite maison, supported her parents, and promised twelve hundred livres of rente to the baby. Persenat's attachment is all the more surprising as both he and his mistress were old demimonde hands.[19] Many patrons were infatuated wildly with their mistresses. According to the police reports, the comte de Hoyn was "in love with" the "charms" of Demoiselle Gallodier and visited her three times a day.[20] The marquis de Sabran was so in love with the dancer La Petite Louison that "he lost his head." He offered her twenty-four hundred livres as a pot-de-vin and six hundred livres a month honoraires. The police identify her as Louise O'Murphy, former mistress to Louis XV.[21] The comte de Klinglin grew "more in love [with Demoiselle Agathe] every day."[22] The duc d'Olonne was "fully in love" with his mistress, Demoiselle Amédée.[23]

We see evidence of the language of love in personal correspondence. The married marquis de Sade wrote to his mistress, Demoiselle Colet, an actress in the Comédie-Italienne: "It is difficult to see you without loving you, and even more difficult to love you without saying so. . . . My happiness is in your hands, I cannot live without you anymore."[24]

It is possible that such evidence of love, brought to us directly or filtered through police sources, was another manifestation of the growing sentimentalism of the period, that patrons were falling in love left and right because it was the vogue to express oneself in this manner. Mistresses, however, were poor recipients of such sentiments. Sentimentalist discourse demanded equality between the partners. Sentimental relationships were supposed to be transparent. Women in sentimentalist discourse were simple and naturally virtuous, while mistresses were not.[25] Moreover, patron love or infatuation could not possibly have been experienced without the heavy fear of dissimulation. Dames entretenues, whether in fiction, the work of diarists and moralists, or the police reports, almost always were constructed as integrally mercenary beings. For the inspectors, a mistress could not genuinely reciprocate a patron's love or affection; patrons who believed otherwise only fooled themselves and, perhaps more important, subjected themselves to public ridicule. In following the affair of Demoiselle Saron, a dancer in the Opéra, and Pierre Durey Harnoncourt, father-in-law of Louis-Bénigne-François Bertier de Sauvigny, the intendant of Paris, Inspector Marais wrote: "She [Saron] is unrelenting towards this old man who is ruled by imbecility and whose brain is filled with the idea that this girl loves him. More likely, she loves his écus." That Saron truly could feel such love was inconceivable. Even Harnoncourt's grandson (a future intendant of Paris) told her that she looked ridiculous.[26]

In the inspectors' telling, love was the exclusive province of the patron, and it functioned as nothing more than a lever to the contract, enabling a mistress to "draw" more and more from her foolish lover. Other commentators agreed that mistresses were constitutionally incapable and indeed professionally disinclined to love back. The comte de Tilly wrote in his memoirs about his father's friend's mistress, who was simply "following the rule" in detesting her patron.[27] Casanova claimed that the "mercenary beauties" of France were superior to those in Dresden in what he called "the art of pleasing, which chiefly consists in appearing to be in love with the man who has found them attractive and pays them."[28] According to Marais, at least one dame entretenue concurred, arguing that reciprocated love was impossible. The inspector reported that Demoiselle Dumirey, in the face of the efforts of the financier Charles Bernard de Marville to "attach her to him intimately," claimed she did not understand how any woman who was paid could possibly love her patron nor take any pleasure from him. Marais conveyed her sentiments, "love demands equality. A kept woman is exactly like a jewel that lends itself for the convenience of a rich man, but without any affection toward him and which he can exchange for another whenever he wants."[29]

In making the mistress a mercenary entity, the inspectors took something that was fundamental to the patron–mistress relationship—that vague emotional and sometimes domestic experience—and reduced it to a commercial construct. In her discussion of the relationships of servants and masters, Sarah Maza allows for a different interpretation of this particular patron–mistress dynamic. Maza argues that while servants were largely focused on being paid, their masters expected obedience and loyalty, indeed "not just formal obedience but an allegiance that extended even beyond their time in service."[30] These differing expectations can be understood, she argues, "if we take into account the dangers and promises that shaped a servant's working life." While masters were acutely aware of their servants' "vulnerability," servants "looked upon their occupation as a temporary plight, a prelude to a better life."[31] There are many parallels between the master-servant and patron-mistress relationship, beginning with a contract that specifies certain forms of service in exchange for pay and over which is laid the expectation of a sort of emotional bond. Patrons also were well aware of the vulnerability of their mistresses, whom they protected from poverty, from arrest, or other harassment, and from being forced by economic circumstances into a brothel or onto the street. Perhaps because they were participating in an open sex market, patrons thought their mistresses should be grateful or that such protection might translate into affection if not love. And mistresses, like servants, viewed their position as a means to an end rather than an *état*, perhaps resenting the requirement of emotional as well as sexual compliance.

Maza, however, does give examples in which servants claimed to have affection for their masters.[32] And the police did ignore their idealized portrait of the kept woman on enough occasions to see individual mistresses as loving and living happily with their patrons. A police mouche reported that Demoiselle Rosalie Astraudi and the comte d'Egmont "were crazy about one another and live together in perfect harmony."[33] Marais believed that the Comédie-Italienne actress Anne-Marie Véronèse, called Coraline, "loved" the comte de la Marche "for himself."[34] The long on-again, off-again affair of Demoiselle Agathe and Christophe Klinglin is another instance in which the police write of true affection between patron and mistress.[35]

Yet if the patron-mistress relationship was discursively constructed as being emotionally bankrupt, one has to wonder whether patrons actually cared. Despite his considerable experience in the demimonde (and his education, which would have made him aware of its discursive rendering) did the comte d'Egmont expect Astraudi to love him when the two finalized their contract? Perhaps part of the satisfaction men found in these relationships was not necessarily in being loved but in the reliable pretense of it. In supporting a mistress, a patron created a universe of which he was purportedly the center. Requiring a facade of feeling was a continuous and rather profound exercise of power on the part of the patron. Because it touched on interior life and required a new sort of compliance, it could be considered more weighty than a patron's putative control over his mistress's sexuality or his very real ability to control her physical environment.[36] We have been tracing the various and complicated ways in which mistresses resisted this exercise of power, as well as demarcating the parameters within which patrons accepted such resistance. Mistresses had some formal power, namely the power to leave, but this power was diminished by economic need. That same economic need often drove infidelity, forcing the patronocentric version of the relationship to contend with a competing mistresscentric one. Fighting, in which some couples engaged often, also challenged the primacy of the patron. But both parties agreed, at least out loud, that only the patronocentric world existed.

Moreover, absent from their relationship were many of the power struggles that would have dominated the patron's life outside of his mistress's company. In the context of increasing authority over the individual, William Reddy discusses the emergence in this period of "emotional refuges," specifically the salon, the Masonic lodge, friendship, and the affective marriage. "These freely chosen connections between persons were based not on family, office, or rank, but on merit or personal inclination. The rigidity of etiquette was ostentatiously set aside in favor of a more open, more egalitarian manner, which, as the eighteenth century wore on, became increasingly sentimental."[37] Perhaps the patron-mistress relationship was another form of emotional refuge. Lenard Berlanstein concurred in arguing that as the demands of family, state, and church were "imposing greater discipline and constraint on individuals," male aristocrats developed a greater sense of self that "found expression in higher expectations for affection and intimacy within a privatized sphere of domestic life." It was with theater women, he argued, that male aristocrats "pursued their own happiness, disregarding formal social obligations."[38] All but a few kept women were removed from le monde, and hence they had no bearing on the constant collective quest for position and advantage that was the ethos of the elite. Spending time with a mistress must have been a form of freedom for many of these men.

But perhaps the opposite is also true. The patron-mistress relationship was not just a space in which the patron could escape the exercise of a certain form of power. It was a place in which he could exercise another form of it. Dena Goodman recently argued that marital success (and the happiness of wives) depended on "how the man she had married exercised the power he now held over her, and on her own willingness to accept the legitimacy of that power."[39] One wonders if happiness was similarly situated for husbands. Mistresses may have exercised informal power within relationships, but they were not wives, protected by dowries, kin networks, a marriage contract, social convention, and the law. Patrons could and did reclaim property, imprison, rape, and beat mistresses with impunity. Beyond the sex, company, real or pretended love, and food and fun, perhaps the exercise of this particular form of power was enjoyable in its own right.

In terms of the private experience of mistress keeping, the benefits for the patron could be considerable: sex and the company of a woman to whom he was attracted, affection real or feigned, a person on whom to dote affection, and the chance to exercise power over another while being free from the control of kin networks and the inexorable push for position and power. Some of these experiences, such as those of love and lust, were the bread and butter of extramarital affairs, regardless of the partners. Others were facilitated by the particular structure of the demimonde, in which patrons had affairs with paid agents who wore a cloak of respectability, over whom they could legitimately exercise sexual and personal power with no fear of social or political consequences. But they were not without risks. In being with a dame entretenue, patrons faced a significant moral hazard, that the women in whom they invested emotionally were faking reciprocity. In other words, in terms of private life, the greatest risk a patron faced was loss of money and possibly hurt feelings; that is, of course, unless he fell madly in love.

✒ Relationships on the Margins

For most patrons, like Poupelinière, the private experience of keeping a mistress mainly fell within the parameters outlined above. Poupelinière visited Dallière a few times a week, paid her according to their contract, and took his meals at her apartment, but never slept there. While the police reports provide few hints of how Poupelinière felt about Dallière, that the fermier was willing to take the dancer back even after she had cheated on him so openly and in spite of his own intolerance for infidelity suggests he liked her a great deal.

But what of Tourmont? Did his relationship with Dallière fit the generalized pattern of mistress keeping? A sizeable minority of men had relationships with their mistresses that did not; the day-to-day experience of these affairs was qualitatively different. The two most common types of these marginal relationships were those in which a patron was madly in love with his mistress and those, like the relationship of Tourmont and Dallière, in which patron and mistress lived together in a form of concubinage.

✒ Mad Love

Some patrons fell madly in love with their mistresses or with women they wished to have as mistresses. What marked these relationships in particular was not only the intensity of emotion, which was no doubt felt by other men. It was the compulsive and manic way in which it was expressed. These patrons showered their mistresses with expensive gifts. They spent excessively, often until they were forced to stop, either because they had nothing left and could no longer obtain credit or because they were forcibly removed from the situation. Such was the case with Michel-François Roussel, the nineteen-year-old nephew or son of a fermier général (his identification in the records is unclear), who had an affair with the dancer Catherine Ponchon. At the time Roussel shows up in the police reports, in the winter of 1756, Ponchon was being maintained by several other patrons. At best, Roussel would have occupied a tertiary position, yet he immediately "overwhelmed" Ponchon with very costly presents including a horse, a cabriolet, a bracelet with his portrait in miniature surrounded by diamonds (estimated at eight thousand to ten thousand livres), and other jewelry that was "in fashion." Despite Ponchon's busy schedule, Roussel came to see her twice a day, renting a carriage to do so. The value of his gifts left Meusnier wondering if the young man had borrowed from usurers. Ponchon also worried about Roussel's spending, specifically the possibility that Roussel's family might have her incarcerated to stop it. Despite being sick and on leave from the Opéra, the dancer demanded reinscription on the academy's rolls.[40] Roussel's spending did not go unnoticed by the man Meusnier assumed was the boy's father, who tried sending his Roussel away from the capital in the winter of 1756. Perhaps Roussel never left, or perhaps he returned, because later that spring the police reported he was in town, again giving extravagant gifts to Ponchon.[41] It is not clear what happened, but it seems that Roussel's family was able finally to contain the young man's spending because, in December, the police listed Roussel only as one of Ponchon's visitors, suggesting that the dancer was allowing him access in exchange for gifts of lesser value.[42]

Like Roussel, many of these patrons went to great lengths to be with their mistresses, often returning to visit following exile or imprisonment. After trying to elope with his mistress, Rosalie Astraudi, in the fall of 1753, Sieur Féron was arrested at the request of his family and imprisoned at the abbey of Saint-Germain-des-Prés. Following his release in the spring (1754), he began secretly to visit the actress again. Meusnier reported that Féron was "more crazy than ever over Demoiselle Astraudi despite the indifference she seem[ed] to feel towards him," and that he visited her at least every other day. Féron had lost his commission in the army. He was living in a rented room with only a single servant, and yet he managed to find the money for "extravagant" gifts to send to Astraudi. Distraught by her feelings for him, he announced that he would fall on his sword in front of her, at which point Astraudi supposedly laughed. Despite the histrionics, by the summer of 1754,

Astraudi had taken Féron back in some subsidiary position to her new patron, the duc de Montmorency. Nevertheless, Féron continued to send Astraudi thousands of livres' worth of gifts. We hear no more of him after this.[43]

Most of these men were young and inexperienced in the ways of the demimonde. Few appear to have maintained previous mistresses. Yet they tended to pair with women who, if not older, certainly had been working in the demimonde for a while. There was a six-year age difference between Roussel and Ponchon. When his affair with Ponchon caught police attention (because Ponchon was under surveillance), Meusnier at first had difficulty identifying Roussel and then, I believe, did so incorrectly, signs that if he had an amorous history it was hardly a notorious one. Ponchon, in contrast, had started working as an elite prostitute and professional mistress ten years earlier and, by the time she met Roussel, was an accomplished kept woman, having been maintained at honoraires of twelve hundred livres. That she had been able to juggle two very powerful patrons, the chevalier de Mocenigo, ambassador of Venice, and Monsieur de la Houssaye, in addition to several greluchons, for several years suggests that she was strategically brilliant and very skillful.

Police and other commentators understood the patron's love as truly felt, but dangerous, and not just because it could result in financial or marital disaster. Féron was not alone in threatening to kill himself. According to Meusnier, Cotelle de Grandmaison, "lost in his love" for Demoiselle Le Chesne who rejected him, was ready to poison himself.[44] Yet in these cases there is no evidence that any of these mistresses reciprocated their patrons' feelings. This was certainly the view of the police. Meusnier called the marquis d'Amanzé a "type of idiot," as, in a matter of months, he spent whatever he could of his large inheritance, in addition to one thousand borrowed louis, on the dancer Demoiselle Hernie. His family used a lettre de cachet to exile him to Île Sainte-Marguerite for a year, "where he had all the time in the world to think of his love."[45]

For inspectors Meusnier and Marais, such relationships, while extreme, were rare. They made up but a handful of the thousands of pairings that the inspectors tracked. For other policing agents, these types of relationships were the logical and probable outcome of any patron-mistress engagement. In his treatise, *La Police de Paris en 1770*, police commissioner Jean-Baptiste-Charles Le Maire argued that kept women were dangerous by definition because they supported themselves by bankrupting men. Le Maire's treatise was a manual written at the request of Austrian empress Maria Theresa, who wanted to establish her own police force. The commissioner instructed, in the case of kept women, that the police were to take action whenever a man "recovered his senses," realized that he had been duped, and sought the intervention of the magistrate. This magistrate, then, was to stop the woman and punish her, all the more severely if she had taken advantage of the man's naïveté.[46] Other commentators built on the image of the kept woman as rapacious, taking advantage of young, wealthy men by ensnaring them and feigning love until nothing remained of their fortunes and their innocence.

In the midst of this experience, however, one has to wonder what the patron felt. As he dodged his family, he spent all of his money on a mistress with whom he was in love, but who might have been asking him to schedule his visits so as to accommodate other patrons. Was he aware of the larger discourse that identified him very specifically as a fool, as weak and emasculated, not in love with a feeling, caring person but with a mercenary construct that could destroy in a manner of weeks the wealth a family had acquired over the course of generations? Did these men think their mistresses loved them? Or was it that, as in the case of the chevalier de Grieux, protagonist of *Manon Lescaut*, who learned that his mistress had betrayed him and would again, they simply did not care? These relationships show an intensity of feeling well evident in other eighteenth-century sources, which also had a great deal to say about the power of passion. In these instances, however, it was a love that, contrary to the newer ideas of marriage and Enlightenment ideas of reason, was irresponsible, reckless, and impulsive—a fiery loss of control, which was the base of a strong antimistress critique.

✎ Concubinage

At the other end of the attachment spectrum were patron–mistress relationships that were a form of concubinage, in which a man and woman who are not married to each other share an enduring, intimate life together, usually, but not always, by cohabitating. Jean-Louis Flandrin argues that, whereas marriage was "a social institution by which families of the same standing entered into an alliance to perpetuate themselves, concubinage was a personal union, an affair of love, at least on the part of the man."[47] In the demimonde, a small but significant proportion of mistresses did live in concubinal relationships with their patrons.[48] These relationships tended to last years, typically ending only because of a change in external circumstances, such as death or sudden financial reversal. Jean-Baptiste Ledoux, *receveur des tailles de l'élection de Paris*, maintained Demoiselle Désirée, a former model in the Opéra corps de ballet, until her death in childbirth, after more than twelve years as his mistress.[49] Marie-Thérèse Biancolelli, an actress in the Comédie-Italienne, was maintained by the marquis d'Hauteville for more than seven years. He left her only when he traveled to Switzerland as part of the French diplomatic mission in 1744. In contrast to the "mad love" relationships, these unions were depicted as being mutually loving and respectful. Meusnier called Biancolelli and d'Hauteville's relationship "very serious."[50] The inspector reported that Dame de Metz and Monsieur Darbonne, *grand maître des eaux et fôrets*, "continue to live together in perfect union," and a year later, he added that they "have supported each other for more than three years with all the pleasures of a novelty."[51]

As opposed to the general practice in which a patron visited his mistress several times a week at her place, spending the rest of his time without her company, these couples built lives together, creating daily routines that allowed them to spend much of their time in each other's company. D'Egmont and Astraudi, for example, took most of their meals with her family, in a house she leased, and spent every night at his petite maison in the village of Chaillot. They left town each night on which she performed, returning to Paris on the day of her next performance.[52] Some of these couples cohabitated, as did the chevalier Christophe-Louis Pajot de Villers and the Opéra singer Demoiselle Lablotière.[53] While D'Egmont and Astraudi's schedule was organized around her theatrical career, some mistresses retired from the stage to live quietly with their patrons. Demoiselle Mainville (also called Rozette) left the Opéra-Comique to live with the duc de Crussol. Perhaps Crussol was not willing to share his mistress with an audience. While time on the stage increased a dame entretenue's sexual capital and enhanced her patron's status, it also left her the object of male desire and longing. Working in the theater took time and focus away from her patron. But retirement was significant. It cut kept women off from an independent source of income and a pool of potential candidates for passades and secondary patronage. Leaving the Opéra also exposed kept women to arrest and incarceration via lettre de cachet. In other words, for dames entretenues, leaving the theater was a great show of trust and dedication to the relationship.

In some cases, these couples lived a semiprivate existence, disengaging from Parisian social life. Mainville and Crussol lived on his lands for four years, during which time they had several children, who lived with them and for whom the duke provided. In this case, however, the retirement was not by choice. The duke was forced to retire to his estates after he had his mistress pose as his wife in a criminal attempt to borrow 100,000 livres. To protect Mainville from his family, the duke had her marry his servant.[54]

Patrons who engaged in these relationships form a loose sort of group. They could be sword nobles (Egmont, Hauteville), robe nobles (Tourmont, Pajot de Villers) or wealthy commoners, some of whom, like Ledoux, were in the process of ennoblement. Many, like Tourmont, already were married.

Tourmont was not particularly rich, whereas d'Egmont was. Dames entretenues who became concubines, however, were not from the same sorts of backgrounds as most kept women. They tended to be from middling or theater backgrounds. Lablotière was the daughter of a *bourgeois* of Tours and had herself married a mirror maker. Astraudi and Biancolelli were from theater families. What these women had in common was that they were educated. This was the same particular subpopulation of kept women who married men of means.

These concubinal relationships were not fully domestic in the way that term came to be understood later in the eighteenth century, but they were intimate. The couple lived together, often with their children. They were reported taking pleasure in being together and appear to have cared deeply for one another. Though the mistress continued to be paid, she seemed more like the wife of a love match than a dame entretenue. Sometimes these relationships mimicked marriage so well that they fell victim to marital problems. During the last three years of his relationship with Demoiselle Désirée, Monsieur Ledoux took on a second mistress. He thereby positioned Désirée, then thirty-three, as a wife. But even this second relationship was exceptionally close. The two slept together every night, either at her place or at his.[55] Is it ironic that it was with mistresses and not wives that these elite men found domestic comfort? What should we make of this phenomenon?

Historically, concubinage among the elite happens most often when they are subject to arranged, noncompanionate marriage. In France, concubinage was widespread and at all social levels before the sixteenth century. Priests were often in concubinal relationships. For the elite, it was a form of domestic polygamy. For the poor, it was a legitimate union, even after the French monarchy rejected the Council of Trent's reaffirmation of clandestine marriage in its great decree, the *Tametsi*.[56] The Gallican church began a campaign against concubinage in the sixteenth century. They had the least success among the poor, many of whom continued to live in concubinal relationships, unable to afford the church ceremony that would legally wed them, or perhaps avoiding it for other reasons. Placets for lettres de cachet provide ample evidence of men and women living together as common-law spouses, even while married to other people. By the eighteenth century, the practice of concubinage—as opposed to shorter extramarital affairs—was publicly tolerated among the poor and among certain small sections of the elite.

Exactly how common concubinage was in the eighteenth century has yet to be determined, in part because it is not always easy to identify or define. It was at once tacitly encouraged by the structure of elite marriage and discouraged by the discourse surrounding it. Elite marriage in the early modern

period was part of a family strategy, and while there was increasing con-
demnation of forced marriage, sons and daughters of these families did not
expect to marry for love. Matches were arranged by relatives, and the new-
lywed couple were expected to work together for the advancement of their
families.[57] Ideally they would come to love each other and share an emotional and sexual life; at least, this was the gist of religious treatises on marriage since the Reformation. These calls for a more intimate form of marriage
came in the very centuries historians associate with the emergence of the
modern family, identified by greater affection between spouses, and between
parents and children. Nevertheless, the marital prescription was tempered by
the expectation that, at least among a portion of the highest ranking nobles,
husband and sometimes wife would seek emotional and sexual satisfaction
outside the marriage. In the eighteenth century, from Regency to Revolution, this sexually permissive elite subculture expanded, giving us a "libertine
moment" in which extramarital fornication and adultery were tolerated, and
in some quarters expected, by greater numbers of nobles, wealthy commoners and financiers. After midcentury, moralists and later Revolutionaries
exaggerated the extent and depravity of this subculture as a way to critique
the monarchy and the Old Regime more generally.[58]

Yet in the midst of this libertine moment, the shift toward a more affec-
tionate, tightly knit nuclear unit accelerated with the development of the cult
of the domestic, happy family, a theme that was explored and depicted in
novels, plays, paintings, and treatises. Most scholars point to the publication of
Jean-Jacques Rousseau's back-to-back bestsellers *Émile* and *La Nouvelle Héloïse*
as a watershed moment in the evolution of this cult.[59] This family was based
on a marriage freely chosen by husband and wife because they were in love.
They had many children, whom they loved, and with whom they passed their
hours over seeking the pleasures of urban sociability. While Rousseau did in-
troduce a full articulation of the domestic ideal, it was clearly in evidence
earlier in the century in genre painting and the *bourgeois drame*.[60]

While this new model was situated, at least discursively, as a rejection of both
older aristocratic culture, especially its marital and sexual values, and its libertine offshoot, the degree to which the elite were adopting it is unclear. The
evidence is mixed. Case studies of individual marriages show many that were
companionate and just as many that were not.[61] Scholars point toward bigger
trends against forced marriage and toward the construction of interior architecture that allowed for greater privacy as evidence of change in the nature of
the family, but these are loose associations and not indicative of a qualitative
shift in elite marriage. Moreover, Dena Goodman has shown that spouses in
arranged matches were perfectly able to build companionate relationships.[62]

However, scholars directly addressing the question of the domestication of the elite and their adoption of companionate marriage agreed that it was not happening, at least not en masse, in the eighteenth century. Jean-Louis Flandrin argued that elites in the second half of the eighteenth century "dreamed of instituting the love-match, but they were incapable of doing this as long as their social power remained based on a material patrimony."[63] Margaret Darrow, looking at the letters and memoirs of aristocratic women, argued that the aristocracy consciously and abruptly adopted domesticity later, during the Revolution. They did so in one generation as a calculated response to pre-Revolutionary critiques, in an effort to retain their position as a governing class.[64] Sarah Maza argues that the increasing representation of the domestic family in culture was not, in fact, a measure of a widening dispersion of "bourgeois" family values but instead a cultural response to a problem posed by individualistic and rationalist discourse that threatened to undermine social cohesion. The loving families represented a new social glue; "society could only cohere if the overwhelming power of family love was recognized, portrayed, and extended from the domestic sphere outward."[65]

To the degree that elites embraced new family values, they did not and could not always realize them within the family.[66] Nor were meaningful extramarital relationships limited to the demimonde. Adultery was endemic among the elite, for women as well as for men. Many of these relationships may have been dalliances or linked to political or social gain, but many were not. Several elite women, for example, had lasting and meaningful relationships with philosophes, many of whom avoided marriage out of principle.[67] Perhaps more pertinent is the example of Thérèse Levasseur and Jean-Jacques Rousseau, who spent a lifetime together. And while it is clear that most of the adulterous affairs among the elite were not concubinage, they did appear to be modern relationships, fashioned by individuals who spent time together because they enjoyed each other's company. The "domesticity" of which Rousseau wrote was growing for some of the elite, ironically, from outside of marriage. To achieve this with a professional mistress was almost mocking Rousseau's image of domesticity, especially given his view of theater women, who, he claimed, were vain, artificial, and corrupt.[68]

❧ The "Public" Lives of Patrons

Regardless of what a patron felt about his mistress, his experience as a patron was shaped by more than the social practices and the internal dynamics of his own relationship. It was equally informed by its public meaning, which was multivalent, shifting, messy, and even contradictory. Keeping a mistress could enhance a patron's status as an essential component of his performance of masculinity. Or it could detract from it, bringing him dishonor. The effect of mistress keeping on a patron's image depended on which public was doing the judging and on the how the patron comported himself. Expectations of comportment were relative. Some men, such as *grandees*, were supposed to keep mistresses; the practice was institutionalized, as it was for the king, with the maîtresse-en-titre. Other men, such as clerics, could not keep mistresses under any circumstances without scandal. Complicating matters, sexual codes among the Parisian elite that determined the legitimacy and meaning of mistress keeping were not consistently tied to occupational or social groupings.

Public meaning no doubt informed how an entreteneur perceived his status and behavior as a patron. But the diversity of views around mistress keeping leaves us with the impossible task of trying to figure out which attitudes a patron may have internalized. The sources give away little on the subject of patron subjectivity. What we can track, however, is his public behavior. Some patrons worked to be noticed, for example, by getting their mistresses on the stage. Others tried to hide their affairs. Examining how patrons situated their relationships and engaged with their peers as patrons does not necessarily tell us how they felt. There are any number of reasons aside from feelings of shame why, for example, a patron might have tried to hide his affair. Nevertheless, looking at behavior performed specifically for the benefit of others gives us a sense of how a patron thought his actions might be perceived, and this was an important part of the male public experience of galanterie. Let us start with the patrons who hid their relationships and then move on to those who tried to flaunt them.

✦ Hidden Affairs

In this study, less than a tenth of patrons in the police reports were shown trying to hide their affairs. Some went to considerable lengths to do so. The chevalier de Mocenigo hid his identity as the patron of Catherine Ponchon from the police for months by meeting her at her petite maison, arriving on foot and without a domestic (and hence without telltale livery or an identifiable coach), wrapped in a large coat.[69]

Some patrons, especially younger ones, hid their activities specifically from their parents. Secrecy was often the only way they could continue relationships that parents sought to end. The father of the comte de Tilly shipped his son off to school when he suspected that the boy was sexually attracted (at age nine) to his nurse. At thirteen, after the comte had begun a sexual relationship with a girl in the village, his father sent him away again, but not before he was lectured by his aunt "on the dangers of certain kinds of liaisons, and on the opprobrium which was attached to seducers."[70] In other cases, it was not in order to teach sexual propriety or to avoid a bad reputation that parents intervened so much as to prevent certain practical outcomes. Parents particularly worried about excessive spending, which could damage family finances, or about a strong emotional attachment, which might lead to marriage. Since the family goals of preserving wealth and honor were shared by the state, anxious parents could and did obtain lettres de cachet to incarcerate their disobedient sons.

Many patrons kept their affairs secret not only from their fathers but also from their wives. Letellier, a bureaucrat with the army in Flanders, hid his five-year affair with Demoiselle Blot from his spouse.[71] In another example, the comte Christophe de Klinglin met Demoiselle Agathe in the brothel of Madam Paris. He paid her debts, set her up as his mistress in an apartment, and eventually moved her into a convent in Colmar so that he could visit her without his wife knowing.[72] Monsieur de Montreuil, former *président de la Troisième Chambre de la Cour des Aides*, kept his affair with Catherine de la Ferté secret from his wife, the formidable Madam de Montreuil, Sade's mother-in-law.[73] Why did they do it? In Letellier's case, hiding his affair was probably necessary to its continuance. He was a chief clerk in the distribution of supplies to the French army in Flanders, a position that would have enabled him to amass some wealth. That his wife was a seamstress, however, suggests that Letellier was of humbler stock than most patrons and from a social group that was scandalized by mistress keeping. Letellier was also a regular visitor at the brothel of Madam Paris. He was at least fifty-five years old and was supporting two households. In theory, a wife could procure a lettre de cachet to incarcerate a husband, but it would have been difficult, as she would need the support of male relatives.[74] We have seen from the lettres de cachet published by Farge and Foucault that some wives did pursue such action, but only when their husbands' actions were so irresponsible as to threaten truly the physical survival of the family, which it is unlikely Letellier was doing. More likely, his actions would have been considered scandalous by his peer group, both because its sexual ethics included marital fidelity and because Letellier was being financially irresponsible, even if not ruinously so.[75] But if Letellier's secrecy is understandable, what should we make of the behavior of Klinglin, Montreuil, and Mocenigo, all of whom were married nobles?

Christophe de Klinglin was from an old, powerful Alsatian family that had helped Austrian and then French monarchs rule the province for centuries. By the time he met Demoiselle Agathe, he was fifty years old, married with children and, as first president of the Conseil Souverain of Alsace, held one of the two highest administrative posts in region. His brother, François-Joseph, held the other. As chief magistrate of Strasbourg, François-Joseph had a brilliant but highly corrupt administration. Although he built palaces and was deeply involved in the arts, he was arrested eventually and tried for corruption by Louis XV. Both brothers were familiar figures in the demimonde. Police records show Christophe frequenting the brothel of Madam Paris. His brother, in his youth, had had a celebrated affair with the French actress Adrienne Lecouvreur, which produced a child. It is believed that François-Joseph ended the affair in order to get married.[76] In short, the Klinglins were hardly a family that condemned mistress keeping generally. The timing of Klinglin's affair, however, suggests that, like his brother, Christophe did not think open mistress keeping was the purview of a married man or, perhaps, that his wife did not. The comte resumed his affair with Agathe publicly only after his wife's death. As a noble, the comtesse would have been habituated to the idea that sexual satisfaction was found beyond the marriage bed. That does not mean that she accepted it. Mathieu Marraud, in his discussion of marital separation among the Parisian nobility, points out that couples' toleration of sexual permissiveness varied.[77] For some, longstanding affairs led to separation; for others, they were not problematic. The nobility was heterogeneous in any number of ways, one of which was in their codes of sexual decorum.

We do not know specifically why Klinglin felt a need to hide his affair from his wife, and hence we cannot know the grounds on which he thought her disapproval rested—financial, social, personal, moral, religious, or even medical. However, we know much more about the attitudes of Madam de Montreuil, wife of Claude-René de Montreuil, toward mistress keeping because of her ongoing conflict with her son-in-law, the marquis de Sade, over his own extramarital sexual activity.[78]

In 1764, the marquis de Sade began to have (neither particularly violent nor remarkable) affairs with dames entretenues, and La Présidente (Madam de Montreuil) did little. One biographer of the family claims that she "may have looked on such frolics as the price she had to pay for having married her daughter to a high-ranking nobleman."[79] But when Sade became seriously attached to and began to maintain Demoiselle Colet, La Présidente broke up the relationship by giving Sade proof of his mistress's infidelity. A year later, in 1765, Sade took his new mistress, Demoiselle Beauvoisin, to his ancestral estates in Provence and passed her off as his wife. La Présidente clearly was furious and wrote to his uncle, Abbé Sade. She said, "I didn't think such demented passions could lead to such excessive indecency. . . . His covert infidelities are an affront to his wife and to me, but this public offence that confronts the entire province is an insult to his neighbors and will be of irreparable harm to him if it becomes known up here."[80] La Présidente sought to keep the affair from her daughter so as to maintain the emotional intimacy of the marriage and to protect her daughter from humiliation. She also was trying to preserve Sade's own reputation and hence his (and her daughter's) future.

La Présidente's objections were based on concern for the viability of her daughter's marriage, put at risk through Sade's serious attachment and his fraud, which publicly usurped her daughter's rights and thereby damaged her reputation. If La Présidente found the mistress keeping of her son-in-law, an aristocrat, to be both scandalous and an emotional betrayal of his marriage, she would have been horrified by the same behavior in her husband. Le Président, even if he thought he had a right to a mistress, clearly was incapable of standing up to his wife. Madam de Montreuil thoroughly dominated her husband. She controlled her family's finances and business dealings and "generally ruled over her family as if it were the world's most orderly and important kingdom."[81] What would have landed Le Président in even deeper trouble, were his wife to find out, was the cost of his affair. His mistress's husband suspected Montreuil had given her 300,000 livres over the five years they were together, money he acquired by selling some of his wife's possessions including diamonds, a gold watch, and a gold tobacco box.[82] In keeping a mistress, Montreuil was not only offending his wife's sense of propriety, he was stealing from her.

We might consider a second possibility with the Montreuils, that the different attitudes toward mistress keeping espoused by husband and wife represent an uneven embrace of the permissive sexual behavior associated with much of the Parisian nobility, as the family integrated into it. La Présidente considered the union of the Montreuils with the ancient sword family of Sade a social coup. It was the first such marriage for the family. The Montreuils were robe nobles, having been ennobled on both sides within a half-century.[83] Le Président's father, Jacques-René Cordier de Launay, a treasurer, had purchased the baronial lands of Montreuil around the time of his son's marriage. La Présidente, Marie-Madeleine Masson de Plissay, was herself the daughter of an esquire, royal counselor, and secretary. The marriage was a hard push into the sword nobility.

The effort of wealthy families to attain patents of nobility demanded considerable sexual and financial asceticism over many generations. The family had to acquire wealth, then manage their fertility and arrange inheritance so as to pass on that wealth as intact as possible to each new generation. The goal required sexual discipline, as families had to limit the number of heirs. It dictated marital choice, sometimes preventing a child from marrying at all. In other words, individual family members had to sacrifice personal desires to the greater needs of the family. Speaking of the eighteenth century, Robert Nye argues that "a specifically bourgeois notion of family honor emerged from the repetition of these strategies. . . . The acquisition of a noble title was only, in certain respects, a glittering veneer that did not replace, but rested on, the bourgeois honor that earned it and preceded it."[84] Sarah Maza and David Garrioch have since challenged the notion that there was a "bourgeoisie" in the eighteenth century and consequently undermined the idea that we can attribute a class-specific set of values to them.[85] But Nye's larger point about the kind of multigenerational discipline required by these families, whatever we might call it, is well taken. Clearly, mistress keeping was antithetical to this ethos.

I am not suggesting that Le Président feared his wife because they were robe nobles who by definition championed an antilibertine sexual ethic, one he was failing to uphold. In fact, looking across the police reports, about a third of the patrons—maybe even more as many of the patrons are not fully identifiable—were robe nobles. Moreover, there is no correlation in the reports between patterns of mistress keeping and social divisions among the elite.[86] Instead, what is at question is whether there was an assimilation process at work. If we agree with Nye, both that a certain asceticism was required and that it would not "disappear overnight," perhaps Le Président was moving more quickly than his wife to embrace certain aspects of their Parisian noble lifestyle.[87]

There is a vast literature on assimilation, but little of it deals with sexual ethics.[88] From individual studies, however, we see that some elites were quick to take up this particular aspect of aristocratic culture, often in advance of ennoblement. Rochelle Ziskin showed how the first generation of financiers living at Place Vendôme in the late seventeenth century adopted some of the public symbols of nobility while they "retained certain customs considered to be bourgeois. Among these may have been the sharing of a bedroom by husband and wife."[89] Ziskin is referring specifically to Antoine Crozat, who, while keeping a bed in his wife's bedroom, also had a mistress, as did many of his peers, including the banker Samuel Bernard. Bernard had a long affair with Demoiselle Fontaine, with whom he had three daughters.[90] By second generation, argues Ziskin, the practice of sharing a bedroom disappeared at the Place Vendôme.[91] Both of Bernard's sons, the comte de Coubert and Président Rieux, were rarely without high-profile mistresses. By this time, financiers had become an archetype of the patron in contemporary literature.

Assimilation is a difficult argument to make, not least because of the dynamism and heterogeneity of the elite in this period. There were established noble families, for example, who were adopting new models of companionate marriage or who had limited tolerance for sexual permissiveness. There were nonnoble families that tolerated adultery. But if we assume that for some rising families living nobly also included the possibility of living a different sexual ethos, we can also see that assimilation proceeded at different speeds.

If Montreuil's motives for secrecy are clear, what do we make of the behavior of the chevalier de Mocenigo, ambassador of Venice and member of an old aristocratic family? His desire to hide his affair seems to be linked to his position as a diplomat. Other diplomats tried to keep their mistress keeping secret as well. Russian prince Belonsiski was so worried that his wife would discover his affair with Demoiselle Lacour and report him to the Russian ambassador that the prince reportedly planned to meet with Marais to troubleshoot the problem.[92] A baron attached to the Lithuanian mission visited Demoiselle La Chanterie in secret, afraid that the grand chamberlain of Lithuania would tell his family about his "derangement." While some of these diplomats may have come from societies in which mistress keeping was considered scandalous, for most, money was probably the issue. Diplomats regularly wrote home asking for more money, pleading that they were broke—a case that would be hard to sustain in the face of mistress keeping.

What all three of these cases have in common was the illicit use of funds. Letellier spent money that should have supported his wife. Montreuil spent money that belonged to his wife. Mocenigo spent money that was supposed to go toward his work. In spending money on their mistresses, these men violated the one rule that transcended social and cultural divisions within the elite: having a mistress should not interfere with a man's ability to fulfill his duties. This principle shaped much of the public meaning of mistress keeping and helps explain why it was considered the domain of bachelors who did not have families to support. Mistress keeping was thought inherently dangerous to the ordered regulation of one's affairs. A weak or enamored patron, or even a self-aware patron in the hands of a skilled mistress, easily could let himself spend more than he could afford. The critique, then, from every quarter was not specifically of mistress keeping, but of a consequent loss of control—the loss of oneself to one's desires or the manipulation of them by another—within the relationship.

This generalized critique of mistress keeping had a specific iteration in the debate over luxury, which suggested that keeping a mistress, in any way, was problematic because it caused weakness. Enlightenment writers evinced a wide-ranging fear that luxury would damage aristocratic fortunes in an age when the mercantile classes were gaining economically.[93] Many also linked the consumption of luxury to a decline in manners and especially in masculinity, which, they argued, bode poorly for France's military future and global power. According to Mercier, men who indulged in luxury were weak, effeminate, and poor soldiers.[94] Like other thinkers, he associated useless spending of money on luxury goods with the useless spending of seminal fluid on prostitutes. Prostitutes who weakened their clients without providing them with children thus exposed another danger of luxury: depopulation. Mercier was especially hard on kept women, particularly those of the Paris Opéra, claiming that they were agents enervating France.[95]

✒ Making Affairs Public

If a small number of patrons hid their affairs, for many others public recognition was an important part of the experience. This was especially true in the context of the theater. Lenard Berlanstein argues that keeping a theater woman "symbolized the unification of exalted status with masculine prowess." A patron could expect to be acknowledged by his mistress from the stage. She would wear the jewelry he bought her and possibly direct any declarations of love towards him and not her costar.[96] So desirable was such a mistress that her patron, according to Casanova, was willing to accept "some of her infidelities provided she does not throw away what he gives her and that she does not cuckold him too brazenly; the nobleman who keeps her seldom objects to her fancy man [greluchon], and in any case he never goes to sup with his mistress without letting her know in advance."[97]

With theater women, then, several systems of status are at play. Men derived status by being recognized publicly as patrons of the eighteenth-century equivalent of movie stars. These women were, if not beautiful, then charismatic and on public display. They had exceedingly high sexual capital. They were officially desirable. Being the patron of such a woman was like owning a splendid carriage, except that in this case, the carriage could chose its owner, conferring even more status. It was an act of conspicuous consumption made more meaningful by the jewels, dresses, or carriages he might give her and which she, in turn, would publicly display. She was a rare and expensive object that he had consumed, conspicuously, and this reflected both his wealth and his taste. This was the case even if she was not well known, but was beautiful and well attired—anything to suggest that she was expensive. As an act of conspicuous consumption, mistress keeping became part of the noble as a "public man."

In speaking of nobles, Cissie Fairchilds argues that "all aspects of their style of life—their extravagant dress, their lavish hospitality, their enormous houses with their entrances, staircases, and rooms arranged to overawe visitors— functioned as public proclamations of their place at the apex of the social hierarchy." Fairchilds argues that central to this representation were servants who "provided opportunities, with their rich liveries and their sheer profusion, for further displays of wealth; they also created "what E. P. Thompson has called a 'theater of rule,' demonstrating constantly to the world the obedience and deference they—and, by implication, everyone else—owed to their masters."[98] Mistresses similarly performed both functions. To publicly display a mistress was to publicly display (at least putative) control over another person, over not just their labor but also their sexuality and emotions, their essential person. This was especially the case with a mistress in high demand.

If a theater woman with high sexual capital was a "conquest" for a patron, one which enhanced his own status, it was not a conquest as imagined in libertine literature.[99] In these works, protagonists were aristocrats (rather than members of an amalgamated elite) who sought sexual partners exclusively of their own social class. The purpose and style of seduction was based either on revealing the hypocrisy of social conventions and contemporary sexual morality, or on manipulating them for the sole purpose of pleasure. The very set of social conventions so disturbing to libertines was absent in the demimonde. In fact, it was often because of their violation of these social conventions that women ended up as elite prostitutes in the first place. If anything stood as an obstacle between the emergence of desire and its fulfillment, it was not modesty; it was money (and sometimes another patron). Nor was it, for the most part, vanity, another target of libertine protagonists. Aside from the stars of the stage, there were very few women in the demimonde who were in the position to reject suitors for other than monetary reasons, and, with the exception of these cases, there was no "conquest." Rather than revealing the hypocrisy of the conventions that governed sexual morality, mistress keeping, as a form of prostitution, actually shored up these conventions by dividing "good" women from "bad."

But libertinism more broadly defined did inform the public experience of mistress keeping for a group of men and women in the demimonde who formed a sort of libertine core. This group populated brothel parties and balls, and threw petits soupers. They can be identified as libertine not because of any larger agenda addressing the social conventions of sex, but because they were more invested in the pursuit of pleasure, especially outside of the confines of social convention, than were most patrons and dames entretenues. For many of these men and women, their relationships had meaning because they were public. The patron-mistress relationship served them as another form of sociability within a group. This is best exemplified by the phenomenon of the "reconciliation party," a fête thrown by an ex-lover or greluchon to celebrate the reuniting of a couple that had broken up. For example, Monsieur de Pressigny threw a party for Monsieur Courval and Demoiselle Aubin to celebrate their getting back together. Both Courval and Aubin made public vows to change the behavior that had led to their separation. In attendance was the libertine core. Re-creating the couple required public acknowledgement.[100] In another instance, the Baron Wangen was "charged with reuniting" his former mistress, Demoiselle Masson, a singer in the Opéra, with her patron, the comte de Rochefort. To celebrate their reunion, Wangen threw a party as well.[101] These were often big events, with fireworks and a feast, as if marking the ways in which the small community was healing itself.

Relationships with kept women carried a variety of meanings, some of which were contradictory. In their relations with Demoiselle Dallière, Tourmont, Poupelinière, and Villeclos each could have expected love, companionship, pleasure, and the enhancement (or loss) of status. Perhaps Poupelinière was searching for a significant relationship with Dallière. About Villeclos we know nothing except that he was the kind of man many kept women married (and then separated from). Tourmont seemed to care deeply about his mistress.

Collectively, mistress keeping provided three services for patrons: pleasure, status enhancement, and intimacy. That mistresses provided pleasure in the form of sex and companionship is hardly surprising. Pleasure was their business, and as such it was not historically specific, although the kinds of pleasure and their meaning most certainly were. However, the relationship of patrons to the second two services was deeply rooted in the changing attitudes toward marriage and sexuality in the eighteenth century. That mistresses could confer status was a function of a libertine ethos. Mistress acquisition could demonstrate not just wealth and taste, but in some instances serve as a symbol of sexual prowess. It demonstrated masculinity. That mistress keeping could, in other cases, impugn status shows that this ethos was not embraced by all, that there were multiple sexual codes in operation within the elite.

Did embarrassment over mistress keeping represent an embrace of newer ideas of marriage? This is a question the evidence does more to complicate than to answer. The idea that companionship, and emotional and sexual intimacy should come from within marriage and not outside it was not an idea invented by Rousseau. It was basic stock of Reformation (and then Counter-Reformation) writings on marriage. And the church's attack on functional polygamy was largely successful. From this vantage point, the explosion and regularization of mistress keeping, alongside a pervasive, almost compulsive adultery within the elite, was a phenomenon unique to the mid-eighteenth century. Cases in which patrons sought to hide their affairs may not have been related to newer ideas but rather to older ones, including the need to hide adultery from a wife whose wealth supported the marriage. But newer ideas were also at work. That some patrons had emotionally intimate lives with their mistresses rather than their wives suggests elite marriage had not yet become an exclusive site for Rousseauian marriage.

What this evidence highlights, then, is the heterogeneity of the elite, who were contending with different sexual codes including post-Reformation ideals, libertinism and domesticity. Perhaps most important, patterns of mistress keeping do not line up with social distinctions among the elite. Sword nobles hid affairs. Robe nobles had them openly. What we are left with is the mandate to think about sexual behavior and morals as categories of analysis within the elite.

The full picture of these relationships, however, must wait until we examine the mistresses' experience of them. And it is to that which we now turn.

➶ CHAPTER 7

Sexual Capital and the Private
Lives of Mistresses

According to police reports, Marie Lemaignon, known professionally as Demoiselle Brillant, had a spectacular debut in the demimonde. In 1742—Brillant was sixteen or thereabouts—she managed to ruin her very first patron, something usually accomplished by dames entretenues only when they were older and had a better sense of their own sexual worth. The patron, François Roblastre de Beaulieu, intendant (steward) of the maréchal de Belle-Isle, spent apparently all he had on singing lessons for his young mistress and bribes to ensure her entry into the Opéra-Comique. That Beaulieu's family subsequently had him incarcerated at Saint Lazare for doing so only enhanced the girl's reputation.[1]

Brillant's theatrical debut increased her sexual capital and hence her choice of patrons. She eventually settled on Lenoir de Monteau, a wealthy fermier général, and if we are to believe Inspector Meusnier, who was following the case, it was in the course of this relationship that Brillant fell in love and quietly married someone else.[2] Her husband, a man named Bureau, was the oboe player at the Opéra-Comique. They tried to keep their marriage secret. Nevertheless, it soon became general knowledge "and did her considerable harm. No one appeared to be in the mood to pay the piper," wrote Meusnier. Brillant's attachment to her husband upset her patrons. Monteau "complained about it more than once, but since his exhortations did not produce the result for which he was waiting," and Brillant refused to separate from her husband, Monteau left her.

By 1749, Brillant's situation was so bleak that she sold her furniture to pay some debts and joined a French acting troupe in London. The move changed little. As in France, Brillant was able to attract wealthy patrons, but her "affairs of the heart" quickly drove them away. In January 1750, she promised to retire from the theater to live with Laval, the rich son of a member of Parliament, who provided her with an English teacher, a house, and a large stipend. One police report even suggested that the couple was engaged (apparently Laval was unaware of Bureau).[3] But after a few months, Laval left Brillant because of her relationship with a greluchon, the brother-in-law of a French police commissioner, who, in the words of La Jannière, the French police agent reporting on her actions, "was not in the position to pull her out of poverty."[4]

Eighteen months after leaving, Brillant returned to Paris (in 1750 she was probably twenty-six years old), now on the arm of her husband, Bureau. Two years later, she debuted with great success at the Comédie-Française and then found Bureau a position as an oboe player with the musketeers. What became of their marriage? Meusnier reported a piece of malicious gossip: Bureau had stumbled on his wife "at work" sometime that same year and left her.[5] Not coincidentally, it was only after their separation that Brillant rejoined the ranks of the best-paid women in the demimonde.

The array of Brillant's lovers—those who paid her, those whom she paid, those whose connections to her were purely personal—raises the larger question of the relationship between Brillant's professional and private lives. Was it possible for women who sold sex and intimacy to claim and to create sexually intimate private lives for themselves? What were the implications of both the claim and the effort to do so? What do the decisions of Demoiselle Brillant and other dames entretenues about whom to charge, whom to pay, whom to marry, and how to balance the relationships off of each other reveal about the connections between these licit and illicit sexual worlds? In other words, how did Demoiselle Brillant and other kept women construct private lives and what were their goals in doing so?

It is too early to speak of private life as it came to be understood in the nineteenth century, based in the home and family, differentiated against a public commercial and political sphere. In the mid-eighteenth century, especially for working people and artisans, the family was an economic unit as well as an affective one. Master artisans lived and ate with their apprentices alongside their own children, selling their goods perhaps from a workshop but just as often from their own living quarters. Even sexual reputation played into commercial prospects; a woman's sexual honor was important to her ability to function as a businesswoman. But while marital relationships could have enormous public significance, they were also the essential core of eighteenth-century private life, as the exclusively sanctioned site of sexual activity. That core was unstable, at least for a subset of the elite. Many patrons were married. Mistress keeping—the outsourcing of sexual pleasure and intimacy to a secondary relationship—put elite marriage into a marriage system in which the meanings of public and private sexuality were confused.

The dividing line between the private and professional sexual lives of mistresses was similarly unclear. Husbands pimped their wives. Dames entretenues married and continued to work. Greluchons, while "lovers of the heart," were also an intrinsic and public part of the demimonde economy. For kept women, relationships existed on a spectrum from those that were clearly professional, and hence public, to those that clearly were personal, and hence private. As is evident in the case of Demoiselle Brillant and indeed many others including Demoiselle Varenne—whose effort to marry her longtime greluchon so captivated Inspector Marais—dames entretenues engaged in both short- and long-term intimate irregular relationships. Some ended in marriage. Most did not. In both cases, kept women financed these "private" relationships with money earned as professional mistresses. Thus for dames entretenues, the factor that most shaped their "private" lives was the same as that which was central to the practice of their public ones: sexual capital.

With respect to marriage and prostitution, we might consider there to be two types of sexual capital. Female virginity was a form of sexual capital. Probity enhanced its value. Technically, this sexual capital was not the possession of the virgin herself but rather that of her father who could sue for financial damages should his daughter be raped or seduced.[6] Women working away from home, however, assumed ownership of this asset and took legal action to protect it by filing paternity suits, for example. In principle, with the sexual consummation that accompanied a wedding, this primary sexual capital was entirely invested in the marriage and hence converted into other forms of capital, namely social and economic. The wife's sexual labor became the exclusive property of her husband. What was left to women was sexual honor, maintained by following the rules of sexual decorum. Sexual honor was not fungible. It could not be turned into something else. Rather, it was a social attribute which women possessed but which also reflected on the honor of their spouses and parents. In practice, however, married women did have sexual capital, but only within the context of adultery. Brillant, though married, explicitly charged Laval for her sexual services. The cost was the loss of whatever sexual honor remained to her. In the demimonde, high sexual capital allowed kept women to engage in different kinds of nonprofessional intimate relationships including, ironically, marriage. Yet, once married, they risked losing control of the very asset that got them there.

Looking at mistress keeping and the marriage system from the perspective of dames entretenues enables us to tease out connections among prostitution, irregular relationships, and marriage. It helps us to explore what galanterie meant for kept women and understand the kinds of private lives they sought to create for themselves.

☛ Procuring Husbands and Wayward Wives

In a sample of 265 dossiers, a little more than one-quarter of the women were married while under police surveillance. Given that reporting often stopped right as these women hit the age of marriage—and that it sometimes stopped because a subject married—it is likely many kept women wed later, when they were no longer of interest to the police. Of the married demimondaines, slightly more than 40 percent followed the same course as Demoiselle Brillant and married only after having become a dame entretenue. In contrast, about a quarter of the women were married *before* entering the demimonde. (For the rest, the police reports do not tell us when the marriage occurred). The two groups of women came from the same types of lower and lower-middling backgrounds and in roughly the same proportions. However, they made very different sorts of matches. The experiences of these women highlight the relationship between sexual capital and agency, as well as the ways in which marriage, which was supposed to secure women financially and socially, diminished both.

Those who married first are hardly distinguishable from the population at large. Brides married grooms of similar social standing to that of their own fathers. Catherine Darlington, for example, married the comte de la Ferté, a man of the same rank and position as her stepfather.[7] Demoiselle Lyonnais, whose father was the ticket taker at the Strasbourg Comédie, married a dancer in the Paris Opéra, where she herself entered the corps de ballet in the years following.[8] Studies of marriage in Paris and other French cities show this to be a fairly typical pattern.[9] These marriages, then, appear to be like any other in this period. They were attempts by two families or two persons to combine fortunes and establish a new household that could provide its members with economic and social security. The issue for the police was in understanding how these particular women eventually became elite prostitutes. In telling their stories, the inspectors linked the private relationship of marriage to professional sex work. The issue for us is slightly different; it is to assess ownership of sexual labor, and hence sexual capital, within marriage.

Not surprisingly, Inspectors Meusnier and Marais thought in each case that resorting to prostitution was a function of bad character; either the wife or the husband was utterly and constitutionally unsuited for marriage. The police depicted over half of the women in this sample as too sexually active or ambitious, or both, to have their various wants satisfied within the confines of matrimony. The affairs of Demoiselle Marquis, called *La Belle Cordonnière* on account of her marriage to a *cordonnier* (cobbler), supposedly drove her husband to abandon her.[10] In 1750, Demoiselle Letellier left her husband, also a cordonnier, to try her luck with the army in Flanders.[11] A man the police identify as Sieur Bourcharla had his wife, the singer l'Hériter, incarcerated for more than two years for her alleged sexual libertinism. She was released only after he died. When Meusnier began reporting on her shortly thereafter, her hair, having been clipped in jail, was still too short to sport contemporary fashions.[12] According to the inspectors, these women left marriage for prostitution. The relationship between the two was sequential. As such, it represented a shift in ownership of sexual labor, from husband to wife as she moved from an economy of sexual honor incorporated in marriage to one of sexual capital. The inspectors show these women as agentic; they were able to exploit their own sexual labor for fun and profit, although we have no idea what occasioned their turn to prostitution in the first place, or whether it was even voluntary.

The virtuous wives in the sample often were married to "bad subjects"—literally mauvais sujets—who pushed their wives into prostitution themselves or provided for the family so poorly, if at all, that the wife was shown to have no other choice.[13] For example, Marais reported that a man he identified only as Sieur Sauval prostituted his wife. The couple's fortunes had declined after he lost his position in the King's Guard, and they had no choice but to live with her impoverished mother. "This frugal life did not at all suit the so-called Sieur Sauval," wrote Marais, "and I have been assured that he forced his wife to be maintained, and consequently to accept the 'tributes' of Sieur Olivier, the *garde-meuble chez le roi* (keeper of the king's wardrobe). [Olivier] supported her for four years."[14]

The inspectors' reliance on character as an explanatory device is not particularly revealing of the relationship of prostitution to marriage beyond presenting a chronology. But their reports do make clear that, for whatever the reason, at some moment something went seriously wrong in each of these marriages. And when it did, these particular women had few resources to help them. Many married women who later became dames entretenues did not have living parents. By the time of their first recorded instance of prostitution in Paris, at least half of married elite prostitutes had lost their mothers (as opposed to less than a tenth in the sample at large), and at least a quarter had lost their fathers as well. Parents often played important support roles in the marriages of their children. Marriages of working people in this period were constantly threatened by the desertion or death of one or the other spouse and, always, by poverty. The lettres de cachet examined by Farge and Foucault attest both to the fragility of the personal relationship and to the extraordinary efforts of spouses and their families to keep marriages intact.[15] Families often provided additional financial resources when those of the couple failed to support them. These could be cash or material goods, a place to stay or social connections that could help the husband or wife find a position. When couples had trouble, families might side with one of the spouses in an effort to force husband and wife back together, even appealing to the king when they thought it necessary. And, when the marriage was going to fail, families might intervene in an effort to minimize the damage.

In addition to being without one or both of their parents, it is likely that many of these women also were without secondary support systems of friends and associates. This is because women who entered the demimonde already married tended to have married young, on average at age eighteen. These women likely would have had less opportunity before marriage to work away from home and develop the skills and connections that could have helped them later. This stands in contrast to most women of such humble social origins, who tended to marry at about age twenty-five, after having worked for ten or more years to accrue a suitable dowry. In the process, they became embedded in larger networks of co-workers, neighbors, compatriots, and employers.[16] As older, more mature women, they would have had greater self-confidence and a greater ability to find work.

The sample of women who married and then became dames entretenues is small. Their particular stories might be explained by nothing more than a specific combination of events and personalities. Nevertheless, familiar patterns emerge from the documents about the relationship of prostitution to social isolation. The failure of these marriages—either their dissolution or their inability to serve as a unit that protected its members—caused the wife to enter the demimonde.[17]

If Sauval's intention was to keep his family fed from his wife's earnings as a prostitute, then the project failed. Few of these marriages endured. The husband's effort to launch a professional sex life for his wife destroyed their private one. Marais claimed that Sauval's pimping broke his wife emotionally. "After such betrayal by her husband, whom she had married only for love, Madame Sauval came to hate him and no longer cared what he did."[18] When Olivier stopped maintaining her, Marais claimed, Sauval forced his wife into other relationships. Years later, when he finally got back on his feet, having found a position with the navy in Brest, his wife refused to follow him there. She preferred, instead, to stay with her current patron in Paris.[19]

In prostituting his wife, Sieur Sauval manipulated the model of the family economy in which husbands relied on spousal labor to create products or services that linked the family to the marketplace. It was not Dame Sauval's ability to weave, however, which her husband was selling. Rather, he capitalized her sexual labor, which, by definition, was his exclusive property and inalienable. By forcing her to go with Olivier, Sieur Sauval pushed his wife into the economy of sexual capital and then lost control of the very asset he was exploiting, though doing so was illegal. In the police reports, procured wives like procured daughters eventually established full ownership of their own sexual labor. Not surprisingly, the disintegration of these marriages helped the careers and hence the professional lives of married kept women; it increased their sexual capital. Brillant's career picked up only after her separation from Bureau.

⚓ The Profitability of Marriage

When we compare married women who became demimondaines to other women from the same social background, we find that they stood out in a number of ways. They married young. They had few resources. The solution to their financial problems was truly fantastic and most probably the product of random chance. Ironically, the other portion of this sample—the twenty-eight kept women who married—fit the working-class model. They left home (or began to work) at age fifteen, worked for ten years, and then married in their mid- to late twenties. The crucial difference, of course, was that they were not milliners or domestics, but elite prostitutes, and that particular career choice greatly influenced who, and possibly when, they would marry. The difference was a function of the relationship between sexual capital and sexual honor.

Profiting from the exploitation of their own sexual capital, brides who worked as dames entretenues appear to have been wealthier at marriage than other women from the same background. According to Olwen Hufton, working-class women were lucky, extremely lucky, if by their mid-twenties they had saved 100 livres in cash.[20] Some dames entretenues, as in the case of Demoiselle Varenne, managed to amass 250 times that in yearly income alone. At age twenty-five she had up to 15,000 livres in rente as well as what the police called "considerable personal goods."[21] But items in hand were not the full extent of her fortune. Like other working women, Varenne had acquired human capital—skills, a reputation, and the tools of her trade— and this too must be considered in evaluating her total wealth. Quite a few kept women had significant sexual capital at the eve of marriage, as reflected in the salaries they commanded from clients. For example, shortly before her marriage to the king's apothecary, the pregnant actress Adelaide-Louise-Pauline Hus was able to wrangle 1,200 livres from her former patron, Bertin de Blagny for every month of her pregnancy, and this was *after* he had left her.[22] In another example, Louise-Madeleine Lany was paid 1,000 livres a month by her patron in the same year as her marriage.[23]

Beyond their actual savings, the value of their possessions, and their earning potential, two-thirds of married demimondaines had a fourth asset, one which was important to consider in assessing their wealth at marriage; this was membership in a theater company. For women from similar backgrounds, guild membership (or even just guild access) with an artisanal skill set was itself a dowry. While not property in the way guild membership was, being inscribed on the rolls of the Royal Academy of Music or the theater companies conferred numerous other securities and protections, not the least of which was financial, and these also must be factored into any calculation of fortune. Among these securities was occasional debt coverage. More than once the treasurer of the Opéra bailed out an indebted performer whose creditors threatened to have her jailed. In addition, singers and dancers were paid, though not always very much. Lead performers fared better, and eight of the demimondaines who married were lead singers or dancers. Marie-Jeanne Lemière, principal dancer in the Opéra, had a base salary of sixteen hundred livres during the year of her marriage. Soloist singers Demoiselles Chevalier and Romainville each earned three thousand livres.[24]

Not every kept woman who married, however, was at the top of her profession. Suzanne Elizabeth LeGrand (Beaumont), for example, tended to collect from her patrons honoraires of around three hundred livres a month. But she was still meeting her living expenses. In fact, all but one for whom such data are available seemed to be supporting themselves without much trouble. Most had enough wealth to live comfortably and did not lack for patrons. But while bridal dames entretenues may have had more wealth than their nonprostitute counterparts, they did not have sexual honor, still considered to be a prerequisite for a respectable match. Their careers as elite prostitutes and, for many of them, their status as actresses and performers put them outside of the traditional social hierarchy. While it made them celebrities of a sort, it stripped them of any social respectability, and this in turn severely limited their marriage options. What kind of men married kept women?

About a third of these women married men of higher social status than their own fathers. Five women married officeholders or nobles. Another two married high-level servants of nobles, though one of these marriages was a sham. The duc de Crussol, like Louis XV, had his mistress marry one of his domestics. Only two women married low-paid, semiskilled workers— one a public scribe and the other a domestic—exactly the kind of men they might have married had they never been prostitutes.

The rest of the group married socially marginal men. Like Brillant, whose case study opened this chapter, ten theater women married theater men. Eight of those ten married men in their same troupe. These were obvious pairings; the couples worked in the same industry and saw each other on a daily basis. The social stigma attached to theater women would not have been so much of a problem for theater men, as they shared the worst of it, and prostitution was endemic in the theater subculture. Another two women married men who were or had been in the army or musketeers. The sexual morals of these men were thought so disreputable that any woman found in their company was automatically assumed to be a prostitute. The last six women married men who were unemployed. For example, Vidaud, the husband of the dancer Delisle, no longer had any position, nor any income beyond his four hundred livres pension. In fact, his marriage contract suggests he had little of anything—no significant property, rente or cash— whereas his wife owned "considerable" furniture and other movable goods.[25] Another ex-soldier, the American Lesther, had been a musketeer but "retired" shortly before marrying his wife, Françoise Villemin, and living off of her savings.[26] In sum, fewer than a third of those women who married after entering the demimonde wed men who were socially respectable. Half of the sample married men who might have been able to support them, though probably at lower standards than those at which they had once supported themselves. The rest married men they had to support.

How do we explain these marriages? Let us begin with the question of why any man might want to marry a dame entretenue. In some cases he did not, at least not exactly; he married an actress, a dancer, or a singer. Perhaps the celebrity of a woman like Comédie-Italienne star Rosalie Astraudi, who married a nobleman, combined with her identity as an artist (not to mention her beauty, talent, and charisma), were enough to dampen any aversion to her sexual history. These qualities, however, were not enough for the public. Men who married actresses opened themselves up to enormous ridicule. Similarly, theater men who married theater women were marrying artists, and equally important, within their own profession. But for those brides who had never been on the stage, either their partners were insensitive to issues of sexual honor, or they were encouraged to become so by a promise of money or perhaps love.

For brides, marrying up does not require explanation, nor perhaps does marrying a man of similar fortune. However, why some of these women married poor men or those without prospects is more curious. It is possible they did so because marriage was normative for women in their mid-twenties, a poor match being better than no match at all. For these women, then, mistress keeping was part of the marriage system only as a form of work, a means to accrue a dowry, even if this was not the intent from the outset. Yet marriage involved a big risk for these women. Before assuming they married because women married and because perhaps they thought that, as prostitutes, they were lucky to do so, we have to look critically at what marriage offered these women and think about what kinds of private lives they were trying to build.

Let us begin with financial prospects, as marriage was fundamentally an economic union. For several demimondaines, marriage offered an immediate increase in wealth. A far greater number, however, married men of lesser or no fortune, thereby risking their own. For the majority, it was a complex calculation. Marriage might have appeared to offer long-term financial security, but it also carried the risk inherent in turning one's own property over to another for management.

According to the *Coutume de Paris*, the customal that determined civil law in the Ile-de-France, married women did not control most of their own property; their husbands did.[27] When a couple married, each donated a portion of his or her goods to the *communauté de biens*, a fund that was supposed to enable the newlyweds to establish themselves as an independent economic unit. Exactly what each spouse would include was stipulated in the marriage contract. The husband alone had the power to manage the fund. He was able to alienate it, use it as collateral, even spend it, though he could not alienate the portion constituted by his wife's dowry without her permission. She, on the other hand, had no rights over the communauté, and it was largely as a consequence of this that she could likewise take no legal action on her own; that is, she could not borrow, pay debts, or make contracts without her husband's express authorization. Her legal personality was assimilated to his.[28]

For women who married as legal adults—the age of majority was twenty-five—wedlock resulted in a significant loss of financial control over their own wealth. This was because a single, adult woman, a *jeune-fille majeure*, had the same general property rights as a man. She could sell or borrow against what she owned. She could engage in any legal action, including bringing suits and making contracts, both of which were necessary parts of financial management.[29] Of course, a wife did not have to put all her property into the communauté, though the larger her dowry, the greater her prospects for marriage. She could donate only a portion. She also could demand a complete separation of goods (*séparation des biens*), meaning a full exclusion of all her real estate (*immeubles*), though this was rare among working-class people. But even a séparation des biens allowed a certain intrusion on her property rights. Her husband retained the right to administer any immeubles, whether they were excluded or not. The only goods over which a married woman retained complete control were those that related to any commercial enterprise she might have had separate from her husband's affairs.[30]

Since most kept women were legal adults at the time of marriage, many took a risk in marrying. The median age of first marriage for kept women was 27.7, and the mean was 25. Not every husband was able to (or even wanted to) maintain the integrity of the communauté. Placets for lettres de cachet filed by wives and extended families provide countless examples of husbands who dissipated the communauté. Marie Lecocq asked the lieutenant general of police to incarcerate her husband, Henry Petit, via lettre de cachet because he had sold all their belongings to buy alcohol.[31] Jeanne Catry similarly claimed that her husband, Antoine Chevalier, had sold all of the couple's clothes for the same purpose.[32] These wives took action to preserve what remained of the communauté. In the years 1728 and 1758, about half of the cases in which a wife asked for the incarceration of her husband concerned dissipation of communal property.[33]

Several affianced dames entretenues must have suspected their future husbands of being poor money managers, or perhaps they simply wanted to retain control over their own goods. According to police reports, Demoiselle Delisle put only her furniture, worth 21,000 livres, into the communauté, while keeping out her rente (18,000 livres) and Opéra pension (400 livres).[34] Cécile Rotisset, the Opéra star known as Romainville, also demanded a partial separation of goods at her marriage to Étienne-Pierre Masson de Maisonrouge, a receveur général des finances, even though he was thought to be the wealthier of the two. Her dowry was a large house on the rue des Bons-Enfants that Maisonrouge had given to her some years previously; 100,000 livres in cash; a rente of 30,000 livres, which was to pay for the expenses of the house; and ten royal lottery tickets. What did she leave out of the communauté? The marriage contract listed all of her private property. This included 90,000 livres of diamonds, 124,000 livres of furniture, 22,000 livres of silver, and seventy-one dresses (nineteen for spring and autumn, eighteen for summer, twenty-four for winter, and ten others). The decorations alone for each dress could cost thousands of livres.[35]

How profitable was marriage for these women? Delisle married a man of lesser fortune. Romainville, on the other hand, married a man of immense wealth. Most cases, however, are not as clear as either one of these. Even if we assume the husband was a competent manager, it is difficult to determine to what degree most kept women who wed profited financially from their marriages because of the difficulty of assessing sexual capital. For example, in the mid-1750s, Rosalie Astraudi, the twenty-six-year-old star of the Comédie-Italienne, was at the peak of her career. Sometime around the beginning of 1756, she married a nobleman. As a measure of his wealth, the husband was reported to have 30,000 livres in rente in his possession. Astraudi's previous patron had given her thirty thousand livres in gifts and cash over the course of a single winter.[36] If Astraudi could earn in a few months what her husband earned annually, was it a good financial decision to marry him? We do not know what other financial or material resources the groom might have had at his disposal. Nor do we know for how much longer Astraudi would have been able to draw thirty thousand livres from a patron as age and eventual retirement from the stage depreciated her worth as a dame entretenue. On the other hand, once Astraudi married she no longer had to work. In fact, she retired immediately from the demimonde, and she left the stage within a year. Perhaps marriage was a good investment for her. Aside from her husband's fortune, were she to outlive him she was guaranteed by her marriage contract a lump sum of forty thousand livres in cash in addition to a very generous dower.

The problem of sexual capital makes age of marriage a useful category through which to examine the relationship between kept women and the economic benefits of marriage. Astraudi married at about the same age as most women from working-class or artisan backgrounds. Like so many of them, she ceased to engage in her premarital career once wed. But whereas a seamstress or a domestic could remain at work for decades if she did not find a husband (and even if she did), Astraudi and other femmes galantes could not. Being a professional mistress was a young woman's career. Statistics on the age of retirement for dames entretenues are impossible to calculate from the police dossiers, though Meusnier and Marais rarely reported on women older than twenty-eight. Those few who remained objects of surveillance into their mid-thirties tended to be the most notorious and successful kept women of their day. Nevertheless, the police described the physical appearance of these older women in the most unflattering terms.

The inspectors, however, had a point. By their late twenties, many of these women would have had rotted teeth, a fact brought home by regular descriptions of the "belles dents" of younger women. Their bodies would have been tired by multiple childbirths, bouts of venereal disease, and even worse, its often disfiguring mercury cure. Even in perfect health, they still had to compete against teenagers who were being marketed aggressively by a range of profiteers, from their mothers to the city's madams. Fragonard's paintings of round and voluptuous women contrast sharply with the preferences of men like Casanova, who called a girl's middle teens "ambrosial."[37] The public concurred. The contrast is greater than one would assume. Girls aged fourteen and fifteen seemed to have been the most sexually desirable in the demimonde.[38] At least, that was when they were sold as virgins or entered into their first relationships. A fifteen-year-old female body in the eighteenth century, however, would have been significantly less sexually developed than the body of a fifteen-year-old girl today. The average age of menarche in the second half of the eighteenth century was sixteen. It decreased to thirteen by the latter half of the twentieth century.[39] Casanova's quarry were a far cry from the pneumatic images of Fragonard. So we must wonder if kept women married in their late twenties because that was the custom among women of their social background. Or did it have to do with approaching retirement?

For many, that retirement was only approaching; it had not arrived. Theater women continued to perform for a decade after marriage, whether they had retired from prostitution or not. From police reports, theater women married on average at age twenty-nine, and these women retired from the theater on average at age thirty-eight. As for the rest, more than half for whom the data are available chose to keep working as elite prostitutes. Retirement status at marriage can be established for eighteen of the twenty-eight women in this sample (of demimondaines who married). Two had left the demimonde some time before marriage. Six kept women retired at marriage (though four of them eventually went back to being professional mistresses). The remaining ten women kept working as prostitutes.

The career of Agathe Rigotier (known professionally as Zélie or Dorval) actually improved after her marriage. She wed at age twenty-six. Her husband was a marquis and sixty years her senior. But rather than use her marriage to lead a different sort of life, she capitalized on her new title to improve the one she had. Now the marquise d'Aubard, she was able to command far greater sums from her patrons than she could previously. Her first postnuptial patron was a young nobleman, son of the provisional commissioner of the Department of Bordeaux. Meusnier wrote:

> It is said that she is making him pay quite dearly for the honor of having a marquise as a mistress. In less than six months, not only did she have him dissipate all that he had brought with him to Paris, but after having had him demand money from his family under various pretexts, she is now making him contract more than 15,000 livres in rente. After hearing these stories, his father has now come to Paris, and I am assured, he has the intention of incarcerating his son.[40]

The nobleman was succeeded by a man named Dupré, who began his relationship with Rigotier by giving her twelve thousand to fifteen thousand livres' worth of furniture for her apartment and 600 livres honoraires.[41]

Astraudi and Rigotier married at around the same age. Why did one retire and the other not? No real pattern emerges from the documents. Those who left the demimonde at marriage were no older on average than those who stayed. Several did marry men whose wealth eclipsed their own earnings as elite prostitutes. Most, however, did not. The money earned by such wives would have been welcome even though the most genetically fortunate among them could hardly have expected to work for more than a few additional years. It is tempting to argue that these women married in their mid to late twenties because that is when women of their social backgrounds married. Aware that their careers would be ending, they wanted to secure their futures by finding husbands even if they were not yet ready for retirement. One's prospects for marriage decreased with age. In her discussion of widows, Olwen Hufton points out that only 20 percent of those over forty ever remarried.[42] But if this hypothesis is true, and marriage was part of a long-term financial plan for survival, how then do we explain the third of the sample who married men of lesser or no fortune?

About a third of the husbands in the sample were unemployed, or became so shortly after marriage. They relied on their wives' savings or earnings for financial support. Thérèze Brébant, for example, had used savings accrued as a kept woman to buy an apprenticeship with a fashion merchant, but then left, at the behest of her sister, to work with her in making linen. The business faltered and Brébant, to stave off poverty, agreed to marry an acquaintance of her brother-in-law, a man named Despures. The plan did not work. As Despures was a man "made to be comfortable," in Marais's estimation, Brébant was forced to work at brothel parties so as better to support the couple.[43] Despures's seeming inactivity, however, was unusual among this particular group of men. The rest of the unemployeds actively planned, hustled, and manipulated their social connections, however distant, to better their positions and find a post. For example, Moreau, the unemployed husband of provincial actress Suzanne Elizabeth LeGrand (Demoiselle Beaumont), had used his mother's connection to the duc de la Rochefoucault to secure a position of some sort in the French Caribbean colonies.[44] Former captain Philippe Durocher de Mandeville, who counted the brothers Fleury among his protectors, tried, in vain, to get a position with the Compagnie des Indes. But Moreau waited more than a year to secure his post, and Mandeville never got his. And so, like most of the unemployeds, they were plagued by money problems, despite their wives' earnings. LeGrand and Moreau dealt with their financial problems in fairly typical fashion. They borrowed and then hid when the creditors came to the door. Still unmarried, the couple disappeared one day in October 1750. Everyone in the district assumed that they had gone to America. LeGrand had borrowed a total of three thousand livres from various people, ranging from a local Jewish lender to a café owner. The couple had run off to Guernsey to marry, leaving their creditors befuddled.[45]

The women who married unemployed men could not have been unaware of their spouses' financial situation. Did they hope things would improve? Had Moreau and Mandeville spoken convincingly of their social connections, assuring their fiancées of a certain job? It is possible, but the way in which Meusnier and Marais describe these men casts at least some doubt over their characters. Moreau was described as a libertine, a mauvais sujet, but with a "pretty face."[46] Marais described Thérèze Brébant's husband as lazy, a drunk, and a wife beater.[47] The dancer Delisle's husband, Vidaud, was "a man of pleasure, a charming debauché."[48] Even those who earned their keep were not spared the inspectors' disdain. Meusnier said that the Opéra dancer Rabon's marriage to her fellow dancer Pitro was "foolish" and that her husband proved it as he very quickly "wasted" what remained of her money, furniture, and jewels.[49]

The poor reputation of these particular men raises the question of respectability. If LeGrand did not marry for money, could she have married Moreau to elevate her social status? In a society that had little room for single adult women, marriage even to a mauvais sujet was probably more socially acceptable than remaining unwed. But marriage, even to a man of superior status, did not automatically confer respect. With Rigotier, it had the opposite effect. Marais wrote that after her marriage (to the marquis) she "affected airs of grandeur that were intolerable to everyone. The public calls her 'marquise' only in mockery."[50] For those women at the very top of the demimonde, and especially the great talents of the stage like Astraudi and Romainville, who carried out their love lives circumspectly, marriage was more a reflection of their status than an enhancement of it.

It is unlikely that LeGrand married Moreau to erase any stain incurred from her life as a kept woman. She did not retire at marriage. Moreover, she married a man with a bad reputation, and the couple behaved dishonorably both before and after they wed. The explanation probably lies elsewhere. LeGrand and Moreau had been lovers for two years prior to marrying. While LeGrand worked, she kept Moreau as her boyfriend. Men like Moreau— broke, voraciously feeding off of their wives, mauvais sujets, socially marginal— were a fixture in the demimonde and in the lives of kept women. These were the exact same type of men who served as greluchons, "lovers of the heart" or "boyfriends," which kept women often had, and usually supported, while serving as mistresses to other men. Even the nature of the relationships was similar, based on exploitation and often violence. A number of the husbands, in addition to Moreau, actually had affairs with their wives in this capacity for several years preceding marriage. Others, like Rabon's husband, Pitro, served as greluchons to several other women. Perhaps, then, Brillant married Bureau and LeGrand married Moreau because of a connection fostered through their experiences of *greluchonnage*. Greluchonnage was at the core of private life for kept women and, at the same time, an essential part of their public one. As such, it both reflected and helped to build sexual capital.

❧ Greluchons

In reporting on Demoiselle Hypotite, Inspector Meusnier wrote, "In addition to her Monsieur, Fournier de Bellevue, she has the young Monsieur Boule, as either a greluchon or a *farfadet*. The difference between a greluchon and a farfadet is that the first ordinarily pays less than the Monsieur, whereas the second is absolutely free." Despite such clarity, Inspector Meusnier typically used the word *greluchon* to refer to any number of different arrangements, and he used *farfadet* not at all.[51] The word *greluchon* has a murky origin. In the mid-sixteenth century, there was a faux Saint Greluchon in central France. A wooden statue of him in the Diocese of Bourges (at Gargilesse) was the object of pilgrimage for infertile women who hoped to cure themselves by drinking a tea brewed from shavings made of the statue's phallus. A severe comment on the virility of French husbands, greluchon came to mean "gigolo."[52]

By early in the eighteenth century, the word denoted a lover of the heart, a boyfriend, someone with whom a kept woman had a relationship based on sexual attraction or even love, as opposed to monetary gain.[53] From this perspective, these relationships were personal, not commercial. Yet such affairs were never purely sentimental, no matter how romanticized they may have been in literature. Money was an organizing factor. Someone always was paid. In the police reports about half the greluchons paid their mistresses, while the other half were paid by them. The direction of the money flow determined the power dynamics within the relationship, though often in contradictory ways.

The men who became greluchons generally fit a specific profile. They were described as being quite physically attractive, "big, well made, with a handsome face," like the greluchon of dance student Demoiselle Montfreville.[54] They also were depicted, generally, as scoundrels. They came from both the lowest and the highest echelons of society. About 30 percent could be considered to be socially marginal as they were theater men, servants, or unemployed. Another large group was made up of men in the King's Guards and musketeers. These were the greluchons *mangeants* (eating greluchons). Another third of the men were part of the amalgamated elite of eighteenth-century society: nobles, army officers, and government officials, or their sons. These were greluchons *payants* (paying greluchons).

Paying greluchons usually offered small gifts. Occasionally, they gave cash, but never honoraires. The "charming" Monsieur Grandville, an officer in the King's Guard, gave Opéra dancer Louise Régis (known professionally as Raye) a blue satin negligee worth 3 louis (72 livres).[55] Monsieur Tisserand gave singer Dallière a dress worth 500 livres. As if out of some novel, these two lovers met secretly. They had an elaborate means of communicating, involving two intermediaries and a compartment in the Opéra box of the duc d'Orléans.[56] This was by necessity. As we have seen in the case of Dumas and Gautier, being caught in flagrante delicto with a greluchon (or news of having been so) could create problems in a patron-mistress relationship. Demoiselle Raye, for instance, lost a patron in this manner. In the summer of 1761, the marquis de Romey returned from his estates to Paris and made arrangements (i.e., he lied to his wife) to spend the night with Raye. He planned to give the dancer 480 livres in the morning for services rendered. Shocking all, Raye "entirely refused" his proposition, "claiming not to be in the habit of sleeping with men." Thinking this was odd, Marais had her house watched. Monsieur Violet, Raye's greluchon, was spotted entering her place at 11:00 p.m. The police presumed he had spent the night. Romey apparently was informed of this and was furious. He swore never to see Raye again. Marais concluded, "This demoiselle will not be long in regretting [her decision] if Monsieur de Romey keeps his promise, because her creditors are overwhelming her and pressing her on every front."[57]

In terms of patron retention, a greluchon was a risky proposition, but the risk was not fully contained in the problem of bad planning and consequent discovery. Some kept women could not control their greluchons. It was not just Violet's untimely appearance that caused Raye to lose her patron. By making his presence in her house too obvious, Violet managed to chase off Romey's successor. Later, Raye's new greluchon, Grandville, openly quarreled with her then-patron, the extremely wealthy financier François Fontaine de Cramayel, causing the latter to break off relations. For Raye, the loss was significant. Marais wrote at the start of their relationship, "In order to satisfy her creditors, Demoiselle Raye is in dire need of keeping hold of this financier for a long time. But I hardly believe she will be able to. She has a mother who loves luxury a bit too much and the expenses of her house are capable of cracking even the strongest safe." Cramayel was paying the cost of the household as well as giving her expensive gifts. After Cramayel left, Raye arranged to keep seeing Grandville, but only if he gave her 10 louis (240 livres) a month and promised not to cause her any more trouble.[58]

What was Raye doing? Was she in love with Violet or with Grandville? Whatever she may have felt, she proved herself unable to create a stable life with either of them. Not only did the affairs with her greluchons rapidly collapse, but Raye continued to recruit new patrons despite the disruptive presence of these men. Was Raye simply reckless? Or was it more a question of establishing a private life outside of the confines of her professional one? These questions, for Raye and for kept women like her who took on greluchons for limited financial profit, are immeasurably complicated by an examination of those kept women who actually paid greluchons for their company.

A very few among this second group treated the men they paid as gigolos or toys. One such woman was Demoiselle Deschamps. At the Opéra in August of 1761, Deschamps and a fellow dancer began an argument as to who "possessed" the greluchon Vesian, a clerk with the tax farms.[59] Deschamps won and kept the company of the young man. Vesian, perhaps encouraged by this fight over him, thought that it was he who controlled Deschamps and not the other way around. Marais reported that the man was vain and liked "a good time" and that "as long as a woman has grand airs, a carriage, is showy and has a lot of diamonds, little does it matter whether she is pretty or ugly. And he claimed that Deschamps's reputation is such that he will be able to get her to do whatever he wishes. But I scarcely believe that he will succeed in this. This woman is a true Messalina and as soon as she perceives that he is stumbling, she will get rid of him as she has so many others."[60] Indeed, within a month Marais reported that Deschamps was madly in love with another man, the chevalier de Rupière. Given the way in which Deschamps "won" Vesian, he may have been nothing more than the trophy in a competition between two women trying to prove their positions in the demimonde.[61]

With Rupière, however, Deschamps found herself enmeshed in an entirely different power dynamic. She reportedly was "obsessed" with the chevalier. Marais, with his usual inclination toward crude description, described Rupière as "a very likeable young man" who was known in the demimonde, above all, for "his ability to vigorously serve a mistress." It was for this quality, he claimed, that Deschamps privileged the chevalier over his competitors; she was known to have "a big appetite." In short, Deschamps and Rupière reversed roles. Deschamps was the patron. She was strengthened vis-à-vis Rupière in that she had the money he needed. She was weakened by the fact that it was she who desired him. According to Marais, Rupière had told all of his friends that he did not like Deschamps at all. Furthermore, he was known to be attached to a prostitute who worked for Brissault. Rupière, for his part, had the power to accept or refuse Deschamps's overtures, but, as happened also with so many kept women, his decision was informed by his impressive debt. For Rupière, the decision to be a kept man was a business move. Marais characterized him as a "resourceful man. . . . He satisfied [Deschamps's] vanity and profited from her weakness for him, in order to straighten out his finances, which had been destabilized by all his past romantic adventures. She loaned him 5,000 livres with which he paid off several creditors."[62]

Like so many patrons, Deschamps chose to conduct this particular affair at one of Brissault's petites maisons. She wanted to hide her affair from her patron, a man the police identify as Monsieur Salis, a Swiss officer who was spending a great deal on her.[63] What risk did Deschamps run? Discovery, especially of the fact that she was giving her patron's gifts to her paid lover, could have ended her lucrative relations with Salis. But Deschamps probably could have replaced him without much trouble. (We do not know if she did, as reporting on her stopped soon thereafter.) Her particular position as a sexual commodity in the demimonde protected her. Professionally, she risked little in being discovered by Salis except the short-term inconvenience of finding another patron.

Women who paid their greluchons, however, often faced a second, far more insidious financial risk than that which came with exposure. Many, even some of the most powerful, allowed themselves to be bankrupted by these men. Before her marriage, Rosalie Astraudi kept a man named Monchenu, an *exempt* (officer) of the King's Guard. "He cost her a lot. It was he who totally ruined her. She is currently in a wretched state, ever more indebted, selling things without knowing whether she will have enough money," claimed a police mouche.[64] Demoiselle Brillant found herself in a similar situation. While in England with a French theatrical troupe, the *comedienne* suddenly found herself patronless, and the police employee observing her there reported, rather dramatically, "Brillant is dying of hunger with her two greluchons."[65] Why did Brillant and Astraudi endanger their financial well-being in this manner? For Astraudi, the question is even more pressing, as she was her family's breadwinner. Was it love? Obsession? Bad planning?

Perhaps Brillant and Astraudi, for once, simply found themselves on the other side of that sexual equation in which the patron allowed every possible resource to be drawn from him by his mistress until he had nothing left. If so, this is significant. It meant that Brillant and Astraudi, like Deschamps, were sexual consumers just as much as were the patrons who supported them. Only women at the very top of their professions—these were usually stars of the stage—could do this. They were able to use the very sexual capital from which they had accrued wealth and status within the demimonde to assume the privileges, and follies, of the men in their world. Deschamps on the one hand, and Astraudi and Brillant on the other, represent different varieties of patrons. The case of Deschamps paralleled that of the majority of men, who, from pride, good planning, or some other aspect of character, managed not to allow their attachments to their mistresses to lead to financial ruin. Brillant and Astraudi represented the sort who did.

The actions of Brillant, Astraudi, and Deschamps underscore the power dynamic that defined the patron-mistress relationship, the tension between sexual desire and money. That women—if only a few—could assume either side of this relationship brings into question the degree to which this dynamic was inherently or entirely gendered. The actions of Brillant and her colleagues show that those driven by their own desires to purchase the sexual services of another were not always men. Nor were those who manipulated this desire to their advantage always women. But the exchange of traditional places in this relationship was not necessarily absolute. In the autumn of 1756, Meusnier reported a rumor that Opéra singer Marie-Madeleine Jendrest (known professionally as Chefdeville) had an "eating greluchon who punished her when she did not engage in paying affairs."[66] Whether this rumor was based on any sort of truth we probably will never know. Nevertheless, observations of this kind do appear here and there throughout the police dossiers. Furthermore, it is the model of an "eating greluchon" whose control of his keeper extended beyond the manipulation of the latter's sexual desire in which we are interested. In this model, Chefdeville's greluchon is neither a commodity, nor a toy. He was a pimp. Regardless of what else went on between the couple, he specifically directed his patron to have affairs (we assume, to earn money) and punished her when she did not. A mistress did not exert this sort of control over her patron. The very idea that an Opéra singer could be pushed around by a man who was not paying her and to whom she was not married—in other words, a man to whom she had no recognizable obligations whatsoever—recasts, again, the gender question. Confusing it further, Chefdeville was married and had had sufficient self-confidence and social standing to have her husband incarcerated seven years earlier via lettre de cachet for his abusive behavior.[67] Female patrons did not possess every aspect of the power that came with that position when it was occupied by a man. In these cases, the apparent gender role reversal was incomplete.

On the other hand, when a female patron presented all of the power of a male patron, the event did not pass without comment. We have seen how the inspectors wrote of the entrance of most women into the demimonde within two highly structured narratives: either she was a slut seeking adventure or an unfortunate with no other options. In making Deschamps (and they applied these descriptors to a number of other women) a "Messalina," "obsessed," and "with a big appetite," they continued to caricature female sexual desire; if it existed, it was without bounds.[68] The idea that mistresses took on greluchons because they wanted to have more sex lays bare the elemental contradiction in the greluchon-mistress relationship. It was both fundamentally public and status oriented, and inherently private and personal.

Finally, one wonders what Deschamps, Brillant, and Astraudi hoped to gain from paying men for sex and companionship. If these relationships were about love, they also must have been about control. All three women had numerous paying greluchons as well as many men who would have taken any patronal position offered to them. But there is another possibility. Not every dame entretenue had a greluchon. However, the greater her sexual capital, the greater the possibility that she would. Was it simply that women with high sexual capital had these affairs because they could get away with them? Or did having these affairs actually increase their sexual capital? That the most elite dames entretenues paid their greluchons suggests the latter possibility. In a sense, then, greluchons were a part of the demimondaine image. They were much like diamond earrings or a carriage, which most kept women sought, but which only the most successful acquired. They were a desired commodity, not only for their intrinsic qualities but also because they represented status. This theory might explain the patterned nature of the relationships. Although such a conclusion might simply be a consequence of the nature of police reporting, it also is possible that these particular behaviors were part of the self-representation of kept women. They advertised their sexuality and suitability as mistresses by having affairs with young, handsome men whose careers or lifestyles labeled them virile.

✒ Greluchonnage and Romantic Partnerships

Greluchon–kept woman relationships may have helped to cultivate a certain public image for various dames entretenues. Yet by their very existence they constituted a private romantic life for many of the same women. Greluchons were like boyfriends. Dames entretenues had affairs with these men because they found them personally desirable. By definition, a greluchon stood in opposition to a patron with whom sexual and romantic relations were work. In taking a greluchon, a demimondaine established the boundaries of a patron's ownership and separated her professional and private lives. However, the greluchon's roles of public image-maker and boyfriend often were inseparable, making it difficult to place the private side of these relationships in a separate analytical category. The problem is compounded by the fluidity of the patronal categories. Greluchons occasionally became patrons, and vice versa. Nevertheless, it was largely through greluchons that kept women were able to link their intimate lives with their sexual ones, even if the process had a certain public meaning.

This linkage did not appear to be very successful most of the time. The collective impression left by the police reports and by contemporary observers like Casanova and Barbier was that greluchon-mistress relationships fell into two categories. They either were sexual dalliances devoid of any emotional content or they were intense, passionate love affairs. Neither type tended to last very long, either falling apart on its own accord or being sacrificed to professional exigencies. The relationship of Deschamps to Vesian might be an example of a dalliance. Casanova felt himself to be similarly toyed with by Demoiselle Coraline (Anne-Marie Véronèse), an actress in the Comédie-Italienne. In love with the actress, he began to visit her at odd hours, "but odd hours, too, belong to the proprietor; so I would sometimes be there at the time the prince [of Monaco] came to see her." Casanova eventually began spending his evenings with the couple, and after a few months Coraline at last agreed to an assignation. They planned to go hunting together on the outskirts of Paris. On the way, their carriage met that of a (male) friend of Coraline, and she decided on the spot to go with him instead, leaving Casanova alone and humiliated. When the latter bitterly complained to a friend, he was informed that what happened was quite "within the rules, for there is not a fancy man to whom something of the sort is not bound to happen, and who, if he is intelligent, is not willing to put up with it."[69]

As for intense love affairs, the relationship of Opéra soloist Chevalier (Marie-Jeanne Fesch) with Sieur Lagarde Landivisau, a captain in the Gray Musketeers, might qualify. She was supposedly "in love" with the captain, and Meusnier reports that the feeling was mutual. "For two to three months they have not lost sight of each other," wrote the inspector.[70] The singer LaBlotière was "folle" (crazy) about Le Petit Abbé, a violin player in the Opéra. For his part, he once attacked one of her patrons to protect her.[71] Perhaps Demoiselle Raye (Louise Régis, the dame entretenue who claimed to be not "in the habit" of sleeping with men so that she could put off her patron in favor of her boyfriend) was in love with her greluchon Violet and was willing to endure his reckless behavior even if it meant losing patrons.

The reporting on Raye is not detailed enough to ascertain her motives. But in the case of Demoiselle Lyonnais (Marie-Françoise Rempon), a dancer in the Opéra, it is. While maintaining a career as a demimondaine, Lyonnais had a long-term relationship with the singer Favier, who was married with a family of his own. The story that emerges from her dossier is that her career was a way to maintain both her quality of life and her relationship with her boyfriend. The ways in which she wove her relationship with Favier into her professional life provide a third model of greluchon-nage, after the "eating" and "paying" greluchons. This model might help to explain why at least some kept women married during their careers and why they married men of little or no fortune.

Both Lyonnais and Favier worked in the Opéra. Lyonnais, long separated from her husband, was a soloist and received a yearly salary of at least two thousand livres. She also had significant income from patrons. From at least the fall of 1748, she was maintained by the very generous comte de Vin-timille, who was captain of his own regiment. Vintimille provided Lyonnais with a monthly stipend. He gave her gifts and paid the costs of her house-hold, including servants' wages. Favier, on the other hand, with a wife and children to support, never earned more than six hundred livres a year.[72] For whatever reason, and despite his constant and not insignificant difficulties with creditors, he was willing to forgo even this income, repeatedly trying to resign his appointment with the Royal Academy of Music.

It is difficult to calculate what Lyonnais's support of Favier might have meant in monetary terms. What she provided changed as her circumstances did. At first, it was just food. Beginning in the spring of 1749, Favier took all his meals at Lyonnais's house. To deflect suspicion, he passed himself off as her music teacher. Providing meals was no small thing. Food expendi-tures generally consumed one-half to two-thirds of a family's total earnings; the poorer the family, the greater the percentage of its income was devoted to feeding itself.[73] Moreover, a comte's table—and it was a comte's table be-cause it was financed by Vintimille, who also ate there—certainly would have been better provisioned than that of a singer in the Opéra choir with a family to feed. Favier could have expected to eat meat only once a week, if even that often.

By the fall of 1750, Lyonnais was pregnant with Favier's child, and, oddly, this created an opportunity for her to increase her support. Favier "forced" Lyonnais to rent a house in Passy for her confinement and then moved in with his family. Meusnier wrote, "Favier's wife and children are there continuously and we are well informed that it is Lyonnais who sup-ports the entire family, at the expense of Monsieur de Vintimille, who goes almost every day to Passy to keep Lyonnais company."[74] The baby, delivered in November, was a girl. Vintimille thought the child his. Lyonnais claimed that it was Favier's, but had the comte stand at her side as the father while Favier held the infant under the baptismal fonts as its godfather. Six months later, in the spring of 1751, Vintimille and Lyonnais separated. Whatever the cause, Meusnier was sure that Favier was preventing any sort of recon-ciliation. "Favier has more than ever established himself as the head of her

house." Moreover, by this time, Lyonnais was not only feeding and sheltering Favier, but also preventing his creditors from seizing what furniture he
had left by locking up the items at her house. "With this arrangement, Favier's wife and children are in a rented room. As for Favier, he sleeps more
willingly at Lyonnais's than with his wife."[75]

The disappearance of Vintimille marked the end of Lyonnais's bounty
years. In that time, Favier had proved such an economic burden that Lyonnais
emerged from the three-year maintenance having saved very little money.
When she was unable to procure a new patron quickly, she was no longer
able to pay the couple's bills. She engaged in various passades and eventually,
in February 1752, accepted a contract to dance with a troupe in Prussia for
twelve thousand livres a year, six times her current salary. Favier, for his part,
still could not get released from his contract so that he could accompany
her. Did she go? We do not know. She was back in Paris in the fall of 1754,
however, finally having landed a new patron, a Polish count who paid her
five hundred livres a month. He went to her house three to four times a week
but never slept there. "Things could indeed continue on this footing," wrote
Meusnier, "as long as the count doesn't realize he has a substitute. Favier is
leaving his mark on everything."[76] Police reporting ended soon thereafter.

In many ways, Favier fits the profile of a greluchon mangeant. With a
single exception, to which we will return later, he relied on Lyonnais for his
subsistence (and for that of his family) as well as for a certain degree of protection from his creditors. She earned the money for that subsistence by
working exclusively as a dancer and a kept woman. But, in other ways, the
relationship between Lyonnais and Favier did not conform to the model.
First, it lasted a long time, at least six years, which was the entire period of
police observation. Secondly, it played a greater role in Lyonnais's life than
greluchon–kept woman relationships typically did in the lives of most
dames entretenues. Astraudi and Brillant may have allowed themselves to be
bankrupted by their greluchons. Deschamps may have been "in love" or
"obsessed" with various men. Yet none of these women organized their
professional lives around maintaining a particular greluchon, as Lyonnais
appeared to do. There was also the one instance in which Favier did pay for
something. In the summer of 1755, in Meusnier's last entry on Lyonnais, he
reports that she had a huge party at her house with fireworks and that Favier
paid for the festivities.[77] Last, the power dynamics are difficult to determine.
Lyonnais was neither a Deschamps, who had power over her greluchon, nor
a Chefdeville, who was controlled by hers. In fact, there is no convincing
evidence that either one of the partners made all of the central decisions
in the relationship. Favier certainly had some control over his patron.

Meusnier claims that he "forced" her to rent a house in Passy, for his use. Yet Meusnier also wrote that Lyonnais gave her "consent" to her lover, allowing him to store some furniture at her house, thereby preventing what little he had left from being seized by those to whom he owed sizeable debts.

The relationship between Favier and Lyonnais might present a third model of greluchonnage; here is a greluchon–kept woman relationship in which the private and personal element was emphasized over the public element. They were in an irregular relationship, the kind Anne Michelet was in with Vielbans. Relationships of this type were uncommon. Fewer than five women kept the same greluchon for more than a year. Favier was the only married greluchon among them. But if both he and Lyonnais had been single, would they have married? It is certainly possible.

Greluchonnage contributed to the professionalization of galanterie by enabling kept women to link their sexual and emotional lives outside of work. However, greluchonnage was also an important part of the economy of the demimonde. The inseparability of the public and private functions of greluchons echoes, if not exaggerates, the ways in which public and private, commercial and familial, were interwoven in this period. What was considered private, however, was marital sexual behavior and emotional engagement, even though the consequences of both had enormous public importance. And for kept women, it was exactly these elements that made up their work life. Yet their "private life" was defined by the same sets of behaviors, though not entirely.

In her study of seamstresses, the historian Clare Crowston makes the point that most scholarship on marriage looks at the process of spousal selection only from the perspective of the groom, "assuming that the woman had little choice in selecting her mate and that her career was subsumed by her husband's." She continues: "As a result, we know little about the role of women's work in creating unions or the potential for autonomous female occupations within married life. The particular considerations working women may have brought to matrimony, or the overall stakes at risk for women in the choice of a mate, also remain unclear."[78] If we expand "mate" to include boyfriends, the circumstances of kept women's lives and the wide-ranging limitations they faced may have made these particular calculations even more difficult.

Some married and although they married around the same age as women from similarly modest backgrounds, the evidence suggests that fewer than half made wise financial decisions in doing so. What were they up to? The sample size is so small that individual choices and circumstances have to be considered. But regardless of their particular feelings, for these women elite prostitution functioned in much the same way as domestic service did; that is, it was work taken by girls that earned them money with which they could get married. The implications of this are significant. It suggests that the disability inherent in sexual dishonor was mitigated, in these cases, by wealth. This is nothing new, historically. Police records are filled with cases of fathers paying to marry off their dishonored daughters. What is unique about these cases is that the money belonged to the brides themselves. In other words, these women were able to capitalize on their very lack of sexual honor and their sexual capital to earn enough wealth (and in some cases celebrity) as prostitutes to marry.

Some clearly married for personal reasons, namely love, companionship, or perhaps sexual attraction. Brillant, after all, "fell in love with her husband." It is as good a guess as any as to why some wealthy women ran off and married good-looking men whom they knew to be wastrels. But there is another possibility. If, in their jobs, kept women were responsible, at least occasionally, for creating together with their patrons a happy loving relationship, what of their own lives? If the affair of Favier and Lyonnais is any sort of indicator, it would appear that at least some kept women were looking for partners with whom they could establish this sort of intimacy, and that they had to use their wealth to create it.

But whether Brillant married out of love, attraction, the desire for companionship, stability, or perhaps increased respectability, she did not insulate her marriage from her career. Examining the love affairs of Demoiselle Brillant, it often is impossible to determine not which were "professional," but which actually were private. Someone paid someone in most of her relationships. None seemed to be privileged steadily over the others for long. We have no idea where Brillant's "heart" lay. But at a very basic level, Brillant's marriage and cohabitation with Bureau professionalized her work as a mistress; it set clear limits on the meaning of her relationship with Monteau.

That professionalization, however, was qualified. We already have seen how some patron-mistress relationships were serious affairs of deep love and attachment. It was further qualified by the confused "private" status of a kept woman's relationships with her family, friends, and lovers. Many of these relationships, like that of Favier and Lyonnais, were not isolated from the workings of the demimonde but functioned through it. Greluchons increased sexual capital and created reputations. Mothers pushed daughters into prostitution. Husbands pimped wives. For women from laboring and artisanal backgrounds, work life and private life hardly were distinct. Marital choice, the dynamics of marriage, arrangement of living quarters, and even perceptions of sexual behavior all affected women's work opportunities and informed the shape of the work once procured.

However, for most women, sex life and work life were distinct spheres. Consequently, for demimondaines, the specific ways in which work and private life reflected each other were unique. For money, dames entretenues set up homes with patrons, creating, in some instances, a domestic space. They had sex and, on occasion, feigned or even felt love and affection as part of a profession that operated by clearly established rules. It is tempting to argue that private and professional sexual relationships created each other. But we must argue simultaneously that these relationships also existed on a continuum from public to private, from professional to personal, and that somewhere along that continuum is where the heart lay.

Conclusion

In the spring of 2012, after the elections that swept the Socialists to power, France's women's rights minister, Najat Vallaud-Belkacem, proposed abolishing prostitution in France and across Europe. Selling sex in France is legal, although solicitation, which includes standing in revealing clothing in a place known for prostitution, was banned in 2003 in a law introduced by then interior minister, Nicolas Sarkozy. Brothels were outlawed in 1946. Vallaud-Belkacem's proposal, which criminalizes the purchase of sex, quickly reopened a debate over the status of prostitutes. The "prostitute problem" has a long history. The question of whether prostitutes were criminals or victims, vice loving or exploited, guilty or innocent, informed the writing not only of inspectors Meusnier and Marais, but of those of their contemporaries who scribbled anything about prostitution, no matter the genre. The modern iteration of the debate, however, made possible by the labor and women's movements, emerged in France and elsewhere only in the 1970s.

In support of Vallaud-Belkacem's proposal, government officials and various nongovernmental agencies pointed to the alarming number of women forced into prostitution through trafficking and argued that drug addiction and childhood sexual trauma left many others with no option but to become prostitutes. Criminalization advocates highlighted the enduring, violent conditions in which many of these women work as evidence that prostitution could not possibly be anything but coerced. In opposition to the proposed law, individual sex workers and sex-work union leaders argued that prostitution is both a choice and a profession, nothing more than a way to pay bills. Rejecting feminist claims that prostitutes are oppressed and should be rescued, these sex workers asserted that they were liberated and subverting male privilege rather than extending it.[1]

French intellectuals and feminist powerhouses also weighed in on the larger issue on both sides, as did editorial pages and the public at large.[2] At issue are a number of practical problems. One is whether to treat "independent" sex workers, those who choose prostitution, separately from those who are clearly victims. Another concerns the effect of the proposed measures, should they become law, on the safety of sex workers, who would be forced underground where they would be easy prey for pimps and without recourse against violent clients. But underpinning the debate is a larger philosophical issue as to whether it is possible for a woman to voluntarily choose prostitution or whether sex work is by its very nature so exploitative and dehumanizing that even those who think they are making a free choice have been conditioned into it. The question concerns why women become prostitutes and then what kind of control they can exert over their lives, as such. At base, it is the same question of agency that shadows much of this work.

Of course, the parameters of any discussion of prostitution and agency are necessarily very different in the context of the eighteenth century. This is especially the case when we think historically about what constituted coercion. With the exception of girls who were sold into the sex trade, the choice/coercion formula—however accurate it may be for the present—simply cannot be applied to the eighteenth century. The constraints faced by women, and indeed by most men, were already so numerous that few had a great deal of career choice. Less choice did not necessarily mean greater discontent, but it could, especially for those women who were required by their families or their own economic need to take on employment or marry men they disliked. Most women had no way out of violent marriages. Some had no alternative but to work in dangerous industries or, given the endemic poverty of the era, to eke out a precarious existence on the streets. Under these conditions, coercion does not carry its modern connotation as the antithesis of freedom, but rather, exists as a basic part of the fabric of eighteenth-century life.

This is especially the case when we evaluate prostitution against other work possibilities for women. Was prostitution so much worse than the life of an itinerant rag picker, for example? Those who wrote about prostitution in the eighteenth century would have said yes, as they imagined not the physical and psychological hardships of sex work but its moral ones. Prostitution stripped women of respectability. It ostracized them from society and barred them from marriage, with all its social and economic benefits. Yet these assumptions were not entirely true. Some prostitutes married or at the very least found themselves in irregular relationships. Moreover, being a dame entretenue (as opposed to a street walker) afforded some women greater choice about how to live their lives than what was experienced by those from similar backgrounds. While this does not mean that prostitution was a positive outcome for women, it does contextualize its burdens and costs in relationship to the few options that most women did have.

The question of agency is at the heart of this book not only because it frames much contemporary thinking about prostitution, especially elite prostitution, but because it is a central question we ask about women's experiences in the past. Historians of women explore the means by which women negotiated the various gendered constraints to which they were subject. In doing so, historians make these constraints visible. The object is not to determine what was good or bad for women, but rather to illuminate the ways in which gender was a form of power in shaping the lives of men and women. It is in the nexus of these two problematics—the agency of prostitutes and workings of gender—that this book's subject lies. A study of prostitutes, triply disempowered by gender, class, and occupation, further demonstrates how sexual status was also a form of power. Dames entretenues were successful despite so many obstacles because of their sexual capital and not their sexual honor.

I have argued that what allowed kept women to become financially self-sufficient heads of household, for however long, was the ambiguity of the contract. The contract structured the patron-mistress relationship as a financial one, but in not stipulating the mistress's duties and hence defining her as a prostitute, it allowed for the possibility that the relationship was not merely transactional. The contract was a flexible instrument that enabled patrons to express their affections materially. Many did and a few so generously that they enriched their mistresses. The contract was what distinguished the patron-mistress relationship from others, making the dames entretenues into a group that we can study. But, in many ways the patron-mistress relationship was not unique. Muddling the definition of prostitution, the patron-mistress relationship was similar to marriage, on the one hand, and irregular relationships on the other. It is in these comparisons that our assessment of the agency of kept women must take place.

The contractual basis of the patron-mistress relationship makes it akin to marriage. Both were financial relationships in which the material exchange is clearly defined and linked to sexual obligation. In both there may have been a hope by either party for an emotional connection, the parameters of which were defined by social expectation and not by contract. Both could be sites of sexual pleasure and intimacy, and in some cases, domesticity. Of course, the differences are obvious. One relationship was socially, religiously, and officially sanctioned; the other—though widely tolerated and even supported by the police—was not. The financial and social protections afforded wife and widow were inscribed in law. Custom dictated financial and social protections for mistresses, but patron compliance with these terms was voluntary. Marriage was a permanent relationship, a site of human and financial reproduction. It was a means of allying families and transferring property, and a way to make new couples self-sustaining economic entities. The patron-mistress relationship was temporary and meant to be a site of pleasure, in which the production of children was problematic. Wealth transferred to the mistress enhanced the patron's reputation or brought him happiness but it carried no benefit to his family. Whatever the patron gave her was lost to his family forever. Patrons chose their mistresses whereas few were able to choose their wives. Mistresses had less choice over their patrons, but most would have been similarly constricted, had they never become prostitutes, in choosing a husband. Marriage compelled a wife to relinquish ownership of her sexual labor. Elite prostitution left its possession in the hands of the mistress.

When we take the patron-mistress construct out of the context of marriage, however, and think of it from the perspective of irregular romantic attachments, we see a spectrum of relationships in which the constellation of economic, sexual, and emotional exchange are configured differently. This confuses the definition of prostitution. While street walking—the single sale of sexual services—clearly was prostitution, what should we make of the relationship of Anne Michelet with Vielbans, or even that of Thérèse Levasseur with Rousseau? Anne and Thérèse had sex and cohabitated with men to whom they were not married in return for financial support, and they did so in part because they had few other options. Today, in thinking about the exchange of sex for material support, the dividing line between what is and what is not prostitution seems to involve considerations of sentiment and intention. But in an era in which people did not necessarily marry or even pair for love, and in which most women were dependent on such relationships for their survival, how should we evaluate mistress-work in terms of agency?

In the array of sexual relationships ranging from street walker and customer to that of husband and wife, mistresses occupied a unique position.

They were women who sold sex, of course. And, for payment that usually included the establishment or maintenance of a household, they also sold their company and sometimes even their love. Wives provided company and affection too, also in return for a household, but as part of the network of exchanges that constituted marriage. Unlike wives, however, kept women acquired these households without marrying and so did not face the irrevocable conversion of their sexual capital into social and economic capital. Dames entretenues, then, were able to exchange sex, company, and affection for a household, yet retain control over their sexual capital, which they successfully exploited to build professional and intimate lives for themselves. The frailty of the family structure, loopholes in economic regulation, police participation, and shifting ideas of marriage all created a space in which it was possible for socially marginalized girls to become independent heads of household, revealing the significance of sexual capital as a form of power. As part of a well-defined market, sustained in part by police participation, dames entretenues could enhance their own sexual capital and hence afford themselves more choices with regard to whom they took as partners and how they lived their lives.

We should not, however, exaggerate the extent of the degree of choice they possessed. Very few had the choice of saying no to a patron. And if they did, their financial needs made it hard to say no for long. Dames entretenues were subject to the whims of their patrons, the police, and sometimes their families, to the ravages of venereal disease, and to their own habits of consumption which left most in staggering debt. While relentless acquisition of luxury items was characteristic of the demimonde, it threatened the financial well-being of kept women, who could work no more than ten years, as much as did venereal disease or the lettre de cachet. When dames entretenues reached their late twenties or early thirties, their choices were grim. Some married. Those who had managed their wealth during their careers opened dress shops or became madams themselves. For many others, there was no choice but to continue selling sex. As their sexual capital decreased with age, these women found themselves moving down the prostitution hierarchy to streetwalking, with its inherent dangers. And so while kept women may have been able to exercise sexual and other forms agency for the period of their careers, this became an impossibility for most when those careers ended.

Yet, for a decade in their lives, sometimes more, women who would otherwise have been streetwalkers, dying young on the streets or in the Hôpital, were able to exercise a modicum of choice in their sexual partners and in doing so were able to support themselves. The cost was social respectability but the benefit—beyond food on the table and a place to sleep—was the chance at a future. That future did not encompass a reintegration into the artisanal world from which these women came but held out the possibility of a place—as a madam, a dress shop owner or a wife—in a more flexible urban community with decidedly less rigid sexual codes. Is this where Demoiselle Varenne ended her days? We don't know but we can only hope.

❧ ABBREVIATIONS

A.N.   Archives Nationales.

ARM   *L'Académie royale de musique au XVIIIe siècle; documents inédits découverts aux Archives Nationales.* Edited by Émile Campardon. 1884. 2 vols. Reprint. New York: Da Capo Press, 1971.

B.A.   Bibliothèque de l'Arsenal.

B.N.   Bibliothèque Nationale.

Larchey   *Documents inédits sur le règne de Louis XV; ou . . . le journal des inspecteurs de M. le lieutenant de Police de Sartines: première série, (1761–1764).* Bruxelles: E. Parent, 1863. Partial publication of mss. 11357–60 of the Bibliothèque Nationale de France.

Piton   *Paris sous Louis XV: rapports aux inspecteurs de police au roi.* Edited by Camille Piton. 5 vols. Paris: Mercure de France, 1908–15.

☙ NOTES

Introduction

1. Inspector Meusnier's reports can be found in the Bibliothèque de l'Arsenal (henceforth, B.A.) ms. 10242, Dossier of Demoiselle Varenne (*dite* Bentheim), reports dating from 21 September 1752 to 17 December 1756. Inspector Marais's report is in Bibliothèque Nationale (henceforth B.N.) ms. 11358, *Notes sur différentes dames entretenues* (henceforth *Notes*), 26 February 1762. Also found in Lorédan Larchey, *Journal des inspecteurs de M. de Sartines* (Bruxelles, 1863), 103–4 (henceforth Larchey). The story that follows comes from these documents.

2. B.N. ms. 11358, *Notes*, 26 February 1762. This was not the first time Varenne tried to marry secretly. According to Inspector Meusnier, in August of 1755, she tried to liquidate all of her assets, gifts given to her by her current patron, in order to marry another army officer, this time in Anjou. The "marriage project" failed. B.A. ms. 10242, Dossier of Demoiselle Varenne (dite Bentheim), 28 August 1755.

3. Other terms for a professional mistress included *femme galante, fille entretenue, fille d'Opéra, courtisane, courtisane du bon ton,* and *demoiselle du haut trottoir,* each with its own variations. The police used these words interchangeably and in no perceivable pattern. Dictionary definitions offer little more precision. The term *galant* is similarly vague. In the late seventeenth century, a *galant* was a man who sought to please women or was, in fact, the lover of a married woman. The female version, the *galante,* was a flirt, "une femme coquette." *Dictionnaire de l'Académie Française,* 1st ed. (1694), s.v. "galant." By 1762, *galant* had taken on a more sinister tone.

4. Some scholars argue that there were different kinds of *dames entretenues.* In studying police files, historian Erica-Marie Benabou identified thirteen separate categories of subject. There is no question that different ideal types emerge through the reports, but to start with their differences ignores what they have in common and the ways in which their work was regularized. Erica-Marie Benabou, *La Prostitution et la police des moeurs au XVIIIᵉ siècle* (Paris, 1987), 362–69.

5. Ibid., 280–319. Walkowitz made a similar discovery in her study of prostitutes in nineteenth-century Britain. Judith Walkowitz, *Prostitution and Victorian Society: Women, Class, and the State* (Cambridge, 1982), 21.

6. Throughout this study I use the term *demimonde.* There is no single term in eighteenth-century sources that describes the world of elite prostitution and mistress keeping. Referring to a different set of sexual relations than the one under study here, Alexander Dumas *fils* coined the term (as "demi-monde") in a play by the same name in 1855. By the 1870s, however, the term had come to refer to "femmes galantes, entretenues" (Émile Littré, *Dictionnaire de la langue française* [Paris, 1872–77]). It is used

in current scholarship in reference to eighteenth-century dames entretenues and their patrons. See L. L. Bongie, *From Rogue to Everyman: A Foundling's Journey to the Bastille* (Montreal, 2004).

7. *Dictionnaire de l'Académie Française*, 4th ed. (1762), s.v. "galante" and "galanterie."

8. On theater women as mistresses and the link between the theater and the demimonde, see Lenard R. Berlanstein, "Women and Power in Eighteenth-Century France: Actresses at the Comédie Française," in *Visions and Revisions of Eighteenth-Century France*, eds. Christine Adams, Jack R. Censeor, and Lisa Jane Graham (University Park, 1997), 160–63, and Berlanstein, *Daughters of Eve: A Cultural History of French Theater Women from the Old Regime to the Fin-de-Siècle* (Cambridge, MA, 2001), 33–58; Virginia Scott, *Women on the Stage in Early Modern France, 1540–1750* (Cambridge, 2010), 28–37, 246–74; Martine de Rougemont, *La Vie théâtrale en France au XVIIIe siècle* (Paris, 1988), 193–212; Pamela Cheek, *Sexual Antipodes: Enlightenment Globalization and the Placing of Sex* (Stanford, 2003), 50–53.

9. Berlanstein examines this question in *Daughters of Eve*, 39–53. The hyperelite mistresses were a fixation for the nineteenth-century French historians Jules and Edmond Goncourt who wrote books on the dancer Marie-Madeleine Guimard, actress Mademoiselle Clairon, and singer Sophie Arnould and who claimed their accomplishments, among those of other women, for denoting the eighteenth century as "the century of women." Also see Ivor Guest, *Ballet of the Enlightenment: The Establishment of the Ballet d'Action in France, 1770–1793* (London: 1996).

10. Abbé Prévost, Antoine François, *L' Histoire du chevalier des Grieux et de Manon Lescaut* (1731).

11. On the emergence of royal mistresses, see Kathleen Wellman, *Queens and Mistresses of Renaissance France* (New Haven, 2013). On sexuality at court, see Fanny Cosandey, *La Reine de France: symbole et pouvoir, XVe–XVIIIe siècle* (Paris, 2000); Jeffrey Merrick, "The Body Politics of French Absolutism," and Thomas Kaiser, "Louis le Bien-Aimé and the Rhetoric of the Royal Body," in *From the Royal to the Republican Body: Incorporating the Political in Seventeenth and Eighteenth-Century France*, eds. Sara E. Meltzer and Kathryn Norberg (Berkeley, 1998); Jeffrey Merrick, *Order and Disorder in the Ancien Régime* (Newcastle, 2007) and Alain Viala, *La France galante: essai historique sur une catégorie culturelle* (Paris, 2008). Also see some of the many popular biographies on the mistresses of Louis XIV and Louis XV including Evelyne Lever, *Madame de Pompadour: A Life*, trans. Catherine Temerson (New York, 2002); Christine Pevitt, *Madame de Pompadour: Mistress of France* (New York, 2002); and Jacques Levron, *Trois soeurs pour un roi, ou, La cour de Versailles au début du règne de Louis XV Paris* (Paris, 1982).

12. See Nina Kushner, "Concubinage: An Overview" and Kushner, "Concubinage: A Comparative History," in *Oxford Encyclopedia of Women in World History* (New York, 2008), 4:467–79.

13. See Wellman, *Queens and Mistresses*, passim.

14. Mercier distinguished five categories of kept women (*filles d'Opéra, filles entretenues, demoiselles, grisettes,* and *courtisanes*) on the basis of how "decently" they conducted their affairs, on their pride, and on the danger they posed to the health

and finances of their patrons and the nation. Louis-Sébastien Mercier, *Tableau de Paris* (1781–89; repr., Paris, 1994), 3:588, 3:594, 3:602–3, 3:619.

15. *Dict. l'Acad. Fr.*, 4th ed. (1762), s.v. "courtisane."

16. Denis Diderot and Jean le Rond d'Alembert, eds., *Encyclopédie ou Dictionnaire raisonné des sciences, des arts et des métiers, par une Société de Gens de lettres* (Paris, 1761–85), s.v. "courtisane."

17. See Nina Kushner, "Courtesans: Overview," and Nina Kushner and Wai-Yee Li, "Courtesans: A Comparative History," in *Oxford Encyclopedia of Women*, 4:495–98 and 4:498–502. Also see Margaret F. Rosenthal, *The Honest Courtesan: Veronica Franco, Citizen and Writer in Sixteenth-Century Venice* (Chicago, 1992); Martha Feldman and Bonnie Gordon, eds., *The Courtesan's Arts: Cross-Cultural Perspectives* (New York, 2006); and Kathryn Norberg, "Prostitutes," in *History of Women in the West: Renaissance and Enlightenment Paradoxes* (Cambridge, MA, 1993), 458–75.

18. There were a few exceptional dame-entretenue theater women, including Marie-Madeleine Guimard and Sophie Arnould, who held salons. On the salonnières, see Dena Goodman, *The Republic of Letters: A Cultural History of the French Enlightenment* (Ithaca, 1994); Steven Kale, *French Salons: High Society and Political Sociability from the Old Regime to the Revolution of 1848* (Baltimore, 2004); and Antoine Lilti, *Le Monde des salons: sociabilité et mondanité à Paris au XVIIIe siècle* (Paris, 2005).

19. On medieval prostitution, see Jacques Rossiaud, *La Prostitution médiévale* (Paris, 1988); and Leah Otis-Cour, *Prostitution in Medieval Society: The History of an Urban Institution in Languedoc* (Chicago, 1985). For the eighteenth century, see Benabou, *Moeurs*. On the nineteenth and twentieth centuries, see Jill Harsin, *Policing Prostitution in Nineteenth-Century Paris* (Princeton, 1985); and Alain Corbin, *Les Filles de noce: misère sexuelle et prostitution: 19e et 20e siècles* (Paris, 1975).

20. Philip Nord, review of *Policing Prostitution in Nineteenth-Century Paris*, by Jill Harsin, *Journal of Modern History* 59, no. 2 (June 1987): 386. In reducing the prostitute to an object, the regulationist approach can discursively replicate the regimes meant to circumscribe such subjects. Modern scholars who have treated the dames entretenues outside of the framework of regulation have done so peripherally and often writing about these women as the police did, representing their affairs as funny or prurient. Such an approach doubly objectifies the subject. It invites us to join in reducing her to entertainment. See, for example, Robert Muchembled, *Les Ripoux des Lumières: Corruption policière et Révolution* (Paris, 2011), passim.

21. This argument is implicit and may not have been her intent. Benabou died before completing her study, and her research was compiled into a book by several of her colleagues.

22. See, for example, Luise White, *The Comforts of Home: Prostitution in Colonial Nairobi* (Chicago, 1990).

23. The literature produced by the debate, mainly between sex workers and feminists, is extensive. For the position of sex workers, see Gail Pheterson, ed., *A Vindication of the Rights of Whores* (Seattle, 1989), 144–72, 173–201; Frederique Delacoste and Priscilla Alexander, eds., *Sex Work: Writings by Women in the Sex Industry* (Pittsburgh, 1987); Jill Nagle, ed., *Whores and Other Feminists* (New York, 1997). For an overview of feminist positions, see Linda Lemoncheck, *Loose Women, Lecherous*

Men: A Feminist Philosophy of Sex (New York, 1997); Louise Gerdes, ed., *Prostitution and Sex Trafficking / Opposing Viewpoints* (Detroit, 2006); and Gayle Rubin, "Thinking Sex: Notes for a Radical Theory of Sexuality," in *Pleasure and Danger: Exploring Female Sexuality*, ed. Carole S. Vance (Boston, 1984). Also see Noah D. Zatz, "Sex Work/ Sex Act: Law, Labor, and Desire in Constructions of Prostitution," *Signs: Journal of Women in Culture and Society* 22, no. 2 (winter 1997): 277–308; Carole Pateman, *The Sexual Contract* (Stanford, 1988), 189–218; Christine Overall, "What's Wrong with Prostitution? Evaluating Sex Work," *Signs: Journal of Women in Culture and Society* 17, no. 4 (summer 1992): 705–24.

24. The concept was developed in Olwen Hufton, "Women and the Family Economy in Eighteenth-Century France," *French Historical Studies* 9, no. 1 (spring 1975): 1–22; and Louise A. Tilly and Joan Scott, *Women, Work and Family*, 2nd ed. (New York, 1987).

25. The financial success of kept women was not unique. A growing number of studies of the eighteenth century have identified women who were able to support themselves outside of marriage, who were heads of household, or whose careers were the center of the family economy. See Lauren R. Clay, *Stagestruck: The Business of Theater in Eighteenth-Century France and Its Colonies* (Ithaca, 2013); Clare Haru Crowston, *Fabricating Women: The Seamstresses of Old Regime France, 1675–1791* (Durham, 2001); Daryl Hafter, "Female Masters in the Ribbonmaking Guild of Eighteenth-Century Rouen," *French Historical Studies* 20, no. 1 (winter 1997): 1–14; Nancy Locklin, *Women's Work and Identity in Eighteenth-Century Brittany* (Burlington, 2007); Janine Lanza, *From Wives to Widows in Early Modern Paris: Gender, Economy, and Law* (Burlington, 2007); Rene Marion, "The *Dames de la halle:* Community and Authority in Early Modern Paris" (Ph.D. diss., Johns Hopkins University, 1994). The question of "successful women" is the subject of Daryl Hafter and Nina Kushner, eds., *Enterprising Women: Agency, Gender and Work in Eighteenth-Century France* (Baton Rouge, forthcoming).

26. Timothy J. Gilfoyle, "Prostitutes in History: From Parables of Pornography to Metaphors of Modernity," *American Historical Review* 104, no. 1 (February 1999): 137–38 and Kathryn Norberg, "Prostitutes."

27. These are stored in B.A. mss. 10234–44, 10248, 10251–53, 10256, 11846, and the Bibliothèqué Nationale (B.N.) *fonds français*, mss. 11357–60.

28. On Mercier as a writer, see *Panorama of Paris: Selections from* Le Tableau de Paris *by Louis-Sébastien Mercier*, ed. Jeremy Popkin (University Park, 1999), 1–17. Giacomo Casanova, *History of My Life*, trans. Willard R. Trask, 12 vols. (Baltimore, 1997); Alexandre Comte de Tilly, *Mémoires du comte Alexandre de Tilly pour servir à l'histoire des moeurs de la fin du XVIIIᵉ siècle*, ed. Christian Melchior-Bonnet (Paris, 1965); Jean-François Marmontel, *Mémoires de Marmontel: Mémoires d'un père pour servir à l'instruction de ses enfants*, ed. Maurice Tourneux, 3 vols. (Paris, 1891).

29. Edmond Jean François Barbier, *Chronique de la Régence et du règne de Louis XV (1718–1763) ou Journal de Barbier*, 8 vols. (Paris, 1857); Louis Petit de Bachaumont, François Pidansat de Mairobert, and Barthélemy François Joseph Moufle d'Angerville, *Mémoires secrets pour servir à l'histoire de la République des Lettres en France depuis 1762 jusqu'à nos jours*, 18 vols. (London, 1777–89). On the *Mémoires secrets*, see Robert S. Tate, *Petit de Bachaumont: His Circle and the* Mémoires secrets (Geneva,

1968); Jeremy D. Popkin and Bernadette Fort, eds., *The* Mémoires secrets *and the Culture of Publicity in Eighteenth-Century France* (Oxford, 1988). For a discussion of the construction and depiction of sexuality in the *Mémoires secrets*, see Jeffrey Merrick, "Sexual Politics and Public Order in Late Eighteenth-Century France: The *Mémoires secrets* and the *Correspondance sècrete*," *Journal of the History of Sexuality* 1, no. 1 (1990): 68–84, and Cheek, *Sexual Antipodes*, 48–62.

30. On the destruction and reconstitution of the archive, see Frantz Funck-Bretano, *Catalogue des manuscrits de la Bibliothèque de l'Arsenal*, vol. 9, *Archives de la Bastille* (Paris, 1896), xxix–xl.

31. Emmanuel Le Roy Ladurie, *Montaillou, village Occitan de 1294 à 1324* (Paris, 1975); Carlo Ginzburg, *The Night Battles: Witchcraft and Agrarian Cults in the Sixteenth and Seventeenth Centuries*, trans. John and Anne Tedeschi (Baltimore, 1983), xviii. Ginzburg used a similar method in analyzing the interrogation of Menocchio, the protagonist of *The Cheese and the Worms: The Cosmos of a Sixteenth-Century Miller*, trans. John and Anne Tedeschi (Baltimore, 1980).

32. See, for example, Robert Darnton, "A Police Inspector Sorts His Files: The Anatomy of the Republic of Letters," in *The Great Cat Massacre and Other Episodes in French Cultural History* (New York, 1985); Arlette Farge, *Subversive Words: Public Opinion in Eighteenth-Century France*, trans. Rosemary Morris (University Park, PA, 1995); and Lisa Jane Graham, *If the King Only Knew: Seditious Speech in the Reign of Louis XV* (Charlottesville, 2000). Other examples include Steven L. Kaplan, "Réflexions sur la police du monde du travail, 1700–1815," *Revue Historique* 261 (1979): 17–77; and Bongie, *Rogue*.

33. Natalie Zemon Davis, *The Return of Martin Guerre* (Cambridge, MA, 1983), 572.

34. This was Davis's strategy in *The Return of Martin Guerre*. She "embedded" the story of Martin Guerre "in the values and habits of sixteenth-century village life and law, to use them to help understand the central elements of the story and to use the story to comment back on them." Natalie Zemon Davis, "On the Lame," *American Historical Review* 93, no. 3 (June 1998): 572. For a critique of this technique, see Robert Finlay, "The Refashioning of Martin Guerre," *American Historical Review* 93, no. 3 (June 1988): 553–71.

1. The Police and the Demimonde

1. This is Antoine-Jean Amelot de Chaillou (1732–95) son of Jean-Jacques Amelot de Chaillou who had been secretary of state for foreign affairs (1737–44). At the time of this report, Antoine-Jean Amelot was a *maître de requêtes*.

2. B.A. ms. 10241, Dossier of Demoiselle St. Hylaire (dite Fatime, *née* Gabrielle Liberre), 20 March 1755.

3. The police are referring to Wilhelm Heinrich II, prince of Nassau-Saarbrücken. B.A. ms. 10237, Dossier of Demoiselle Maupin, 22 March 1755.

4. Meusnier's reports, like many other police papers, were stored in the archive of the Bastille, which was ransacked when the citadel was stormed on 14 July 1789. Despite an effort by Revolutionaries to recover these documents, it is clear that in the case of the Département des femmes galantes dozens of dossiers and countless

reports within dossiers remain missing. For example, although Meusnier followed 150 women in 1755, there were thirty more on whom he had written reports in 1753 or 1754 and in 1756. It is possible, then, that at least some of these thirty women had been the subjects of reports in 1755, and that those particular reports were subsequently lost. When Marais inherited and inventoried Meusnier's files in 1758, he listed sixty-six that are now lost.

5. Robert Darnton made the same observation with respect to the report writing of Meusnier's contemporary, Joseph d'Hemery, inspector of the book trade. Darnton, "Inspector," 160.

6. An excellent summary of different arguments in this vein can be found in Clive Emsley, *Policing and Its Context, 1750–1870* (London, 1984).

7. Alan Williams's complete list of departments: calf market, spectacles, bourse, pawnbrokers and usurers, charlatans, gambling, wet nurses, criminal investigation and mendicancy, military affairs, *librairie* (publications), foreigners, circles and clubs, horse market, prostitutes and kept women, confidence men (*escrocs*), Les Halles, pederasty, poultry market, hay and fodder, prisoners of state, police prisoners, the *maisons de force*, native Protestants, foreign Protestants, and livestock market. Williams, *The Police of Paris: 1718–1789* (Baton Rouge, 1979), 101. Williams did not include a department of *délits d'opinion* (crimes of opinion), which Lisa Jane Graham discusses in her work *If the King*, 27.

8. Francis Freundlich, *Le Monde du jeu à Paris, 1715–1800* (Paris, 1995), 44–72.

9. Michel Rey, "Police et sodomie à Paris au XVIIIᵉ siècle: du péché au désordre," *Reveu d'histoire moderne et contemporaine* 29 (1982): 113–24; Rey, "L'art de 'raccrocher' au XVIIIᵉ siècle," *Masques* 24 (1984–85); and Rey, "Parisian Homosexuals Create a Lifestyle, 1700–1750: The Police Archives," *Eighteenth-Century Life: Unauthorized Behavior in the Enlightenment*, ed. Robert McCubbin, special edition of *Eighteenth-Century Life* 9 (May 1985).

10. Robert Darnton has written extensively on the policing of the book trade. See, for example, "Inspector."

11. Graham, *If the King*, 27.

12. Williams, *Police of Paris*, 115–24; Vincent Milliot, *Un Policier des Lumières: suivi de Mémoires de J.C.P. Lenoir, ancien lieutenant général de police de Paris écrits en pays étrangers dans les années 1790 et suivantes* (Seyssel, 2011), 222–35; Justine Berlière and Vincent Milliot, *Policer Paris au siècle des Lumières: les commissaires du quartier du Louvre dans la seconde moitié du XVIIIᵉ siècle* (Paris, 2012).

13. The commissioners were respected and trusted to a much greater degree than other police cadres. Arlette Farge and Jacques Revel, *The Rules of Rebellion: Child Abductions in Paris in 1750*, trans. Claudia Miéville (Cambridge, MA, 1991), 30. Also see Milliot, *Un Policier*, 252–64.

14. Jean-Baptiste-Charles Le Maire, *La Police de Paris en 1770: mémoire inédit composé par ordre de G. de Sartine sur la demande de Marie-Thérèse*, ed. Augustin Gazier (Nogent-le-Rotrou, 1879), 42–63; Williams, *Police of Paris*, 4–104; Milliot, *Un Policier*, 252–58.

15. Williams, *Police of Paris*, 95.

16. Ibid., 104–11. The most comprehensive work describing the milieu of the mouche is L. L. Bongie's history of Charles de Julie. As Julie worked for Meusnier,

Bongie recreates in great detail the operations and general working environment of Meusnier and several other inspectors. Bongie, *Rogue*, 105–66. Also see Patrick Wald Lasowski, *Le Traité des mouches secrètes* (Paris, 2003); and Paul d'Estrée, "Un Journaliste policier: le chevalier de Mouhy," *Revue d'histoire littéraire de la France* (1897): 195–238.

17. Milliot, *Un Policier*, 188.

18. Denis Diderot, *Mémoires pour Catherine II*, in *Oeuvres complètes*, ed. Roger Lewinter (Paris, 1969–73), 10:702–3, quoted in Bongie, *Rogue*, 54. Williams estimates that under Lenoir there were 340 spies working for the police during which time Paris had a population of more than 500,000. Williams, *Police of Paris*, 111.

19. Deriving from the Latin "polis," it was defined in the sixteenth century in Robert Estienne's *Dictionnaire francois-latin* (Paris, 1549) as "the . . . government of a republic." In the course of the seventeenth century, the definition narrowed, coming to be closely associated with the government of a city. Pierre Richelet defines "police" in his *Nouveau dictionnaire françois* (Rouen, 1719) as "regulation of a city." Williams, *Police of Paris*, 8–9. The duties of the police were famously outlined in Nicolas Delamare and Le Cler du Brillet, *Traité de la police* (Paris, 1719–1738).

20. Benabou, *Moeurs*, 161–64. Pamela Cheek offers a compelling interpretation of the cultural work effected by the reports. Cheek, *Sexual Antipodes*, 62–77.

21. Robert Muchembled, *Les Ripoux*, 67. For a critique of Muchembled, see Vincent Milliot, "Le Déshonneur de la police?" *La Quinzaine littéraire* 1031 (February 2011).

22. Le Maire, *La Police de Paris en 1770*, 92. Le Maire's treatise was a manual written at the request of Austrian Empress Maria Theresa who wanted to establish her own police force.

23. Marc-René de Voyer d'Argenson, *Rapports inédits du lieutenant de police René d'Argenson* (1891; repr., Liechtenstein, 1972); Letter from Pontchartrain to d'Argenson, 10 February 1706 in *Correspondance administrative sous le règne de Louis XIV*, eds. G. B. Depping and Guillaume Depping (Paris, 1850–55), 2:821–22.

24. Robert Darnton, *The Devil in the Holy Water or the Art of Slander from Louis XIV to Napoleon* (Philadelphia, 2010), 110.

25. Pamela Cheek, "Prostitutes of 'Political Institution,'" *Eighteenth-Century Studies* 28, no. 2 (1994–95): 193–95.

26. See *Paris sous Louis XV: rapports des inspecteurs de police au roi*, ed. Camille Piton, 5 vols. (Paris, 1908–15), 1:8 (henceforth Piton) and Larchey, ix.

27. B.N. ms. 11358, *Notes*, 10 September 1761 (Larchey, 48). Auguste-Louis Bertin de Blagny (1725–88) came from a family of financiers and held the position of *receveur général des revenus casuels et deniers extraordinaires* from 1758.

28. Darnton, "Inspector," 146, 160.

29. In private correspondence, Jacob Melish observed a similar writing style in the report of the Parisian sergeant Alexandre Arnoul. After having arrested a tavern keeper as ordered, the sergeant submitted not the brief report that was required, but a page-and-a-half suspenseful narrative, complete with observations and brief descriptions of people and their emotional reactions. A.N. series Y, ms. 12249, *Procès verbal contre Guillier*, 18 February 1670.

30. Williams, *Police of Paris*, 19–25, 41–44.

31. Jacob Soll, *The Information Master: Jean-Baptiste Colbert's Secret State Intelligence System* (Ann Arbor, 2009), 67–71.

32. Ibid., 132.

33. While several of the lieutenants general had been intendants before taking over the police, only two, Marc-Pierre de Voyer d'Argenson (1720, 1722–24) and René Hérault (1725–40), ever held both positions.

34. Soll, *Information Master*, 137–39.

35. Letter from Pontchartrain to d'Argenson, 10 February 1706 in Depping, *Correspondance administrative*, 2:821–22.

36. Milliot, *Un Policier*, 151–55; Williams, *Police of Paris*, 39–42.

37. Williams, *Police of Paris*, 5–7.

38. Milliot, *Un Policier*, 150, 163–68.

39. For a discussion of the tumult of the period and its relationship to policing, see Robert Darnton, *Poetry and the Police: Communication Networks in Eighteenth-Century Paris* (Cambridge, MA, 2010), 46–55 and 129–88.

40. Ibid. 46–55.

41. Lever, *Pompadour*, 115.

42. Darnton, *Poetry*, 55.

43. The influence of the marquise was a major political issue at midcentury. For an overview of reactions, see Lever, *Pompadour*, 70–138. Writers blamed her for the kingdom's problems; she was thought to have corrupted the king.

44. Williams, *Police of Paris*, 60, ff. 83. Later, in 1758, Pompadour had Berryer promoted to the position of minister of the navy, which he was awarded over her old enemy, the comte de Maurepas. Also see Lever, *Pompadour*, 244.

45. Darnton, *Poetry*, 41.

46. René-Louis de Voyer, marquis d'Argenson, *Journal et mémoires du marquis d'Argenson* (Paris, 1858), 6:108, quoted in Darnton, *Poetry*, 42.

47. Paolo Piasenza, "Juges, lieutenants de police et bourgeois à Paris aux XVIIᵉ et XVIIIᵉ siècles," *Annales* 45, no. 5 (1990): 1198. He makes similar arguments in "Opinion publique, identité des institutions, 'absolutisme.' Le problème de la légalité à Paris entre le XVIIe et le XVIIIᵉ siècle," *Revue d'historique* 118, t. 290 (1993): 97–142. He expands the argument in *Polizia e città: strategie d'ordine, conflitti e rivolte a Parigi tra Sei e Settecento* (Bologne: 1990); R. Cheype, *Recherces sur le procès des inspecteurs de police, 1716–1720* (Paris, 1975). On the relationship between commissioners and inspectors, see Milliot, *Un Policier*, 253, 258–67.

48. Farge, *Subversive Words*, 3, 18.

49. B.A. ms. 10260; Michel Rey, "Police et sodomie"; and "L'art de 'raccrocher.'"

50. Milliot, *Un Policier*, 176–79.

51. Alan Williams argues that the lieutenant generalcy was established in part to deal with the threat posed by the lower classes and *gens sans aveu*. Williams, *Police of Paris*, 189–237. Also see Milliot, *Un Policier*, 184; Kaplan, "Réflexions"; and Michel Foucault, *Discipline and Punish: The Birth of the Prison*, trans. Alan Sheridan (New York, 1979), 304.

52. Vincent Denis and Vincent Milliot, "Police et identification dans la France des Lumières," *Genèses, sciences sociales et histoire* 54 (March 2004): 8–9; Milliot, *Un Policier*, 175, 184.

53. Ibid., 184.

54. Foucault, *Discipline and Punish*, 213–15.

55. Milliot, *Un Policier*, 183.

56. See the letter from Minister Ponchartrain to Lieutenant General d'Argenson dated February 10, 1706. Depping, *Correspondance administrative*, 2:821–22.

57. B.A. mss. 10246, 10261, 10264, 10267. From 1755 to 1757, Meusnier headed a sting operation that arrested priests *in flagrante delicto* with prostitutes in low-end brothels. The priests were not from the elite social milieu. Because the *procès verbaux* produced by these arrests described the priests' sexual activities in graphic detail—which was rare in police reports—and because they focused on the conditions under which the priest ejaculated, they could be used to calculate degrees of sin. Most of the priests were released to their orders, usually within a few hours. All this suggests that the operation had less to do with the state policing of clerical sexuality than with the intense midcentury struggles within the church. For an overview, see Benabou, *Moeurs*, 121–54.

58. Ibid., 104, 114–15.

59. In making this argument I disagree with Benabou whose analysis of prostitution does not distinguish the Département as being administratively separate from other efforts to police prostitution. For evidence of a quarter-based system see A.N. series Y, ms. 9475, "Rolle des prisonniers et prisonneres detenus de police en prisons de Paris arresté par M. le Lt Géneral de police le mercredy 7 juillier et raporté a l'audience de police tenu le 9 du mois de Juiliet 1756." Also see A.N. series Y, mss. 9451A, 9451B, 9628. In his notes, the last lieutenant general, Jean-Charles-Pierre Lenoir, implied that under his watch, policing high and low level prostitution fell to two different departments. The notes marked "département des filles" concern issues related to common prostitution, while those with the marginalia of "département des femmes galantes" related information about engagements with kept women. *Mémoires de J.C.P. Lenoir, ancient Lieutenant général de police de Paris, écrit en pays étrangers dans les années 1790 et suivantes*, ms. 1423, fol. 55, (Milliot, *Un Policier*, 1027–30).

60. On Meusnier, see Bongie, *Rogue*, passim; Paul d'Estrée, "Un policier homme de lettres: L'Inspecteur Meusnier (1748–1757)," *Revue rétrospective: receuil de pièces intéressantes et de citations curieuses*, nouvelle série, sixième semestre (July–December 1892): 217–76; Robert Shackleton, "Deux policiers au XVIIIᵉ siècle: Berryer et d'Hemery," *Thèmes et figures du siècle des Lumières: mélanges offerts à Roland Mortier*, ed. Raymond Trousson (Genèva, 1980), 251–58. Benabou, *Moeurs*, passim, and Robert Muchembled, *Les Ripoux*, passim, the subject of which is the life and career of Inspector Meusnier.

61. Barthélemy-François-Joseph Moufle d'Angerville, *La Vie privée de Louis XV, ou principaux événemens, particularités et anecdotes de son regne* (London, 1781); Paul d'Estrée, "Un policier homme."

62. Bongie, *Rogue*, 72.

63. B.A. ms. 10252. Some have been reprinted in Gaston Capon, *Les petites maisons galantes de Paris, au XVIIIᵉ siècle, folies, maisons de plaisance et vide-bouteilles; d'après des documents inédits et les rapports de police* (Paris, 1902).

64. Of the 2,160 reports on women of the theater, 71 percent were on women of the Opéra, 15 percent Comédie-Française, 7 percent Comédie-Italienne, and 7 percent Opéra-Comique.

65. B.A. ms. 10237, *État present des actrices de l'Opéra*, 1 September 1752. Also see Berlanstein, *Daughters of Eve*, 43 for a discussion of a different list.

66. Opéra administrative records are incomplete for this period. Salaries for several years are listed in Bibliothèque-Musée de l'Opéra, mss. PE 17T, PE 205 and CO 511 and in the A.N. series AJ, mss. 13/17, 13/19 through 13/21. Claude Alasseur found that the principal singers and dancers were paid on average six times more than men and women in the choruses. Opéra salaries rose over the course of the century (as did those in the Comédie-Française) so that by century's end, principals were earning as much as six thousand livres and had the opportunity to supplement these earnings with various bonuses, but these salaries still lagged behind those of the Comédie-Française. Martine de Rougemont, *La Vie théâtrale*, 202, 193–93. Also see Claude Alasseur, *La Comédie française au 18e siècle; étude économique* (Paris, 1967), 111–22, 147–50.

67. Apprentice actors, those without a full or even partial share in the company, might earn between fifteen hundred and two thousand livres annually. Those with shares in the company earned considerably more, although those earnings, despite royal subvention, could vary considerably by year. But in general, the income of actors and actresses climbed over the course of the century, especially after 1760. Lauren Clay found that in 1765, an actress with a full share in the Comédie-Française earned more than ten thousand livres a year. By the mid 1780s, with the general rise in salaries, this figure had climbed to twenty-six thousand livres. Clay, *Stagestruck*, 137–41; Scott, *Women on the Stage*, 261–62; and H. C. Lancaster, "The Comédie-Française, 1701–74: Plays, Actors, Spectators, Finances," *Transactions of the American Philosophical Society* 41 (1951): 593–96. On Opéra salaries, see A.N. series AJ mss. 13/17, 13/19 through 13/21.

68. Casanova, *My Life*, 3:193.

69. Virginia Scott and Lenard Berlanstein disagree as to the extent and meaning of actresses' extramarital sexual activities. They also disagree as to the relative power of actresses. Scott thought actresses lost authority within the Comédie-Française over the course of the eighteenth century while Berlanstein did not. Scott, *Women on the Stage*, 38–58, 247–68; Berlanstein, "Women and Power," 160–63, and *Daughters of Eve*, 33–58. For the position of actresses in the Paris theater and beyond, see Clay, *Stagestruck*, passim, and Rougemont, *La Vie théâtrale*, 193–212. On the power of women in the Opéra, see Guest, *Ballet of the Enlightenment*, passim.

70. Most streetwalkers had other professions, usually in the garment trades, and tended to engage in prostitution when they could not earn enough through licit means. Benabou, *Moeurs*, 280–319.

71. B.A. ms. 10237, Dossier of Demoiselle Catherine Ponchon, 6 February 1756.

72. Compare Meusnier's conception of identity to that of Inspector d'Hemery who in writing on writers considered "a network of family relations, clientages, and 'protections.'" Darnton, "Inspector," 164–65. On the construction of identity more broadly in the Old Regime, see Vincent Denis, *Une Histoire de l'identité: France, 1715–1815* (Seyssel, 2008).

73. That these narratives are similar to those found in fiction has not escaped scholarly attention. See Cheek, "Prostitutes of 'Political Institution,'" 204, 210–11, and *Sexual Antipodes*, 65–69.

74. B.A. ms. 10243, Dossier of Demoiselle Magdelain, 2 January 1754.

75. Alexandre Dumas's *La Dame aux camélias* (1848) was a highly sentimentalized and sympathetic portrait of a kept woman. The play version of the novel became the basis for Verdi's *La Traviata*, first performed in 1853.

76. B.A. ms. 10253, Report from d'Osment, 16 March 1750.

77. Ibid., Report from Hecquet, not dated; Benabou, *Moeurs*, 177.

78. These are B.A. mss. 10252, 10253. On the use of nonpolice personnel as spies, see Milliot, *Un Policier*, 180–82.

79. Benabou, *Moeurs*, 210–66.

80. B.A. ms. 10253, Report from d'Osment, 10 April 1756.

81. For an example, see d'Osment's report to Berryer, B.A. ms. 10253, 25 October 1750.

82. These are in B.A. ms. 10234; Bongie, *Rogue*, 86.

83. For more on La Jannière and his relationships with Meusnier and Inspector d'Hemery, see Bongie, *Rogue*, 111–12.

84. B.A. ms. 10238, Meusnier's correspondence with Berryer, 3 June 1751.

85. B.N. ms. 11358, Dossier of Demoiselle Le Clair, 27 June 1760 (Piton, 1:170).

86. B.A. ms. 10241, Dossier of Demoiselle St. Hylaire (dite Fatime, née Gabrielle Liberre), 20 March 1755.

87. *Mémoires de J.C.P. Lenoir*, Titre II: *Moeurs* (Milliot, *Un Policier*, 500–503).

88. See, for example, the royal edicts of 1656, 1673, 1684, and 1689 that founded and set policy for the Hôpitals Généraux.

89. The primary exception to this was the operation to arrest libertine priests. Benabou argues that the police did intervene in cases of elite prostitution but does not cite any instances. I found no cases of police intervention ex officio.

90. B.N. ms. 11358, Dossier of Julie Morel, 1 November 1760.

91. B.A. ms. 10238, Dossier of Demoiselle Virginie (née Catherine Mahüe), 29 April 1754, 26 October 1754, and 12 November 1754.

92. B.A. ms. 10242, Dossier of Demoiselle Lambertiny, 28 [month illeg.] 1750.

93. B.A. ms. 10238, Dossier of Demoiselle Beaumont (née Suzanne Elizabeth LeGrand), 4 January 1751. Also see Bongie, *Rogue*, 106–110.

94. Ibid., Letter from Beaumont to Meusnier, 20 December 1750.

95. Ibid., 4 January 1751.

96. B.A. ms. 10253, Report from d'Osment, 12 October 1757. Capon thought this letter was from Madame Payen. Gaston Capon, *Les Maisons closes au XVIIIᵉ siècle. Académies de filles et courtières d'amour, maisons clandestines, matrones, mère-abbesses, appareilleuses et proxénètes* (Paris, 1903), 16. Also see Benabou, *Moeurs*, 102.

97. B.A. ms. 10243, Dossier of Dame Perrin de Metz, 23 November 1752, 28 November 1752 and 12 April 1753. Also see Benabou, *Moeurs*, 169.

98. B.A. ms. 10243, Dossier of Geneviève Longagne, 29 November 1756; Benabou, *Moeurs*, 100–1. Muchembled has a different interpretation of Meusnier's relationship to his wife than either myself or Benabou. He claims that the couple worked throughout their lives to grow and sustain Meusnier's criminal enterprises. Muchembled, *Les Ripoux*, passim.

99. B.A. ms. 10238, Report on a petite maison, 26 August 1751.

100. Paul d'Estrée, "Une colonie Franco-Russe au XVIIIe siècle," *La Revue des revues* XIX (1896): 1–16. For the investigation, see B.A. ms 12300, 12301. Muchembled expands on d'Estrée's argument and bases much of his thesis on the idea that Meusnier, in collusion with his wife, Marais, and a number of others, faked his death and then came back to work for the police as Lieutenant General Lenoir's secretary. Muchembled, *Les Ripoux*, passim.

101. B.A. ms. 10253, Report from d'Osment, 12 October 1757. Benabou discusses this report as well. See Benabou, *Moeurs*, 102.

102. A.N. series Y, ms. 15645, Papers of Commissioner Sirebeau, 25 April 1758, quoted in Benabou, *Moeurs*, 102.

103. B.N. ms. 11358, *Notes*, 10 July 1761 (Piton, 1:329).

104. Benabou, *Moeurs*, 103.

105. B.A. ms. 12436, Letter of Sartine to Lenoir, 5 June 1755, quoted in Williams, *Police of Paris*, 95. Jean du Barry was a famous pimp who managed the career of Jeanne Bécu, the future comtesse du Barry, the last maîtresse-en-titre of Louis XV. To qualify Jeanne as a royal mistress, Louis had her marry du Barry's brother, Guillaume, and ennobled the family.

106. Alexis de Tocqueville, *The Old Régime and the French Revolution*, trans. Stuart Gilbert (New York: 1955), 61.

107. Foucault, *Discipline and Punish*, 195–228.

108. Milliot, *Un Policier*, 269–300; See, for example, Francois Antoine Chevrier, *Paris, histoire véridique, anecdotique, morale et critique, avec la clef* (La Haye, 1767); Anne-Gédéon La Fitte, marquis de Pellepore, *Le Diable dans un Bénitier et la métamorphose du Gazetier cuirassée en mouche* (London, 1784); and Louis Pierre Manuel, *La Police de Paris dévoilée par l'un des adminstrateurs de 1789.* 2 vols. (Paris, 1793).

109. Arlette Farge and Michel Foucault, *Le désordre des familles: lettres de cachet des Archives de la Bastille au XVIIIe siècle* (Paris, 1982); David Garrioch, "The People of Paris and their Police in the Eighteenth Century: Reflections on the Introduction of a 'Modern' Police Force," *European History Quarterly* 24, no. 4 (1994): 511–35.

110. David Garrioch, "The Police of Paris as Enlightened Social Reformers," *Eighteenth-Century Life* 16 (1992): 56–57; Milliot, *Un Policier*, 269–387.

2. Leaving Home

1. B.A. ms. 10238, Dossier of Anne Michelet, 28 July 1754.

2. By the 1780s, around 3,500 people moved to Paris each year. Colin Jones, *Paris: Biography of a City* (New York, 2004), 207. The population of Paris at mid-century is a subject of contention. Daniel Roche estimates that it was 500,000 in the years 1700–14 and between 600,000 and 700,000 on the eve of the Revolution. Daniel Roche, *The People of Paris: An Essay in Popular Culture in the 18th Century*, trans. Marie Evans (Berkeley, 1987), 19–20. On the journey to Paris, see Richard Cobb, *Paris and Its Provinces, 1792–1802* (London, 1975). On adjustment from village to city living, see Daniel Roche, *France in the Enlightenment*, trans. Arthur Goldhammer (Cambridge, MA, 1998), 180–86.

3. Michael Sonenscher, *The Hatters of Eighteenth-Century France* (Berkeley, 1987), 23–25.

4. Olwen Hufton, *The Poor of Eighteenth-Century France: 1750–1789* (Oxford, 1974), 26–28; David Garrioch, *Neighborhood and Community in Paris, 1740–1790* (New York, 1986), 127–28; Adeline Daumard and François Furet, *Structures et relations sociales à Paris au milieu du XVIIIe siècle* (Paris, 1961), 33; Cissie Fairchilds, *Domestic Enemies: Servants and Their Masters in Old Regime France* (Baltimore, 1984), 24; Jacqueline Sabattier, *Figaro et son maître: maîtres et domestiques a Paris au XVIIIe siècle* (Paris, 1984), 17–36.

5. Anne followed the late age of marriage determined by the accumulation of a dowry. On this model and marriage age, see J. Hajnal, "European Marriage Patterns in Perspective," in *Population in History: Essays in Historical Demography*, eds. D. V. Glass and D.E.C. Eversley (London, 1969); Etienne Gautier and Louis Henry, *La Population de Crulai, paroisse normande* (Paris, 1958); Jean-Louis Flandrin, *Families in Former Times: Kinship, Household, Marriage, and Sexuality*, trans. Richard Southern (Cambridge, 1976), 185–86; Olwen Hufton, "Family Economy," 7; and Michael W. Flinn, *The European Demographic System, 1500–1820* (Baltimore, 1981), 124–27. This typicality has been challenged by Hans Medick, "The Proto-Industrial Family Economy: The Structural Function of Household and Family during the Transition from Peasant Society to Industrial Capitalism," *Social History* 1, no. 3 (October 1976): 303–4. Also see Tilly and Scott, *Women, Work, and Family*, 41–42, 91–92.

6. Although the police spell his name as "Vieilban," Anne's lover might well have been Jean de Vielbans, *écuyer*, and seigneur de Pommiers, who was a Black Musketeer at this time.

7. Dominique Godineau, *The Women of Paris and Their French Revolution*, trans. Katherine Streip (Berkeley, 1988), 18–24.

8. B.A. ms. 10238, Dossier of Anne Michelet, 28 July 1754.

9. Pierre Henri de Tourmont, 1708–69. Made président in 1742 and held the post until 1760.

10. B.A. ms. 10238, Dossier of Anne Michelet, 19 March 1756. Louis-Antoine-Auguste, prince de Rohan-Cabot. He died in the September Massacres (1792) during the French Revolution.

11. The scholarship on marriage in the early modern period is extensive. A good overview is presented in Olwen Hufton's *The Prospect before Her: A History of Women in Western Europe, 1500–1800* (New York, 1995). The bibliographical essay on pages 577–82 lists most of the major works on the subject. Jeffrey Watt summarizes the debates on marriage in *The Making of Modern Marriage: Matrimonial Control and the Rise of Sentiment in Neuchâtel, 1550–1800* (Ithaca, 1992), 1–23. For a summary of the debates over family size and changes in the emotional content of relationships between family members, see Jack Goody, *The European Family: An Historico-Anthropological Essay* (Oxford, 2000). For an overview of marriage as a social institution in eighteenth-century France, see Suzanne Desan, "Making and Breaking Marriage: An Overview of Old Regime Marriage as a Social Practice," in *Family, Gender, and Law in Early Modern France*, eds. Suzanne Desan and Jeffrey Merrick (University Park, 2009). The volume includes some of the most recent work on the topic.

12. Hufton, *Poor*, 26.

13. It was unusual but not as rare as previously thought. Clare Crowston and Nancy Locklin both have found "spinster clusters" and other evidence of single

women supporting themselves through work. Crowston, *Fabricating Women*, 89; Nancy Locklin, *Women's Work*, 43–44, 98.

14. On women who married after having had an illegitimate child with another partner, see Jacques DePaux, "Les filles-mères se marraient-elles? L'Exemple de Nantes au XVIIIᵉ siècle," in *Aimer en France 1760–1860: actes du colloque international de Clermont-Ferrand*, eds. Paul Villaneix and Jean Ehrard (Clermont-Ferrand, 1980), 2:525–31. On marrying without a dowry, see Medick, "Proto-Industrial Family," 303–4.

15. Garrioch, "Verbal Insults in Eighteenth-Century Paris," in *The Social History of Language*, eds. Peter Burke and Roy Porter (New York, 1987), 104–19, and Garrioch, *Neighborhood and Community*, 39.

16. Daniel Jousse, *Traité de la justice criminelle de France* (Paris, 1771), 3:727.

17. Dowry rates were regionally variable. For an overview, see Hufton, "Family Economy," 6–8. For individual examples, see Sarah Maza, *Servants and Masters in Eighteenth-Century France: The Uses of Loyalty* (Princeton, 1983), 80, and Crowston, *Fabricating Women*, 351.

18. Olwen Hufton found that the combined resources of husband and wife were insufficient to meet the couple's needs in 50 to 90 percent of cases, depending on the region. Hufton, *Poor*, 37.

19. Medick, "Proto-Industrial Family."

20. For a discussion of servant hierarchies, see Jeffry Kaplow, *The Names of Kings: The Parisian Laboring Poor in the Eighteenth Century* (New York, 1972); Fairchilds, *Domestic Enemies*, 24–38; Godineau, *Women of Paris*, 55–56; and Natacha Coquery, *L'Hôtel aristocratique: le marché du luxe à Paris au XVIIIᵉ siècle* (Paris, 1998), 70–76.

21. B.A. ms. 10240, Dossier of Demoiselle Marie-Antoinette Moreau, 7 March 1750.

22. On theater families, see Hannah Marian, *The Pre-Romantic Ballet* (London, 1974), and Gaston Capon, *Les Vestris; le "diou" de la danse et sa famille 1730–1808* (Paris, 1908).

23. B.A. ms. 10237, Dossier of Demoiselle Minot, 6 November 1748.

24. Hufton, *Poor*, 24. For a discussion of who constitute the "menu peuple," see James R. Farr, *The Work of France: Labor and Culture in Early Modern Times, 1350–1800* (Lanham, 2008), 47–78. Farr includes servants in this category, which I do not. Also see Kaplow, *Names of Kings*, 3–65.

25. See, for example, the hierarchies of Nicolas-Edme Rétif de la Bretonne, *Les Parisiennes* (Neuchâtel, 1787), 26–44 and Mercier, *Tableau*, 11:1060–1063. For discussions of social hierarchy and socio-professional classifications in eighteenth-century Paris, see Roche, *People of Paris*, 36–63; Daumard and Furet, *Structures*, 15–41, and Annik Pardailhé-Galabrun, *The Birth of Intimacy: Privacy and Domestic Life in Early Modern Paris*, trans. Jocelyn Phelps (Philadelphia, 1991), 22–39. For seventeenth-century France, see Farr, *Work of France*, 3–7.

26. Berlanstein, *Daughters of Eve*, 57–58; Scott, *Women on the Stage,* 38–58. The French church excommunicated actors, who legally were branded with *infamia*. Only retirement from the stage, an order of the King, or an act of Parlement could reverse the excommunication. On the efforts of various actresses to improve their status, see Mercier, *Tableau*, 3:521, and Casanova, *My Life*, 3:125.

27. B.A. ms. 10242, Dossier of Demoiselle Regnault (née Marie Jeanne Treppier), 14 August 1753.

28. B.A. ms. 10240, Dossier of Demoiselle Marie-Antoinette Moreau, 7 March 1750.

29. B.A. ms. 10243, Dossier of Demoiselle Gagnon (née Marguerite Madeylaine Jacob St. Priest), 8 March 1753.

30. B.A. ms. 10237, Dossier of Demoiselle Martigny (dite Massu), 1 July 1753.

31. B.N. ms. 11358, Dossier of Demoiselle Crousol, *la cadette*, 21 November 1760 (Piton, 1:243–45).

32. Hufton, *Poor*, 115.

33. Milliot, *Un Policier*, 187; Denis, *L'identité*, passim.

34. See for example the confession of Jacques Catery, a servant arrested for solicitation of a *mouche*. B.A. ms. 10260, Dossier of Jacques Catery, 17 December 1749–17 January 1750.

35. Cheek, *Sexual Antipodes*, 70–71.

36. For an overview of the types of work available to girls and women, the female work cycle, and migration, see the work of Olwen Hufton, *Prospect*, 74–101; "Women, Work and Family," in *A History of Women in the West*, eds. Natalie Zemon Davis and Arlette Farge (Cambridge, MA, 1993), 3:17–26; and "Family Economy," 1–11. Also see Godineau, *Women of Paris*, 43–51.

37. Hufton, "Family Economy," 4–8; Daryl Hafter, "Women Who Wove in the Eighteenth-Century Silk Industry of Lyon," in *European Women and Preindustrial Craft*, ed. Daryl Hafter (Bloomington, 1995), 31–42; and Natalie Zemon Davis, "Women in the Crafts in Sixteenth-Century Lyon," in *Women and Work in Preindustrial Europe*, ed. Barbara A. Hanawalt (Bloomington, 1986), For women in industrial production in other parts of France, see Reed Benamou, "Women and the Verdigris Industry in Montpellier," *European Women and Preindustrial Craft*, 3–15; Judith Coffin, *The Politics of Women's Work: The Paris Garment Trades, 1750–1915* (Princeton, 1996); Gay Gullickson, *Spinners and Weavers of Auffay: Rural Industry and the Sexual Division of Labor in a French Village, 1750–1850* (Cambridge, 1986); Hafter, "Female Masters," 1–14; Hafter, *Women at Work in Preindustrial France* (University Park, 2007); Locklin, *Women's Work*, 47–81; and Tessie Liu, *The Weaver's Knot: The Contradictions of Class Struggle and Family Solidarity* (Ithaca, 1994).

38. Hufton, *Poor*, 28; Farr, *Work of France*, 59.

39. Hufton, "Family Economy," 4.

40. Ibid.

41. Hufton, *Poor*, 92–99.

42. Daniel Roche, "Nouveaux Parisiens au XVIIIᵉ siècle," *Cahiers d'histoire* 24, no.3 (1979): 10. Cissie Fairchilds confirmed this finding in her study on servants in Paris. Fairchilds, *Domestic Enemies*, 61–64. Sarah Maza found similar patterns with respect to female migration and service in Aix and Toulouse. Maza, *Servants and Masters*, 37–40. Jeffry Kaplow summarizes some of the older literature on Parisian in-migration. Kaplow, *Names of Kings*, 30–34.

43. Daniel Roche, *People of Paris*, 23–28. Also see Jean-François Dubost, "Les étrangers à Paris au siècle des Lumières," in *La Ville Promise: mobilité et accueil à Paris, fin XVIIᵉ-début XIXᵉ siècle*, ed. Daniel Roche (Paris, 2000), 238–41.

44. Of the 143 women for whom the police recorded geographic origin, 114 (79.7 percent) were from urban areas. Of these, 72 (50.3 percent of the total) were from Paris. Forty-two (29.3 percent) were from other cities.

45. B.N. ms. 11358, Dossier of Julie Brebant, 18 January 1760.

46. Cobb, *Provinces*, 21.

47. Roche, *People of Paris*, 27.

48. Garrioch, *Neighborhood and Community*, 30–33.

49. B.A. ms. 10236, Dossier of Demoiselle La Neuville (née Geneviève Châtelain), 18 June 1755.

50. B.A. ms. 10237, Dossier of Edmée Liotard, 10 September 1753.

51. B.N. ms. 11358, Dossier of Demoiselle Julie Morel, 11 January 1760.

52. Ibid., Dossier of Marie-Louise Prévost (dite Daubigny), 25 July 1760 (Piton, 1:185–87).

53. François Lebrun, "Amour et mariage," in *Histoire de la population française*, eds. Jacques Dupâquier et al., 4 vols. (Paris, 1988): 2:314.

54. Arlette Farge, *Fragile Lives: Violence, Power, and Solidarity in Eighteenth-Century Paris*, trans. Carol Shelton (Cambridge, MA, 1993), 26–41. Other studies of petitions for seduction and abandonment, *déclarations de grossesses* and paternity suits, have found similar patterns. See Nicole Castan, "Inégalités sociales et differences de condition dans les liaisons amoureuses et les tentatives conjugales," in *Aimer en France*, 513–34; Marie-Claude Phan, "Typologie d'aventures amoureuses d'après les déclarations de grossesse et les procédures criminelles enregistrées à Carcassonne de 1676 à 1786," in *Aimer en France*, 503–11; Cissie Fairchilds, "Female Sexual Attitudes and the Rise of Illegitimacy: A Case Study," *Journal of Interdisciplinary History* 8, no. 4 (spring 1978): 627–67; Françoise Fortunet, "Sexualité hors mariage à l'époque révolutionnaire: Les mères des enfants de la nature," in *Droit, histoire et sexualité*, eds. Jacques Poumarède and Jean-Pierre Royer (Lille, 1987): 187–99; Godineau, *Women of Paris*, 47–48; and Maza, *Servants and Masters*, 89–91.

55. The Ordinance of Blois (1579, arts. 40–42) raised the age of majority and criminalized clandestine marriage with a minor as a particular type of rapt, *rapt de séduction*. The Ordinance of 1639 (art. 169) expanded the law to cover children even if they were no longer legal minors. François-André Isambert et al., *Recueil général des anciennes lois françaises depuis l'an 420 jusqu'à la révolution de 1789* (Paris, 1821–33): 14:391–2, 16:273–4, quoted and discussed in Sarah Hanley, "Engendering the State: Family Formation and State Building in Early Modern France," *French Historical Studies* 16, no. 1 (spring 1989): 9–10. Also see Jousse, *Traité*, 3:705–52. For a discussion of the development of the crime of *rapt de séduction* see James Richard Farr, *Authority and Sexuality in Early Modern Burgundy, 1550–1730* (New York, 1995), 97–99.

56. Flandrin, *Families*, 132–34. For an analysis of the relationship of these rules to the evolution of paternal authority, the "family-state" compact, see Hanley, "Engendering the State"; Hanley, "Family and State in Early Modern France: The Marriage Pact," in *Connecting Spheres: Women in the Western World, 1500 to the Present*, eds. Marilyn J. Boxer and Jean H. Quataert (New York, 1987); and Hanley, "The Monarchic State in Early Modern France: Marital Regime, Government and Male Right," in *Politics, Ideology, and the Law in Early Modern Europe: Essays in Honor of J. H.*

Salmon, ed. Adrianna Bakos (Rochester, 1994). For an overview of the church's position see James Brundage, *Law, Sex, and Christian Society in Medieval Europe* (Chicago, 1987), chapter 11.

57. Castan, "Inégalités sociales," 514.

58. B.N. ms. 11358, Dossier of Demoiselle Monginet, 12 December 1760.

59. B.A. ms. 10238, Dossier of Demoiselle Prioré, 13 February 1756.

60. B.N. ms. 11358, Dossier of Julie Morel, 11 January 1760.

61. Ibid., Dossier of Demoiselle Monginet, 12 December 1760. Anne Nicolas Robert de Caze (1718–93) held numerous positions in the financial bureaucracy and has been portrayed as a wastrel who spent inordinate amounts on mistresses. See, for example, Henri Thirion, *La vie Privée des financiers au XVIIIᵉ siècle* (Paris, 1895), 195.

62. Mercier, *Tableau*, 3:594.

63. Abbé Prévost, *Histoire du chevalier des Grieux et de Manon Lescaut* (1731; reprint, Paris, 1995); Anonymous, *Histoire de Mademoiselle Brion, dite comtesse de Launay* (1754; reprint, Paris, 1968). Even those fictional prostitutes forced or tricked into prostitution, like Fanny Hill, whose novel was a best seller in France, soon discovered an inspiring love of sex that shaped the rest of their careers. John Cleland, *Fanny Hill, or, Memoirs of a Woman of Pleasure* (1748; reprint, New York, 1985).

64. Godineau, *Women of Paris*, 43–4.

65. Maza, *Servants and Masters*, 111.

66. B.N. ms. 11358, Dossier of Demoiselle Bourcelles (née Marie Viot), 11 January 1760.

67. Hufton, *Poor*, 20.

68. [Claude Villaret], *La Belle Allemande, ou les galanteries de Thérèse* (Paris, 1755), 32–34.

69. Garrioch, *Neighborhood and Community*, 70, 85.

70. Farge, *Fragile Lives*, 28. Two-thirds of these pregnancies were the result of sexual relations between social equals. One-third were with men of higher social status. Sarah Maza found that female servants accounted for at least 40 percent of reported illegitimate pregnancies in Nantes and between 50 and 67 percent in Aix. Maza, *Servants and Masters*, 89. Benabou estimated that in Paris 60 percent of "fille-mères" were servants. Benabou, *Moeurs*, 300–06.

71. Phan, "Typologie d'aventures," 504–5. Also see Fairchilds, *Domestic Enemies*, 164–80.

72. This typology comes from Cissie Fairchilds's examination of the *déclarations de grossesse* in Aix. "Relationships of equality" were between social equals. "Relationships of inequality" were with men who offered economic inducement or were of greater social rank. Fairchilds, "Female Sexual Attitudes," 635.

73. Flandrin, *Families*, 142–43; Hufton, *Poor*, 30–31, ff. 1; Jousse, *Traité*, 3:715. Godineau found that while most masters dismissed servants they impregnated, 13 percent actually recognized children from these unions. Godineau, *Women of Paris*, 48.

74. Hufton, *Poor*, 312; Benabou, *Moeurs*, 303–4.

75. Garrioch, *Neighborhood and Community*, 33.

76. Jousse, *Traité*, 3:280. "Le bruit public" was not sufficient proof on its own and had to be coupled with evidence of indecent actions, dress or "something similar."

77. B.A. ms. 10242, Dossier of Demoiselle Deperville, 23 August 1752.

78. B.A. ms. 10238, Dossier of Demoiselle Rosalie Blondet (dite Rougi), 20 February 1756.

79. Ibid., 26 March 1756.

80. Farge, *Fragile Lives*, 31.

81. B.A. ms. 10241, Dossier of Marie Marguerite de Villers, 10 September 1752.

82. Phan, "Typologie d'aventures," 506–7.

83. DePaux, "Les filles-mères?"

84. Rousseau discusses his relationship with Thérèse and her family in his *Confessions* (1782). See also Charly Guyot, *Plaidoyer pour Thérèse Levasseur: servante, maîtresse et épouse de J.-J. Rousseau* (Neuchatel, 1962); Maurice Cranston, *Jean-Jacques: The Early Life and Work of Jean-Jacques Rousseau: 1712–1754* (Chicago, 1991); and Leo Damrosch, *Jean-Jacques Rousseau: Restless Genius* (Boston, 2007).

85. Godineau, *Women of Paris*, 23.

86. Benabou, *Moeurs*, 275–82. Clare Crowston did a similar survey of women sent to Saint-Martin in the seven weeks between December 1771 and February 1772 and found that almost a third of those arrested declared themselves to be linen workers. (The next largest groups were laundresses, domestic servants, and tailors' workers). Crowston, *Fabricating Women*, 107.

87. Crowston, *Fabricating Women*, 76. For a breakdown of female occupations in Revolutionary Paris and a discussion of earlier work on the topic see Godineau, *Women of Paris*, 53–93.

88. Dominique Godineau has the impression that after a year or two of cohabitation, some couples would marry. If they remained together for that long and did not marry, they never would. Ibid., 19–20.

89. Hufton, "Family Economy," 10.

90. B.N. ms. 11358, Dossier of Henriette Dubois l'Écuyer, 30 May 1760 (Piton, 1:160–62).

91. B.N. ms. 11238, Dossier of Marie-Barbe-Sophie Faillon (dite La Forest), 15 August 1760 (Piton, 1:195–96).

92. Crowston, *Fabricating Women*, 345; Daumard and Furet, *Structures*, 74–75.

93. B.A. ms. 10237, Dossier of Demoiselle Blanchard, 1 November 1752.

94. Ibid., Dossier of Demoiselle Minot, 30 June 1749; Ibid., Dossier of Demoiselle Blanchard, 1 November 1752.

95. Ibid., 1 November 1752. Jean-Denis Duprès was called "le petit Duprès" so as not to confuse him with Louis Duprès, the principal male dancer of the Opéra until 1751.

96. On *marchandes de modes*, see Jennifer Jones, *Sexing La Mode: Gender, Fashion and Commercial Culture in Old Regime France* (Oxford, 2004), 154–60; Crowston, *Fabricating Women*, 68–69, 108; Daniel Roche, *The Culture of Clothing: Dress and Fashion in the "Ancien Régime,"* trans. Jean Birrell (Cambridge, 1996), 307. Much of the following discussion comes from Jones.

97. Mercier, *Tableau de Paris*, 6:1478–79, quoted in Jones, *Sexing La Mode*, 155.

98. Jones, *Sexing La Mode*, 156.

99. Mercier, *Tableau*, 3:620, 6:1478.

100. Ibid., 8:337–40. See also Jones, *Sexing La Mode*, 159.

101. They were also in the Place de Victoires, which was not a locale of particular importance to the demimonde.

102. Jones, *Paris*, 183. Also see Coquery, *L'Hôtel aristocratique*, 48–56 for shop locations and 187–209 for the residence patterns of Paris's elite.

103. Jones, *Sexing* La Mode, 151. Also see François Boucher's painting, *La Marchande de Modes* 1746 (64 x 53 cm. Nationalmusuem, Stockholm, Sweden). I am thankful to Dena Goodman who brought this to my attention.

104. B.N. ms. 11358, Dossier of Jeanne Demoiselle Béroud (dite Fouassier), 23 April 1760 (Piton, 1:158–60). This is most likely Andre-Antoine, vicomte de Sabran, who was a major in the gendarmes in 1757 and was wounded and captured in battle in 1759.

105. B.A. ms. 10242, Dossier of Demoiselle Regnault (née Marie Jeanne Treppier), 14 August 1753.

106. Benabou, *Moeurs*, 307–19; Crowston, *Fabricating Women*, 108; Hufton, *Poor*, 311–13; Godineau, *Women of Paris*, 13.

107. B.A. ms. 10235, Dossier of Demoiselle Roux (dite Cénie, Charmer, Chaumart), 26 April 1752. Her patron was Henry Hyde, Viscount Cornbury (28 November 1710–28 May 1753), who worked to garner French support for a Stuart invasion of southern England. He was a descendant of Edward Hyde, the governor of New York and New Jersey, who was thought to have dressed as a woman.

108. B.A. ms. 10235, Dossier of Demoiselle Alart, 5 November 1756. On the remarkable career of the female director Madame Destouches (Destouches-Lobreau), see Clay, *Stagestruck*, 108–13, 121, 128–29.

109. B.A. ms. 10238, Dossier of Anne Michelet, 5 November 1756.

110. Hufton, *Poor*, 32.

3. Being Sold into the Demimonde

1. B.A. ms. 10238, Dossier of Demoiselle Louise de la Tour (née Devaux), 1 June 1753, note by Devaux.

2. Ibid., 14 June 1753.

3. Ibid., 19 June 1753.

4. Ibid., 14 June 1753.

5. Ibid.

6. François Aleil, "La Prostitution à Clermont au XVIIIᵉ siècle," in *Aimer en France*, 479–92.

7. B.N. ms. 11358, Dossier of Demoiselle Noël, 18 July 1760 (Piton, 1:180–81). This was probably Claude Dominique Rondé who held the position of *joaillier du roi* and *garde des diamants de la Couronne* from 1753 until 1760, when he died.

8. Pardailhé-Galabrun, *Birth of Intimacy*, 29–31.

9. B.A. ms. 10235, Dossier of Marie Emilie Duneboc de Carville, 2 August 1749.

10. Guest, *Ballet of the Enlightenment*, 22–23.

11. B.A. ms. 10239, Dossier of Demoiselle Dumont, 16 January 1756. Antoine-Gaspard-Grimod de la Reynière (1687–1756), fermier général from 1721 to 1756, and *administrateur-général des postes et relais de France* (postmaster general), amassed 14 million

livres by his death. He was a patron of the arts, kept a lavish townhouse in Paris, and had a chateau in Monceaux. His protection within the postal service allowed Voltaire to dispatch manuscripts through the mail. Colin Bailey, *Patriotic Taste: Collecting Modern Art in Pre-Revolutionary France* (New Haven, 2002), 207.

12. "Economy of makeshifts" is a phrase used by Olwen Hufton to describe how impoverished families did whatever was necessary to survive. Hufton, *Poor*, 15.

13. In his study of prostitution in Clermont, François Aleil found that it was usually mothers, and especially widows, who sold their own daughters into prostitution. "La Prostitution," 483.

14. B.N. ms. 11358, Dossier of Marie Boujard (dite Belleville), 1 March 1760 (Piton, 1:119–21). In this entry, Marais claims that Marie's father had died in the Hôtel Dieu a year before his wife prostituted Marie. In the next entry (26 September 1760) he refers to both parents as living.

15. Bandol was from a provincial robe family, the son of François de Boyer who had been *président à mortier* of the Parlement of Provence. According to nineteenth-century historians Gaston Capon and R. Yves-Duplessis, Bandol's mistress, la petite Pàges, who was the younger sister of Marie-Anne Pàges (Demoiselle Deschamps), fled and hid in a convent in 1759, supposedly because Bandol repeatedly sodomized her. At the time Bandol met Marie Boujard, he was married and soon thereafter experienced significant financial difficulties. Executors of his mother's estate sued him for dissipation of funds. See Jean-Baptiste Denisart, Armand-Gaston Camus, and Jean B. Bayard, *Collection de décisions nouvelles et de notions relatives à la jurisprudence*, vol. 8 (Paris, 1789), 8:215–17; Gaston Capon and Robert Yves-Plessis, *Paris galante au dix-huitième siècle; fille d'Opéra, vendeuse d'amour: histoire de Mlle Deschamps (1730–1764)* (Paris, 1906), 156.

16. B.N. ms. 11358, Dossier of Marie Boujard (dite Belleville), 1 March 1760 (Piton, 1:119–21).

17. Ibid. All the inspector said was that the surgeon found "un large étonnant," meaning that her vagina was "surprisingly wide." Refusal to pay was a common reaction when the buyer believed himself duped. According to the diarist Barbier, the man who slept with the Opéra dancer Dazincourt, believing he had paid for her virginity, demanded some of his money back when he thought he had been tricked. Dazincourt refused to pay, and the couple took their dispute to another singer, Demoiselle Carton, to adjudicate. Carton famously said "quand la toile est levée, on ne rend plus l'argent," referring to the Opéra practice that once the curtain goes up, the audience cannot get its money back. Barbier, *Chronique de la régence*, 3:242.

18. There is no information on how much parents earned when they sold their children themselves.

19. Mathieu-François Pidansat de Mairobert, *L'Espion Anglois, ou correspondance secrète entre milord all eye et milord all'ar*, 10 vols (London, 1779–84), 2:352–66.

20. B.N. ms. 11358, Dossier of Demoiselle Crousol, la cadette, 21 November 1760 (Piton, 1:243–45).

21. B.A. ms. 10235, Dossier of Demoiselle Alart, 5 November 1756.

22. B.N. ms. 11358, Dossier of Demoiselle Godeau, 7 March 1760 (Piton, 1:126–27).

23. Ibid., Dossier of Demoiselle Crousol, la cadette, 21 November 1760. This was Charles Godefroy de la Tour d'Auvergne (1706–71). The notary may have been Auguste-Amable Sibire (1730–72), notary and *conseiller du Roi* 1759–72.

24. B.A. ms. 10236, Dossier of Demoiselle Deschamps (née Marie-Anne Pagès), 15 September 1755. Contrary to what is commonly believed, this was not Samuel-Jacques Bernard, son of the famous financier Samuel Bernard, who inherited 33 million livres in 1739 and declared bankruptcy in 1751. Samuel-Jacques Bernard died in 1753 while Deschamps's relationship with Coubert continued until the end of 1755. It was Coubert's grandson son, Jacques-Samuel-Oliver Bernard (1730–1801).

25. B.A. ms. 10238, Dossier of Dame Perrin de Metz, 28 November 1752, Letter from Montbrun.

26. Casanova, *My Life*, 3:138–39.

27. Marquis d'Usson de Bonnac (1717–1778), colonel of his own regiment who was later promoted to lieutenant general and made governor of Brouage. Opéra historian Émile Campardon, who found and published this document, claims Petite commissioned it. However, throughout his many compendia on theater performers, Campardon tended to take satirical pieces at face value. *Factum pour Mlle Petit, danseuse de l'Opéra révoquée, complaignante au public* (Émile Campardon, *L'Académie royale de musique au XVIIIe siècle* (Paris, 1884), 2:233, henceforth *ARM*).

28. [Denis-Laurian Turmeau de la Morandière], *Représentations à M. le lieutenant général de police de Paris sur les courtisannes à la mode et les demoiselles du bon ton* (Paris, 1762), 9. Also see Capon and Yves-Plessis, *Deschamps*, 25–7.

29. B.N. ms. 11358, Dossier of Demoiselle Raye, l'aînée (Rey, née Louise Régis), 14 December 1759.

30. *ARM*, 2:247–56.

31. B.N. ms. 11358, Dossier of Demoiselle Raye (Rey, née Louis Régis), 14 December 1759.

32. Ibid., Dossier of Marie Dascher (dite La Belle Cauchoise), 25 January 1760 (Piton 1:111–13), 21 February 1761 (Piton, 1:198–99), and 23 August 1761 (Larchey, 16–17). In these reports, Marais refers to one man as the marquis de Voyer d'Argenson and later as the marquis de Voyer, and then just as Voyer. These titles refer to two different people: Marc-René de Voyer de Paulmy d'Argenson (1722–82), to whom I think Marais was referring, was called the marquis de Voyer and sometimes the comte de Paulmy. Son of the secretary of war, Voyer was made the governor of the Château de Vincennes in 1754. He should not be confused with his cousin, Antoine-René de Voyer de Paulmy (1722–87) the marquis de Paulmy, who became the third marquis d'Argenson in 1757.

33. B.N. ms. 11358, Dossier of Demoiselle Crousol, la cadette, 21 November 1760 (Piton, 1:243–45).

34. According to Jousse, "Les pères et mères qui prostituent leur filles, doivent être punis de peine capitale, et quelquefois même du dernier supplice." Jousse notes that in Roman law, prostituting children abrogated *puissance paternal*. Legal theorist M. Guyot argues, "On prétend aussi que les pères et les mères qui prostituent leurs filles doivent être puni de peines emportant, morte civile comme les galères ou le bannissement à perpétuité." Jousse claims, however, the seriousness of the crime can be mitigated if the parents were driven to it by poverty, or if they did

not profit at all and the child consented. Jousse, *Traité*, 3:813–14; M. Guyot, *Répertoire universel et raisonné de jurisprudence civile, criminelle, canonique et bénéficiale* (Paris, 1780), 38:466.

35. *Ordonnance* of 1639.

36. See chapter 2, footnotes 56 and 57.

37. For an overview of children's and parents' legal rights and their duties toward each other, see Henry Taudière, *Traité de la puissance paternelle* (Paris, 1898), 58–70; Flandrin, *Families*, 137–39. For a discussion of *puissance paternelle* (paternal power) in customary law, which governed Paris, see Paul Ourliac and J. de Malafosse, *Historie du droit privé*, vol. 3, *Le Droit familial* (Paris, 1968), 69–75.

38. *Encyclopédie*, 1st ed., s.v. "fils de famille" and "puissance paternelle."

39. Flandrin, *Families*, 134–40.

40. Jeffrey Merrick, "Fathers and Kings: Patriarchalism and Absolutism in Eighteenth-Century French Politics," *Studies on Voltaire and the Eighteenth Century* 308 (1993): 281–303; Merrick, "Patriarchalism and Constitutionalism in Eighteenth-Century Parlementary Discourse," *Studies in Eighteenth-Century Culture* 20 (1990): 317–30; and Merrick, "Marital Conflict in Political Context: Langeac vs. Chambonas, 1775" in *Family, Gender and Law*, 137–82. The idea that patriarchalism should serve as the basis of royal authority found some of its most persistent and eloquent proponents in the eighteenth century, specifically, Jacques-Bénigne Bossuet, *Politique tirée des propres paroles de l'Écriture Sainte à Monseigneur le Dauphin* (Paris, 1709), and Jacob Nicolas Moreau, *Les devoirs du prince, réduits à un seul principe, ou discours sur la justice* (Versailles, 1775).

41. The literature produced by the modernization debate is extensive. A good summary can be found in Goody, *The European Family*. André Burguière and François Lebrun also offer a good overview of the general trends in research in "101 familles d'Europe," in *Histoire de la famille*, eds. André Burguière et al. (Paris, 1986), 2:11–94.

42. Closer emotional relations between parents and children are now considered part of the family's modernization, and this subject has generated considerable scholarship. For an overview of the historiography of childhood, see Hugh Cunningham, "Histories of Childhood," *American Historical Review* 103, no. 2 (October 1998): 1195–1208. For differing views on mother-child relations, see Elizabeth Badinter, *Mother Love: Myth and Reality: Motherhood in Modern History* (New York, 1980) and Lesley Walker, *A Mother's Love: Crafting Feminine Virtue in Enlightenment France* (Lewisburg, 2008).

43. Pardailhé-Galabrun, *Intimacy*, 65–67.

44. Farge, *Fragile Lives*, 52–3.

45. Ibid., 55–62; Arlette Frage and Jacques Revel, *The Vanishing Children of Paris: Rumor and Politics before the French Revolution*, trans. Claudia Miéville (Cambridge, MA, 1991).

46. For general works, see Andre Chassaigne, *Des lettres de cachet sous l'ancien régime* (Paris, 1903); Claude Quétel, *Une légende noire: les lettres de cachet* (Paris, 2011); Quétel, *De par le roy: essai sur les lettres de cachet* (Toulouse, 1981); Farge and Foucault, *Le Désordre des familles*; Franz Funck-Bretano, *Les Lettres de cachet: étude suivie d'une liste des prisonniers de la Bastille, 1659–1789* (Paris, 1903); Brian Strayer,

Lettres de Cachet and Social Control in the Ancien Regime, 1659–1789 (New York, 1992).

47. Farge and Foucault, *Le Désordre des familles*, 18.

48. Archives de la préfecture de police de Paris (A.P.P.) ms. A/B/364.

49. Marguerite Langlois, arrested 22 August 1756, A.P.P. ms. A/B/363.

50. Ibid., Catherine l'Equiller (Femme Chaveau), arrested 15 February 1756.

51. Farge and Foucault, *Le Désordre des familles*, 164.

52. Francine du Plessix Gray, *At Home with the Marquis de Sade: A Life* (New York, 1998).

53. B.A. ms. 10238, Dossier of Dame Perrin de Metz, 23–28 November 1752.

54. Ibid., 28 November 1752.

55. This was possibly Claude-Gédéon-Denis Dumetz de Rosnay, *president à la chambre des comtes*, who was a client of Lafosse.

56. B.A. ms. 10252, Report from Lafosse, 2 November 1755 (Capon, *Maisons closes*, 151).

57. B.A. ms. 10253, Report from Lafosse, not dated (Capon, *Les Maisons closes*, 138–39).

58. Benabou, *Moeurs*, 168–69.

59. B.A. ms. 10235, Dossier of Demoiselle Roux (Cénie), 26 April 1752 and 8 October 1752.

60. B.N. ms. 11358, Dossier of Julie Morel, 11 January 1760.

61. A.N. series Y, ms. 14330, papers of Commissioner Leger, 30 August 1767, quoted in Benabou, *Moeurs*, 349.

62. B.A. ms. 10238, Dossier of Louise de la Tour (née Devaux), 14 June 1753.

63. B.N. ms. 11358, Dossier of Demoiselle Marie Boujard (dite Belleville), 1 March 1760.

64. B.A. ms. 10235, Dossier of Demoiselle Roux (Cénie), 26 April 1752.

65. Pardailhé-Galabrun, *Intimacy*, 34. Daniel Roche, looking at death inventories in Paris, estimated that the average age of marriage was between twenty-seven and thirty. Roche, *People of Paris*, 60.

66. B.A. ms. 10235, Dossier of Demoiselle Amédée (Belgrant), 14 August 1749.

67. Ibid., 4 January 1750. The patron was Charles-Anne-Sigismond de Montmorency-Luxembourg, duc d'Olonne (1721–77). He was made a *maréchal général des camps et armées du roi* in 1748. Shortly after these reports, in June of 1750, the king exiled the duke to his lands in Normandy and the duke abandoned Amédée.

68. B.A. ms. 10235, Dossier of Rosalie Astraudi (Astrodi), 28 June 1750. In another example, the Vestris clan worked as a team to advance the family's fortunes using sexual affairs and positions in various theater companies across Europe from the 1730s through the 1750s. B.A. ms. 10237, Dossier of Violante Vestris. Report by Buhot, 1749. Also see Gaston Capon, *Les Vestris; Le "diou" de la danse et sa famille, 1730–1808, d'après des rapports de police et des documents inédits* (Paris, 1908). Astraudi's patron, comte d'Egmont (Casimir Pignatelli), was rising in the army at this time, under Richelieu's protection. His affair with Astraudi ended in 1753. In 1756, he married the duke's daughter, who was very active in the arts.

69. A.N. series Y, ms. 12156, papers of Commissioner Louis Cadot (*ARM*, 2:31–33).

4. Madams and Their Networks

1. B.N. ms. 11358, Dossier of Marie Boujard (dite Belleville), 1 March 1760 (Piton, 1:119–21).

2. This was probably Nicolas-Joseph Revengé de Bompré, born in 1726. As part of the Régiment de Cavalerie de Levis, Persenat fought in the Seven Years' War, during which he was awarded the cross of Saint Louis (in 1760). He was eventually made *maréchal de camp* and captain of the *gardes de roi de Pologne*.

3. B.N. ms. 11358, Dossier of Marie Boujard, 26 September 1760 (Piton, 1:222).

4. Police toleration was common in polities in which prostitution was illegal. In medieval England, for example, many towns had laws that both criminalized prostitution, which was seen as abhorrent, and regulated its practice, which was thought to be necessary to the peaceful functioning of society and the protection of the honor of respectable women. See Ruth Mazo Karras, *Common Women: Prostitution and Sexuality in Medieval England* (New York, 1996), 13–47. In the nineteenth century, police and state authorities regulated prostitution as a way both to contain it and provide specific male populations with sexual outlets. See Corbin, *Filles de noces*; Judith Walkowitz, *Victorian Society*; and Philippa Levine, *Prostitution, Race and Politics: Policing Venereal Disease in the British Empire* (New York, 2003).

5. These reports can be found in B.A. ms. 10252 and 10253. Some of them have been transcribed and printed in Gaston Capon, *Les Maisons closes*.

6. B.A. ms. 10253, Dossier of Madam Dufresne, client lists for June, July and August 1753.

7. Ibid., Dossier of Madam d'Osment, client lists for September, October and November 1750.

8. Casanova, *My Life*, 3:150.

9. B.A. ms. 10253, Dossier of Madam Montbrun, client lists for July and August 1752.

10. Benabou characterized the relationship of these madams to the police as one of patronage. Benabou, *Moeurs*, 179.

11. Contemporaries were aware that the madams were taking notes and forwarding them to the police. See Charles Théveneau de Morande, *La Gazette Noire par un homme qui n'est pas blanc ou oeuvres posthumes du gazetier cuirassé* (Paris, 1784), 89–90, quoted and analyzed by Cheek, "Prostitutes of Political Institutions," 195–97.

12. Charles Bernardin de Menildot, marquis de Vierville, made *maréchal de camps et armées du roi* in 1759. His daughter was the marquise de Barbentane who was a writer.

13. B.N. ms. 11358, *Notes*, 24 July 1761 and 31 July 1761 (Piton, 1:336 and 342).

14. B.A. ms. 10252, Report from Lafosse, 2 November 1755 (Capon, *Les Maisons closes*, 151).

15. Benabou, *Moeurs*, 175–76.

16. B.A. ms. 10253, Report from d'Osment, 20 March 1757 and 12 October 1757 (Capon, *Les Maisons closes*, 16–21). Capon claims that Madam Payen was the author of these reports. For a different interpretation of the encounter, see Benabou, *Moeurs*, 239–42.

17. B.A. ms. 10253, Report from d'Osment, 12 October 1757.

18. Lauren Clay, *Stagestruck*, chapters 4–5.

19. The idea that eighteenth-century populations manipulated those who policed them has been explored by David Garrioch, "People of Paris," 511–35.

20. Edict of Orléans, 1560, article 101. Later royal ordinances that tried to suppress prostitution and pimping or which set up regimes for its punishment include that of 1660, 1684, 1687, and 1713. For legal glosses on "maquellerage," see Jousse, *Traité*, 3:810–16 and Guyot, *Répertoire universel*, 38:461–69. See Benabou, *Moeurs*, 21–30 and 38–49 for an overview of the laws against prostitution and pimping and for a discussion of their enforcement.

21. B.A. ms. 11326, Dossier of Madam Lacroix, no date (Capon, *Les Maisons closes*, 54).

22. For some night raids led by Meusnier and Commissioner Boullanger that resulted in the arrest of prostitutes or the breakup of brothels, see A.N. series Y, ms. 12659, Papers of Commissioner Claude Louis Boullanger, 1 October 1760: Procès Verbal de visitte de nuit et emprisonment de filles de Debauche.

23. On police court and transport of prostitutes to prison, see Mercier, *Tableau*, 3:598–99 and Benabou, *Moeurs*, 60–65.

24. B.A. ms. 10252, Report from Lafosse, no date (Capon, *Les Maisons closes*, 142).

25. Barbier, *Chronique de la régence*, 5:159. Barbier said that the house passed to Carlier "qui est apparemment autorisée." Also see Capon, *Les Maisons closes*, 40, 49–52, and Benabou, *Moeurs*, 178.

26. Additionally, madams may have apprised Meusnier of these sales in the effort to win his good will. Both Lafosse and Montbrun appear to have offered virgins they were brokering into relationships to Meusnier for his sexual use. B.A. ms. 10238, Dossier of Dame Perrin de Metz, 28 November 1752 and 14 June 1753; B.A. ms. 10252, Report from Lafosse to Inspector Meusnier, 2 November 1755 (Capon, *Les Maisons closes*, 151–52).

27. B.A. ms. 11069, Dossier of Madam Ricard (Capon, *Les Maisons closes*, 237–38) and Benabou, *Moeurs*, 50.

28. Barbier, *Chronique de la régence*, 4:448–49; Jousse, *Traité*, 3:813. Also see Benabou, *Moeurs*, 46–51, for a discussion of the case.

29. Benabou, *Moeurs*, 49–53.

30. Jousse, *Traité*, 3:810–16.

31. A.N. series Z^2, ms. 3039. For contemporary reporting on the scandal, see Pidansat de Mairobert, *L'Espion Anglois*, 2:50–64. Mairobert accused Gourdan of having tried to procure a married noblewoman once before, on behalf of Sieur Dongé, a fermier général. He also named Madam Grenier and not Madam Montigny as the third defendant. Madam Gourdan was a popular subject of satire. See Charles Théveneau de Morande, *Le Porte-feuille de Madame Gourdan, dite la Comtesse,*

pour servir à l'histoire des moeurs du siècle, et principalement de celles de Paris (Paris, 1783). Also see Benabou, *Moeurs*, 51.

32. D'Argenson, *Journal et mémoires*, 7:109.

33. Mercier, *Tableau*, 7:14.

34. Some contemporaries developed plans to control the problem of prostitution via containment, the most famous of which was Nicolas-Edme Rétif de la Bretonne, *Le Pornographe* (London, 1769). The idea of containment was an active part of official nineteenth-century prostitution policies, by which prostitutes were to register and often live in brothels that were walled off from the public. Corbin, *Filles de noces*, passim.

35. B.N. ms. 11358, Dossier of Marie-Barbe-Sophie Faillon, 15 August 1760.

36. B.A. ms. 10252, Report from Lafosse, no date (Capon, *Les Maisons closes*, 143).

37. Ibid., Report from Montbrun, 26 January 1753.

38. B.A. ms. 10253, Dossier of Montbrun (on the front of her file in Meusnier's hand). Benabou provides biographies of several other madams, *Moeurs*, 237–59. Historians debate whether we can use the terms "gay" and "lesbian" to refer to sexualities in the mid-eighteenth century.

39. According to Durocher, Monsieur Baudouin tried to move back in with his wife after learning of her success. She resisted, and they both filed complaints with the police. B.A. ms. 10252, Report on Baudouin by Inspector Durocher, 20 October 1752.

40. Muchembled claims that Meusnier wrote this autobiography as well as many of d'Osment's reports as the madam was a "double agent" working for him. Muchembled argues that d'Osment's reports were false but he provides no actual evidence for this argument. Muchembled, *Les Ripoux*, 242–53.

41. B.A. ms. 10253, Report from d'Osment, 10 October 1750. Kathryn Norberg, "An Eighteenth-Century Madam: Marie-Madeleine d'Ossement" (paper presented at the annual meeting for the Western Society for French History, Boulder, CO, October 2009). The name d'Osment has multiple spellings in the police reports.

42. Mercier, *Tableau*, 7:11–21.

43. Barbier, *Chronique de la régence* (1851 ed.), 3:122 (Capon, *Les Maisons closes*, 41). The Charpentier edition (1857), which is used as a source throughout this book, deleted the section on Madam Paris from Barbier's entry of March, 1750.

44. Casanova, *My Life*, 3:151.

45. Archives de la Seine, Lettre de ratification, carton 975 (Capon, *Les Maisons closes*, 191).

46. Mairobert, *L'Espion Anglois*, 2:50–64.

47. B.A. ms. 10252. Report from Madam Montbrun, January 1754.

48. See, for example, Marmontel's discussion of Saxe and his mistresses in Marmontel, *Mémoires*, 107–17.

49. B.A. ms. 10252, Report of Montbrun, 7 April 1753. On contemporary terminology, see Alexa Albert, *Brothel: Mustang Ranch and Its Women* (New York, 2001), 19.

50. B.A. ms. 10252, Report from Lafosse, 19 March to 23 March 1755 (Capon, *Les Maisons closes*, 138–39). Capon claims the letters are undated. Lafosse explained

Helvétius's presence by saying his wife was about to have a son. She also claimed that he had released his wife from her "conjugal duties," turning to their chamber maid instead. On the philosophe's sexual relations with his wife, see Meghan Roberts, "Cradle of Enlightenment: Family Life and Knowledge Making in Eighteenth-Century France" (Ph.d. diss. Northwestern University, 2011), 282.

51. B.A. ms. 10252, Report from Lafosse, 11 July, no year (Capon, *Les Maisons closes*, 140).

52. Ibid. This was Claude-Etienne Bidal (1719–92), made *maréchal de camp* in 1748 and was married in 1755 to Anne-Louise Charlotte de Pajot.

53. B.A. ms. 10252, Reports from Baudouin and Durocher, 17 August 1753.

54. Ibid., Reports from Babet, November and December, 1754.

55. B.A. ms. 10253, Reports from Montbrun, September 1752.

56. B.A. ms. 10252, Report from Durocher on Baudouin, 7 September 1753.

57. Casanova, *My Life*, 3:150–51.

58. Barbier, *Chronique de la régence*, 3:122 (1851 ed.) (Capon, *Les Maisons closes*, 41).

59. B.N. ms. 11358, *Notes*, 6 February 1761 (Piton, 1:291–92).

60. B.A. ms. 10253, Report from Montbrun, June and September 1752.

61. B.N. ms. 11358, *Notes*, 31 July 1761 (Piton, 3:339–40).

62. B.A. ms. 10253, Report from Montbrun, no date.

63. Ibid., Report, 16 March 1750. (The author seems to be d'Osment, but the report says Maison left from chez Lasalle. Nancy was a frequent customer at d'Osment's brothel.

64. B.A. ms. 10252, Report from Lafosse, no date (Capon, *Les Maisons closes*, 141).

65. Théveneau de Morande, *Le Porte-feuille*, 7–8.

66. B.A. ms. 10252, Report from Montbrun, 26 January 1753.

67. B.A. ms. 10235, Dossier of Eléonore Boismilon (dite Vanosse), 11 September 1754.

68. B.A. ms. 10252, Report of Durocher on Baudouin, 21 September 1753 and B.A. ms. 10243, Dossier of Demoiselle Marquis, 9 April 1754. Of Spanish descent but having been born in France, Ximènes (1728–1817) was a soldier in his youth but quit the army after the battle of Fontenoy (1745) and then became a respected playwright, author of *Don Carlos*, and a poet. He was good friends with Voltaire. He married in 1768.

69. B.A. 10252, Report on *petites maisons*, August 1752.

70. See for example Lafosse's description of a petit souper at the house of Monsieur Cury, *intendant des menus plaisirs de roi*. B.A. ms. 10252, Report from Lafosse, 6 May 1754 (Capon, *Les Maisons closes*, 146–48).

71. Of the sixty-four women who attended these fifty-three soupers, forty-four are identifiable. Thirteen were pensioners, and the rest were theater women or kept women. B.N. ms. 11358, *Anecdotes Galantes*, 16 February 1761 through 22 January 1762.

72. B.A. ms. 10252, Report from Durocher on Baudouin, 31 August 1753.

73. Ibid., Report of Montbrun (Desparvier), 27 January 1754.

74. Marquis de Sailly, for example, had dinner parties with prostitutes provided by Madam Fleurance at his house at the Barrière Blanche. B.A. ms. 10252, *État des petites maisons*, August 1754.

75. Of the fifty-three events listed between February 1761 and January 1762, Marais recorded the location of forty-six of them. Of these, twenty-three were held at petites maisons (eight of which were rented by madams). Fourteen petits soupers were held in brothels—those of Varenne, Brissault, Dupuis and Hecquet. The rest were held in private residences.

76. Gaston Capon, *Les petites maisons galantes de Paris, au XVIIIe siècle, folies, maisons de plaisance et vide-bouteilles; d'après des documents inédits et des rapports de police* (Paris, 1902).

77. The ways in which dames entretenues used these houses to keep their affairs secret became a metaphor for the philosophe Marmontel in describing the secrecy of his landlord, the salon hostess Madam Geoffrin. "Elle avoit un appartement dans un convent de religieuses et une tribune à l'église des Capucins, mais avec autant de mystère que les femmes galantes de ce temps-là avaient des petites maisons." Marmontel, *Mémoires*, 2:50–52.

78. Capon, *Les Maisons closes*, 163.

79. B.A. ms. 10252, *État des peittes maisons scituées aux environs de Paris avec les noms des propriataires et de ceux qui les occupents au premiet julliet 1752*, 1 July 1752.

80. *Histoire de Mademoiselle Brion dite comtesse de Launay* (1754; reprint, Paris, 1968), 39.

81. B.A. ms. 10236, Dossier of Demoiselle Deschamps, l'aînée, 20 February 1753.

82. B.A. ms. 10243, Dossier of Demoiselle Betrand, 2 February 1751.

83. B.A. ms. 10252, Inspector Durocher's report on Baudouin, 16 November 1753.

84. Ibid., Report from Montbrun, 9 February 1757.

85. On businesswomen and property managers, see James Collins, "The Economic Role of Women in Seventeenth-Century France," *French Historical Studies* 16 (fall 1989), 456–57; Crowston, *Fabricating Women*, passim; Hafter, *Women at Work*, passim; Hafter, "Female Masters"; Julie Hardwick, *The Practice of Patriarchy: Gender and the Politics of Household Authority in Early Modern France* (University Park, 1998), 77–142; Hardwick, *Family Business: Litigation and the Political Economies of Daily Life in Early Modern France* (Oxford, 2009), 128–82; Lanza, *Widows*, 122–52; Locklin, *Women's Work*, passim; and some of the essays in *Enterprising Women*, including Jacob Melish, "The Power of Wives: Managing Money and Men in the Family Businesses of Old Regime Paris"; Rafe Blaufarb, "The Phenomenon of Female Lordship: The Example of the comtesse de Sade"; Jane McCleod, "Printer Widows and the State in Eighteenth-Century France"; and Jennifer Palmer, "Colonial Transformations: Gender and the Family in the Age of Transatlantic Commerce."

86. Claude de Ferrière, *Corps et compilation de tous les commentateurs anciens et modernes sur la Coutume de Paris* (Paris, 1714), article 235.

87. On relationships of madams to pensionners and for a discussion of life inside the brothel, see Benabou, *Moeurs*, 223–33.

88. B.A. ms. 10253, Report from Hecquet, no date. Also see Benabou, *Moeurs*, 177.

89. Ibid., Report from d'Osment, 16 March 1750.

90. Ibid.

91. Casanova, *My Life*, 3:151.

92. Deschaux was missing three teeth in the front of her mouth. B.A. ms. 10235, Dossier of Geneviève-Agnès Deschaux (dite Beaufort), 12 September 1755.

93. Rétif de La Bretonne, *Le Pornographe*, 486–87, quoted in Benabou, *Mœurs*, 224.

94. B.A. ms. 10238, Dossier of Demoiselle Virginie (née Catherine Mahüe), 12 November 1754.

95. Benabou, *Moeurs*, 409–10.

96. For an overview of the symptoms and treatment for both syphilis and gonorrhea, see Linda E. Merians, "Introduction," *The Secret Malady: Venereal Disease in Eighteenth-Century Britain and France*, ed. Linda E. Merians (Lexington, 1996), 7–9. For the state of medical knowledge, see Susan P. Conner, "The Pox in Eighteenth-Century France," in *Secret Malady*, 15–33. For attitudes toward venereal disease, see Kathryn Norberg, "From Courtesan to Prostitute: Mercenary Sex and Venereal Disease, 1730–1802," in *Secret Malady*, 34–50; and Benabou, *Moeurs*, 407–30.

97. With a 20 percent margin of error. Benabou, *Moeurs*, 411.

98. Hardwick, *Family Business*, 128–82, quote is on 136.

99. Benabou, *Moeurs*, 225.

100. Mercier, *Tableau*, 7:11–21, quoted in Popkin, *Panorama of Paris*, 142–43; Casanova, *My Life*, 3:151.

101. B.N. ms. 11358, *Notes*, 1 January 1762 (Larchey, 88).

102. Ibid., 27 November 1761 (Larchey, 64–65).

103. B.N. ms. 11358, Dossier of Demoiselle Marie Boujard (dite Belleville), 1 March 1760 (Piton, 1:119–21).

104. Ibid., Dossier of Demoiselle Marie Lelache (dite Deschamps), no date.

105. Capon, *Les Maisons closes*, 230–31.

106. B.A. ms. 10252, Reports on Baudouin by Inspector Durocher, 5 December 1752 to 21 March 1753. Antoine-René de Voyer de Paulmy d'Argenson was called the marquis de Paulmy until he succeeded his father as the marquis d'Argenson in 1757. He kept mistresses and he visited Lafosse's brothel, repeatedly expressing worry that the madam would report his actions to Meusnier. See B.A. ms. 10252, Report from Lafosse, no date (Capon, *Les Maisons Closes*, 143). His cousin, Marc-Renè de Voyer de Paulmy d'Argenson, son of the secretary of war, was called both the marquis de Voyer and the comte de Paulmy, and hence is also a possible, but less likely, candidate.

107. Morande, *Port-feuille*, 5–6.

108. B.A. ms. 10252, Reports on Baudouin by Inspector Durocher, 3 November 1752 to 16 December 1752. Jean-Baptiste-François de Montmorin, marquis de Saint-Hérem (1704–79). In 1750 he was a lieutenant general in the army in addition to being *gouverneur et capitaine de chasses de Fontainebleau*. He was also a widower, and would remarry in 1761.

109. B.N. ms. 11358, Dossier of Demoiselle Beauvoisin, 20 April 1762 (Larchey, 115). Antoine-Antonin de Grammont (1722–1801). At the time he wanted to sleep with Demoiselle Beauvoisin, Grammont was married to Béatrix de Choiseul-Beaupré, sister of the duc de Choiseul, former minster of war and foreign affairs.

110. B.A. ms. 10252, Report of Madam Baudouin, 28 September 1753 (Capon, *Maisons closes*, 127–28).

111. B.A. ms. 10235, Dossier of Geneviève-Agnès Deschaux (dite Beaufort), 12 September 1755 and 21 January 1756.

112. B.A. ms. 10240, Dossier of Demoiselle Agathe (dite Marbourg), 30 April 1749 to 19 November 1753.

113. B.N. ms. 11358, Dossier of Marie Dascher (dite La Belle Cauchoise), 25 January 1760 (Piton 1:111–13), 21 February 1761 (Piton, 1:198–99), and 23 August 1761 (Larchey, 16–17).

114. B.A. ms. 10237, Dossier of Demoiselle Judith Leoni (dite Matini), 22 May 1752.

5. Contracts and Elite Prostitution as Work

1. B.A. ms. 10236, Dossier of Demoiselle Gautier, la cadette, 28 August 1753 and 6 April 1754. Dumas de Corbeville (1724–54) was from a finance family. His father, Claude-François Dumas, *écuyer*, seigneur of Corbeville was also a fermier général and his mother was the from the Grimod family, who were also financiers. Yves Durand, *Les Fermiers généraux au XVIIIe siècle* (Paris, 1996), 276.

2. B.A. ms. 10237, Dossier of Demoiselle Raime, 17 April 1754 and 21 August 1754. In the file on Gautier, Inspector Meusnier claimed that the apartment was rented for six hundred livres and the furniture for six hundred livres. In the file on Raime he claimed that the same apartment cost twelve hundred livres in rent and that the furniture was owned. It is possible that Raime was given an extra floor on which to live and that her furnishings were both rented and owned.

3. Although ownership of Dumas's post was contested after his death (in July 1765) the post was immediately given to Charles Guillaume Le Normant d'Étiolles, husband of the marquise de Pompadour. A month later, in August, the police reported that d'Étiolles became Raime's patron as well. They were together until police reporting stopped in 1757 and had one child. Barbier, *Chronique de la régence*, 6:39; B.A. ms. 10237, Dossier of Demoiselle Raime, 12 August 1754 to 7 January 1757.

4. See, for example, *Histoire de Mademoiselle Brion*, 135–36.

5. For "bail," see the song about Mademoiselle Dazincourt (*ARM*, 1:100). In his satire on the contract, Turmeau de la Morandière uses the term "arrangements." Turmeau de la Morandière, *Représentations* (Paris, 1762), 27.

6. The primary definition of the word *commerce* is unchanged from the first edition of the *Dict. l'Acad. Fr.* (1694) through the most current edition (1935). In the 1694 edition, the second entry concerns dishonest or illegal dealings: "On dit fig. d'Un homme qui se mesle de quelque chose qui n'est pas honneste. *Qu'Il fait un mauvais, un meschant, un vilain commerce, un sale & honteux commerce.* & par ironie, *un joli, un beau commerce.*" By 1798, the editors had added several new meanings including "On dit. *Avoir commerce, être en commerce avec . . .* Et il s'entend en mauvaise part, quand on parle de personnes de différens sexes." By 1835 "commerce" had come to mean "d'une liaison illicite entre deux personnes de sexes différens."

7. *Dict. l'Acad. Fr.*, 5th ed. (1798), s.v. "honoraires." Occasionally, the police used "appointemens" in place of *honoraires*. According to the *Encyclopédie* (1:554) the two terms were synonyms.

8. *La Belle Allemande*, 1, 40, and 142.

9. Erica-Marie Benabou took a different sample and found only slightly different proportions. Benabou counted 517 contracts in the portion of Marais's reports published by Larchey in *Journal des inspecteurs*. Benabou, *Moeurs*, 337–38.

10. Bauchamont, *Mémoires secrets*, 3:287–88

11. Badinter, *Mother Love*, 47; Crowston, *Fabricating Women*, 91; Sonenscher, *Work and Wages*, 204; Darnton, *The Literary Underground of the Old Regime* (Cambridge, MA, 1982), 48.

12. Sonenscher, *Work and Wages*, 183–84.

13. Lauren Clay, "Provincial Actors, the Comédie-Française, and the Business of Performing in Eighteenth-Century France," *Eighteenth-Century Studies* 38, no. 4 (summer 2005): 651–79.

14. Maza, *Servants and Masters*, 103. Also see Fairchilds, *Domestic Enemies*, 54–58.

15. B.N. ms. 11358, Dossier of Demoiselle Crousol, la cadette, 21 November 1760 (Piton, 1:243–45).

16. Ibid., Dossier of Demoiselle Geneviève Vallée (dite Dupin), 1 August 1760 (Piton, 3:191–93).

17. Ibid., Dossier of Demoiselle Sire (dite Dornay), 27 November 1761 (Larchey, 68).

18. Bachaumont, *Mémoires secrets*, 3:323. Louis-Léon-Félicité de Brancas (1733–1824), duc de Villars and duc de Lauraguais after 1755. Lauraguais was known for spending extravagantly on mistresses and for having a long affair with the singer Sophie Arnould, with whom he had four children.

19. Benabou, *Moeurs*, 340–41. Her 1790 rental statistics were taken from Marcel R. Reinhard, *Nouvelle histoire de Paris, la Révolution 1789–1799* (Paris, 1971), 42.

20. B.A. ms. 10238, Dossier of Demoiselle Leoville, 26 November 1756.

21. B.N. ms. 11358, Dossier of Demoiselle Chédeville, 6 February 1761 (Piton, 1:287–88). Despite the similarity in name and possibility of the inspectors confusing military titles, this could not be General Stepan Fyodorovich Apraksin who commanded Russian forces during the Seven Years' War and was accused of treason in 1757. The general died in 1758. Chédeville is not the same person as the principal singer Marie-Madeleine Jendrest, known professionally as Chefdeville.

22. Capon and Yves-Plessis, *Deschamps*, 70, 90.

23. The basic work on Guimard is still Edmond de Goncourt, *La Guimard, d'après les registres des menus-plaisirs, de la bibliothèque de l'Opéra, etc.* (Paris, 1893). Also see Ivor Guest, "Letter from London: Guimard's Farewell to the Stage," *Dance Chronicle* 18, no. 2 (1995): 207–15 and Guest, *Ballet of the Enlightenment*; Capon republished Guimard's "clippings" in *ARM*, 1:366–90. On the cost of the furniture, see Kathryn Norberg, "Goddesses of Taste: Courtesans and Their Furniture in Late-Eighteenth-Century Paris," in *Furnishing the Eighteenth Century: What Furniture Can Tell Us about the European and American Past*, eds. Dena Goodman and Kathryn Norberg (New York, 2007), 99.

24. B.A. ms. 10236, Dossier of Demoiselle Gallodier, la cadette, 13 August 1756. Gravelles held that position from 1753 until 1766.

25. B.A. ms. 10236, Dossier of Marie Perette Granier, 9 January and 16 January 1754. Auguste-Simon Brissart (1726–79) was from and married into families of

fermiers généraux. Becoming a fermier général in 1750, Brissart dispensed enormous sums on dames entrerentues, especially filles d'Opéra, including Demoiselles Caroline, Chaumart, and Deschamps on whom the police estimated him to have spent 500,000 livres. Durand, *Les Fermiers généraux*, 341.

26. A.N. series Y, ms. 12997, papers of Commissioner Charles-Alexandre Ferrand, déclaration de grossesse, 10 June 1775 (*ARM*, 2:109–10).

27. *ARM*, 1:371.

28. Sonenscher, *Work and Wages*, 186.

29. Clay, "Business," 661.

30. Sarah Maza, *Servants and Masters*, 163.

31. Steven Kaplan, "Réflexions," 57.

32. Daniel Roche, "Work, Fellowship, and Some Economic Realities of Eighteenth-Century France," in *Work in France: Representations, Meaning, Organization, and Practice*, eds. Steven L. Kaplan and Cynthia J. Koepp (Ithaca, 1986), 60.

33. B.A. ms. 10237, Dossier of Catherine Ponchon, 7 February 1756 and 9 April 1756. This is probably Michel-François Roussel, the future marquis de Courcy. If so, Meusnier mistook for Roussel's first cousin, Jacques-Jérémie Roussel (1712–76), for his father. Paris-based Jacques-Jérémie Roussel (1712–76) became a fermier général in 1750 and bought the chateau de la Celle from the marquise de Pompadour. Jacques-Jérémie became the younger Roussel's father-in-law when he married his daughter to the young libertine. Apparently, Jacques-Jérémie was not much better at managing his own money than was his cousin/son-in-law. His financial mismanagement led to calls for his resignation in 1767. His chateau was taken by creditors. Rumor deemed his 1776 drowning a suicide. Durand, *Fermiers généraux*, 159, 192.

34. B.A. ms. 10238, Dossier of Demoiselle Pelissier, 5 January 1754.

35. Mercier, *Tableau*, 3:588–90; Turmeau de la Morandière, *Répresentations*, 44–48.

36. "entre-vifs, pure, simple et irrévocable." A.N. series Y, ms. 404 (*ARM*, 1:11–12).

37. This is taken from Sonenscher, *Work and Wages*, 195.

38. Turmeau de la Morandière, *Répresentations*, 28–37.

39. A.N. series Y, ms. 13114, papers of Commissioner Bernard-Louis-Philippe Fontaine, 28 January 1762 (*ARM*, 2:46–48).

40. *ARM*, 2:55.

41. The auction was preceded by a public viewing which proved so popular, it lasted for three days. Barbier described both the auction and Deschamps's possessions. Barbier, *Chronique de la régence*, 7:244–45.

42. Capon and Yves-Plessis, *Deschamps*, 194–95.

43. *ARM*, 1:371.

44. A.N. series Y, ms. 11009, Papers of Commissioner Jean-François Hughes, 9 October 1768 (*ARM*, 2:96).

45. Ibid., 23 January 1768 (*ARM*, 2:49).

46. A.N. series Y, ms. 10876, Papers of Commissioner Pierre Thiérion, 13 November 1759 (*ARM*, 1:19–20).

47. Barbier thought the altercation was between Deschamps and Dame Roger but as Capon and Yves-Plessis rightly point out, Deschamps at this time had her own

house on the rue de Four and was not taking rooms in someone else's lodging. Barbier, *Chronique de la régence*, 6:226–7; Capon and Yves-Plessis, *Deschamps*, 106–10.

48. Marmontel, *Mémoires*, 2:66–70.

49. By midcentury there were several novels depicting the lives of dames entretenues, including *L'Histoire du chevalier des Grieux et de Manon Lescaut* (1731) by Abbé Prévost.

50. B.N. ms. 11358, Dossier of Demoiselle Dubois (l'aînée), 8 January 1762 (Larchey, 89).

51. The duc de Montmorency was outraged when Astraudi told him of his father's threat. In response, he immediately went to see his father's mistress, the dancer Vestris, and similarly threatened to have her incarcerated were she to continue seeing Luxembourg. Both father and son continued their relationships regardless, and neither made good on his promise to have the other's mistress arrested. B.A. ms. 10235, Dossier of Demoiselle Rosalie Astraudi (Astrodi), 27 April 1754.

52. For an overview of the history of pornography in France, see Lynn Hunt's article "Obscenity and the Origins of Modernity, 1500–1800," in *The Invention of Pornography: Obscenity and the Origins of Modernity, 1500–1800*, ed. Lynn Hunt (New York, 1993), 9–45.

53. Robert Darnton, *The Forbidden Best-Sellers of Pre-Revolutionary France, 1769–1789* (New York, 1995), 63–64. For descriptions of these works and excerpts, see section II. Also see Cheek, *Sexual Antipodes*, 66–67.

54. Bette Talvacchia, *Taking Positions: On the Erotic in Renaissance Culture* (Princeton, 1999), 96–98.

55. These same inspectors, especially Meusnier, wrote impressively graphic depictions of the sex acts engaged in by libertine priests apprehended by the police. B.A. ms. 10261.

56. B.A. ms. 10243, Dossier of Demoiselle Rabon (Dame Pitro), 17 July 1753. Italian nobleman, Victor Amadeus I, prince de Carignano (1690–1741) was an habitué of both the Opéra and the demimonde, and frequently had mistresses.

57. B.N. ms. 11358, *Notes*, 1761 (probably 21 February 1761).

58. B.A. ms. 10237, Dossier of Demoiselle Puvigné, fille, 4 March 1753.

59. B.A. ms. 10235, Dossier of Demoiselle Coraline (née Anne-Marie Véronèse), 12 November 1755. The couple had two children.

60. Tilly, *Mémoires*, 51.

61. The child was later naturalized as Aurore de Saxe. This incident was not the first time in which Marmontel had an affair with a mistress of the maréchal. The *philosophe* had also been the lover of Marie-Gabrielle Hévin de Navarre while she was in the pay of the maréchal. Marmontel claims that Saxe was not angry with him over the first affair but was furious about the second. Marmontel, *Mémoires*, 1:125–27.

62. Darnton, "Inspector," 170.

63. B.N. ms. 11358, *Notes*, 10 July 1761 (Piton, 1:330).

64. Ibid., 23 January 1761 (Piton, 1:275). From a family of financiers, Ferrand assumed his post in 1751. He was both a friend of and related to the marquise de Pompadour. Durand, *Les Fermiers*, 266, 545.

65. B.N. ms. 11358, Dossier of Demoiselle Crousol, la cadette, 21 November 1760 (Piton, 1:243–45).

66. B.A. ms. 10237, Dossier of Demoiselle Romanville, 18 July 1750.

67. Barbier, *Chronique de la régence*, 5:160–61. Also see Bongie, *Rogue*, 339.

68. B.A. ms. 10235, Dossier of Rosalie Astraudi, 12 December 1755.

69. B.N. ms. 11358, *Notes*, 6 November 1761 (Larchey, 57–58).

70. B.A. ms. 10236, Dossier of Marie-Anne Pagès (dite Beauchamp), 17 August 1752; Capon and Yves-Plessis, *Deschamps*, 37–47, 77–79; Durand, *Les Fermiers*, 342–43; Ruth Plaut Weinreb, *Eagle in a Gauze Cage: Louise d'Épinay femme de lettres* (New York, 1993), 14–16; and Louise d'Épinay's autobiographical novel, *Histoire de Madame de Montbrillant: Les Pseudo-mémoires de Madame d'Épinay*, ed. G. Roth, 3 vols. (Paris, 1951). D'Épinay infected his wife with venereal disease. In her autobiographical novel, she details her husband's adultery with dames entretenues and describes him as a scoundrel.

71. Capon and Yves-Plessis, *Deschamps*, 39.

72. *Mémoires secrets*, 14:281–84 (*ARM*, 2:287–88).

73. B.A. ms. 10235, Dossier of Angelique Coignard (dite Beauchamps), 10 and 17 July 1751.

74. A.N. series Y, ms. 11006, papers of Commissioner Jean-François Hughes, 9, 10 and 11 March 1765 (*ARM*, 1:1–5). Three days after the initial complaint, the count had returned almost all of the items to Adélaide, and both parties promised not to pursue their cases against each other. The commissioner makes no note as to why. As the dossier system was no longer operative in 1765, Inspector Marais did not report the incident.

75. B.A. ms. 10238, Dossier of Demoiselle Beaumont (née Suzanne Elizabeth LeGrand), 12 February and 6 June 1750. Meusnier identifies the German noble as Baron Wolf. Bongie claims he was Baron de Wolfsdorf, a Lutheran canon from Leipzig. Bongie, *Rogue*, 107.

76. B.A. ms. 10238, Dossier of Agathe Rigotier (dite Zélie), 29 and 30 August 1755.

77. Clay, *Stagestruck*, 10, 132–35, 160–62.

78. For example, when the singer Marie-Jeanne Lemière wished to leave the duc de Grammont, who had sequestered her on his lands near Orléans, she felt that she could do so only by rejoining the Opéra and thereby coming under the king's protection. This was realized through an elaborate ruse. Lemière used the pretext of going to Mass one Sunday to meet secretly with the Opéra's directors, and from there she escaped to Paris. She refused to see Grammont again until she was inscribed safely on the theater's rolls. B.A. ms. 10237, Dossier of Marie-Jeanne Lemière, 8 October 1756.

79. For the ways in which a courtesan's rejection of a patron or client could have social and political ramifications, see Guido Ruggiero, "Who's Afraid of Giuliana Napolitana? Pleasure, Fear, and Imagining the Arts of the Renaissance Courtesan," in *The Courtesan's Arts*, 280–93.

80. On terms used to describe ranked patrons, see Bachaumont, *Mémoires secrets*, 3:298.

81. B.A. ms. 10237, Dossier of Catherine Ponchon, 6 February 1756. Claude Charles Jacques le Pelletier de la Houssaye (1726–64) was from a robe noble family.

His relative Felix le Pelletier de la Houssaye had been comptroller-general of finances in 1720, under Louis XV.

82. See Pierre-Ambroise-François Choderlos de Laclos, *Les Liaisons dangereuses* (1782; reprint, Paris, 2006).

83. B.N. ms. 11358, *Notes*, 23 January and 21 February 1761.

84. Ibid., 1 January 1762 (Larchey, 86).

85. Mercier, *Tableau*, 7:16–17.

86. Pierre Bourdieu, "Forms of Capital," in *Handbook of Theory and Research for the Sociology of Education*, ed. J. G. Richardson, trans. Richard Nice (New York, 1986), 241–58. Catherine Hakim, "Erotic Capital," *European Sociological Review* 26, no. 5 (October 2010): 499–518; and *Erotic Capital: The Power of Attraction in the Boardroom and Bedroom* (New York, 2011).

87. See, for example, Morag Martin, *Selling Beauty: Cosmetics, Commerce, and French Society, 1750–1830* (Baltimore, 2009) and Aileen Ribeiro, *Facing Beauty: Painted Women & Cosmetic Art* (New Haven, 2011).

88. B.A. ms. 10237, Dossier of Demoiselle Raime, 16 March 1754.

89. B.A. ms. 10235, Dossier of Marie-Thérèse Biancolleli, 17 January 1753.

90. B.A. ms. 10241, Dossier of Demoiselle de Villers, 10 September 1752.

91. *Dict. l'Acad. Fran.*, 4th ed. (1762), s.v. "vif."

92. B.N. ms. 11238, Dossier of Demoiselle Lelache, 11 January 1760.

93. B.A. ms. 10235, Dossier of Demoiselle Brillant, 23 November 1753.

94. Ibid., 21 January 1757. Emmanuel-Dieudonné de Hautefort, marquis d'Hautefort (1700–77) who was ambassador to Vienna in 1750.

95. Kathryn Norberg, "Goddesses of Taste," 97–100.

96. Abbé Clément, *Cinq années littéraires* (Berlin, 1760), 2:15, quoted in Capon and Yves-Plessis, *Deschamps*, 39.

97. B.N. ms. 11358, *Notes*, 26 March 1762 (Larchey, 107); A.N. series Y, ms. 13114, Papers of Commissioner Bernard-Louis-Philippe Fontaine, 28 January 1762 (*ARM*, 2:44–48).

98. B.N. ms. 11358, Dossier of Demoiselle Raye, l'aînée, 14 December 1759, 21 March 1760, 23 January 1761, 21 February 1761 and 2 October 1761.

99. B.A. ms. 10236, Dossier of Demoiselle Deschamps, 19 September 1755.

100. Casanova, *My Life*, 3:193–94.

101. B.A. ms. 10236, Dossier of Demoiselle Marie Hernie, 26 December 1752.

102. B.A. ms. 10235, Dossier of Marie-Thérèse Biancolelli, 17 January 1753.

103. Ibid., Dossier of Demoiselle Cupis de Camargo, 5 December 1753.

104. See, for example, the description of Camargo published in the *Spectacles de Paris pour l'année 1771* (*ARM*, 1:88).

105. Marmontel, *Mémoires*, 1:118.

106. Pietro Aretino, *Sei giornata: Ragionamento della Nanna e della Antonia (1534); dialogo nel quale la Nanna insegna a la Pippa* (1536).

107. Bourdieu, "Forms of Capital," 243.

108. Ibid. 246–47. Bourdieu argued that cultural capital could exist in three forms: embodied, objectified, and institutionalized. Cultural capital in the objectified state was in "the form of cultural goods (pictures, books, dictionaries, instruments,

machines, etc.).'' In the institutionalized state, it was in the form of academic qualifications.

109. Ibid., 252.

6. Male Experiences of Galanterie

1. B.A. ms. 10236, Dossier of Demoiselle Dallière (née Louise Pimperelle), 23
January 1750 and 24 April 1750.

2. Ibid., 23 August 1750.

3. Ibid., 2 April 1751 and 4 April 1751.

4. Ibid., 30 October 1753.

5. The entire Tourmont/Dallière story is recounted in Berlanstein's *Daughters of
Eve*, 45.

6. Barbier, *Chronique de la régence*, 3:46; Émile Campardon, *Le Cheminée de la
Madame de la Poupelinière* (Paris, 1880); and Casanova, *History of My Life*, 3:214, 335.
Madame de la Poupelinière died not long afterwards from breast cancer, which
many initially thought she was faking to win her husband's sympathy. Richelieu
supposedly provided her with a pension until her death. Madame de la Poupelinière
was also the lover of the comte de Sade, father of the marquis de Sade.

7. Berlanstein, *Daughters of Eve*, 33–39 and Mathieu Marraud, *La Noblesse de Paris
au XVIIIe siècle* (Paris, 2000), 148–49.

8. Berlanstein used a similar but slightly different frame to analyze male experiences of libertinism. He argued that ''libertinism had no one pattern, no one meaning. It was a practice that revolved around three poles of uneven and variable
import: reputation, money and sentiment.'' Berlanstein, *Daughters of Eve*, 45.

9. B.A. ms. 10235, Dossier of Demoiselle Amédée (dite Belgrant), 16 October
1750.

10. On courtesans as performers and entertainers in the early modern era, see the
works listed in the Introduction, endnote 17. There is a well-developed literature on
courtesans as entertainers in the ancient world. For a helpful and insightful discussion
of their role in ancient Athenian society and culture, see James Davidson, *Courtesans
and Fishcakes: The Consuming Passions of Classical Athens* (New York, 1997).

11. Roger Duchêne, *Ninon de Lenclos, ou, la manière jolie de faire l'amour* (Paris,
2000) and Duchêne, *Ninon de Lenclos: la courtisane du Grand Siècle* (Paris, 1984).

12. Albéric Deville, *Arnoldiana, Ou Sophie Arnould et ses contemporaines: recueil
choisi d'anecdotes piquantes de réparties et de bon mots de Mlle. Arnould* (Paris, 1813).

13. B.N. ms. 11358, Dossier of Demoiselle Suzanne Delille, 9 May 1760 (Piton,
1:153–55).

14. Mercier, *Tableau*, 12:1536–38.

15. This was the conclusion of Erica-Marie Benabou who found no cultural
objects among the possessions of kept women listed in their post death inventories.
Benabou, *Moeurs*, 381–82. Also see Berlanstein, *Daughters of Eve*, 40.

16. Martine Sonnet, ''A Daughter to Educate,'' in *A History of Women*, 124–28.
For more details, see Sonnet, *L'Éducation des filles au temps des Lumières* (Paris, 1987).

17. Compare Lenclos's letters to the one Suzanne Elizabeth LeGrand (Demoiselle Beaumont) wrote to Meusnier in 1750 asking for permission to come back to

Paris. LeGrand wrote well, but even aided by the police spy and writer Charles de Julie, she was not the writer Lenclos was. Charles Henry Robinson, *Life, Letters, and Epicurean Philosophy of Ninon de L'Enclos, the Celebrated Beauty of the Seventeenth Century* (Chicago, 1903). B.A. ms. 10238, Dossier of Demoiselle Beaumont (née Suzanne Elizabeth LeGrand), letter to Meusnier, 20 December 1750, and Bongie, *Rogue*, 106–110.

18. .B.A. ms. 10248, Dossier of Demoiselle Gautier, la cadette, Letter from Vanboorn de Lescard, no date. On constructions of desire in the eighteenth century, see Anna Clark, *Desire: A History of European Sexuality* (New York, 2008), chap. 7.

19. B.N. ms. 11358, *Notes*, 15 May 1762 (Larchey, 124).

20. B.A. ms. 10236, Dossier of Demoiselle Gallodier, l'aînée, 12 November 1755.

21. B.N. ms. 11358, *Notes*, 1759, not dated (Piton, 1:293–94). Five years later, Sabran left Louise following the birth of their baby, "unmoved by the love he knew she had for him," according to Marais. Ibid., 16 March 1764 (Piton, 2:46). This is most likely Louis-François, marquis de Sabran (b. 1731). Another possibility is Andre-Antoine, vicomte de Sabran since Piton refers to Sabran as "victome" in his 1764 *Notes*.

22. B.A. ms. 10240, Dossier of Demoiselle Agathe (dite Marbourg), 9 October 1749.

23. B.A. ms. 10235, Dossier of Amédée (dite Belgant), report from a mouche, 12 October 1750.

24. Sade to Colet, 16 July 1764, quoted in Gray, *At Home*, 72.

25. On sentimentalism, see William M. Reddy, *The Navigation of Feeling: A Framework for the History of Emotions* (Cambridge, 2001), especially chapter 5, and David Denby, *Sentimental Narrative and the Social Order in France, 1760–1820* (Cambridge, 1994).

26. Larchey, *Journal*, 314, quoted in Benabou, *Moeurs*, 342. Both Larchey and Benabou claim Harnoncourt was the father of Louis-Bénigne-François de Bertier de Sauvigny (1737–89). But Harnoncourt was the family name of his mother. His father-in-law, Pierre Durey d'Harnoncourt (1682–1769) would have been the right age to be the man Inspector Marais claimed Demoiselle Saron was manipulating.

27. Tilly, *Mémoires*, 51.

28. Casanova, *My Life*, 3:217.

29. B.N. ms. 11359, *Notes*, 5 August 1763 (Larchey, 303). Also see Benabou, *Moeurs*, 342. Charles Bernard de Marville was *receveur général de la generalité d'Amiens* from 1754. He died in 1782, supposedly bankrupt.

30. Maza, *Servants and Masters*, 161.

31. Ibid., 105.

32. Ibid., 159.

33. B.A. ms. 10235, Dossier of Rosalie Astraudi, report from a mouche, 15 December 1750. The comte d'Egmont was Casimir d'Egmont Pignatelli (1727–1802). At the time he was with Astraudi, he was a brigadier, and he eventually rose to be an army lieutenant general. His relationship with Astraudi ended in 1753. In 1756 he married the daughter of the duc de Richelieu, comtesse Septimanie d'Egmont Pignatelli, who would become a patron of arts and letters.

34. B.N. ms. 11358, *Notes*, 23 January 1761 (Piton, 1:278–79).

35. B.A. ms. 10240, Dossier of Agathe (dite Marbourg), reports from 30 April 1749 to 4 November 1751.

36. Reddy, *Feeling*, 141.

37. Ibid., 149–52.

38. Berlanstein, *Daughters of Eve*, 42.

39. Dena Goodman, "Marriage Choice and Marital Success: Reasoning About Marriage, Love, and Happiness," in *Family, Gender, and Law*, 49.

40. B.A. ms. 10237, Dossier of Catherine Ponchon, 27 February 1756 and 9 April 1756.

41. Meusnier contradicts himself in his reporting, claiming that Roussel was set to leave Paris on 19 February 1756. But a week later, on 27 February, Meusnier reported that Ponchon was in a new relationship with someone he later identified as Roussel. B.A. ms. 10237, Dossier of Catherine Ponchon, 7 February 1756 and 27 February 1756.

42. Ibid., 24 December 1756.

43. B.A. ms. 10235, Dossier of Rosalie Astraudi, 30 October 1753, 15 November 1753, 4 April 1754, 9 May 1754 and 20 August 1754.

44. B.A. ms. 10238, Dossier of Demoiselle Le Chesne, 16 April 1756.

45. B.A. ms. 10236, Dossier of Demoiselle Hernie, 26 December 1752.

46. Le Maire, *La Police de Paris en 1770*, 92.

47. Flandrin, *Families*, 181.

48. For discussion of theater women in long-term loving relationships, see Scott, *Women on the Stage*, 259–60.

49. B.N. ms. 11358, *Notes*, 19 March 1762 (Larchey, 111).

50. B.A. ms. 10235, Dossier of Marie-Thérèse Biancolelli, 17 January 1753.

51. B.A. ms. 10237, Dossier of Demoiselle Metz, 18 December 1755 and 17 December 1756.

52. B.A. ms. 10235, Dossier of Rosalie Astraudi, 28 June 1750.

53. B.A. ms. 10236, Dossier of Demoiselle Lablotière, 25 September 1752 and 20 April 1753. The relationship lasted between fifteen and thirty months. On Pajot de Villers, see Jeffrey Ravel, "The Coachman's Bare Rump: An Eighteenth-Century French Cover-Up," *Eighteenth-Century Studies* 40, no. 2 (winter 2007): 279–308. Lablotière was a singer in the Opéra chorus until 1751. A.N. series AJ, ms. 13/18.

54. B.A. ms. 10238, Dossier of Demoiselle Mainville (dite Rozette), 28 April 1751. It was unclear if Mainville and the domestic, Pagin, had been lovers. They certainly were later, and Pagin turns up as the domestic of one of her patrons, the comte de Clermont. Other sources have Mainville married to Opéra violinist Joseph Labbé de Saint-Sévint. *ARM*, 2:27.

55. B.N. ms. 11358, *Notes*, 19 March 1762 (Larchey, 111).

56. Farr, *Authority and Sexuality*, 92–123.

57. Guy Chaussinand-Nogaret, *The French Nobility in the Eighteenth Century: From Feudalism to Enlightenment*, trans. William Doyle (Cambridge, 1985), 117–29. For an example, see Sara Chapman, *Private Ambition and Political Alliances: The Phélypeaux de Pontchartrain Family and Louis XIV's Government, 1650–1715* (Rochester, 2004).

58. There is considerable scholarship on representations of and responses to aristocratic and royal libertinism. See, for example, Olivier Blanc, *Les Libertines: plaisir au temps des Lumières* (Paris, 1997); Margaret Darrow, "French Noblewomen and the New Domesticity, 1750–1780," *Feminist Studies* 5, no.1 (spring 1979): 41–42; Chantal Thomas, *The Wicked Queen: The Origins of the Myth of Marie-Antoinette* (New York, 1999). Also see, Lynn Hunt, "The Many Bodies of Marie-Antoinette: Political Pornography and the Problem of the Feminine in the French Revolution," and Elizabeth Colwill, "Pass as a Woman, Act Like a Man: Marie-Antoinette as Tribade in the Pornography of the French Revolution" in *Marie Antoinette: Writings on the Body of a Queen*, eds. Dena Goodman (New York, 2003).

59. Jean-Jacques Rousseau, *Julie ou la Nouvelle Héloïse* (1760; reprint, Paris, 1999); Rousseau, *Émile: ou de l'éducation* (1762; reprint, Paris, 1966). For a brief summary of Rousseau's vision of marriage, see Dena Goodman, "Marriage Choice," 46. For a more thorough analysis see Lieselotte Steinbrügge, *The Moral Sex: Women's Nature in the French Enlightenment*, trans. Pamela E. Selwyn (New York, 1995), 55–82; and Joel Schwartz, *The Sexual Politics of Jean-Jacques Rousseau* (Chicago, 1984).

60. For a discussion of the evolution of domesticity in genre paintings and their purchase, see Richard Rand, "Love, Domesticity, and the Evolution of Genre Painting in Eighteenth-Century France," and Anne L. Schroder, "Genre Prints in Eighteenth-Century France: Production, Market and Audience," in *Intimate Encounters: Love and Domesticity in Eighteenth-Century France*, ed. Richard Rand (Princeton, 1997), 3–19. For an analysis of the *drame bourgeois*, see Sarah Maza, "The 'Bourgeois' Family Revisited: Sentimentalism and Social Class in Pre-Revolutionary French Culture," in *Intimate Encounters*, 39–47.

61. For evidence of companionate marriages across class in the eighteenth century, see Watt, *Modern Marriage*, 210–17; Dena Goodman, "Marriage Choice"; Margaret Darrow, "Popular Concepts of Marital Choice in Eighteenth-Century France," *Journal of Social History* 19, no. 2 (winter 1985): 267; and Jeffrey Merrick, "The Family Politics of the Marquis de Bombelles," *Journal of Family History* 21 (1996): 503–18.

62. Spousal choice was not predictive of marital experience. See Goodman, "Marriage Choice," 27. That Parisians desired greater familial intimacy and hence wanted quarters that afforded them privacy is the argument of Annick Pardailhé-Galabrun in *The Birth of Intimacy*. How increased demand for privacy bore on the qualitative nature of relationships in the home, however, is not clear. See Maza, "The 'Bourgeois' Family," 41, and Flandrin, *Families*, 94.

63. Flandrin, *Families*, 171–73.

64. Darrow, "French Noblewomen," 43.

65. Sarah Maza, "The 'Bourgeois' Family," 39.

66. This was an observation of Dena Goodman, made in conversation.

67. The contention that a true *philosophe* had to be a bachelor is challenged by Meghan Roberts's study of the family and marital lives of several philosophes. Roberts, "Cradle of Enlightenment," passim.

68. Jean-Jacques Rousseau, *Lettre à d'Alembert sur les spectacles* (1758; reprint, Paris, 1993).

69. B.A. ms. 10237, Dossier of Catherine Ponchon, 6 February 1756.

70. Tilly, *Mémoires*, 3:45–46.

71. B.A. ms. 10235, Dossier of Demoiselle Blot (dite Letellier), 7 September 1749 and 10 November 1750.

72. B.A. ms. 10240, Dossier of Demoiselle Agathe, 10 September 1749.

73. B.A. ms. 10243, Dossier of Catherine de la Ferté (dite Darlington), 3 June 1751.

74. Farge and Foucault, *Le Désordre*, 32–35, 154; Chassaigne, *Des lettres de cachet*, 245–48; Funck-Bretano, *Les Lettres de cachet*, chap. 2.

75. On bourgeois codes of honor and sexual propriety in the eighteenth century, see Robert A. Nye, *Masculinity and Male Codes of Honor in Modern France* (Berkeley, 1998), 15–31.

76. Eugene Muller, *Le Magistrat de la ville de Strasbourg: les stettmeisters et ammeisters de 1674 à 1790, les préteurs royaux de 1685 à 1790 et notices généalogiques des familles de l'ancienne noblesse d'Alsace depuis la fin du XVIIe siècle* (Strasbourg, 1862), 171; François-Christophe-Honoré de Klinglin, *Mémoire de Monsieur Klinglin, préteur royal de la ville de Strasbourg* (Grenoble, 1754); Pierre Germain, *Adrienne Lecouvreur: tragédienne* (Paris, 1983), 53–54, 189–94.

77. Marraud, *La Noblesse de Paris*, 150–51.

78. Gray, *At Home*, passim. Maurice Lever similarly depicts the couple. Maurice Lever, *Sade: A Biography*, trans. Arthur Goldhammer (San Diego, 1993), 100–01, 114, 209–10.

79. Gray, *At Home*, 58–59, 74. Gray argues that there were very different standards of sexual behavior for robe and sword nobles. Robe nobles, especially women, more closely adhered to the standards of their bourgeois roots, while sword nobles (court aristocracy) engaged in more extramarital affairs.

80. Letter from la présidente de Montreuil to the abbé de Sade, 17 July 1765, quoted in Gray, *At Home*, 81.

81. Ibid., 49, 54–55.

82. B.A. ms. 10243, Dossier of Marie Catherine de la Ferté, 3 June 1751.

83. Lever, *Sade*, 100, ff. 30.

84. Nye, *Masculinity*, 35–39.

85. Sarah Maza, *The Myth of the French Bourgeoisie: An Essay on the Social Imaginary 1750–1850* (Cambridge, MA, 2003); David Garrioch, *The Formation of the Parisian Bourgeoisie, 1690–1830* (Cambridge, MA, 1996), 1–14.

86. There is a considerable literature on the subject of divisions within the elite. For an overview of the state of current research, see Jay M. Smith, "Introduction," in *The French Nobility in the Eighteenth Century: Reassessments and New Approaches*, ed. Jay M. Smith (University Park, 2006), 1–15. Also see Gail Bossenga, "A Divided Nobility: Status, Markets, and the Patrimonial State in the Old Regime," in the same volume.

87. Nye, *Masculinity*, 39.

88. On the specific question of sexual behavior, see Nye, *Masculinity*, 31–46. For more general works on the Parisian nobility and questions of assimilation, see Marraud, *La Noblesse de Paris;* Natacha Coquery, *"Hôtel aristocratique*; and Rochelle Ziskin, *The Place Vendôme: Architecture and Social Mobility in Eighteenth-Century Paris* (New York, 1999), 49–50.

89. Ziskin, *The Place Vendôme*, 49–50.

90. Ibid., 122, ff. 31.

91. Ibid., 50.

92. B.N. ms. 11358, *Notes*, 26 June 1761 (Piton, 1:323–24).

93. There is an extensive literature on the question of luxury in this period. For a general overview, see Renato Galliani, *Rousseau, le luxe, et l'idéologie nobiliaire: étude socio-historique* (Oxford, 1989); Christopher Berry, *The Idea of Luxury: A Conceptual and Historical Investigation* (Cambridge, 1994); Sara Maza, "Luxury, Morality, and Social Change: Why There Was No Middle-Class Consciousness in PreRevolutionary France," *Journal of Modern History* 69, no. 2 (June 1997): 199–229. Also see Saint Lambert, *Encyclopédie*, s.v. "luxe"; John Shovlin, "The Cultural Politics of Luxury in Eighteenth-Century France," *French Historical Studies* 23 no. 4 (autumn 2000): 577–606.

94. Mercier, *Tableau*, 2:265.

95. Ibid., 3:588–90.

96. Berlanstein, *Daughters of Eve*, 40–41, 46.

97. Casanova, *My Life*, 3:193–94.

98. Fairchilds, *Domestic Enemies*, 12–13.

99. For an overview of this literature, see Michel Feher, "Introduction," in *The Libertine Reader: Eroticism and Enlightenment in Eighteenth-Century France*, ed. Michel Feher (New York, 1997), 10–47.

100. B.N. ms. 11358, *Notes*, 10 July 1761 (Piton, 3:330–31).

101. B.N. ms. 11358, *Notes*, 25 December 1761 (Larchey, 80–81).

7. Sexual Capital and the Private Lives of Mistresses

1. B.A. ms. 10235, Dossier of Demoiselle Brillant, 23 October 1753. François Roblastre, seigneur de Beaulieu was the son of François Roblastre, who was the chief supplier of firewood to the king.

2. Although Meusnier spells the name of this patron as "Montau," this may have been Antoine Isaac Le Noir de Monteau, son of Guillaume Le Noir de Cindré. Antoine's brother, Lenoir de Cindré, is mentioned quite frequently in the police reports. The Lenoirs were a family of fermier généraux.

3. Ibid., 30 January 1750 and 5 March 1750.

4. Ibid., 5 March 1750.

5. Ibid., 23 October 1752.

6. Fathers could sue for the loss of a daughter's virginity and be awarded financial compensation. See Hufton, *Prospect*, 57–58, 268–275.

7. B.A. ms. 10253, Dossier of Marie Catherine de la Ferté, 24 May 1751.

8. B.A. ms. 10237, Dossier of Demoiselle Lyonnais (née Marie-Françoise Rempon), 18 November 1748 and 18 September 1750.

9. Clare Crowston makes this point in her study of Parisian seamstresses, *Fabricating Women*, 348–49. Julie Hardwick found that women from notarial families in seventeenth-century Nantes married men from the same narrow social backgrounds. Hardwick, *Practice of Patriarchy*, 11–12. Regarding the relationship between parental occupation and spousal choice, Cissie Fairchilds suggests that those women from villages who remained in contact with their families after having gone to large cities to work as low-level servants often would return home to marry men, probably

peasants, chosen by their parents. Fairchilds, *Domestic Enemies*, 83. For a general break-down of marriage choice in Paris see Daumard and Furet, *Structures*, 73–83.

10. B.A. ms. 10243, Dossier of Demoiselle Marquis, 9 April 1754.

11. B.A. ms. 10235, Dossier of Demoiselle Blot (Letellier), 11 October 1750.

12. B.A. ms. 10237, Dossier of Demoiselle l'Hériter (Dame Bourcharla), 11 December 1754.

13. In his study of prostitution in Clermont, François Aleil found many cases in which husbands acquiesced to or supported their wives' work as prostitutes. Aleil, "La Prostitution," 482–84.

14. B.N. ms. 11358, Dossier of Dame Sauval, 24 October 1760 (Piton, 1:227–30).

15. Farge and Foucault, *Le Désordre des familles*, 23–154.

16. Olwen Hufton, "Women, Work and Family," 17–26. For how the need for a dowry impacted women in various industries, see additionally Crowston, *Fabricating Women*, 351–54, and Fairchilds, *Domestic Enemies*, 81–91. That neighbors would help was certainly a possibility. See Arlette Farge, *Fragile Lives*, 9–20. In their study of police abductions in 1751, Farge and Revel showed the importance of neighbors in helping families recover children. Arlette Farge and Jacques Revel, *Rules of Rebellion*.

17. When a couple failed to support themselves, elite prostitution was an odd alternative. The thousands of requests for lettres de cachet now stored in the Archive of the Arsenal evince a wide variety of outcomes for women of failing marriages, even for those with few resources. Some ran away with other men. Others became street walkers. Street walking and general low-level, casual prostitution were much more immediate experiences for men and women of the working milieu. The particular husbands and wives in this small sample probably chose elite prostitution as the remedy for their financial problems (or financial desires) because they happened to have the opportunity to do so.

18. B.N. ms. 11358, Dossier of Dame Sauval, 24 October 1760 (Piton, 1:227–30).

19. That was not the end of it. When Dame Sauval would not follow her husband to Brest, he actually began legal proceedings against her and eventually gained custody of two of their three children. Ibid.

20. Hufton, "Family Economy," 9.

21. B.N. ms. 11358, Dossier of Demoiselle Varenne (dite Bentheim), 26 February 1762 (Larchey, 103–4). This is an average. The years she was employed steadily, she probably earned much more.

22. B.N. ms. 11358, *Notes*, 2 October 1761 (Larchey, 39).

23. B.A. ms. 10236, Dossier of Louise-Madeleine Lany, 11 August 1754.

24. A.N. series AJ mss. 13/17 and 13/19 through 13/21. Also see chapter 1, footnote 67.

25. B.A. ms. 10236, Dossier of Demoiselle Delisle, 11 September 1754.

26. B.A. ms. 10241, Dossier of Demoiselle Lesther (née Françoise Villemur), 15 November 1752.

27. Claude de Ferrière, *Corps et compilation*, articles 236–37.

28. Eighteenth-century legal scholar Robert Pothier argued that it was on this basis that a husband's authority over his wife's legal personality was established. Were she able to make contracts, she could endanger the communauté or challenge

her husband's control over it, thus sowing discord within the household. As the household was the constituent unit of the kingdom, its control, and not Biblical injunction per se, was the practical root of husbandly authority. Robert-Joseph Pothier, *Traité de la communauté, auquel on a joint un traité de la puissance du mari sur la personnelle et les biens de la femme* (1774), vol. 5, *Oeuvres de Pothier* (Paris, 1825), 1–39. Also see Paul Ourliac and Malafosse, *Le Droit Familial*, vol. 3, *Histoire du droit privé* (Paris, 1968).

29. Léon Abensour puts these rights into historical perspective in *La Femme et le feminisme avant la Révolution* (1923; reprint, Geneva, 1977).

30. She had certain rights as a *marchande publique*. See Hafter, *Women at Work*, 25–26.

31. Farge and Foucault, *Le Désordre des familles*, 104–6.

32. Ibid., 95–98.

33. Ibid., 23–154.

34. B.A. ms. 10236, Dossier of Demoiselle Delisle, 11 September 1754.

35. A.N. Minutier Central, LXXIV, 3333, 2 February 1752, quoted in Jean Delay, *Avant Mémoire*, vol. 3, *La Fauconnier* (Paris, 1982), 167–68.

36. B.A. ms. 10235, Dossier of Rosalie Astraudi (Astrodi), report by Desnoyez, 20 August 1754 and 27 February 1755.

37. Casanova, *My Life*, 3:173.

38. Virginia Scott noted that after 1750, the average age of a girl debuting in the Comédie-Française decreased from twenty to seventeen, but that the company included girls as young as thirteen. Scott, *Women on the Stage*, 263.

39. Elise de La Rochebrochard, "Age at Puberty of Girls and Boys in France: Measurements from a Survey on Adolescent Sexuality," *Population: An English Selection* 12 (2000): 55.

40. B.A. ms. 10238, Dossier of Agathe Rigotier (dite Dorval, Zélie, marquise d'Aubard), 17 September 1756.

41. Ibid.

42. Hufton, *Prospect*, 222. Also see Lanza, *Widows*, 155–61 for a more general discussion.

43. B.N. ms. 11358, Dossier of Thérèze Julie Brébant, 18 January 1760.

44. B.A. ms. 10243, Dossier of Guinebauld de Millière, l'ainée, 15 July 1756.

45. B.A. ms. 10238, Dossier of Demoiselle Beaumont (née Suzanne Elisabeth Legrand), 14 October 1750 and 16 October 1750.

46. Ibid.

47. B.N. ms. 11358, Dossier of Thérèze Julie Brébant, 18 January 1760.

48. B.A. ms. 10236, Dossier of Demoiselle Delisle, 5 February 1755.

49. B.A. ms. 10243, Dossier of Demoiselle Rabon (Dame Pitro), 17 July 1753.

50. B.N. ms. 11358, Dossier of Agathe Rigotier (dite Dorval, Zélie, marquise d'Aubard), 25 December 1759 (Piton, 1:267).

51. B.A. ms. 10243, Dossier of Demoiselle Hypotite, 14 February 1753. This was the only entry in which I found the word *farfadet*.

52. *Le Grand Robert de la Langue Française: Dictionnaire alphabétique et analogue de la Langue Française, de Paul Robert*, 2nd ed., (1985) s.v. "*greluchon*." The etymology is traced back, in one case, to "grelot," meaning "testicle."

53. *Dict. l'Acad. Fran.*, 4th ed. (1762) "Nom qu'on donne à l'amant aimé & favorisé secrétement par une femme qui se fait payer par d'autres amans. Il est familier & libre."

54. B.A. ms. 10237, Dossier of Demoiselle Montfreville, 26 January 1751.

55. B.N. ms. 11348, *Notes*, 1 January 1762 and 19 February 1762 (Larchey, 85, 102).

56. B.A. ms. 10238, Dossier of Demoiselle Adélaide, 28 August 1753.

57. B.N. ms. 11358, *Notes*, 10 July 1761(Piton, 1:329).

58. Ibid., 25 December 1761, 1 Jaunary 1762, 19 February 1762, (Larchey, 81–82, 85; Piton 1:102).

59. Antonio Francesco Soleri de Vesian, brother of Louise Vesian, a dancer at the Comédie-Italienne.

60. B.N. ms. 11358, *Notes*, 7 August 1761 (Larchey, 9–11).

61. The police report another instance in which Brillant competed with a fellow dame entretenue. In 1753, she drew in passers-by at the Comédie-Française to judge whether she or her friend Demoiselle Retz (maybe Rais) was the most "brilliantly" dressed. B.A. ms. 10236, Dossier of Demoiselle Deschamps (née Marie-Anne Pàges), 17 August 1753.

62. B.N. ms. 11358, *Notes*, 11 September 1761 (Larchey, 29).

63. Ibid., 25 September 1761 (Larchey, 35).

64. B.A. ms. 10235, Dossier of Demoiselle Astraudi, 20 August 1754, report to Meusnier by Desnoyez.

65. B.A. ms. 10235, Dossier of Demoiselle Brillant, 30 January 1750, report from La Jannière to Meusnier.

66. B.A. ms. 10235, Dossier of Demoiselle Chefdeville (née Marie-Madeleine Jendrest), 3 September 1756.

67. A.N. series Y, ms. 11,116, Papers of Commissioner Charles-François Cleret, 14 July 1749 (*ARM*, 116–17).

68. This was a common construction of female desire. For further discussion of this theme, see Thomas Laqueur, *Making Sex: Body and Gender from the Greeks to Freud* (Cambridge, MA, 1990); Dena Goodman, ed., *Marie-Antoinette:Writings on the Body of a Queen* (New York, 2003); Lynn Hunt, *Family Romance of the French Revolution* (Berkeley, 1992), 113–15.

69. Casanova, *My Life*, 3:148–50.

70. B.A. ms. 10235, Dossier of Dame Chevalier (Marie-Jeanne Fesch), 2 September 1756.

71. B.A. ms.10236, Dossier of Demoiselle Lablotière, 6 September 1750.

72. A.O. mss. AJ/13/17 and AJ/13/19–21 list Lyonnais's annual income as 2200 livres when all forms of remuneration are included.

73. Daniel Roche, *Histoire des choses banales: naissance de la consommation dans les sociétes traditionnelles XVIIe–XIXe siècle* (Paris, 1997), 67–91. Roche analyzes the speculative budgets of families at various social levels put forward by economists in the eighteenth century who were interested in calculating a tax base.

74. B.A. ms. 10237, Dossier of Demoiselle Lyonnais (née Marie-Françoise Rempon), 17 August 1750. In the previous entry (30 May 1750), Meusnier claims, erroneously it seems, that Favier had forced Lyonnais to take an abortifacient, which

ended her pregnancy. Lyonnais gave birth three months later. Virgina Scott also discusses the long term relationship of actresses, Scott, *Women on the Stage*, 259.

75. Ibid., 2 April 1751.

76. Ibid., 1 January 1752, 9 February 1752, 18 April 1754, and 4 October 1754.

77. Ibid., 14 August 1755.

78. Crowston, *Fabricating Women*, 347.

Conclusion

1. Angelique Chrisafis, "How Prostitution Became France's Hottest Social Issue," *The Guardian*, 24 September 2012; "End of the World's Oldest Profession? Women's Rights Groups Seek to Ban Prostitution Across the EU," *International Business Times* (US ed.), 4 December 2012; "L'interdiction de la prostitution est une chimère," *Le Nouvel Observateur: Sociètè*, 22 August 2102; "On the Game: France and Prostitution," *The Economist* (US), 14 July 2012.

2. "Ces feminists qui plaident pour l'abolition de la prostitution," *Le Point*, 7 July 2012.

✒ SELECTED BIBLIOGRAPHY

Primary Sources Consulted

Archival Sources

Archives Nationales
series Y: mss. 9451A, 9451B, 9475, 9628, 14330.
series AJ: ms. 13/1, 13/17–21.
Archives de la Préfecture de Police
series A/B: mss. 362–64, 404, 432.
Bibliothèque de l'Arsenal
Archives de la Bastille: mss. 10027–29, 10042–58, 10135, 10138, 10142–46,
  10175–76, 10180, 10230, 10234–44, 10247, 10248, 10250–53, 10256,
  10260–61, 10268, 10293, 11846, 12690.
Bibliothèque Historique de la Ville de Paris
mss. 637, 719–12.
Bibliothèque de la Mazarine
mss. 2387, 2393.
Bibliothèque du Musée de l'Opéra
series CO: mss. 511, PE 17 T, PE 205 (122).
Bibliothèque Nationale
Fonds français: mss.11357–60, 13709–12.

Print Sources

Académie Française. *Dictionnaire de l'Académie Française*, 1st–5th eds. Paris:
  1694–1798.
Almanach Royal. Paris: D'Houry [etc.], 1719–89.
Anonymous. *Histoire de Mademoiselle Brion dite comtesse de Launay*. 1754. Reprint,
  Paris: Tchou, 1968.
Bachaumont, Louis Petit de, Mathieu-François Pidansat de Mairobert, and
  Barthélemy-François-Joseph Mouffle d'Angerville. *Mémoires secrets pour servir*
  à l'histoire de la République des Lettres en France depuis 1762 jusqu'à nos jours. 18
  vols. London: Chez John Adamsson, 1777–89.
Barbier, Edmond Jean François. *Chronique de la régence et du règne de Louis XV*
  (1718–1763), ou, Journal de Barbier. 8 vols. Paris: Charpentier, 1857.
Boislisle, Arthur Michel de, ed. *Lettres de M. de Marville, lieutenant général de police,*
  au ministre Maurepas (1742–1747). 3 vols. Paris: H. Champion, 1896–1905.
Campardon, Émile. *Les Spectacles de la foire; théâtres, acteurs, sauteurs et danseurs de*
  corde, monstres, géants, nains, animaux curieux ou savants, marionnettes, automates,

figures de cire et jeux mécaniques des foires Saint-Germain et Saint-Laurent, des boulevards et du Palais-Royal, depuis 1595 jusqu'à 1791; documents inédits recueillis aux archives nationales. Paris: Berger-Levrault et cie., 1877

———. *Les Comédiens du roi de la troupe française pendant des deux derniers siècles: documents inédits recueillis aux Archives Nationales.* Paris: H. Champion, 1879.

———. *Les Comédiens du roi de la troupe italienne pendant les deux derniers siècles.* Paris: Berger-Levrault et cie, 1880.

———. *L'Académie royale de musique au XVIIIᵉ siècle; documents inédits découverts aux Archives Nationales.* 1884. 2 vols. Reprint, New York: Da Capo Press, 1971.

Capon, Gaston. *Les Maisons closes au XVIIIᵉ siècle. Académies de filles et courtières d'amour, maisons clandestines, matrones, mères-abbesses, appareilleuses et proxénètes.* Paris: H. Daragon, 1903.

Casanova, Giacomo, chevalier de Seingalt. *History of My Life.* Translated by Willard R. Trask. 12 vols. Baltimore: Johns Hopkins University Press, 1997.

Chevrier, Francois Antoine. *Paris, histoire véridique, anecdotique, morale et critique, avec la clef.* La Haye: 1767.

Cleland, John. *Fanny Hill, or, Memoirs of a Woman of Pleasure.* 1748. Reprint, New York: Oxford University Press, 1985.

D'Alembert, Jean le Rond, and Denis Diderot. *Encyclopédie; ou, Dictionnaire raisonné des sciences, des arts et des métiers, par une société de gens de lettres.* Lausanne: Societes typographiques, 1780–82.

D'Argenson, Marc-René de Voyer. *Rapports inédits du lieutenant de police René d'Argenson (1679–1715) publiés d'après les manuscrits conservés à bibliothèque nationale.* 1891. Reprint, Liechtenstein: Kraus Reprints, 1972.

———. *Notes de René d'Argenson, Lieutenant général de police; Intéressantes pour l'histoire des moeurs et de la police de Paris à la fin du règne de Louis XIV.* Paris: Imprimerie Emile Voitelain et Cie, 1866.

D'Argenson, René-Louis de Voyer. *Journal et mémoires du marquis d'Argenson.* Edited by E.J.B. Rathery. 5 vols. Paris: Jules Renouard,1864.

D'Épinay, Louise. *Histoire de Madame de Montbrillant: Les Pseudo-mémoires de Madame d'Épinay.* Edited by G. Roth. Paris: Gallimard, 1951.

Delamare, Nicolas, and Le Cler du Brillet. *Traité de la police.* 4 vols. Paris: Chez M. Brunet, 1719–38.

Denisart, Jean-Baptiste, Armand-Gaston Camus, and Jean B. Bayard, eds. *Collection de décisions nouvelles et de notions relatives à la jurisprudence.* Vol. 8. Paris: Chez la Veuve Desaint, 1789.

Depping, G. B., ed. *Correspondance administrative sous le règne de Louis XIV.* 4 vols. Paris: Imprimerie nationale: 1850–55.

Dumas, Alexandre, fils. *La Dame aux camélias.* 1848. Reprint, Paris: Gallimard, 1974.

———. *Le Demi-Monde: comédie en cinq actes, en prose*, 1855. Reprint, Paris: Michel Lévy Frères, 1875.

Ferrière, Claude de. *Corps et compilation de tous les commentateurs anciens et modernes sur la Coutume de Paris.* 4 vols. Paris: H. Charpentier, 1714.

Guyot, M. *Répertoire universel et raisonné de jurisprudence civile, criminelle, canonique et bénéficiale.* 24 vols. Paris: Panckoucke, 1780.

Isambert, François-André, Athanase Jourdan, and M. Decrusy. *Recueil général des anciennes lois françaises, depuis l'an 420 jusqu'à la révolution de 1789.* 29 vols. Paris: Plon frères, 1821–33.

Jousse, Daniel. *Traité de la justice criminelle de France.* 4 vols. Paris: Chez Debure Père, 1771.

Klinglin, François-Christophe-Honoré de. *Mémoire de Monsieur Klinglin, préteur royale de la ville de Strasbourg.* Grenoble: André Giroud, 1754.

Laclos, Choderlos de, Pierre-Ambroise-François. *Les Liaisons dangereuses.* 1782. Reprint, Paris: Editions Flammarion, 2006.

La Fitte, Anne-Gédéon, marquis de Pellepore, *Le Diable dans un Bénitier et la métamorphose du Gazetier cuirassée en mouche, ou tentatice du Sieur Receveur, Inspecteur de la Police de Paris, chevalier de Saint-Louis . . .* London: 1784.

Larchey, Lorédan, ed. *Documents inédits sur le règne de Louis XV; ou . . . le journal des inspecteurs de M. de Sartines: première série, (1761–1764).* Paris: E. Parent, 1863. Partial publication of mss. 11357–60 of the Bibliothèque Nationale de France.

Le Maire, Jean-Baptiste-Charles. *La Police de Paris en 1770: mémoire inédit composé par ordre de G. de Sartine sur la demande de Marie-Thérèse.* Edited by Augustin Gazier. Nogent-le-Rotrou: G. Daupeley, 1879.

Le Moyne, Nicolas Toussaint [Des Essarts]. *Dictionnaire universel de police.* 7 vols. Paris: Moutard, 1786–89.

Littré, Émile *Dictionnaire de la langue française.* Paris: Éditions Universitaires, 1872–77.

Mairobert, Mathieu-François Pidansat de. *L'Espion Anglois, ou correspondance secrète entre milord all eye et milord all'ar.* 10 vols. London: John Adamson, 1779–84.

——. *La chronique scandaleuse, ou mémoires.* Edited by Octave Uzannee. Paris: A Quentin, 1879–83.

Marmontel, Jean-François. *Mémoires de Marmontel: mémoires d'un père pour servir à l'instruction de ses enfants.* 2 vols. Edited by Maurice Tourneux. Paris: Librairie des Bibliophiles, 1891.

Menetra, Jacques-Louis. *Journal de ma vie: compagnon vitrier au XVIIIᵉ siècle.* Edited by Daniel Roche. Paris: A. Michel, 1998.

Mercier, Louis-Sébastien. *Le Tableau de Paris.* Edited by Jean-Claude Bonnet. 12 vols. 1781–89. Reprint, Paris: Mercure de France, 1994.

Moufle d'Angerville, Barthélemy-François-Joseph. *La Vie privée de Louis XV, ou principaux événemens, particularités et anecdotes de son regne.* 4 vols. London: J. P. Lyton, 1781.

Piton, Camille, ed. *Paris sous Louis XV: rapports aux inspecteurs de police au roi.* 5 vols. Paris: Mercure de France, 1908–15. Partial publication of mss. 11357–60 of the Bibliothèque Nationale de France.

Pothier, Robert-Joseph. *Traité de la communaté, auquel on a joint un traité de la puissance du mari sur la personne et les biens de la femme* (1774). Vol. 5. *Oeuvres de Pothier contenant les traités du droit français.* Paris: Bechet ainé, 1825.

Prévost, Abbé. *Histoire du chevalier des Grieux et de Manon Lescaut.* 1731. Reprint, Paris: GF Flammarion, 1995.

Rétif de la Bretonne, Nicolas-Edme. *Le Pornographe.* London: J. Nourse, 1769.

——. *Les Parisiennes; ou, XL caractères généraux pris dans les moeurs actuelles, propres à servir à l'instruction des personnes-du-sexe; tirés des mémoires du nouveau Lycée-des-moeurs.* Neuchâtel: Guillot, 1787.

Rousseau, Jean-Jacques. *Lettre à d'Alembert sur les spectacles.* 1758. Reprint, with an introduction by Marc Launay, Paris: Flammarion, 1993.

——. *Julie ou la Nouvelle Héloïse.* 1760. Reprint, Paris: Gallimard, 1999.

——. *Émile: ou de l'éducation.* 1762. Reprint, Paris: Flammarion, 1966.

——. *Les Confessions.* 1789. Reprint, edited by Jacques Voisin, Paris: Éditions Garnier frères, 1964.

Taudière, Henry. *Traité de la puissance paternelle.* Paris: L. A. Pedone, 1898.

Théveneau de Morande, Charles. *Le Porte-feuille de Madame Gourdan, dite la Comtesse, pour servir à l'histoire des moeurs du siècle, et principalement de celles de Paris.* Paris: 1783.

——. *La Gazette noire par un homme qui n'est pas blanc, ou oeuvres posthumes du gazetier cuirassé.* Paris: 1784.

Tilly, Alexandre de. *Mémoires du comte Alexandre de Tilly pour servir à l'histoire des moeurs de la fin du XVIIIᵉ siècle.* Edited by Christian Melchior-Bonnet. Paris: Mercure de France, 1965.

Tocqueville, Alexis de. *The Old Régime and the French Revolution.* Translated by Stuart Gilbert. New York: Doubleday, 1955.

Turmeau de la Morandière, Denis-Laurian de. *Représentations à M. le lieutenant général de police de Paris sur les courtisannes à la mode et les demoiselles du bon ton.* Paris: 1762.

[Villaret, Claude]. *La Belle Allemande, ou les galanteries de Thérèse.* Paris: 1755.

Selected Secondary Sources

Alasseur, Claude. *La Comédie française au 18e siècle; étude économique.* Paris: La Haye Mouton, 1967.

Aleil, François. "La Prostitution à Clermont au XVIIIᵉ siècle." In *Aimer en France 1760–1860: actes du Colloque international de Clermont-Ferrand,* vol. 2, edited by Paul Viallaneix and Jean Ehrard. Clermont-Ferrand: Association des publications de la faculté des lettres et des sciences humaines de Clermont-Ferrand, 1980.

Badinter, Elizabeth. *Mother Love: Myth and Reality: Motherhood in Modern History.* New York: Macmillan, 1980.

Benabou, Erica-Marie. "Amours 'vendus' dans Paris à la fin de l'Ancien Régime: 'clercs libertins' police et prostituées." In *Aimer en France 1760–1860: actes du Colloque international de Clermont-Ferrand,* vol. 2, edited by Paul Viallaneix and Jean Ehrard. Clermont-Ferrand: Association des publications de la faculté des lettres et des sciences humaines de Clermont-Ferrand, 1980.

——. *La Prostitution et la police des moeurs au XVIIIᵉ siècle.* Paris: Librairie Académique Perrin, 1987.

Berlanstein, Lenard R. "Women and Power in Eighteenth-Century France: Actresses at the Comédie Française." In *Visions and Revisions of Eighteenth-Century France,* edited by Christine Adams, Jack R. Censer, and Lisa Jane Graham. University Park: Pennsylvania State Press, 1997.

———. *Daughters of Eve: A Cultural History of French Theater Women from the Old Regime to the Fin-de-Siècle.* Cambridge, MA: Harvard University Press, 2001.

Berlière, Justine, and Vincent Milliot. *Policer Paris au Siècle des Lumières: les commissaires du quartier du Louvre dans la seconde moitié du XVIIIe siècle.* Paris: Ecole des Chartes, 2012.

Bongie, L. L. *From Rogue to Everyman: A Foundling's Journey to the Bastille.* Montreal: McGill-Queen's University Press, 2004.

Bourdieu, Pierre. "Forms of Capital." In *Handbook of Theory and Research for the Sociology of Education,* edited by J. G. Richardson, translated by Richard Nice. Westport, Greenwood Press, 1986.

Burguière, André, and François Lebrun. "101 familles d'Europe." In *Le choc des modernités,* vol. 2 of *Histoire de la famille,* edited by André Burguière et al. Paris: Armand Colin, 1986.

Capon, Gaston. *Les petites maisons galantes de Paris, au XVIIIe siècle, folies, maisons de plaisance et vide-bouteilles; d'après des documents inédits et des rapports de police.* Paris: H. Daragon, 1902.

———. *Les Vestris; le "diou" de la danse et sa famille 1730–1808; d'après des rapports de police et des documents inédits.* Paris: Société du Mercure de France, 1908.

Capon, Gaston, and Robert Yves-Plessis. *Paris galante au dix-huitième siècle: fille d'Opéra, vendeuse d'amour: Histoire de Mlle Deschamps (1730–1764).* Paris: Plessis, 1906.

Castan, Nicole. "Inégalités sociales et différences de condition dans les liaisons amoureuses et les tentatives conjugales." In *Aimer en France 1760–1860: actes du Colloque international de Clermont-Ferrand,* vol. 2, edited by Paul Viallaneix and Jean Ehrard. Clermont-Ferrand: Association des publications de la faculté des lettres et sciences humaines de Clermont-Ferrand, 1980.

Chaussinand-Nogaret, Guy. *The French Nobility in the Eighteenth Century: From Feudalism to Enlightenment.* Translated by William Doyle. Cambridge: Cambridge University Press, 1985.

Cheek, Pamela. "Prostitutes of 'Political Institution.'" *Eighteenth-Century Studies* 28, no. 2 (1994–95): 193–219.

———. *Sexual Antipodes: Enlightenment Globalization and the Placing of Sex.* Stanford: Stanford University Press, 2003.

Clay, Lauren. "Provincial Actors, the Comédie-Française, and the Business of Performing in Eighteenth-Century France." *Eighteenth-Century Studies* 38, no. 4 (summer, 2005): 651–79.

———. *Stagestruck: The Business of Theater in Eighteenth-Century France and Its Colonies.* Ithaca: Cornell University Press, 2013.

Cobb, Richard. *The Police and the People.* Oxford: Oxford University Press, 1970.

———. *Paris and Its Provinces, 1792–1802.* London: Oxford University Press, 1975.

Conner, Susan P. "The Pox in Eighteenth-Century France." In *The Secret Malady: Venereal Disease in Eighteenth-Century Britain and France,* edited by Linda E. Merians. Lexington: University of Kentucky Press, 1996.

Collins, James. "The Economic Role of Women in Seventeenth-Century France." *French Historical Studies* 16, no 2 (fall 1989): 436–70.

Coquery, Natacha. *L'Hôtel aristocratique: Le marché du luxe à Paris au XVIIIᵉ siècle.* Paris: Publications de la Sorbonne, 1998.

——. *Tenir boutique à Paris au XVIIIe siècle: luxe et demi-luxe.* Paris: Éd. du Comité des travaux historiques et scientifiques, 2011.

Cosandey, Fanny. *Le Reine de France: symbole et pouvoir, XVe et XVIIIe siècle.* Paris: Éditions Gallimard, 2000.

Cortey, Matilde. *L'Invention de la courtisane au XVIIIᵉ siècle dans les romans-mémoires des filles du monde de Madame Meheust à Sade, 1732–1797.* Paris: AP editions arguments, 2001.

Cranston, Maurice. *Jean-Jacques: The Early Life and Work of Jean-Jacques Rousseau: 1712–1754.* Chicago: University of Chicago Press, 1991.

Crowston, Clare Haru. *Fabricating Women: The Seamstresses of Old Regime France, 1675–1791.* Durham: Duke University Press, 2001.

Damrosch, Leo. *Jean-Jacques Rousseau: Restless Genius.* Boston: Mariner Books, 2007.

Darnton, Robert. *The Literary Underground of the Old Regime.* Cambridge, MA: Harvard University Press, 1982.

——. *The Great Cat Massacre and Other Episodes in French Cultural History.* New York: Vintage, 1985.

——. *The Forbidden Best-Sellers of Pre-Revolutionary France, 1769–1789.* New York: Norton, 1995.

——. *The Devil in the Holy Water or the Art of Slander from Louis XIV to Napoleon.* Philadelphia: University of Pennsylvania Press, 2010.

——. *Poetry and the Police: Communication Networks in Eighteenth-Century Paris.* Cambridge, MA: Belknap Press, 2010.

Darrow, Margaret H. "French Noblewomen and the New Domesticity, 1750–1850." *Feminist Studies* 5, no. 1 (spring 1979): 41–65.

——. "Popular Concepts of Marital Choice in Eighteenth-Century France." *Journal of Social History* 19, no. 2 (winter 1985): 261–72.

Daumard, Adeline, and François Furet. *Structures et relations sociales à Paris au milieu du XVIIIᵉ siècle.* Cahiers des Annales, no. 18. Paris: A. Colin, 1961.

Davis, Natalie Zemon. *The Return of Martin Guerre.* Cambridge, MA: Harvard University Press, 1983.

——. "On the Lame." *American Historical Review* 93, no. 3 (June 1998): 572–603.

Delumeau, Jean, and Daniel Roche, eds. *Histoire des pères et de la paternité.* Paris: Larousse, 1990.

Denby, David. *Sentimental Narrative and the Social Order in France, 1760–1820.* Cambridge: Cambridge University Press, 1994.

Denis, Vincent. *Une Histoire de l'identité: France, 1715–1815.* Seyssel: Champs Vallon, 2008.

Denis, Vincent, and Vincent Milliot, "Police et identification dans la France des Lumières." *Genèses, Sciences sociales et histoire* 54 (March 2004): 4–21.

DePaux, Jacques. "Les filles-mères se maraient-elles? L'Exemple de Nantes au XVIIIᵉ siècle." In *Aimer en France 1760–1860: International de Clermont-Ferrand*, vol. 2, edited by Paul Viallaneix and Jean Ehrard. Clermont-

Ferrand: Association des publications de la faculté des lettres et des sciences humaines, 1980.

Desan, Suzanne. "Making and Breaking Marriage: An Overview of Old Regime Marriage as a Social Practice." In *Family, Gender, and Law in Early Modern France*, edited by Suzanne Desan and Jeffrey Merrick. University Park: Pennsylvania State University Press, 2009.

D'Estrée, Paul. "Un policier homme de lettres, L'Inspecteur Meusnier (1748–1757)." *Revue rétrospective: recueil de pièces intéressantes et de citations curieuses*, nouvelle série, Sixième semestre (July–December 1892): 217–76.

———. "Une colonie Franco-Russe au XVIIIᵉ siècle." *La Revue des Revues* XIX (1896): 1–16.

———. "Un journaliste policier; le chevalier de Mouhy." *Revue d'histoire littéraire de la France* 4 (1897): 195–238.

———. "Journal du lieutenant de police Feydeau de Marville." *Nouvelle Revue Rétrospective* 6 (1897): 1–24; 97–120; 169–216; 265–88.

Dubost, Jean-François. "Les étrangers à Paris au Siècle des Lumières." In *La Ville promise: mobilité et accueil à Paris, fin XVIIᵉ–début XIXᵉ siècle*, edited by Daniel Roche. Paris: Fayard, 2000.

Duchêne, Roger. *Ninon de Lenclos: la courtisane du Grand Siècle*. Paris: Fayard, 1984.

———. *Ninon de Lenclos, ou, la manière jolie de faire l'amour*. Paris: Fayard, 2000.

Durand, Yves. *Les Fermiers généraux au XVIIIᵉ siècle*. Paris: Maisonneuve et Larose, 1996.

Emsley, Clive. *Policing and its Context, 1750–1870*. London: Macmillan, 1984.

Fairchilds, Cissie. "Female Sexual Attitudes and the Rise of Illegitimacy: A Case Study." *Journal of Interdisciplinary History* 8, no. 4 (spring 1978): 627–67.

———. *Domestic Enemies: Servants and Their Masters in Old Regime France*. Baltimore: Johns Hopkins University Press, 1984.

Farge, Arlette. *Vivre dans la rue à Paris au XVIIIᵉ siècle*. Paris: Gallimard, 1979.

———. *Subversive Words: Public Opinion in Eighteenth-Century France*. Translated by Rosemary Morris. University Park: Pennsylvania State University Press, 1995.

———. *Fragile Lives: Violence, Power and Solidarity in Eighteenth-Century Paris*. Translated by Carol Shelton. Cambridge, MA: Harvard University Press, 1993.

Farge, Arlette, and Michel Foucault. *Le Désordre des familles: lettres de cachet des Archives de la Bastille au XVIIIᵉ siècle*. Paris: Éditions Gallimard, 1982.

Farge, Arlette, and Jacques Revel. *The Rules of Rebellion: Child Abductions in Paris in 1750*. Translated by Claudia Miéville. Cambridge: Polity Press, 1991.

———. *The Vanishing Children of Paris: Rumor and Politics before the French Revolution*. Translated by Claudia Miéville. Cambridge, MA: Harvard University Press, 1991.

Farr, James. *Authority and Sexuality in Early Modern Burgundy*, 1550–1730. New York: Oxford University Press, 1995.

———. *The Work of France: Labor and Culture in Early Modern Times, 1350–1800*. Lanham: Rowman and Littlefield, 2008.

Feldman, Martha, and Bonnie Gordon. *The Courtesan's Arts: Cross-Cultural Perspectives*. New York: Oxford University Press, 2006.

Flandrin, Jean-Louis. *Families in Former Times: Kinship, Marriage, Household and Sexuality*. Translated by Richard Southern. Cambridge: Cambridge University Press, 1976.

Flinn, Michael W. *The European Demographic System, 1500–1820*. Baltimore: Johns Hopkins University Press, 1981.

Finlay, Robert. "The Refashioning of Martin Guerre." *American Historical Review* 93, no. 3 (June 1998): 553–71.

Fortunet, Françoise. "Sexualité hors mariage à l'époque révolutionnaire: Les mères des enfants de la nature." In *Droit, histoire et sexualité*, edited by Jacques Poumarède and Jean-Pierre Royer. Lille: L'Espace Juridique, 1987.

Foucault, Michel. *Discipline and Punish: The Birth of the Prison*. Translated by Alan Sheridan. New York: Vintage Books, 1979.

Freundlich, Francis. *Le Monde du jeu à Paris, 1715–1800*. Paris: Albin Michel, 1995.

Funck-Bretano, Frantz. *Catalogue des manuscrits de la Bibliothèque de l'Arsenal*. Vol. 9. *Archives de la Bastille*. Paris: Librairie Plon, 1892.

———. *Les Lettres de cachet: Etude suivie d'une liste des prisonniers de la Bastille: 1659–1789*. Paris: Hachette 1903.

Garrioch, David. *Neighborhood and Community in Paris, 1740–1790*. New York: Cambridge University Press, 1986.

———. "Verbal Insults in Eighteenth-Century Paris." In *The Social History of Language*, edited by Peter Burke and Roy Porter. Cambridge: Cambridge University Press, 1987.

———. "The Police of Paris as Enlightened Social Reformers." *Eighteenth-Century Life*, 1st ser., 16 (1992): 43–59.

———. "The People of Paris and Their Police in the Eighteenth Century: Reflections on the Introduction of a 'Modern' Police Force." *European History Quarterly* 24, no. 4 (1994): 511–35.

———. *The Formation of the Parisian Bourgeoisie, 1690–1830*. Cambridge, MA: Harvard University Press, 1996.

Gilfoyle, Timothy J. "Prostitutes in History: From Parables of Pornography to Metaphors of Modernity." *American Historical Review* 104, no. 1 (February 1999): 117–41.

Godineau, Dominique. *The Women of Paris and their French Revolution*. Translated by Katherine Streip. Berkeley: University of California Press, 1988.

Goodman, Dena. *The Republic of Letters: A Cultural History of the French Enlightenment*. Ithaca: Cornell University Press, 1994.

———. "Marriage Choice and Marital Success: Reasoning About Marriage, Love, and Happiness." In *Family, Gender, and Law in Early Modern France*, edited by Suzanne Desan and Jeffrey Merrick. University Park: Pennsylvania University Press, 2009.

Graham, Lisa Jane. *If the King Only Knew: Seditious Speech in the Reign of Louis XV*. Charlottesville: University Press of Virginia, 2000.

Gray, Francine du Plessix. *At Home with the Marquis de Sade: A Life*. New York: Simon and Schuster, 1998.

Guest, Ivor. *Ballet of the Enlightenment: The Establishment of the Ballet d'Action in France, 1770–1793.* London: Dance Books, 1996.

——. "Letter from London: Guimard's Farewell to the Stage." *Dance Chronicle* 18, no. 2 (1995): 207–15.

Guyot, Charly. *Plaidoyer Pour Thérèse Levasseur: servante, maîtresse et épouse de J.-J. Rousseau.* Neuchatel: Ides et Calendes, 1962.

Hafter, Daryl. "Women Who Wove in the Eighteenth-Century Silk Industry of Lyon." In *European Women and Preindustrial Craft*, edited by Daryl Hafter. Bloomington: University of Indiana Press, 1995.

——. "Female Masters in the Ribbon Making Guild of Eighteenth-Century Rouen." *French Historical Studies* 20, no. 1 (winter 1997): 1–14.

——. *Women at Work in Preindustrial France.* University Park: Pennsylvania State University Press, 2007.

Hajnal, J. "European Marriage Patterns in Perspective." In *Population in History; Essays in Historical Demography.* edited by D. V. Glass and D.E.C. Eversley. London: E. Arnold, 1969.

Hakim, Catherine. "Erotic Capital." *European Sociological Review* 26, no. 5 (October, 2010): 499–518.

——. *Erotic Capital: The Power of Attraction in the Boardroom and Bedroom.* New York: Basic Books, 2011.

Hanley, Sarah. "Family and State in Early Modern France: The Marriage Pact." In *Connecting Spheres: Women in the Western World, 1500 to the Present*, edited by Marilyn J. Boxer and Jean H. Quataert. New York: Oxford University Press, 1987.

——. "Engendering the State: Family Formation and State Building in Early Modern France." *French Historical Studies* 16, no. 1 (spring 1989): 4–27.

——. "The Monarchic State in Early Modern France: Marital Regime Government and Male Right." In *Politics, Ideology, and the Law in Early Modern Europe: Essays in Honor of J. H. Salmon*, edited by Adrianna Bakos. Rochester: University of Rochester Press, 1994.

Hardwick, Julie. *Practice of Patriarchy: Gender and the Politics of Household Authority in Early Modern France.* University Park: Pennsylvania State University Press, 1998.

——. *Family Business: Litigation and the Political Economies of Daily Life in Early Modern France.* Oxford: Oxford University Press, 2009.

Hufton, Olwen. *The Poor of Eighteenth-Century France, 1750–1789.* Oxford: Clarendon Press, 1974.

——. "Women and the Family Economy in 18th-Century France." *French Historical Studies* 9, no. 1 (spring 1975): 1–22.

——. "Women, Work, and Marriage in Eighteenth-Century France." In *Marriage and Society: Studies in Social History of Marriage*, edited by R. B. Outhwaite. New York: St. Albans Press, 1981.

——. "Le Travail et la famille." In *Histoire des Femmes: XVIe–XVIIIe siècles*, edited by Natalie Zemon Davis and Arlette Farge. Paris: Plon, 1991.

——. "Women, Work and Family." In *A History of Women in the West*, vol. 3, edited by Natalie Zemon Davis and Arlette Farge. Cambridge: Belknap Press, 1993.

——. *The Prospect Before Her: A History of Women in Western Europe, 1500–1800.* New York: Vintage, 1995.

Hunt, Lynn. "Obscenity and the Origins of Modernity, 1500–1800." In *The Invention of Pornography: Obscenity and the Origins of Modernity, 1500–1800,* edited by Lynn Hunt. New York: Zone Books, 1993.

Jones, Colin. *Paris: Biography of a City.* New York: Penguin, 2004.

Jones, Jennifer. *Sexing* La Mode*: Gender, Fashion and Commercial Culture in Old Regime France.* Oxford: Berg, 2004.

Kaiser, Thomas. "Louis *le Bien-Aimé* and the Rhetoric of the Royal Body." In *From the Royal to the Republican Body: Incorporating the Political in Seventeenth and Eighteenth-Century France,* eds. Sara E. Meltzer and Kathryn Norberg. Berkeley: University of California Press, 1998.

Kale, Steven. *French Salons: High Society and Political Sociability from the Old Regime to the Revolution of 1848.* Baltimore: Johns Hopkins University Press, 2004.

Kaplan, Steven L. "Réflexions sur la police du monde du travail, 1700–1815." *Revue historique* 261, no. 569 (1979): 17–77.

——. "Note sur les commissaires de police au XVIIIe siècle." *Revue d'histoire moderne et contemporaine* 28 (October–December 1981): 669–86.

——. "La préfecture de Police [de Paris], trois siècles d'existence." *Liaisons* 309 (1993): 16–9.

Kaplow, Jeffry. *The Names of Kings: The Parisian Laboring Poor in the Eighteenth Century.* New York: Basic Books, 1972.

Kushner, Nina. "Courtesans: Overview." In *Oxford Encyclopedia of Women in World History.* Oxford: Oxford University Press, 2008.

——. "Concubinage: An Overview." In *Oxford Encyclopedia of Women in World History.* Oxford: Oxford University Press, 2008.

——. "Concubinage: A Comparative History." In *Oxford Encyclopedia of Women in World History.* New York: Oxford University Press, 2008.

Kushner, Nina and Daryl Hafter, eds. *Enterprising Women: Agency, Gender and Work in Eighteenth-Century France.* Baton Rouge: Louisiana State University Press, forthcoming.

Kushner, Nina, and Wei-Yee Li. "Courtesans: Comparative History." In *Oxford Encyclopedia of Women in World History.* Oxford: Oxford University Press, 2008.

Lancaster, H. C. "The *Comédie-Française,* 1701–74: Plays, Actors, Spectators, Finances." *Transactions of the American Philosophical Society,* 41 (1951): 593–849.

Lanza, Janine. *From Wives to Widows in Early Modern Paris: Gender, Economy, and Law.* Burlington: Ashgate, 2007.

Lebrun, François. "Amour et mariage." In *Histoire de la population française.* vol. 2, edited by Jacques Dupâquier et al. Paris: Presses universitaires de France 1988.

Lever, Evelyne. *Madame de Pompadour: A Life.* Translated by Catherine Temerson. New York: Farrar, Straus and Giroux, 2002.

Lever, Maurice. *Sade: A Biography.* Translated by Arthur Goldhammer. San Diego: Harcourt Brace and Company, 1993.

Locklin, Nancy. *Women's Work and Identity in Eighteenth-Century Brittany.* Burlington: Ashgate, 2007.

Marian, Hannah. *The Pre-Romantic Ballet*. London: Pitman, 1974.

Marraud, Mathieu. *La Noblesse de Paris au XVIIIe siècle*. Paris: Editions du Seuil, 2000.

Maza, Sarah. *Servants and Masters in Eighteenth-Century France: The Uses of Loyalty*. Princeton: Princeton University Press, 1983.

———. "The 'Bourgeois' Family Revisited: Sentimentalism and Social Class in Pre-Revolutionary French Culture." In *Intimate Encounters: Love and Domesticity in Eighteenth-Century France*, edited by Richard Rand. Princeton: Princeton University Press, 1997.

———. "Luxury, Morality, and Social Change: Why There Was No Middle-class Consciousness in Pre-Revolutionary France." *Journal of Modern History* 69, no. 2 (1997): 199–229.

———. *The Myth of the French Bourgeoisie: An Essay on the Social Imaginary 1750–1850*. Cambridge, MA: Harvard University Press, 2003.

Medick, Hans. "The Proto Industrial Family Economy: The Structural Function of Household and Family during the Transition from Peasant Society to Industrial Capitalism." *Social History* 1, no. 3 (1976): 291–315.

Merians, Linda E., ed. *The Secret Malady: Venereal Disease in Eighteenth-Century Britain and France*. Lexington: University of Kentucky Press, 1996.

Merrick, Jeffrey. *Order and Disorder in the Ancien Régime*. Newcastle, UK: Cambridge Scholars Publishing, 2007.

———. "Patriarchalism and Constitutionalism in Eighteenth-Century Parlementary Discourse." *Studies in Eighteenth-Century Culture* 20 (1990): 317–33.

———. "Fathers and Kings: Patriarchalism and Absolutism in Eighteenth-century French Politics." *Studies on Voltaire and the Eighteenth Century* 308 (1993): 281–303.

———. "The Body Politics of French Absolutism." In *From the Royal to the Republican Body: Incorporating the Political in Seventeenth and Eighteenth-Century France*, edited by Sara Meltzer and Kathryn Norberg. Berkeley: University of California Press, 1998.

———. "Marital Conflict in Political Context: Langeac vs. Chambonas, 1775." In *Family, Gender, and Law in Early Modern France*, edited by Suzanne Desan and Jeffrey Merrick. University Park: Pennsylvania State University Press, 2009.

———. "The Family Politics of the Marquis de Bombelles." *Journal of Family History* 21 (1996): 503–18.

Milliot, Vincent. *Un Policier des Lumières*. Seyssel: Editions Champ Vallon, 2011.

———. "Le Déshonneur de la police?" *La Quinzaine Littéraire* 1031 (February 2011).

Muchembled, Robert. *Les Ripoux des Lumières: Corruption policière et Révolution*. Paris: Seuill, 2011.

Norberg, Kathryn. "Prostitutes." In *Renaissance and Enlightenment Paradoxes*, vol. 3 of *A History of Women in the West*, edited by Natalie Zemon Davis and Arlette Farge. Cambridge, MA: Harvard University Press, 1992.

———. "Goddesses of Taste: Courtesans and Their Furniture in Late-Eighteenth-Century Paris." In *Furnishing the Eighteenth Century: What Furniture Can Tell Us about the European and American Past*, edited by Dena Goodman and Kathryn Norberg. New York: Routledge, 2007.

———. "From Courtesan to Prostitute: Mercenary Sex and Venereal Disease, 1730–1802." In *The Secret Malady: Venereal Disease in Eighteenth-Century Britain and France*, edited by Linda E. Merians. Lexington: University of Kentucky Press, 1996.

Nye, Robert A. *Masculinity and Male Codes of Honor in Modern France*. Berkeley: University of California Press, 1998.

Ourliac, Paul, and J. de Malafosse. *Le Droit Familial*. Vol. 3 of *Historie du Droit Privé*. Paris: Presses Universitaires de France, 1968.

Overall, Christine. "What's Wrong with Prostitution? Evaluating Sex Work." *Signs: Journal of Women in Culture and Society* 17, no. 4 (summer 1992): 705–724.

Pardailhé-Galabrun, Annik. *The Birth of Intimacy: Privacy and Domestic Life in Early Modern Paris*. Translated by Jocelyn Phelps. Philadelphia: University of Pennsylvania Press, 1991.

Pateman, Carole. *The Sexual Contract*. Stanford: Stanford University Press, 1988.

———. *The Disorder of Women*. Stanford: Stanford University Press, 1989.

Phan, Marie-Claude. "Typologie d'aventures amoureuses d'après les déclarations de grossesse et les procédures criminelles enregistrées à Carcassonne de 1676 à 1786." In *Aimer en France 1760–1860: actes du Colloque international de Clermont-Ferrand*, vol. 2, edited by Paul Viallaneix and Jean Ehrard. Clermont-Ferrand: Association des publications de la faculté des lettres et sciences humaines de Clermont-Ferrand, 1980.

Pheterson, Gail, ed. A *Vindication of the Rights of Whores*. Seattle: Seal Press, 1989.

Piasenza, Paolo. "Juges, lieutenants de police et bourgeois à Paris aux XVIIe et XVIIIe siècles." *Annales ESC* 45, no. 5 (September–October 1990): 1189–1215.

———. "Opinion publique, identité des institutions, 'absolutisme'. Le problème de légalité à Paris entre le XVIIe et le XVIIIe siècle." *Revue d'historique* 290, no. 118 (1993): 97–142.

Popiel, Jennifer. *Rousseau's Daughters: Domesticity, Education, and Autonomy in Modern France*. Durham: University Press of New England, 2008.

Popkin, Jeremy. *Panorama of Paris: Selections from* Le Tableau de Paris *by Louis-Sébastien Mercier*. University Park: Pennsylvania State University Press, 1999.

Popkin, Jeremy, and Bernadette Fort, eds. *The* Mémoires secrets *and the Culture of Publicity in Eighteenth-Century France*. Oxford: Voltaire Foundation, 1988.

Quétel, Claude. *De Par Le Roy: essai sur les lettres de cachet*. Toulouse: Privat, 1981.

———. *Une légende noire: les lettres de cachet*. Paris: Perrin, 2011.

Rand, Richard. "Love, Domesticity, and the Evolution of Genre Painting in Eighteenth-Century France." In *Intimate Encounters: Love and Domesticity in Eighteenth-Century France*, edited by Richard Rand. Princeton: Princeton University Press, 1997.

Reddy, William M. *The Navigation of Feeling: A Framework for the History of Emotions*. Cambridge: Cambridge University Press, 2001.

Rey, Michael. "Police et Sodomie à Paris au XVIIIe siècle: du péché au désordre." *Revue d'histoire moderne et contemporaine* 27 (1982): 113–24.

——. "L'art de 'raccrocher' au XVIIIᵉ siècle." *Masques* 24 (1984–85): 92–99.

——. "Parisian Homosexuals Create a Lifestyle, 1700–1750: The Police Archives." In *Eighteenth-Century Life: Unauthorized Behavior in the Enlightenment*, edited by Robert P. Maccubin. Special edition of *Eighteenth-Century Life*, n.s., 9 (May 1985).

Roberts, Meghan. "Cradle of Enlightenment: Family Life and Knowledge Making in Eighteenth-Century France." Ph.d. Diss. Northwestern University, 2011.

Robinson, Charles Henry. *Life, Letters, and Epicurean Philosophy of Ninon de L'Enclos, the Celebrated Beauty of the Seventeenth Century*. Chicago: Lion, 1903.

Roche, Daniel. "Nouveaux Parisiens au XVIIIᵉ siècle." *Cahiers d'Histoire* 24, no. 3 (1979): 3–20.

——. "Work, Fellowship, and Some Economic Realities of Eighteenth-Century France." In *Work in France: Representations, Meaning, Organization, and Practice*, edited by Steven L. Kaplan and Cynthia Koepp. Ithaca: Cornell University Press, 1986.

——. *The People of Paris: An Essay in Popular Culture in the 18th Century*. Translated by Marie Evans. Berkeley: University of California Press, 1987.

——. *France in the Enlightenment*. Translated by Arthur Goldhammer. Cambridge, MA: Harvard University Press, 1998.

——. *The Culture of Clothing: Dress and Fashion in the "Ancien Régime."* Translated by Jean Birrell. Cambridge: Cambridge University Press, 1996.

Rosenthal, Margaret. *The Honest Courtesan: Veronica Franco, Citizen and Writer in Sixteenth-Century Venice*. Chicago: University of Chicago Press, 1992.

Rougemont, Martine de. *La Vie théâtrale en France au XVIIIᵉ siècle*. Paris: Champion, 1988.

Rubin, Gayle. "Thinking Sex: Notes for a Radical Theory of Sexuality." In *Pleasure and Danger: Exploring Female Sexuality*, edited by Carole S. Vance. Boston: Routledge, 1984.

Ruggiero, Guido. "Who's Afraid of Giulana Napolitana? Pleasure, Fear and Imagining the Arts of the Renaissance Courtesan." In *The Courtesan's Arts: Cross-Cultural Perspectives*, edited by Martha Feldman and Bonnie Gordon. Oxford: Oxford University Press, 2006.

Sabattier, Jacqueline. *Figaro et son maître: Maîtres et domestiques a Paris au XVIIIᵉ siècle*. Paris: Perrin, 1984.

Schwartz, Joel. *The Sexual Politics of Jean-Jacques Rousseau*. Chicago: University of Chicago Press, 1984.

Scott, Virginia. *Women on the Stage in Early Modern France, 1540–1750*. Cambridge: Cambridge University Press, 2010.

Soll, Jacob. *The Information Master: Jean-Baptiste Colbert's Secret State Intelligence System*. Ann Arbor: University of Michigan, 2009.

Sonenscher, Michael. *The Hatters of Eighteenth-Century France*. Berkeley: University of California Press, 1987.

——. *Work and Wages: Natural Law, Politics, and the Eighteenth-Century French Trades*. Cambridge: Cambridge University Press, 1989.

Sonnet, Martine. *L'Éducation des filles au temps des lumières*. Paris: Les éditions de cerf, 1987.

———. "A Daughter to Educate." In *Renaissance and Enlightenment Paradoxes*, vol. 3 of *A History of Women in the West*, edited by Natalie Zemon Davis and Arlette Farge. Cambridge, MA: Harvard University Press, 1993.

Steinbrügge, Lieselotte. *The Moral Sex: Women's Nature in the French Enlightenment.* Translated by Pamela E. Selwyn. New York: Oxford University Press, 1995.

Swartz, Robert. *The Policing of the Poor in Eighteenth-Century France.* Chapel Hill: University of North Carolina Press, 1988.

Tallent, Alistaire, "Defying Domesticity: Prostitute Heroines of Eighteenth-Century French Memoir Novels and the Public Sphere." Ph.D. diss., Vanderbuilt University, 2005.

Talvacchia, Bette. *Taking Positions: On the Erotic in Renaissance Culture.* Princeton: Princeton University Press, 1999.

Taudière, Henry. *Traité de la puissance paternelle.* Paris: L. A. Pedone, 1898.

Tilly, Louise A., and Joan W. Scott. *Women, Work, and Family*, 2nd. ed. New York: Metheun, 1987.

Viala, Alain. *La France galante: essai historique sur une catégorie culturelle, de ses origines jusqu'à la Révolution.* Paris: Presses Universitaires de France, 2008.

Walker, Lesley. *A Mother's Love: Crafting Feminine Virtue in Enlightenment France.* Lewisburg: Bucknell University Press, 2008.

Watt, Jeffrey. *The Making of Modern Marriage: Matrimonial Control and the Rise of Sentiment in Neuchâtel, 1550–1800.* Ithaca: Cornell University Press, 1992.

Weinreb, Ruth Plaut. *Eagle in a Gauze Cage: Louise d'Épinay femme de lettres.* New York: AMS Press, 1993.

Wellman, Kathleen. *Queens and Mistresses of Renaissance France.* New Haven: Yale University Press, 2013.

White, Luise. *The Comforts of Home: Prostitution in Colonial Nairobi.* Chicago: University of Chicago Press, 1990.

Williams, Alan. *The Police of Paris, 1718–1789.* Baton Rouge: Louisiana State University Press, 1979.

Zinsser, Judith. *Emile du Châtelet: Daring Genius of the Enlightenment.* London: Penguin, 2006.

Ziskin, Rochelle. *The Place Vendôme: Architecture and Social Mobility in Eighteenth-Century Paris.* New York: Cambridge University Press, 1999.

☙ INDEX